HACKERS

VOCABULARY

해커스 어학연구소

Hackers Vocabulary

초판 1쇄 발행 2006년 6월 20일
초판 11쇄 발행 2010년 8월 2일

지은이 David Cho | 언어학박사 前 UCLA 교수
펴낸곳 해커스 어학연구소
펴낸이 해커스 어학연구소 출판팀
주 소 서울시 서초구 서초동 1316-15 해커스 교육그룹
전 화 02-566-0001
팩 스 02-563-0622
홈페이지 www.goHackers.com
등록번호 978-89-90700-31-5 18740
정 가 15,900원(테이프 별매)

H a c k e r s   V o c a b u l a r y

PREFACE

제2외국어인 영어를 접하면서 많은 사람들이 영어 독해나 문법 혹은 청취 분야를 독립적인 분야로 생각하여 이 각각의 분야를 분리하여 공부하여 성취할 수 있다고 생각하는 오류에 빠지게 됩니다. 더 나아가 독해를 하다보면 단어는 저절로 해결된다고 생각하는 오류에 빠집니다. 그러나 독해나 문법 혹은 청취가 기본적인 단어의 바탕 없이는 어느 한계 이상을 나아갈 수 없는 '모래위의 성 쌓기' 에 불과합니다. 모든 문장이 단어로 구성되어 있기 때문입니다.

그렇다면 정상적인 독해에 요구되는 단어는 어느 선까지일까요? 토플과 토익의 주관사인 ETS에서 수많은 전문가들을 통하여 이 기준에 대한 연구와 시험을 계속해 왔고, 이러한 기준의 충족 여부를 확인하기 위하여 TOEFL이라는 시험을 개발하여 시행해왔던 것입니다. 즉, 토플이라는 시험에서 출제되는 단어들은 미국을 포함한 기타 영어권 대학에서 수학 능력을 위한 기본이 되는 단어일 뿐만 아니라, 기타 영어로 표현된 모든 학문 분야의 기본이 되는 단어라는 뜻입니다. HackersVoca는 이러한 TOEFL 시험에서 최근 수년간에 걸쳐 제시된 단어들과 이 수준의 단어들을 분석하여 이루어진 단어집으로 영어 수학 능력을 키움과 동시에 이러한 영어 수학 능력 측정 시험에 대비할 수 있는 '표준단어집' 이라고 할 수 있을 것입니다.

HackersVoca의 근간은 기출 단어를 중심으로 한 동의어군을 통한 단어 학습입니다. 이러한 접근법이 실제 토플 시험에서 적응력을 향상시켜 왔고, 이 책의 전신인 Hacker Voca로 공부해온 많은 수험생들이 대변하는 실전에서의 높은 정답률이 그 동안 Hacker Voca를 검증해 왔습니다. 기존의 단어책들이 꼭 필요한 단어가 빠져 있거나 불필요한 단어를 싣는 경우가 많은데 비하여 이책은 강의 기간을 포함한 최근 몇년간의 토플 시험등을 검토하여 필요한 단어만을 선택하여 실은 것이 특징입니다.

저는 영어를 공부하는 여러분에게 영어공부의 고전을 제시한다는 마음으로 책을 썼고, 해커스 졸업생들이 이에 동참을 해 주었음을 자랑스럽게 여깁니다. 이 책이 나오기까지 넓게는 저와 함께 공부하며 HackersVoca에 조언을 준 해커스 졸업생들과 실제로 이책의 작업에 직접 참여를 한 우리 해커스 가족들에게 감사를 표합니다. 유학 준비에 바쁘면서도 초판 책의 표지 디자인을 예쁘게 해준 남희(5기), 혼동되는 단어를 보내온 7기 오후반 C팀(팀장 박세진), 삽화를 그려준 유미(16기), 교정을 도와준 명희(10기), 승신(11.5기), '추장' 정하(12기), 수아(13기), 상균(13기), 하나(14기), 세원(14.5기), '하회탈' 신우(14.5기), 도환(15기), 판준(15기), 태동(15기), 은영(15.5기), '잠탱' 지경(16기), 참신한 책구성의 공로자 영석(11.5기), 수시로 책 작업을 도와준 지원(7.5기) 그리고 창현(5기)에게 다시 한번 감사를 표합니다. 은혜(2기), 수경 (13기)은 연구소 일을 맡아 이 책의 마무리까지 최선을 다해 주었습니다. 특히 신선한 아이디어, 정열, 그리고 책임감으로 이 책의 처음부터 끝까지 함께 해 준 혜진(10기)은 이 책이 나오는 데 크나큰 힘이 되었습니다. 더불어 연구소에서 교정 작업을 도와준 승원, 수경 그리고 이 책의 편집과 출판에 조언을 아끼지 않은 혜정님의 도움에 감사드립니다. Academia의 철학의 실천인 이 책이 진정으로 토플과 영어를 공부하는 이들에게 작은 빛과 길잡이가 되기를 기원합니다.

David Cho

Hackers Voca

Contents

Hackers Voca 구성

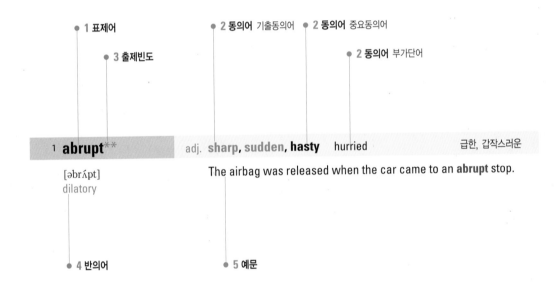

1 표제어

3 출제빈도

2 동의어 기출동의어

2 동의어 중요동의어

2 동의어 부가단어

1 **abrupt**** adj. **sharp, sudden, hasty** hurried 급한, 갑작스러운

[əbrʌ́pt]

dilatory

The airbag was released when the car came to an **abrupt** stop.

4 반의어

5 예문

1	표제어	왼쪽에 가장 큰 글씨의 검정 볼드체로 표시된 것이 바로 표제어입니다. 표제어는 ETS가 주관한 토플 시험에 출제된 기출단어입니다.
2	동의어	표제어의 오른쪽에 일직선으로 표시된 것은 동의어입니다. 녹색 볼드체로 표시된 단어는 기출동의어, 검정 볼드체로 표시된 단어는 중요동의어, 작은 글씨로 표시된 단어는 부가단어입니다. 부가단어가 중요하지 않은 것은 아니며, 시간이 촉박할 경우 학습의 효율성을 높이기 위한 것입니다. 모두 함께 암기하는 것이 가장 좋습니다.
3	출제빈도	표제어 오른쪽의 별표는 출제 빈도의 정도에 따라 한 개에서 세 개까지로 표시하였습니다.
4	반의어	표제어 아랫부분에 작은 글씨로 표시된 것은 표제어의 반의어입니다.
5	예문	단어의 정확한 쓰임을 이해하고 그 의미를 정확하게 파악하는 데 도움이 될 수 있는 예문들을 수록하였습니다.
6	예문해석	예문의 의미를 쉽고 정확하게 파악할 수 있도록 해석을 해당 페이지 하단에 수록하였습니다.
7	연습문제	매일 미니테스트를, 3일마다 그 3일치에 해당하는 종합테스트를 수록하였습니다.
8	쉬어가는 페이지	3일마다 미국 역사, 영시, 재미있는 그림 등을 수록하였습니다. 여러분들의 고된 학습에 편한 쉼터가 되어줄 것입니다.
9	Confu Voca	효율적인 단어 학습을 위하여 자칫 혼동하기 쉬운 단어들을 선별하여 수록하였습니다.
10	인덱스	책 뒷부분에 수록된 해커스 보카의 모든 표제어와 동의어 인덱스를 사전처럼 이용하실 수 있습니다.

Hackers Voca 특징

01
iBT 최신 기출 단어 및 동의어 수록

TOEFL이 달라져도 HackersVoca와 함께라면 걱정하실 필요 없습니다. HackersVoca의 모든 표제어는 실제 시험에 출제되었던 단어들만으로 구성되어 있을 뿐만 아니라 iBT 최신 기출 단어 및 정답이 수록되어 있습니다. 또한 각 표제어들의 출제빈도도 알아보기 쉽게 표시되어 있어 가장 중요한 토플 어휘를 가장 빠른 시간에 익히실 수 있습니다.

02
토플, 편입, 공무원 완벽 대비

TOEFL은 영어권에서 공부하고자 하는 외국인이 반드시 거쳐야 하는, ETS의 검증된 제 분야의 많은 전문가들이 만들어 내는 시험입니다. 다시 말해 TOEFL의 출제 단어들은 미국을 포함한 기타 영어권 대학에서 수학 능력을 위한 기본이 되는 단어일 뿐만 아니라, 기타 영어로 표현된 모든 학문 분야의 기본이 되는 단어임을 알 수 있습니다. HackersVoca는 이러한 토플 기출 단어와 편입시험, 공무원 시험의 기출 단어들이 포함된, 모든 형태의 영어시험에 가장 효과적인 동시에 필수적인 어휘책입니다.

03
빠른 암기가 가능한 편집

단기간에 고득점을 목표로 하고 있지만 어디서부터 손을 대야 할지 고민인 분들도 걱정하실 필요 없습니다. 기출 단어의 정답은 녹색 볼드체로, 중요동의어는 검정 볼드체로 구분하여 필요에 따라 암기하실 수 있습니다. 어느 정도 실력을 쌓으신 뒤에는 중요동의어 오른쪽에 함께 있는 부가단어까지 함께 외우시면 됩니다.

04
표제어의 이해를 돕는 정선된 예문과 해석

해커스 어학 연구소에서 상당한 기간에 걸쳐 엄선하여 수록한 예문들을 통해 표제어의 쓰임과 의미를 정확하게 파악하실 수 있습니다. 또한 해석을 예문의 바로 아래가 아닌 같은 페이지의 하단에 수록해 예문의 의미를 스스로 파악하실 수 있는 기회를 제공함과 동시에 자신의 해석 실력에 대한 빠른 자가진단이 가능하도록 하였습니다.

05

실전을 위한 퀴즈와 테스트

하루치의 단어 뒤에는 퀴즈가 준비되어 있어 그날그날 자가진단을 해보실 수 있습니다. 또한, 3일마다 토플 유형에 가장 가까운 테스트를 통해 실전감각을 유지할 수 있도록 되어 있습니다. 이 외에도 해커스 홈페이지(www.goHackers.com)를 통하여 꾸준히 업그레이드 되는 다양한 문제들은 여러분들의 단어 암기를 더욱 쉽게 도와줄 것입니다.

06

멀티 학습이 가능한 60일 구성

HackersVoca는 하루에 암기하기에 적절한 단어 분량과 60일이라는 학습기간을 제시하여 일정기간의 학습계획을 세우시기에 편리합니다. 또한 기출동의어, 중요동의어 및 부가단어 중에서 선택적으로 암기하는 방법도 있습니다. 이처럼 멀티 학습법이 가능한 것이 HackersVoca의 특징이며 개인별로 공부하는 경우나 스터디를 통해 접근하는 경우 모두 효율적으로 활용하실 수 있는 이유입니다.

07

효과적인 학습을 위한 해커스 보카 테이프와 MP3

HackersVoca 테이프와 MP3는 교재에 있는 최신 기출 단어와 동의어를 정확한 Native Speakers의 발음으로 수록하고 있어 가장 효율적이고 흥미로운 단어 학습을 가능하게 합니다. 또한 정선된 예문 청취를 통해 단어의 정확한 의미 파악과 Listening학습 효과까지 얻으실 수 있습니다. 테이프는 온 · 오프라인 서점에서, MP3는 동영상 전문 사이트 챔프스터디(www.ChampStudy.com)에서 선택하여 구입하실 수 있습니다.

08

해커스 홈페이지를 통한 애프터서비스

해커스 홈페이지(www.goHackers.com)의 보카 Q&A 게시판을 통해 궁금한 사항에 대한 답변을 신속하게 들으실 수 있습니다. 이 외에도 토플자료 게시판등의 유용한 학습자료들을 통해 계속적인 애프터서비스를 받으실 수 있습니다.

Hackers Voca 학습 방법

- 매일 정해진 분량에서 모르는 단어의 앞에 체크하면서 외워 나갑니다. 예문 내에서 그 단어의 뜻과 쓰임새를 확인하도록 합니다. 동의어도 한꺼번에 외워두는 것이 좋습니다.

- 하루치의 분량이 끝나면, 퀴즈를 통하여 확인합니다. 추가로 자료실(www.goHackers.com)에 저장되어 있는 다양한 테스트를 통하여 더욱 철저히 확인할 수 있습니다.

- 다음날이 되면, 같은 방식으로 진행합니다. 물론 처음부터 그 이전 날의 단어까지 누적하여 계속적으로 확인하는 것이 좋습니다. 시간적으로 불가능하다면, 적어도 전날의 단어까지는 확인하는 습관을 들입니다. 이것은 단기간에 확실하게 단어를 암기할 수 있는 가장 좋은 방법입니다.

개별 학습 방법

1

단어는 스터디를 통하여 공부하는 것이 가장 좋습니다. 그러나 여건상 이것이 힘들다면, 자신에게 가장 알맞은 분량을 정하여 꾸준히 해나가야 합니다. 이 경우 다음과 같은 여러 가지 방식이 있습니다.

2

개별 학습 예시

· 날짜 순서대로 암기 : 매일의 꾸준한 학습을 원하시는 경우, 60일로 나누어진 순서에 따라 일정 분량씩 암기하는 방법이 효과적입니다.

· 기출동의어부터 암기 : 기출동의어와 중요동의어가 쉽게 구분하실 수 있도록 표시되어 있으므로, 시간이 촉박한 경우에는 표제어와 기출동의어부터 우선적으로 암기하시면 됩니다. 기출동의어 후에 중요동의어, 부가단어 순으로 본인의 실력과 일정에 맞추어 외우실 수 있습니다.

스터디 학습 방법

1

HackersVoca는 스터디에 가장 적합하게 짜여진 단어책입니다. 다양한 멀티 학습이 가능하므로 반복하여 단어 스터디를 하면서도 지루하지 않고 가장 효율적인 방식으로 단어 암기를 할 수 있을 것입니다. 스터디시에는 좀더 집중적으로 단어에 시간을 투자하여 확실한 성과를 거두도록 하는 것이 좋습니다.

2

스터디를 하게 될 경우, 마찬가지로 각 스터디팀에서 어느 만큼의 분량을 해야 할지를 정해야 합니다. 개별 학습시보다는 좀 더 많은 분량을 정하는 것이 좋습니다. 해커스보카에 나온 테스트는 개인이 단어를 암기하고 확인하기 위해 사용합니다.

3

돌아가면서 매일매일 암기해야 하는 부분에서 단어를 출제하여 시험을 보는 것이 가장 효과적입니다. 이 경우, 틀린 단어에 대해서는 엄격하게 벌칙을 정하여야 합니다. HackerVoca를 외우는 가장 효과적이었던 방법은 '벌금' 이었습니다.

4

해커스 홈페이지(www.goHackers.com)의 '해커스북 자료실' 에 가면 다양한 유형의 문제들이 있을 것입니다.이것을 참조하여 출제자는 허를 찌르는 단어 시험이 되도록, 그리고 문제를 푸는 사람은 그럼에도 불구하고 완벽한 답안이 되도록 단어를 외웁니다.

5

스터디 학습 예시

· 60일에 세 번을 마스터 한다: 스터디는 위에서 이야기했듯이 많은 분량을 소화하도록 하는 것이 좋습니다. 처음에는 이틀치씩, 두번째 확인에서는 3일치씩, 세번째 확인에서는 6일치씩 정한다면, 처음에는 30일, 두번째는 20일, 마지막에는 10일, 즉 60일 동안 세 번 마스터가 가능합니다.

· 40일에 두 번을 마스터 한다: 하루에 3일치씩 전체를 공부합니다. 이렇게 하면 40일만에 두 번 마스터가 가능합니다.

Hackers Voca
토플 시험 문제

The word ______ in the passage is closest in meaning to

1. According to Greek Mythology, when Paris deserted his wife for Helen, he sparked the beginning of the Trojan War.
(A) abominated (B) abandoned (C) disobliged (D) preoccupied

2. Historians attribute the fall of the Roman Empire to the frivolous military spending that lead to rampant inflation.
(A) expensive (B) trivial (C) doubtful (D) indifferent

3. Animals generally live longer in captivity than in the wild.
(A) subsequently (B) earthly (C) drastically (D) largely

4. An animal with canine distemper disorder becomes apathetic, refusing food and water.
(A) abstract (B) considerate (C) indifferent (D) steadfast

5. The Inuit believed that forgetting to provide an offering would anger the gods and result in an unsuccessful hunt.
(A) enrage (B) discard (C) disprove (D) dissent

6. Despite the influence of Islam on the community's legal system, the practice of pre-Islamic traditions remains omnipresent.
(A) shrewd (B) expensive (C) complicated (D) ubiquitous

7. In most Western societies, the practice of child-rearing is performed by the mother and her immediate family.
(A) raising (B) expecting (C) observing (D) resolving

8. The Australian Aborigines perfected the art of basketry despite meager supplies of suitable vegetation.
(A) a lot of (B) incredible (C) scanty (D) plain

9. The younger mountains and adjacent plains were formed during the glaciation process.

(A) adjoining (B) extensive (C) improved (D) consummate

10. In some psychological studies, children are provided with enigmatic pictures designed to evoke an emotional response.

(A) terse (B) puzzling (C) emotional (D) pointed

11. Devout Muslims always begin every prayer with "In the Name of God" in Arabic.

(A) Responsible (B) Covetous (C) Gracious (D) Pious

12. There was some debate over whether or not the railroad would be built in the east or the west in America.

(A) decrepit (B) declaration (C) controversy (D) contrast

13. Contact with poison ivy leaves patches of red and irritated skin.

(A) partitions (B) areas (C) materials (D) parchments

14. A proposal to commemorate the spirit in which America came together after the Sept. 11 terrorist attacks is instead causing a rift between some Pennsylvania residents and lawmakers.

(A) authorizing (B) embarrassing (C) triggering (D) hindering

15. In the early 1800s, Jamaica's internal political strife led to a prolonged period of conflict with its external trade partners.

(A) occult (B) conflict (C) peril (D) reprisal

16. A representative of the army announced that it could quickly deploy up to 3,000 troops to the region if necessary.

(A) separate (B) recall (C) detour (D) position

Answer 1.(B) 2.(B) 3.(D) 4.(C) 5.(A) 6.(D) 7.(A) 8.(C) 9.(A) 10.(B) 11.(D) 12.(C) 13.(B) 14.(C) 15.(B) 16.(D)

Hackers Voca
편입 시험 문제

Choose the synonym of the highlighted word in the sentence.

1. Rescue efforts were hampered by remoteness of the area and by the road damage.
(A) enhanced (B) restricted (C) facilitated (D) stopped

2. If certain herbs are used simultaneously with antibiotics, some infections will not only clear up, but the possibility of reoccurring attacks will decrease.
(A) compatibly (B) continuously (C) concurrently (D) complacently

3. The outcry against the government's policies will subside only if a compromise is reached in the assembly.
(A) die down (B) proceed (C) stand upright (D) be out of order

4. Politicians are well known for being obstinate.
(A) corrupt (B) unrealistic (C) talkative (D) determined

5. Before the advent of a spider-silk marketplace, human web weavers must close the technology gap on their arachnid counterparts.
(A) appearance (B) surge (C) peak (D) close

6. All staff have a responsibility to disseminate their knowledge to any interested person.
(A) spread (B) explain (C) express (D) exhibit

7. Discoveries just as exciting, though perhaps not quite as eerie, are bringing to light extraordinary new aspects of the people who lived in Italy long ago.
(A) interesting (B) valuable (C) weird (D) romantic

8. As a nurse, she was able to alleviate anxiety as well as pain.
(A) relieve (B) enhance (C) aggravate (D) intensify

9. He is an art critic who loathes modern art.

(A) adores (B) relishes (C) detests (D) craves

10. If you are not sure that a person is guilty, don't make suggestions you can't support without tangible proof.

(A) concrete (B) refutable (C) excusable (D) questionable

11. Some people choose jobs which are not lucrative and less-demanding.

(A) disadvantageous (B) challenging (C) profitable (D) time-restricting

12. After all, he himself acknowledged that "dangerous" information is sometimes composed of many pieces of information that are in themselves innocuous.

(A) harmless (B) complicated (C) offensive (D) detrimental

13. The fans argued and pleased but they could not enter the grounds without relinquishing their cell phones.

(A) turning off (B) reclaiming (C) muting (D) surrendering

14. The political incorporation of communities that feel they have a distinct cultural identity provides fertile ground for the emergence of nationalist reaction.

(A) flamboyant (B) productive (C) imminent (D) problematic

15. I think my brother is very adroit as a negotiator.

(A) skillful (B) bashful (C) inexperienced (D) adamant

16. The doctor said that the onset of the disease is gradual.

(A) beginning (B) development (C) close (D) cure

Answer 1.(B) 2.(C) 3.(A) 4.(D) 5.(A) 6.(A) 7.(C) 8.(A) 9.(C) 10.(A) 11.(C) 12.(A) 13.(D) 14.(B) 15.(A) 16.(A)

Hackers Voca
공무원 시험 문제

Choose the synonym of the highlighted word in the sentence.

1. Prostitution is an illicit activity in all states except Nevada.
(A) an unlawful (B) a disgusting (C) a familiar (D) an irresponsible

2. There is a reciprocal relation between goals and data.
(A) mutual (B) inherent (C) exclusive (D) incongruous

3. It was such a great performance from an accomplished actress.
(A) skilled (B) elegant (C) attractive (D) respectable

4. An actor must learn to enunciate his words clearly.
(A) keep (B) cheek (C) prove (D) articulate

5. The seven-year-old boy gave them explicit directions on how to get to the post office.
(A) clear (B) wrong (C) vague (D) implicit

6. We couldn't induce him to set foot on the boat.
(A) preside (B) protect (C) prevent (D) persuade

7. "Korean pop culture skillfully merges Western and Asian values to create its own," said Lui Mei, a Chinese resident in Seoul for three years.
(A) imposes (B) handles (C) purifies (D) blends

8. The jargon in his talk was opaque to me.
(A) attractive (B) suggesting (C) interesting (D) unclear

9. There had always been those on the periphery of the movement who had advocated violence.

(A) influence (B) solidarity (C) fringe (D) perpetuity

10. I predicate my opinion on these points.

(A) base (B) prefer (C) hesitate (D) criticize

11. Pakistan's government has finally admitted that during 1989 ~ 2003 Pakistani nuclear scientists proliferated nuclear weapons-related technologies and equipment.

(A) increased in number (B) became more expensive
(C) changed in philosophy (D) became more crowded

12. They have a reliable method of searching for hidden springs of water.

(A) special (B) creative (C) different (D) dependable

13. At the time dinosaurs thrived near the poles, conditions there were radically different from those today.

(A) wandered (B) summered (C) hibernated (D) flourished

14. The mall looks like a huge shoebox.

(A) excited (B) gigantic (C) foolish (D) dangerous

15. A vacant apartment in Seoul is very difficult to find.

(A) good (B) large (C) empty (D) clean

16. The most spectacular spectacular goal of the match was scored by Harris.

(A) flimsy (B) fragile (C) modern (D) splendid

Answer 1.(A) 2.(A) 3.(A) 4.(D) 5.(A) 6.(D) 7.(D) 8.(D) 9.(C) 10.(A) 11.(A) 12.(D) 13.(D) 14.(B) 15.(C) 16.(D)

DAY Hackers TOEFL **Vocabulary**

1 Hackers Voca

www.goHackers.com

1 **apt***	adj.	1. **inclined, prone, disposed**		~하는 경향이 있는
[ǽpt] disinclined		Chris is **apt** to forget the names of most people.		
inept	adj.	2. **appropriate, proper, suitable**		적당한
		Hotels are **apt** places to give a dinner party.		
2 **astonish****	v.	**surprise, astound, shock**	startle	놀라게 하다
[əstániʃ]		James was **astonished** to be chosen for such a prestigious award.		
3 **chronically**	adv.	**constantly, persistently, continuously**	habitually	만성적으로
[kránikəli]		The **chronically** late employee was punished by his boss.		
4 **daub*****	v.	**coat, cover, plaster, slather**		흠뻑 칠하다
[dɔ́:b]		Jeffrey decorated his room by **daubing** red paint in patches all over his walls.		
5 **domain****	n.	1. **region, area, territory**	realm	지역, 영토
[doumέin]		Sinchi Roca, the second emperor, made no military campaigns to add land to the Inca **domain**.		

apt	Chris는 대부분의 사람의 이름을 잊는 경향이 있다. 호텔은 저녁식사 파티를 열기에 적당한 장소이다.
astonish	James는 그렇게 유명한 상의 수상자로 선정된 것에 대해 놀랐다.
chronically	만성적으로 지각을 하는 직원이 사장에게 징계를 당했다.
daub	Jeffrey는 그의 방에 있는 벽 곳곳에 빨간색 페인트를 칠했다.
domain	두 번째 황제인 Sinchi Roca는 잉카 영토에 땅을 더하기 위한 어떤 전쟁도 수행하지 않았다.

n. 2. **area, field, sphere** 분야, 영역

Once the **domain** of experts, computer programming can be made easy with new software.

6 enthusiastic*

[enθù:ziǽstik]
apathetic

adj. **eager, ardent, zealous** passionate 열성적인

The citizenry was **enthusiastic** about the president's decision to cut taxes by ten percent.

7 extend**

[iksténd]

v. 1. **stretch, reach, range** (어떤 거리까지) 걸쳐 있다

The Sahara desert **extends** far and wide.

shorten

v. 2. **expand, enlarge, increase, prolong, lengthen** 확장하다, 늘리다

Thomas Jefferson **extended** the territory of the United States with the Louisiana Purchase.

8 feat*

[fí:t]

n. **achievement, accomplishment, exploit** 업적

The Taj Mahal is considered a remarkable **feat** of engineering.

9 fulfill**

[fulfíl]

v. 1. **accomplish, achieve, execute** 성취하다

Everyone wants to **fulfill** their wildest dreams.

v. 2. **satisfy, meet** 만족시키다

The contract clauses **fulfilled** our requirements.

10 give over to

phr. **dedicate, devote, commit** 헌신하다, 바치다

John Brown **gave** his life **over to** the cause against slavery.

---

domain — 한때 전문가의 영역이었던 컴퓨터 프로그래밍이 새로운 소프트웨어로 인해 쉬워졌다.
enthusiastic — 시민들은 세금을 10% 감면한다는 대통령의 결정에 대해 열광했다.
extend — 사하라 사막은 멀리 넓게 걸쳐 있다.
Thomas Jefferson은 루이지애나 매입으로 미국의 영토를 확장시켰다.
feat — 타지마할은 공학 기술의 놀랄만한 업적으로 간주된다.
fulfill — 모든 사람들은 자신이 가장 이루고 싶은 꿈을 성취하길 바란다.
그 계약 조항들이 우리의 요구 사항들을 만족시켰다.
give over to — John Brown은 노예제 반대 운동에 생애를 바쳤다.

11 heavy**

[hévi]
light

adj. **ponderous, weighty; burdensome** 무거운 ; 고된

The roof of the cabin collapsed under the **heavy** weight of the snow.

12 hibernation

[hàibərnéiʃən]

n. **sleep, dormancy** 동면

Hibernation in winter is common in certain mammal species.

13 illusion*

[ilúːʒən]

n. **false impression** 착각, 오해

The magician created the **illusion** that the woman's head was removed from her body.

14 intrigue*

[intríːg]
bore

v. 1. **attract, fascinate, interest** (주의 · 관심을) 끌다

Young Albert was **intrigued** by the mysteries of science.

v. 2. **plot, conspire** 음모를 꾸미다

The police didn't believe Jim **intrigued** with the enemy against the government.

15 luxuriant*

[lʌgʒú(ː)əriənt]
withered

adj. **abundant, exuberant, opulent** 무성한, 풍부한

Tracts of **luxuriant** plant life and colonies of teeming insects cover the Amazon river basin.

16 magnitude**

[mǽgnətjùːd]

n. **extent, measure, degree; volume, size, amplitude** 정도 ; 크기

The **magnitude** of an earthquake is measured on the Richter Scale.

17 maintain**

[meintéin]

v. 1. **affirm, contend, claim** 주장하다

Some participants **maintained** that their present situation was worse than before.

heavy	그 오두막의 지붕이 무거운 눈의 무게로 무너졌다.
hibernation	겨울잠은 몇몇 포유류에게서 흔하게 발견된다.
illusion	마법사는 그 여자의 머리가 몸에서 분리된 듯한 착각을 불러일으켰다.
intrigue	어린 Albert는 과학의 미스터리에 관심이 끌렸다.
	경찰은 Jim이 정부에 대항하여 적들과 음모를 꾸몄다는 것을 믿지 않았다.
luxuriant	무성한 식물들과 곤충들로 가득한 동물 군체들이 있는 지역이 아마존 강 분지를 덮고 있다.
magnitude	진도는 리히터 스케일로 측정된다.
maintain	몇몇 참석자들은 그들의 현재 상황이 전보다 더 악화되었다고 주장했다.

v. 2. **sustain, preserve, continue, keep** 지속하다

J.K. Rowling has **maintained** a private life despite the media attention she has received.

18 monitor

[mánitər]

v. **check, examine, inspect** 조사하다

The U.S. Department of Agriculture **monitors** food safety.

19 outbreak*

[áutbrèik]

n. 1. **epidemic** (전염병 등의) 만연, 창궐

The **outbreak** of measles came to be a serious problem.

n. 2. **eruption, explosion, burst** 폭발

The **outbreak** of violence was a sure sign of what was to come.

20 periodically

[pìəriádikəli]

adv. **at intervals, regularly** 주기적으로

The fire alarms are tested **periodically** to ensure they are working properly.

21 release**

[rilí:s]
detain

v. 1. **free, liberate, loose** 해방시키다

Johnson will be **released** from prison tomorrow.

v. 2. **emit, give off, discharge, exude** 뿜다, 방출하다

The burning of fossil fuels **releases** poisonous gases into the air.

v. 3. **loosen, untie, unfasten** (묶인 것을) 풀다

The first-aid worker **released** the tourniquet slowly after the bleeding had stopped.

---

maintain
monitor
outbreak

periodically
release

J.K. Rowling은 그녀가 받은 언론의 관심에도 불구하고 사생활을 유지해 왔다.
미 농림부는 식품의 안전성을 조사한다.
홍역의 창궐은 심각한 문제가 되었다.
폭력의 발발은 앞으로 올 일에 대한 확실한 징조였다.
화재경보기들은 잘 작동되는지 확인하기 위해 주기적으로 점검된다.
Johnson은 내일 감옥에서 석방될 것이다.
화석 연료는 연소할 때 대기 중으로 유독가스를 방출한다.
응급 치료원은 출혈이 멈춘 뒤에 천천히 지혈대를 풀었다.

22 **rendering*****

[réndəriŋ]

n. **performance, presentation, rendition** 연주, 공연

The pianist's new **rendering** of the piece drew rave reviews.

23 **renowned***

[rináund]

adj. **famous, celebrated, eminent, prominent** 유명한

The **renowned** scientist was disgraced when it was discovered that he had lied about his work.

24 **reproduce***

[rì:prədjú:s]

v. 1. **copy, duplicate, imitate** 복제하다

The photograph of the president slipping on ice was **reproduced** in all the major dailies.

perish

v. 2. **breed, multiply, spawn** 번식하다

All living organisms need to **reproduce** to keep their species alive.

25 **rugged**

[rʌ́gid]

adj. **uneven, rough, bumpy** 울퉁불퉁한

The **rugged** terrain proved a challenge for the hikers.

26 **self-sufficient**

[sèlfsəfíʃənt]

adj. **independent** 자급자족하는, 제힘으로 살아가는

People in Western societies are expected to be **self-sufficient** after graduation.

27 **speculative***

[spékjulətiv]

adj. 1. **theoretical, academic** 이론적인

An exact date for the appearance of Homo sapiens remains **speculative**.

adj. 2. **thoughtful, reflective, meditative** 사색적인

Though rather aggressive in his youth, Robert became more **speculative** later in life.

rendering	그 피아니스트에 의한 그 곡의 새로운 연주법은 격찬을 이끌어냈다.
renowned	그 유명한 과학자는 자신의 연구 결과에 대해서 거짓말을 한 것이 드러나자 망신을 샀다.
reproduce	대통령이 빙판에서 미끄러진 사진이 모든 주요 일간지들에 복제되어 실렸다.
	모든 생명체는 그들 종을 유지하기 위해 번식할 필요가 있다.
rugged	울퉁불퉁한 지형은 하이커들의 도전 정신을 시험했다.
self-sufficient	서구 사회에서는 사람들이 졸업 후에는 스스로 생계를 이어가도록 요구받는다.
speculative	호모 사피엔스가 출현한 정확한 날짜는 이론상으로만 남아 있다.
	Robert는 청년시절에는 다소 적극적이었지만, 노년에는 한결 사색적인 사람이 되었다.

28 **stimulate***
[stímjulèit]
discourage

v. **prompt, activate, spur, inspire** 자극하다, 격려하다

The New Deal included federal action to **stimulate** industrial recovery.

29 **subordinate**
[səbɔ́ːrdənət]
dominant

adj. **inferior, subject, dependent** secondary 종속적인

Law should be **subordinate** to morality.

30 **torrential***
[tɔːrénʃəl]

adj. **wild, violent** 격렬한

The village was flooded after eight hours of **torrential** rains.

Quiz

Choose the synonym.

1. apt
2. chronically
3. fulfill
4. subordinate
5. renowned

ⓐ famous, celebrated, eminent
ⓑ subject, inferior, dependent
ⓒ execute, accomplish, achieve
ⓓ habitually, constantly, persistently
ⓔ proper, appropriate, suitable

Answer 1. ⓔ 2. ⓓ 3. ⓒ 4. ⓑ 5. ⓐ

stimulate	뉴딜 정책은 산업의 회복을 자극하기 위한 연방 정부의 조치를 포함했다.
subordinate	법은 도덕에 종속적이어야 한다.
torrential	그 마을은 8시간 동안 격렬한 비가 쏟아진 후에 물에 잠겼다.

DAY 2

Hackers TOEFL **Vocabulary**

Hackers Voca

www.goHackers.com

1 address

[ǽdres]

n. 1. **residence, abode** 주소

A good resume should list the applicant's full name and **address** at the very top of the first page.

[ədrés]

n. 2. **speech, lecture, discourse** 강연

The Gettysburg **Address** illustrates Lincoln's sense of responsibility for others.

2 assume**

[əsú:m]

v. 1. **undertake, take on** 맡다

Roosevelt **assumed** the job of president in 1901.

v. 2. **put on, pretend, affect** ~인 척하다

The criminal **assumed** the identity of a dead mechanic in an attempt to elude police.

v. 3. **think, suppose, presume** ~라고 생각하다, 추측하다

Roger always **assumes** the worst in people.

3 attain**

[ətéin]

v. 1. **reach** 도달하다

Mango trees grow rapidly and can **attain** heights of up to 90 feet.

address	제대로 된 이력서는 지원자의 성명과 주소를 첫 페이지의 맨 위에 싣고 있어야 한다. Gettysburg 연설은 Lincoln의 다른 사람들에 대한 책임감을 보여 주고 있다.
assume	Roosevelt는 1901년에 대통령직을 맡았다. 그 범인은 경찰을 피하기 위해 죽은 기계공의 신분인 척했다. Roger는 항상 사람들의 가장 나쁜 면을 생각한다.
attain	망고 나무는 빨리 자라서 90피트의 높이까지 도달할 수 있다.

v. 2. **achieve, accomplish** 성취하다, 이루다

James **attained** national fame as a leading spokesman for human rights.

4 boast

[bóust]
depreciate

v. **brag, swagger** 자랑하다

Muhammad Ali **boasted** he was the greatest boxer to ever live.

5 capacity

[kəpǽsəti]

n. 1. **volume, dimensions** 용적

All of the lifeboats were filled to maximum **capacity**.

n. 2. **ability, flair, talent** 능력

Jefferson had a great **capacity** for leadership.

6 cede*

[síːd]
defend

v. **yield, surrender, relinquish** 양도하다, 포기하다

After three months of heavy warfare, the French army finally **ceded** victory to the Spaniards.

7 decline*

[dikláin]
accept

v. 1. **refuse, reject, dismiss** 거절하다

Daniel **declined** to go to the movie theater with her.

v. 2. **decrease, fall, fail, weaken** 하락하다, 쇠퇴하다

The singer's popularity has been **declining**.

8 desert*

[dizə́ːrt]
cleave (to)

v. **abandon, forsake** 버리다

Mary was **deserted** by most of her friends after she was found guilty in court.

attain	James는 인권을 위한 성공적인 대변인으로 국가적 명성을 얻었다.
boast	Muhammad Ali는 그가 현존하는 최고의 권투 선수였다고 자랑했다.
capacity	모든 구명보트는 최대한 꽉 차 있었다. Jefferson은 탁월한 지도자적 능력을 갖추고 있었다.
cede	3개월 간의 격렬한 전투 후, 프랑스 군대는 끝내 스페인 군대에게 승리를 양보하였다.
decline	Daniel은 그녀와 함께 영화관에 가는 것을 거절했다. 그 가수의 인기는 하락하고 있었다.
desert	Mary는 법정에서 유죄임이 밝혀지고 난 뒤 대부분의 친구들에게서 버림받았다.

9 **disassemble** | v. **break apart, dismantle, take apart** | 분해하다

[dìsəsémbl]
join

The moving men **disassembled** the large cabinet so they could take it out the narrow door.

10 **dispose*** | v. **array, arrange, order** | 배치하다, 배열하다

[dispóuz]

The interior designer **disposed** the furniture to create a more inviting atmosphere.

11 **dispose of*** | phr. **get rid of** | 처리하다

Area residents can **dispose of** their Christmas trees by dropping them off at the city's recycling center.

12 **erode*** | v. **wear away** | 침식하다, 부식되다

[iróud]

Water can **erode** even the hardest rock into dust.

13 **fairly*** | adv. 1. **reasonably, moderately, tolerably, pretty** | 꽤

[fέərli]
extremely

Mr. Caldwell arrives **fairly** early at work to read the newspaper before the staff arrives.

adv. 2. **impartially** | 공정하게

Judges are expected to conduct all cases **fairly**.

14 **glossy*** | adj. **shiny, bright, glazed, lustrous** | 빛나는, 광택이 나는

[glάsi]
dull

The customer wanted **glossy** prints for her holiday photographs.

15 **grounds** | n. **reasons, rationale, root, basis** | 근거, 이유

[gráundz]

Lawyers questioned the **grounds** for the judge's decision.

---

disassemble	그 이삿짐꾼들은 큰 장식장을 분해하여 그것을 좁은 문 밖으로 옮길 수 있었다.
dispose	인테리어 디자이너는 더 좋은 분위기를 연출하게끔 가구를 배치했다.
dispose of	지역 주민들은 도시의 재활용 센터에 크리스마스트리를 버림으로써 그것들을 처리할 수 있다.
erode	물은 가장 단단한 돌이라도 부식시켜 가는 입자로 만들 수 있다.
fairly	Caldwell씨는 직원들이 도착하기 전에 신문을 읽으려고 꽤 일찍 출근한다.
	판사들은 모든 사건들을 공정하게 처리하도록 요구받는다.
glossy	그 손님은 자신의 휴일 사진이 광택이 나도록 인화되기를 원했다.
grounds	변호사들은 판사의 판결에 대한 근거를 문제 삼았다.

16 **hallmark****
[hɔ́:lmà:rk]

n. **feature, a distinguishing trait** 특징

Clarity is a **hallmark** of good writing.

17 **ideal****
[aidí:əl]
average

adj. 1. **perfect, model, exemplary** 이상적인, 전형의

Julia spent all day shopping with her sisters for the **ideal** wedding dress.

actual

adj. 2. **abstract, theoretical, hypothetical** 관념적인

The physicist developed an **ideal**, purely mathematical model of cosmic light projection.

18 **inhabit****
[inhǽbit]
emigrate

v. **live, occupy, dwell** abide, reside 거주하다

The first people to **inhabit** Cuba were the Ciboney, a friendly tribe related to the Arawak.

19 **laborious**
[ləbɔ́:riəs]

adj. **diligent, industrious** 근면한

Brian deserves to get that promotion since he is a **laborious** worker.

20 **linger***
[líŋgər]

v. 1. **remain, stay, tarry** 남다

Although almost all the guests had left the party, Stephen **lingered** to talk to the host.

hurry, hasten

v. 2. **lag, procrastinate, loiter** drag, delay 꾸물거리다, 질질 끌다

Philip **lingered** over his work till late at night.

21 **loathe****
[louð]
tolerate

v. **abhor, abominate, detest** hate 혐오하다

The reclusive celebrity **loathes** giving interviews and being photographed.

---

hallmark 명료성은 좋은 글쓰기의 특징이다.
ideal Julia는 이상적인 웨딩드레스를 사려고 자매들과 쇼핑하는 데 하루를 다 보냈다.
물리학자는 우주에서 빛을 내보내는 것에 대한 관념적이고 단순히 수리적인 모델을 만들었다.
inhabit 쿠바에 거주한 최초의 민족은 Arawak의 친족이자 우호적인 부족인 Ciboney였다.
laborious Brian은 근면한 사원이므로 그렇게 승진할 만하다.
linger 손님들 대부분이 파티장을 떠났지만 Stephen은 주인과 이야기를 하려고 남았다.
Philip은 밤 늦게까지 꾸물거리며 일을 했다.
loathe 그 은둔한 유명인은 인터뷰하는 것과 사진 찍히는 것을 혐오한다.

22 **mimic***** | v. **copy, imitate, echo** 모방하다

[mímik]

Many insects **mimic** twigs or leaves for protection.

23 **model**** | n. **specimen, prototype, example, pattern** 견본

[mádl]

Some treatments that have worked in the rat **model** have also been successful in humans.

24 **observe*** | v. 1. **watch; perceive, notice** 관찰하다 ; 알아채다

[əbzə́ːrv]

John **observed** the planets with his telescope.

violate | v. 2. **conform, follow, comply** 준수하다

The Fosters **observe** the tradition of a family get-together every last Saturday of the month.

25 **plentiful**** | adj. **abundant, bountiful, rich** 풍부한

[pléntifəl]
scant, scanty, meager

Fish and plankton are **plentiful** in the sea.

26 **preoccupied*** | adj. **engrossed, absorbed** 몰두한

[priːákjupàid]

Jessica was so **preoccupied** with her book that she lost track of time.

27 **property**** | n. 1. **estate, havings, possession** asset 자산

[prápərti]

Albert lost all of his **property** in the fire.

n. 2. **character, characteristic, quality** feature 특성

Prof. Kim was the first to explain to me the **properties** of gas molecules.

---

mimic 많은 수의 곤충들이 자신을 보호하기 위해서 나뭇가지나 나뭇잎을 흉내 낸다.
model 쥐를 모델로 하여 성공했던 몇몇 치료법은 인간에게서도 성공적이었다.
observe John은 망원경으로 행성을 관찰하였다.
Foster 가족은 매달 마지막 토요일에 가족모임을 갖는 전통을 준수한다.
plentiful 물고기와 플랑크톤은 바다에 풍부하다.
preoccupied Jessica는 책에 너무 몰두해서 시간이 가는 줄도 몰랐다.
property Albert는 화재로 전 재산을 잃었다.
김교수는 기체 분자들의 특성들을 나에게 처음으로 설명해 준 사람이었다.

28 recurring* adj. **recurrent** 되풀이되는

[rikə́:riŋ]
isolated

Darcy had to see a therapist because he kept having **recurring** nightmares about drowning.

29 rooted* adj. **ingrained, fixed, embedded** 뿌리 깊은, 정착한

[rú(:)tid]

The problems of the educational system are deeply **rooted** in the lack of competent teachers.

30 thoroughly adv. **completely, perfectly, utterly, entirely** 철저히, 완전히

[θə́:rouli]

The professor covered the subject **thoroughly** in class.

Quiz

Choose the synonym.

1. attain	ⓐ acquire, procure, achieve
2. ideal	ⓑ copy, imitate, echo
3. loathe	ⓒ bountiful, abundant, rich
4. plentiful	ⓓ perfect, model, exemplary
5. mimic	ⓔ abhor, abominate, detest

Answer 1. ⓐ 2. ⓓ 3. ⓔ 4. ⓒ 5. ⓑ

recurring	Darcy는 물에 빠지는 악몽을 계속 되풀이해서 꾸었기 때문에, 치료사의 진찰을 받아야만 했다.
rooted	유능한 교사들이 부족하다는 점에 교육 시스템의 문제들이 깊게 뿌리박혀 있다.
thoroughly	그 교수는 수업에서 그 주제를 철저히 다루었다.

DAY 3

Hackers TOEFL **Vocabulary**

Hackers Voca

www.goHackers.com

1 **afford***	v. **provide, give, grant**	주다
[əfɔ́ːrd]	George's high marks in secondary school **afforded** him many opportunities to enter a good university.	
2 **announce***	v. **proclaim, publish, declare**	공포하다
[ənáuns]	Nixon **announced** his intention to withdraw an additional fifty thousand troops.	
3 **a wide range of***	phr. **a wide variety of**	다양한
	Ancient Egyptians used **a wide range of** cosmetics.	
4 **chance****	n. **probability, likelihood; opportunity**	가능성 ; 기회
[tʃǽns]	There is a good **chance** that Alex will pass the entrance exam.	
5 **chart***	v. **map, plot**	(지도 등을) 작성하다
[tʃɑ́ːrt]	Captain Cook **charted** a steady course across the ocean to Polynesia.	
6 **engage****	v. 1. **promise, contract, pledge**	약속하다
[ingéidʒ] disengage	The young couple announced they were **engaged** to be married.	

afford	중 · 고등학교에서 받은 높은 점수가 George에게 좋은 대학에 입학할 수 있는 많은 기회를 주었다.
announce	Nixon은 추가로 5만 병력을 철수하려는 그의 의도를 공포했다.
a wide range of	고대 이집트인들은 다양한 화장품을 사용했다.
chance	Alex가 입학 시험을 통과할 가능성이 크다.
chart	Cook 선장은 대양을 가로질러 폴리네시아에 이르는 일관된 방향의 경로를 지도로 만들었다.
engage	그 젊은 커플은 그들의 약혼사실을 발표했다.

v. 2. **reserve, book** 예약하다

All the rooms in the hotel are **engaged**.

discharge

v. 3. **hire, employ** 고용하다

The magazine **engaged** the services of several excellent writers to make its articles more interesting.

7 esteem*

[istí:m]
despise

v. **respect, revere; prize, value** 존경하다 ; 중하게 여기다

The singer's patriotism was nationally **esteemed**.

8 evidence*

[évidəns]

n. **proof; sign** 증거 ; 징후

No **evidence** proved that the accused committed homicide.

9 fertile*

[fə́:rtl]
barren

adj. **bountiful, productive, fecund** fruitful 비옥한

The Nile River plain no longer gets its **fertile** soil from the annual flood.

10 generate*

[dʒénərèit]
extinguish

v. **produce, create** 발생시키다

To **generate** enough electricity for the countryside, the mayor had 200 wind turbines built.

11 innate*

[inéit]
acquired

adj. **inborn, natural** 타고난

There are some **innate** differences between men and women.

12 invaluable*

[invǽljuəbl]
worthless

adj. **precious, priceless** 매우 귀중한

Forensic pathology is an **invaluable** science that helps criminologists determine how a person died.

engage	그 호텔의 방들이 모두 예약되었다. 잡지사는 기사를 좀 더 흥미롭게 만들기 위해 훌륭한 작가 몇 명을 고용했다.
esteem	그 가수의 애국심은 전국적으로 존경을 받았다.
evidence	어떤 증거도 그 피의자가 살해를 했다는 사실을 증명하지 못했다.
fertile	나일 강 평야는 더 이상 해마다 일어나는 홍수에 기인한 비옥한 토양을 얻지 못한다.
generate	시장은 도시에서 떨어진 지역에 충분한 전력을 공급하기 위해 200개의 풍향 터빈을 지었다.
innate	남자와 여자 사이에는 몇몇의 타고난 차이점들이 있다.
invaluable	법정 병리학은 범죄학자들이 피해자가 어떻게 사망했는지 알아내도록 도와주는 매우 귀중한 지식 체계이다.

13 **irreparable***

[irépərəbl]
reparable

adj. **irremediable, permanent, irrecoverable** 돌이킬 수 없는

The soldier survived but suffered **irreparable** facial damage.

14 **maxim***

[mǽksim]

n. **saying, proverb; principle** 격언 ; 행동 원칙

The **maxim** "Better late than never" is often used by students who come to class tardy.

15 **object****

[əbdʒékt]
acquiesce

v. 1. **protest, remonstrate** 항의하다

Jane Reagan **objected** to Reagan's increasing political involvement.

[ábdʒikt]

n. 2. **goal, purpose, function** 목적

The main **object** of all marble games is hitting a target by flicking a marble.

16 **outstanding****

[àutstǽndiŋ]

adj. 1. **remarkable, prominent, excellent** eminent 뛰어난

The writer's speech was so **outstanding** that years later people still quote from it.

paid

adj. 2. **unpaid, owing, unsettled** remaining 미결제의

Susan has quite a few **outstanding** debts this month.

17 **patron***

[péitrən]

n. 1. **protector, supporter, advocate** 후원자

Queen Elizabeth II was a **patron** of the arts and sciences.

n. 2. **customer** 고객

Sam and his wife were regular **patrons** of the restaurant, eating there twice a week.

irreparable	그 군인은 살아남았지만 돌이킬 수 없는 안면 상처를 입었다.
maxim	"안 하는 것보다 늦더라도 하는 것이 낫다"라는 격언은 수업에 지각하는 학생들에게 자주 쓰인다.
object	Jane Reagan은 Reagan의 늘어나는 정치 참여를 반대했다. 모든 구슬 게임의 주요 목표는 구슬을 가볍게 쳐서 목표물을 치는 것이다.
outstanding	작가의 연설이 너무나 뛰어나서 수년이 지난 지금도 사람들은 여전히 그것을 인용한다. Susan은 이번 달에 상당히 많은 미결제의 빚을 가지고 있다.
patron	엘리자베스 2세 여왕은 예술과 과학의 후원자였다. Sam과 그의 부인은 그 식당에서 일주일에 두 번은 식사를 하는 단골이었다.

18 **predominate*** v. outweigh, prevail, rule dominate 우세하다, 지배력을 갖다

[pridámənèit]

Service-related companies now **predominate** in a town that was once known for its manufacturing companies.

19 **previous**** adj. prior, earlier, former preceding 이전의

[prí:viəs]
subsequent

Unlike **previous** presidents, Teddy Roosevelt refused to use national force to break strikes.

20 **premise*** n. assumption, supposition 전제

[prémis]

The Chinese legal system works on the **premise** that an accused person is guilty until he is proven innocent.

21 **primitive*** adj. 1. primeval, uncivilized, savage 원시적인

[prímitiv]
civilized

Some **primitive** South American tribes still engage in the practice of cannibalism.

adj. 2. rudimentary 기본적인

The tourist's **primitive** grasp of the language made it difficult for him to communicate with the locals.

22 **proficiency*** n. skill, ability, expertise, mastery 능숙함

[prəfíʃənsi]
incompetence

A specialist must have a high level of **proficiency** in his/her area of expertise.

23 **proposition*** n. suggestion, proposal 제안

[pràpəzíʃən]

Top Republicans abandoned President Bush's drug **proposition** for poor seniors.

24 **questionable*** adj. doubtful, suspicious, dubious 의심스러운

[kwéstʃənəbl]
indisputable

The report's conclusions are **questionable** because the sample used was very small.

predominate	한때 제조업 회사들로 유명했던 한 마을에서 이제는 서비스 관련 기업들이 우세해졌다.
previous	과거의 대통령들과는 달리, Teddy Roosevelt는 파업을 중단시키기 위해 공권력을 이용하는 것을 거부했다.
premise	중국의 법 제도는 피고인이 무죄라는 것이 증명되기 이전까지는 유죄라는 전제하에 적용된다.
primitive	몇몇 남미의 원시 부족은 아직도 사람을 잡아먹는 풍습이 있다.
	그 관광객의 기본적인 언어 이해력이 지역민들과의 의사소통을 어렵게 만들었다.
proficiency	전문가는 자신의 전문 분야에서 고도의 능력을 지니고 있어야 한다.
proposition	고위 공화당 의원들은 가난한 노인들을 위한 부시의 의약 제안서를 포기했다.
questionable	사용된 표본의 크기가 너무 작았기 때문에 그 보고서의 결론은 매우 의심스럽다.

25 rife with* | phr. **full of** | 가득찬, 수없이 많은

The book was so **rife with** errors that readers sent dozens of e-mail messages to complain.

26 shield** | v. **protect, defend, safeguard** guard | 보호하다

[ʃíːld]
expose

Lisa brings an umbrella to **shield** herself from the hot sun during the summer months.

27 solitary** | adj. **isolated, remote, secluded, lonely** | 외딴, 고독한

[sάlitèri]
gregarious

The **solitary** man never spoke to anyone.

28 stick** | v. **cling, adhere** cleave, hold | 달라붙다, 고수하다

[stík]

Because the poster would not **stick** to the wall with glue, Jan used thumb tacks.

29 stimulus* | n. **motivation, incentive, incitement** | 자극, 격려

[stímjələs]

Jack's dream of owning a house is a **stimulus** for him to work hard.

30 stir** | v. **agitate, provoke, rouse** spur, excite | 자극하다

[stə́ːr]

Dale gave rousing speeches during break periods to **stir** the others to go on strike.

31 taboo* | n. **prohibition** | 금기

[tæbúː]
approval

In the Islamic religion, there is a strong **taboo** against marrying non-Muslims.

32 thrive** | v. **prosper, flourish** | 번성하다

[θrάiv]
stagnate

Slavery in America **thrived** because there was a scarcity of labor.

rife with	그 책에는 오류가 너무 많아서 독자들이 수십 통의 항의 이메일을 보냈다.
shield	Lisa는 여름 몇 달 동안 뜨거운 태양으로부터 자신을 보호하기 위해 양산을 가지고 다닌다.
solitary	그 고독한 남자는 어떤 사람에게도 말을 하지 않았다.
stick	풀로는 포스터가 벽에 붙지 않아서 Jan은 압정을 사용했다.
stimulus	집을 갖고 싶다는 Jack의 꿈은 그가 열심히 일하도록 하는 자극이 된다.
stir	Dale은 휴무 기간 동안 고무시키는 연설을 하여, 동맹 파업에 들어가도록 다른 사람들을 선동했다.
taboo	이슬람교에서는 비이슬람교도와의 결혼이 매우 금기시된다.
thrive	미국의 노예제도는 노동력이 부족했기 때문에 번성했다.

33 vagary**

[vέgəri]

n. **uncertainty, sudden desire, caprice, whim** 예측 불허의 변화

The **vagaries** of fashion do not affect how Susan dresses for the office.

34 wane*

[wéin]
increase

v. **decrease, decline, fade** 감소하다, 쇠퇴하다

Betty's interest in art history **waned** after she realized her distaste for classical painting.

35 view*

[vjú:]

n. 1. **outlook, opinion** 견해, 의견

Employees should make their **views** known to their coworkers.

v. 2. **consider, deem, regard** 간주하다

For a long time divorce was **viewed** as socially unacceptable, but today it is the norm in some countries.

Quiz

Choose the synonym.

1. irreparable ⓐ irremediable, permanent, irrecoverable
2. predominate ⓑ uncertainty, caprice, whim
3. solitary ⓒ isolated, remote, secluded
4. stimulus ⓓ motivation, incentive, incitement
5. vagary ⓔ outweigh, prevail, rule

Answer 1. ⓐ 2. ⓔ 3. ⓒ 4. ⓓ 5. ⓑ

vagary
wane
view

패션에 있어 예측 불허의 변화는 Susan이 직장에서 입는 옷에는 영향을 미치지 않는다.
Betty가 자신이 고전 회화에 대해 싫증을 느끼는 것을 깨달은 이후부터, 그녀의 미술사에 대한 관심은 줄어들었다.
직원들은 그들의 의견을 동료들이 알도록 해주어야 한다.
오랫동안 이혼은 사회적으로 받아들여질 수 없는 것으로 여겨졌지만, 오늘날 몇몇 나라에서는 일반적인 것이 되었다.

Hackers TOEFL Voca TEST DAY 01-03

Choose the synonym of the highlighted word in the sentence.

1. The speaker's call for revenge stirred a violent response from the mob.
(A) assembled (B) featured (C) provoked (D) placed

2. Planners decided to dispose apartment buildings as close together as possible to make room for the city's growing population.
(A) arrange (B) placate (C) remove (D) select

3. The Japanese navy was thoroughly defeated at the battle of Midway in 1942.
(A) resolutely (B) utterly (C) possibly (D) previously

4. Hay-on-Wye became a dying town when Welsh agriculture declined.
(A) intensified (B) ameliorated (C) weakened (D) forced

5. The right to vote in a democratic election was extended to women in 1919.
(A) expanded (B) denied (C) protracted (D) altered

6. The defendant's statement was untrue in view of the evidence presented by the prosecution.
(A) maxim (B) stimulus (C) prospect (D) taboo

7. Antibiotics may stimulate the growth of more bacteria.
(A) decline (B) activate (C) remove (D) constrict

8. Mural paintings in a tumulus depict primitive men's activities such as hunting and fishing.
(A) ancient (B) laborious (C) presumable (D) profound

9. Former Los Alamos scientist Wen Ho Lee was released from prison after nine months in confinement.
(A) linked (B) freed (C) announced (D) repressed

10. With the amount of precipitation in the rain forest, it is understandable that vegetation thrives so well.
(A) heals (B) disengages (C) prospers (D) generates

정답 p.419

Pueblo Culture

푸에블로는 북아메리카 남서부에 사는 인디언들로서 지금의 뉴멕시코주· 애리조나주에 해당하는 지역에 살았다. 그들은 농경민으로서 백인이 들어오기 전부터 이미 관개를 하고 있었다. 예전부터 점토를 굳혀 만든 아파트식 취락을 하였으며 지금도 뉴멕시코주의 타오스에 있는 푸에블로족 마을에서 이 종류의 취락을 볼 수 있다. 이전의 바스켓 메이커(Basket Maker)문화와 푸에블로 문화를 합쳐 아나사지(Anasazi)문화라고 하는데, 기하학적 무늬를 넣은 토기와 수백개의 방이 있는 집합주택이 특징이다. 이후 1700년대부터 에스파냐의 영향이 본격화되었지만 이들은 지금까지도 토착문화를 유지해오고 있다.

바스켓 메이커 인디언(100~500)은 수렵 및 채취생활을 하며 동굴이나 석조기둥과 아도비 벽돌로 된 곳에서 살았다. 변형 바스켓 메이커 시기(500~700)에는 농경이 주를 이루면서, 동굴 반지하 가옥이었으며 직선이나 초승달모양으로 운집해 있었다. 발달 푸에블로 시기(700~1050) 또한 직선형· 초승달형 가옥이 운집해 있었으며 이 시기에는 목화 재배가 이루어졌다. 도기 역시 다양한 모양으로 제작되어 바구니의 사용이 점차 줄었다. 고전 푸에블로 시기(1050~1300)에는 협곡과 벼랑을 따라 아파트식 가옥이 형성된 시기이다. 가옥은 벼랑 기슭에 지어졌으나 다른 지역의 가옥과 별반 다르지 않았다. 도기 기술은 고도로 발전했으며 면화나 유카실로 정교하게 직물을 짜는 기술도 있었다. 퇴행 푸에블로 시기(1300~1700)는 남쪽과 동쪽에 거주하던 인디언들이 리오그란데 계곡이나 애리조나의 화이트 산맥지역으로 이동한 시기에 해당한다. 이전 시기보다 더 크게 지어진 가옥은 그 모양이나 건축에 있어서 열악했다. 도기 기술은 여전히 발달했으나 그 모양이 변화되었고, 직물은 그대로 유지되었다. 근대 푸에블로 시기(1700~현재)에는 에스파냐의 영향이 본격화되었다. 에스파냐는 새로운 문화를 강요하여 적대감을 야기했으며, 1600년대에 반란을 일으켰으나 곧 진압되었다. 그 이후 인디언 부족의 수와 마을은 크게 줄었으나 문화와 기술은 현재까지 보존되고 있다.

DAY Hackers TOEFL **Vocabulary**

4 Hackers Voca

www.goHackers.com

1 **achieve****	v.	accomplish, **perform, effect**	성취하다
[ətʃíːv] fail		After working an entire month on the project, the group stepped back to see what they had **achieved**.	
2 **anchor***	v.	hold in place, **secure, fasten**	고정시키다
[ǽŋkər] release		The panel was firmly **anchored** by two large bolts.	
3 **attribute****	v.	1. ascribe, **impute, refer**	~의 탓으로 돌리다
[ətríbjuːt]		The world's increase in energy use can be **attributed** to the population growth.	
[ǽtrəbjuːt]	n.	2. quality, trait, characteristic, property	특성
		Jerry's vast experience is one of the most important **attributes** of his success.	
4 **brisk**	adj.	active, **vigorous, energetic** lively	활기 있는
[brísk] passive		The gourmet cooks from Hong Kong are doing a **brisk** business in Chinatown.	
5 **codify****	v.	classify, **arrange, systematize**	(체계적으로) 정리하다
[kɔ́dəfài] randomize		The Human Genome Project is a scientific initiative that seeks to **codify** all genetic material in the human body.	

achieve	한 달 내내 프로젝트를 수행한 후 그 팀은 한 걸음 물러서서 그들이 성취한 것을 보았다.
anchor	그 패널은 두 개의 커다란 볼트로 단단히 고정되어 있었다.
attribute	세계적인 에너지 사용의 증가는 인구 성장에서 기인하는 것으로 볼 수 있다. Jerry의 풍부한 경험은 그의 성공의 가장 중요한 특성들 중 하나이다.
brisk	음식에 정통한 홍콩 출신의 요리사들은 차이나타운에서 활발한 사업을 하고 있다.
codify	인간 게놈 프로젝트는 인간의 몸 속에 있는 모든 유전적 물질을 체계화하려는 과학적 시도이다.

6 consummate**

[kánsəmət]
incomplete

adj. **superb; complete** 뛰어난 ; 완전한

Pittman's **consummate** dealmaking helped make AOL a marketing powerhouse.

7 descent*

[disént]

n. 1. **falling** 하강

The **descent** from the mountain took a whole day.

n. 2. **origin, blood, lineage** 혈통, 기원

It was estimated that there were fifteen million people of Spanish **descent** in the region.

8 disseminate**

[disémənèit]

v. **spread out, distribute, disperse, scatter** 퍼뜨리다

The rumor was **disseminated** by word-of-mouth.

9 earn

[ə́:rn]

v. **acquire, attain, win** 획득하다

The lawyer **earned** recognition for his work with the poor.

10 emergence

[imə́:rdʒəns]

n. **rise, appearance, advent** 출현, 부상

The **emergence** of Japan as a world power began in the early twentieth century.

11 facilitate*

[fəsílətèit]

v. **make more available (easier)** (일을) 용이하게 하다

Freedom of information laws **facilitate** access to government documents for researchers.

12 fervent*

[fə́:rvənt]
impassive

adj. **passionate, ardent, earnest** 열정적인

The current administration has decided to maintain the education tax in view of the **fervent** support for education.

consummate	Pittman의 뛰어난 계약 체결력이 AOL을 세력 있는 마케팅 회사로 만드는 것을 도왔다.
descent	그 산에서 내려오는데 온종일이 걸렸다. 그 지역에는 천 오백만의 스페인 후손들이 있다고 추정되었다.
disseminate	그 소문은 입으로 퍼뜨려졌다.
earn	그 변호사는 가난한 사람들을 위해 한 일로 인정을 받았다.
emergence	일본은 20세기 초부터 세계 강대국으로 부상하기 시작하였다.
facilitate	정보의 자유에 관한 법은 연구자들이 정부 문서에 접근하는 것을 용이하게 한다.
fervent	현 정부는 교육에 대한 열렬한 지지를 고려하여 교육세를 유지하기로 결정했다.

13 fine**

adj. **slight, subtle, delicate; thin** 미세한, 섬세한 ; 가느다란

[fáin]

Mr. Parkinson sat down with his lawyer to go over the **fine** points of the building contract.

14 frivolous

adj. **trivial, trifling, petty, unimportant** 사소한

[frívələs]

The seemingly **frivolous** affair turned into a major scandal.

15 giant*

n. **ogre** 거인

[dʒáiənt]
dwarf

There is a legend that **giants** live in the red oak forests in California, where they hide from normal humans.

16 golden age

phr. **a period of great achievement** 황금 시대, 전성기

The nineteenth century was the **golden age** of the British Empire.

17 grasp

v. 1. **grip, clutch, grab, seize** 붙잡다

[grǽsp]

Charles **grasped** my hand and pulled me out of the oncoming car's path.

v. 2. **catch, understand, comprehend, apprehend** 이해하다, 파악하다

Few students could **grasp** Professor Benton's physics lecture.

18 hamstrung*

adj. **ineffective, powerless; disabled, crippled, lame** 무력한 ; 불구의

[hǽmstrəŋ]
able, fit

Police officers claim that they are **hamstrung** by regulations and paperwork.

19 haphazard

adj. **random, casual, unplanned, chance** 되는대로의, 우연의

[hǽphæ̀zərd]

Teachers were upset about the school's almost **haphazard** scheduling of classes.

fine	Parkinson씨는 건축 계약서의 세세한 부분을 검토하기 위해 변호사와 함께 자리에 앉았다.
frivolous	겉으로 사소해 보이던 사건이 큰 스캔들로 변했다.
giant	캘리포니아의 붉은 참나무 숲에 거인들이 살고 있다는 전설이 있는데, 이곳은 그들이 일반 사람들을 피해 숨어 있는 장소이다.
golden age	19세기는 대영제국의 전성기였다.
grasp	Charles는 내 손을 잡아서 다가오는 차의 진로에서 끌어내어 주었다.
	Benton 교수님의 물리학 강의를 이해하는 학생은 거의 없었다.
hamstrung	경관들은 규칙과 서류 작업에 의해 자신들이 무력해지고 있다고 주장했다.
haphazard	선생님들은 학교에서 거의 되는대로 짜놓은 시간표 때문에 화가 났다.

20 **incidental** — adj. **minor, secondary; accidental, casual** 중요하지 않은 ; 우연한

[ìnsədéntəl]
essential

The referee, ruling that there was only **incidental** contact between the players, did not call a foul.

21 **initiate**** — v. **start, begin, originate, commence** inaugurate 시작하다

[iníʃièit]
terminate

President Richard M. Nixon **initiated** his new policy of 'Vietnamization.'

22 **make up** — phr. **invent** 창작하다, 창안하다

In their creative writing class, the students were told to **make up** a story about dancing mosquitoes.

23 **manifold*** — adj. **various, multiple, diverse** 가지각색의

[mǽnəfòuld]
single

Social workers deal with **manifold** issues concerning family health and children's well-being.

24 **obliterate**** — v. **delete, erase, efface, eradicate, wipe out** 제거하다

[əblítərèit]
establish

Adolf Hitler tried unsuccessfully to **obliterate** the Jewish race from the face of the Earth.

25 **period**** — n. **time, age, era** epoch 시대

[píəriəd]

The Great Depression was known as the longest and worst **period** of unemployment in American history.

26 **proceed** — v. **advance, progress** 나아가다

[prəsí:d]
recede

The Democrats thought Lincoln was **proceeding** too drastically in his campaign against slavery.

27 **procure*** — v. **obtain, gain, secure** acquire 얻다

[proukjúər]

To **procure** Blake Cobb's phone number, Lenny had to call twenty different people.

incidental	심판은 선수들간의 미미한 접촉이 있었다고 판단하여 파울 선언을 하지 않았다.
initiate	Richard M. Nixon 대통령은 '베트남화' 라는 새로운 정책을 시작했다.
make up	창의적인 글쓰기 수업에서 학생들은 춤추는 모기에 대한 이야기를 창작해 보라는 지시를 받았다.
manifold	사회 사업가들은 가족의 건강과 아동 복지에 관련된 다양한 문제들을 다룬다.
obliterate	Adolf Hitler는 결국 실패로 끝난, 이 지구상에서 유대인을 모두 제거시키려는 시도를 하였다.
period	대공황은 미국 역사에 있어서 가장 긴 최악의 실업 기간으로 알려져 있다.
proceed	민주당원들은 Lincoln이 노예제도에 반대하는 운동에 너무 급진적으로 나아가고 있다고 생각했다.
procure	Blake Cobb의 전화번호를 얻기 위해, Lenny는 20명에게 전화를 해야 했다.

28 professional* adj. **specialized, expert, adept** 전문적인

[prəféʃənəl]
amateur

The first American to become a **professional** sculptor was a woman, Patience Lovell Wright.

29 redundancy* n. **superfluity, extra capacity; wordiness** 여분 ; 장황

[ridʌ́ndənsi]
shortage of

The use of robots may create **redundancy** among human workers.

30 responsible adj. **charged, liable, accountable** answerable 책임이 있는

[rispɑ́nsəbl]
exempt

The truck driver was **responsible** for the terrible accident.

31 sharp** adj. 1. **keen, pointed, shrewd** 날카로운, 예리한

[ʃɑ́ːrp]
dull

Jack asked some **sharp** questions about where the waste is going.

adj. 2. **sudden, abrupt, rapid** 급격한

Korolev did not obscure the reasons for the **sharp** change in plans.

32 supplement** v. 1. **add to** 보충하다

[sʌ́pləmənt]

Joan and Roger looked for fruits that could **supplement** their meat diets.

omission

n. 2. **extension, extra, addition** 추가, 부가

The committee issued a **supplement** to its report in order to clear up unresolved questions.

33 suspend** v. 1. **defer, postpone, delay** procrastinate 연기하다

[səspénd]
precipitate

The committee members **suspended** judgement for the time being.

---

professional	직업적인 조각가가 된 첫 번째 미국인은 Patience Lovell Wright라는 여성이었다.
redundancy	로봇의 이용은 인간 노동력의 과잉상태를 불러 일으킬 수 있다.
responsible	그 트럭 운전기사는 끔찍한 사고에 대해 책임이 있었다.
sharp	Jack은 쓰레기들이 어디로 가고 있는지에 대해 몇 가지 날카로운 질문들을 했다. Korolev는 계획의 급격한 변화에 대한 이유를 숨기지 않았다.
supplement	Joan과 Roger는 고기 위주의 식단을 보충할 수 있는 과일들을 찾았다. 위원회는 해결되지 않은 문제들을 명확히 하기 위해 보고서에 부록을 포함시켰다.
suspend	그 위원회 구성원들은 당분간 판단을 보류했다.

v. **2. interrupt, cease, arrest** stop — 중지하다

The labor union **suspended** its strike this morning.

collapse

v. 3. **hang, dangle, sling** — 매달다

Michael **suspended** the mobile toy from the ceiling.

34 **tailored**** [téilərd]

adj. **adapted, fitted** — 맞추어진

The group members would put together solutions that were **tailored** to their individual problems.

Quiz

Choose the synonym.

1. achieve	ⓐ originate, commence, begin
2. initiate	ⓑ advance, progress
3. proceed	ⓒ delete, erase, efface
4. tailored	ⓓ accomplish, effect, perform
5. obliterate	ⓔ adapted, fitted

Answer 1. ⓓ 2. ⓐ 3. ⓑ 4. ⓔ 5. ⓒ

suspend
그 노동조합은 오늘 아침에 파업을 중지했다.
Michael은 천장에 움직이는 장난감을 매달았다.

tailored
그 단체 구성원들은 그들의 개인적 문제들에 맞추어진 해결책들을 조합하곤 했다.

DAY 5 Hackers Voca

1 **aimlessly****	adv. without purpose, **purposelessly**	목적 없이
[éimlisli]	The patient was found wandering **aimlessly** around the hospital.	
2 **ally***	v. confederate, **affiliate, associate**	~와 동맹하다, 연합하다
[əlái]	Johnson **allied** with hundreds of political organizations to form the new democratic party.	
3 **anonymous****	adj. unnamed, unknown, **innominate**	익명의
[ənɑ́nəməs] named	Nancy was grateful to an **anonymous** reader for some helpful comments.	
4 **anticipate****	v. foresee, predict, expect, **forecast**	예견하다
[æntísəpèit]	Michelle had probably not **anticipated** such results.	
5 **archaic**	adj. primitive, **ancient; antiquated, antique**	원시적인 ; 구식의
[ɑːrkéiik] novel	The tumulus yielded various **archaic** sculpture and porcelain.	
6 **asset**	n. advantage, **resource, benefit**	이점, 장점
[ǽset]	A highly skilled work force is an **asset** to a country's economy.	

aimlessly	그 환자는 병원을 정처 없이 돌아다니는 상태로 발견되었다.
ally	Johnson은 새로운 민주적 정당을 형성하기 위해 수백 개의 정치 조직들과 동맹을 맺었다.
anonymous	Nancy는 몇 가지 도움이 되는 조언을 해준 익명의 독자에게 고마워했다.
anticipate	Michelle은 아마도 그런 결과를 예견하지 못했을 것이다.
archaic	그 고분은 다양한 고대의 조각과 자기류를 내놓았다.
asset	높은 기술을 갖춘 노동력은 국가 경제의 자산이다.

7 **behavior****

[bihéivjər]
misconduct

n. **conduct** 행동

Allen's **behavior** today seems a little bit strange.

8 **ceaseless***

[sí:slis]

adj. **constant, uninterrupted, eternal** 끊임없는

Buddhists see the attainment of perfection as a struggle requiring **ceaseless** effort.

9 **change****

[tʃéindʒ]

v. **alter, vary, turn, convert, metamorphose** 변화시키다

America was **changed** by the diversity of those who settled in the country.

10 **confederacy***

[kənfédərəsi]
adversary, antagonist

n. **ally, alliance, confederation** 연합, 동맹

The president has a typical opinion of what the **confederacy** of neutral nations should do.

11 **cut****

[kʌ́t]

v. **sever, chop** 절단하다

When heated to a very high temperature, hydrogen can be used to **cut** steel.

12 **disturbance**

[distə́:rbəns]

n. **agitation, disorder, confusion** 동요, 혼란

If people suffer from a mental **disturbance**, they can become unstable.

13 **elucidate***

[ilú:sidèit]
confuse

v. **clarify, clear up, enlighten, shed light on** 명료하게 하다

Dr. Magness further **elucidated** the topic of his lecture on mink farming through a series of examples.

14 **encroachment***

[inkróutʃmənt]
defense

n. **invasion, intrusion** 침범

The **encroachment** of genetically modified organisms into the food supply has many American citizens extremely worried.

behavior	오늘 Allen의 행동은 약간 이상해 보인다.
ceaseless	불교도들은 완벽함을 성취하는 것을 끊임없는 노력을 요하는 투쟁으로 여긴다.
change	미국은 정착한 사람들의 다양성에 의해 변화되었다.
confederacy	그 대통령은 중립 국가들의 연합이 무엇을 해야만 하는가에 대한 전형적인 의견을 가지고 있다.
cut	아주 높은 온도까지 달구어지면 수소는 철을 자르는 데 이용될 수 있다.
disturbance	사람들이 정신적 혼란으로 고통을 받으면, 그들은 불안정해진다.
elucidate	Magness 교수는 밍크 사육에 대한 자신의 강의 주제를 일련의 사례를 통해 더욱 명확하게 했다.
encroachment	유전적으로 조작된 생물체의 식량 공급원으로서의 잠식은 많은 미국 시민들로 하여금 심각한 우려를 하게 했다.

15 **entice***

[entáis]
scare

v. **allure, tempt, seduce** 유혹하다

Rene Callie was a 27-year-old man who was **enticed** by the mysterious legend.

16 **equivocally****

[ikwívəkəli]

adv. **ambiguously** 애매하게

Larry mentioned it so **equivocally** that I couldn't understand the exact meaning.

17 **exterminate**

[ikstə́:rmənèit]

v. **extirpate, annihilate, eradicate** 근절하다

The Europeans proceeded to buy out, **exterminate**, or push out the Indians.

18 **fortify***

[fɔ́:rtəfài]
weaken

v. **strengthen, reinforce** 강화하다

To prepare for war, the general had his men **fortify** the walls of the fort.

19 **formerly***

[fɔ́:rmərli]

adv. **previously, before, earlier, once** 이전에

Istanbul was **formerly** known as Constantinople.

20 **immunity**

[imjú:nəti]

n. **exemption, impunity** 면제

While receiving **immunity** from some laws, diplomats are subject to prosecution if they commit a criminal offense.

21 **improve****

[imprú:v]
deteriorate

v. **enhance, refine, enrich** better, ameliorate 개선하다

New York State has taken measures to **improve** its education system.

22 **in retrospect**

phr. **looking back** 되돌아보면, 회상하면

In retrospect, the decision was considered a mistake.

entice	Rene Callie는 신비한 전설에 매혹당한 27살의 남자였다.
equivocally	Larry가 그것을 너무 애매하게 언급해서 나는 그 정확한 의미를 이해할 수 없었다.
exterminate	유럽인들은 인디언들을 사들이거나 멸종시키거나 또는 몰아내기를 계속 진행했다.
fortify	전쟁에 대비하기 위해, 장군은 자기 병사들이 요새의 장벽을 강화하도록 시켰다.
formerly	이스탄불은 이전에는 콘스탄티노플로 알려져 있었다.
immunity	외교관들이 몇몇 법규로부터 면제를 받는 반면, 형사상의 위반을 저지를 경우에는 기소된다.
improve	뉴욕 주는 주 교육 제도를 개선하기 위한 조치를 취해 왔다.
in retrospect	되돌아보면, 그 결정은 실수였다고 생각된다.

23 **lose sight of***

phr. **forget** 잊다

Peter **lost sight of** the fact that he borrowed $1,000 from Jane.

24 **nuts and bolts***

phr. **basics, practical details** 기본

Learning the everyday **nuts and bolts** of life in a new culture is part of what newcomers to America face.

25 **permit***

[pərmít]
prohibit

v. **allow, let** 허락하다

The captain and his men were **permitted** to return to the Virginia settlements.

26 **radical****

[rǽdikəl]
superficial

adj. 1. **fundamental, basic** 근본적인

The achievement of **radical** equality is unrealistic.

adj. 2. **extreme, drastic, revolutionary** 급진적인

Radical social change came about when a revolutionary consciousness was developed.

27 **rarely***

[rέərli]

adv. **extremely seldom, infrequently** 드물게, 좀처럼 ~않는

Although good friends in high school, James and Mike **rarely** see each other these days.

28 **sparse****

[spɑ́ːrs]
rich

adj. **scanty, meager, scarce, limited** 빈약한, 부족한

The vegetation is **sparse** near the summit.

29 **sting**

[stíŋ]

v. **smart, hurt** 얼얼하다, 쓰리다

Sonya hates chopping onions because they make her eyes **sting**.

lose sight of	Peter는 자신이 Jane에게 1,000달러를 빌렸다는 사실을 잊어버렸다.
nuts and bolts	새로운 문화에서 삶의 일상적인 기본을 배우는 것은 미국에 새로이 온 사람들이 직면하는 것의 일부이다.
permit	그 대장과 부하들은 버지니아의 정착지로 돌아오도록 허락을 받았다.
radical	근본적인 평등의 성취는 비현실적이다.
	급진적 사회 변화는 혁명적 의식이 발달했을 때 일어났다.
rarely	James와 Mike는 고등학교에서는 좋은 친구 사이였지만 요즘은 거의 만나지 않는다.
sparse	정상 근처에서는 초목이 희박하다.
sting	Sonya는 양파 써는 것을 싫어한다. 왜냐하면 그것은 그녀의 눈을 따끔거리게 하기 때문이다.

30 support*

[səpɔ́ːrt]
oppose

v. 1. **assist, back, advocate** 지지하다

The government spent more money on public works to **support** the economic recovery.

v. 2. **maintain, sustain, provide for, take care of** 부양하다

Frank **supported** himself in college by working as a bartender.

31 tangible**

[tǽndʒəbl]
intangible

adj. **material, concrete, real, substantial** 실질적인

The ongoing restructuring programs must soon produce **tangible** results.

32 tolerate**

[tálərèit]

v. **endure, stand** bear 견디다

Hoover had **tolerated** a great many hardships in his life.

33 train**

[tréin]

v. **aim, head** ~로 향하게 하다

The firemen **trained** their hoses at the burning building.

34 unambiguous*

[ʌ̀næmbígjuəs]
ambiguous

adj. **clear, distinct, definite** 명확한

Kate praised his **unambiguous** attitude.

35 virtually**

[və́ːrtʃuəli]

adv. 1. **in effect, practically** 사실상

In traditional communities, fashion is **virtually** unknown.

adv. 2. **nearly, almost** 거의

The oldest firestone, **virtually** 10,000 years old, comes from Belgium.

---

support	정부는 경제 회복을 돕기 위해 공공사업에 더 많은 돈을 소비했다.
	Frank는 대학에 다닐 때 바텐더로 일하면서 스스로 생계를 부양했다.
tangible	진행 중인 구조조정 프로그램들은 곧 실재적인 결과들을 산출해 내야만 한다.
tolerate	Hoover는 생전에 상당히 많은 역경을 견뎌야 했다.
train	소방수들은 그들의 호스를 불타고 있는 건물에 향하게 했다.
unambiguous	Kate는 그의 명확한 태도를 칭찬했다.
virtually	전통적인 사회에서 패션은 사실상 알려져 있지 않다.
	거의 만 년이나 된 세계에서 가장 오래된 부싯돌은 벨기에에서 나왔다.

36 **wary****	adj. **distrustful, cautious, heedful** alert	조심(경계)하는
[wέəri] foolhardy	Taiwan's government was **wary** of becoming economically dependent on a political rival.	
37 **wealth***	n. **affluence, abundance, profusion**	풍부함
[wélθ]	Adam's latest book contained a **wealth** of information on constitutional theory.	
38 **wiggle**	v. **move up and down, move from side to side, wriggle**	이리저리 흔들다
[wígl]	To prevent frostbite, those exposed to extreme cold are advised to **wiggle** their fingers and toes to increase blood circulation.	

Quiz

Choose the synonym.

1. archaic	ⓐ ancient, antiquated, antique
2. exterminate	ⓑ clear up, clarify, enlighten
3. elucidate	ⓒ annihilate, eradicate, eliminate
4. tangible	ⓓ move up and down, wriggle
5. wiggle	ⓔ real, substantial, concrete

Answer 1. ⓐ 2. ⓒ 3. ⓑ 4. ⓔ 5. ⓓ

wary	대만 정부는 정치적 경쟁자에게 경제적으로 의존하게 되는 것을 경계했다.
wealth	Adams의 최근의 책은 입헌 이론에 관한 풍부한 정보를 담고 있다.
wiggle	동상을 방지하기 위해서, 극한의 추위에 노출된 이들은 혈액순환을 촉진시키기 위해서 손가락과 발가락을 움직이라고 조언받는다.

DAY Hackers TOEFL **Vocabulary**

6 Hackers Voca

www.goHackers.com

1 **agile*** | adj. **quick, nimble, light** | 민첩한

[ǽdʒəl]
torpid

Brown bears are, for such huge beasts, amazingly **agile**.

2 **ample*** | adj. 1. **sizable, large, spacious, vast** capacious | 넓은

[ǽmpl]
limited

With three bedrooms and two bathrooms, the apartment provided **ample** space for Soren and his sister.

meager

adj. 2. **plentiful, abundant** | 충분한

Richard stocks his refrigerator with an **ample** supply of food and beverages for unexpected guests.

3 **arbitrarily*** | adv. **randomly** | 임의로

[ɑ́ːrbətrèrəli]

The committee modified the rule **arbitrarily**.

4 **attest*** | v. **confirm, support, prove** | 입증하다

[ətést]

John was hired because his past work **attested** his skill.

5 **break with**** | phr. **separate from, discontinue an association** | 관계를 끊다

Mary and Alice are going to **break with** the old accounting firm.

agile	갈색 곰들은 그렇게 큰 동물치고는 놀라우리만치 민첩하다.
ample	세 개의 침실과 두 개의 욕실을 갖춘 그 아파트는 Soren과 그의 여동생에게 넓은 공간을 제공했다.
	Richard는 예상치 못한 손님이 올 것에 대비해 냉장고에 충분한 음식과 마실 것을 넣어 둔다.
arbitrarily	그 위원회는 임의로 그 규칙을 수정했다.
attest	John은 그의 과거 경력이 그의 능력을 입증했기 때문에 고용되었다.
break with	Mary와 Alice는 그 오래된 회계 회사와의 관계를 끊을 것이다.

6 brightness*

[bráitnis]

n. **radiance** 빛

The crystal glass shone with **brightness**.

7 conjure*

[kándʒər]

v. 1. **recall** 불러내다, 상기시키다

The log cabin **conjures** up images of the rugged pioneer days.

v. 2. **implore, supplicate** 간청하다

Matthew **conjured** Sarah to care for his little daughter when he is away.

8 contrive**

[kəntráiv]

v. **invent, concoct, improvise** 고안해내다

Unable to **contrive** an excuse, Sarah did not respond.

9 correspondence**

[kɔ̀ːrəspándəns]

n. 1. **agreement, conformity, harmony** 일치

All Mike can do is to show the **correspondence** of his words and actions.

n. 2. **communication, exchange of letters** (편지로 하는) 통신

CNN reported the results of the **correspondence** between Bush and Blair in an official statement.

10 durable**

[djúərəbl]

adj. **lasting, enduring, constant** 지속적인

Eisenhower could not convert personal loyalty into **durable** support for his party.

11 dwarf

[dwɔ́ːrf]
giant

n. **pygmy** 난쟁이

Johnny's role in the play is one of Snow White's seven **dwarfs**.

brightness	그 크리스털 잔은 환하게 빛이 났다.
conjure	그 통나무 오두막은 고된 개척 시대의 이미지들을 상기시킨다. Matthew는 Sarah에게 그가 없는 동안 어린 딸을 돌봐달라고 간청했다.
contrive	변명할 거리를 생각해내지 못해서, Sarah는 대답하지 않았다.
correspondence	Mike가 할 수 있는 전부는 자신의 말과 행동의 일치를 보여 주는 것이다. CNN은 공식 성명으로 Bush와 Blair 사이의 서신 왕래의 결과를 보고했다.
durable	Eisenhower는 개인적 충성심을 그의 당에 대한 지속적인 지지로 변하게 할 수 없었다.
dwarf	그 연극에서 Johnny의 역할은 백설 공주의 일곱 난쟁이들 중 한 명이었다.

12 enigmatic adj. **puzzling, mysterious, cryptic, perplexing** 알기 어려운

[ènigmǽtik]

Artist Vincent Van Gogh was known for his **enigmatic** personality.

13 extinct** adj. **died out, vanished, defunct** 멸종된

[ikstíŋkt]
extant

Plants and animals are becoming **extinct** at the fastest rate ever known in human history.

14 fabricate* v. **make, build, construct** concoct 만들어내다

[fǽbrəkèit]

The Republicans **fabricated** stories to depict Buchanan as a traitor.

15 flake n. **fragment, bit, chip** 파편

[fléik]
whole

As **flakes** of paint were falling in sections from the old ceiling, Harrison decided to repaint the entire room.

16 harm n. **damage, mischief, detriment** 손해

[há:rm]
benefit

Noise pollution causes a lot of physical and psychological **harm**.

17 innocent adj. **sinless, blameless, guiltless** 결백한

[ínəsənt]
guilty

The army killed thousands of **innocent** civilians.

18 in the course of* phr. **during** ~동안에

Jane met her boyfriend Tom **in the course of** one of her swimming lessons.

19 in vain phr. **unsuccessfully** 헛되이

The effort to impeach the president was made **in vain**.

enigmatic	예술가 반 고흐는 수수께끼 같은 성격으로 유명했다.
extinct	식물과 동물들은 인류 역사상 지금껏 알려진 가장 빠른 속도로 멸종하고 있다.
fabricate	공화당원들은 Buchanan을 배신자로 묘사하기 위해 이야기를 꾸며냈다.
flake	오래된 천장에서 페인트 조각이 분해되어 떨어지게 되자, Harrison은 방 전체를 다시 페인트칠 하기로 결심했다.
harm	소음 공해는 심한 신체적, 정신적인 피해를 유발한다.
innocent	그 군대는 수천 명의 죄 없는 민간인들을 죽였다.
in the course of	Jane은 한 수영 수업 시간 중에 그녀의 남자 친구인 Tom을 만났다.
in vain	대통령을 탄핵시키려는 노력은 허사가 돼버렸다.

20 **inconsequential**	adj. **unimportant, insignificant, petty, trifling**		하찮은, 사소한
[inkὰnsəkwénʃəl]	The assembly's decisions were largely **inconsequential** because the president held most of the power.		
21 **leave**	v. **depart**		떠나다
[lí:v]	James Joyce decided to **leave** Dublin in pursuit of his art.		
22 **liken***	v. **compare, equate, match, parallel**		비유하다
[láikən]	When Jeremiah sits deep in contemplation, it is easy to **liken** his pose to that of Rodin's sculpture 'The Thinker.'		
23 **literally***	adv. **really, actually**		실제로
[lítərəli]	The slave was **literally** unable to speak a word for himself.		
24 **moderate***	adj. **gentle, temperate, reasonable**	mild	온건한
[mάdərət] excessive	The union's **moderate** demands allowed for a quick resolution with the company.		
25 **prolong***	v. **extend, lengthen, protract**		연장하다
[prəlɔ́:ŋ] curtail	Nixon was convinced that the antiwar movement **prolonged** the war.		
26 **purify***	v. **clear, purge, cleanse**		정화하다, 깨끗이 하다
[pjúərəfài] contaminate, pollute	Calgon Carbon Corp. is a maker of air and water **purifying** materials.		
27 **reasonable**	adj. **rational, logical, sensible**		이치에 맞는
[rí:zənəbl] extravagant, absurd	It seems **reasonable** to be tough on habitual criminals.		

inconsequential	대통령이 대부분의 권력을 쥐고 있었기 때문에 의회의 결정은 별로 중요하지 않았다.
leave	James Joyce는 자신의 예술을 위해 더블린을 떠나기로 결심했다.
liken	Jeremiah가 깊은 생각에 잠겨 앉아 있을 때, 그의 자세는 로댕의 조각품 '생각하는 사람'에 쉽게 비유되곤 했다.
literally	그 노예는 실제로 스스로 말 한마디 할 수 없었다.
moderate	노조의 온건한 요구로 사측과 빠른 결의를 이끌었다.
prolong	Nixon은 반전 운동이 전쟁을 연장했다고 믿었다.
purify	Calgon Carbon 회사는 공기와 물 정화 물질을 생산하는 회사이다.
reasonable	상습적인 범죄자들에게 엄격한 것은 이치에 맞는 것처럼 보인다.

28 refined adj. **purified, clarified, distilled** 정제된

[rifáind]
vulgar

Any grain that's not **refined** or polished has health benefits.

29 retain* v. **keep, maintain, preserve** 유지(보유)하다

[ritéin]

Americans must **retain** a copy of their tax forms from the previous three years.

30 scarce** adj. **rare, sparse; scant, deficient** 드문 ; 부족한

[skɛ́ərs]
abundant

Argyrodite is a relatively **scarce** mineral that is found only in Germany and adjoining countries.

31 scope** n. **extent, range** 범위

[skóup]

The professor explained to the class that certain subject matter was outside the **scope** of the course.

32 shabby adj. **ragged, beggarly, poor** 초라한

[ʃǽbi]
spruce

Henry used to wear the **shabby** old hat when he worked in the corn field.

33 short-lived** adj. **lasting for only a short period** 단기간의

[ʃɔ́ːrtlívd]
permanent

The rock star's popularity was **short-lived**.

34 solidify* v. **unify, consolidate** 결속시키다

[səlídəfài]
divide

One wonders when the two Koreas will finally sign a treaty to **solidify** their alliance.

35 substantial** adj. **1. strong, sturdy, solid** 튼튼한

[səbstǽnʃəl]
weak

The Chickasaw Indians lived in **substantial** wooden houses.

refined	정제되지 않은 곡식은 건강에 좋다.
retain	미국인들은 과거 3년 동안의 세금 용지 복사본을 소지하고 있어야만 한다.
scarce	아지로다이트는 오직 독일과 인접 국가에서만 발견되는 비교적으로 드문 광물이다.
scope	교수는 특정 주제가 강의의 범위 밖의 것이라고 설명했다.
shabby	Henry는 옥수수 밭에서 일할 때면 낡고 허름한 모자를 쓰곤 했다.
short-lived	그 록 스타의 인기는 단기간의 인기였다.
solidify	사람들은 언제쯤 남 · 북한이 마침내 자신의 동맹을 결속시키는 협약에 서명할 것인지를 궁금해한다.
substantial	Chickasaw 인디언들은 튼튼한 나무 집에 살았다.

insignificant

adj. 2. **significant, noticeable, considerable** 상당한

A **substantial** number of adults become single parents as a result of divorce.

36 vacant*

[véikənt]
occupied

adj. **empty, void, unoccupied** 텅 빈

The hotel rooms are **vacant** during the winter months because the cold weather deters tourism.

37 wizened*

[wízənd]
blooming

adj. **shriveled, withered, shrunken** 시든, 주름진

The once great chief is now a **wizened** old man.

38 zone*

[zóun]

n. **area, region** 지역

Mr. Gipson was transferred to the Panama Canal **zone** as an executive officer.

Quiz

Choose the synonym.

1. agile	ⓐ unimportant, insignificant, petty
2. enigmatic	ⓑ unify, consolidate
3. inconsequential	ⓒ quick, nimble, light
4. purify	ⓓ puzzling, mysterious, cryptic
5. solidify	ⓔ clear, purge, cleanse

Answer 1.ⓒ 2.ⓓ 3.ⓐ 4.ⓔ 5.ⓑ

substantial	상당수의 성인들이 이혼의 결과 편부 편모가 된다.
vacant	추운 날씨가 관광업을 방해하기 때문에 겨울철 동안에는 호텔 객실이 빈다.
wizened	이제 대추장은 시들시들해진 늙은 노인이다.
zone	Gipson씨는 행정관으로 파나마 운하 지역으로 전출되었다.

Hackers TOEFL Voca TEST DAY 04-06

Choose the synonym of the highlighted word in the sentence.

1. It can be inferred that dinosaurs became extinct because of a global firestorm.
(A) broad (B) predominant (C) accidental (D) vanished

2. Fine shale is perhaps the most significant sedimentary rock covering the earth.
(A) subtle (B) erroneous (C) acid (D) vivid

3. The processes of natural selection ensured the survival of the fittest and improved the quality of the species.
(A) coined (B) bettered (C) shielded (D) aided

4. Manifold sources of information are available on the Internet.
(A) intelligent (B) uniform (C) diverse (D) plain

5. Radical social change can only come about when a revolutionary consciousness is fully developed.
(A) revolutionary (B) urgent (C) eminent (D) latent

6. The ore that contains tin is scarce in southwestern Asia.
(A) coarse (B) judicious (C) rare (D) agile

7. Contrary to the government's expectations, the national economy is on a sharp decline.
(A) manifold (B) sudden (C) ambiguous (D) clear

8. The wooden board was surprisingly substantial enough to hold up the heavy load.
(A) sturdy (B) rare (C) shabby (D) refined

9. The enigmatic nature of surreal art limited its appeal beyond narrow circles.
(A) vexing (B) engaged (C) mysterious (D) transformational

10. In people without heart disease, cholesterol-lowering drugs have not yet been shown to prolong life.
(A) extend (B) strengthen (C) quit (D) delay

정답 p.419

TAKE A BREAK

지하철에서

DAY 7

Hackers TOEFL **Vocabulary**

Hackers Voca

www.goHackers.com

1 **abolish***

[əbɑ́liʃ]
conserve

v. **annul, nullify, revoke** 폐지하다

Congress passed legislation **abolishing** slavery.

2 **adage**

[ǽdidʒ]

n. **proverb, saying, maxim** 속담, 금언

"Life is like a box of chocolates... you never know what you're gonna get" is a memorable **adage** from the movie *Forrest Gump*.

3 **aesthetic****

[esθétik]

adj. **artistic** 미적인

The painting is excellent from an **aesthetic** point of view.

4 **affect****

[əfékt]

v. 1. **influence, act on** ~에 영향을 미치다

The scientists are currently studying how climate **affects** marine animal populations.

v. 2. **pretend, feign, assume** ~인 체하다

Jennifer always **affected** a little stammer when she said anything impudent.

5 **alteration***

[ɔ̀:ltəréiʃən]
preservation

n. **change, modification** 변경

The tailor made an **alteration** to Kelly's wedding dress so that it would drape more loosely about her shoulders.

abolish	국회는 노예제도를 폐지하는 법률을 통과시켰다.
adage	"인생은 초콜릿 상자와도 같아요... 당신은 무엇을 먹게 될지 결코 알 수 없죠"라는 말은 영화 포레스트 검프에 등장했던 기억해둘 만한 명언이다.
aesthetic	그 그림은 미적인 관점에서 상당히 우수하다.
affect	과학자들은 기후가 해양 동물 수에 어떤 영향을 미치는 현재 연구 중이다.
	Jennifer는 염치없는 말을 할 때면 말을 더듬는 척했다.
alteration	재단사는 Kelly의 웨딩드레스를 수선하여 그것이 그녀의 어깨에 좀 더 느슨하게 둘러지도록 하였다.

6 amenity*

[əménəti]

n. **facility, pleasant situation, convenience** 편의 시설

The family chose to stay at the Holiday Inn because it had great **amenities**, such as a hot tub, exercise room, and free parking.

7 approximately**

[əprɑ́ksəmitli]
precisely

adv. **about, roughly, nearly** almost 대략

Central Hudson Electric Utility serves **approximately** 625,000 people in New York State's Mid-Hudson Valley.

8 artisan*

[ɑ́:rtizən]

n. **craftsman** 숙련공

The European Renaissance produced many famous **artisans**, including painters, metalworkers, woodcarvers, and jewelry makers.

9 bear**

[bέər]

v. 1. **carry, transport, convey** 운반하다

Jameson should **bear** the child to the station.

v. 2. **yield, provide, produce** 산출하다, 생기게 하다

The tree is **bearing** a lot of peaches this year.

put down

v. 3. **support, hold, sustain** (무게를) 지탱하다, 견디다

The heaviest barbell John can **bear** is 10kgs.

10 bountiful*

[báuntəfəl]
sparse

adj. **plentiful, abundant, ample, prolific, liberal** 풍부한

Each year a **bountiful** harvest of wheat and corn is produced in the state of Nebraska.

11 constituent

[kənstítʃuənt]

adj. **component, elemental** 구성하는, 구성 요소의

Copper and tin are the **constituent** elements of bronze.

amenity	그 가족은 Holiday Inn에 머물기로 했다. 왜냐하면 거기에는 온수 욕조, 운동할 공간, 무료 주차장과 같은 훌륭한 편의 시설들이 있기 때문이다.
approximately	Central Hudson Electric Utility는 뉴욕 주의 미드허드슨 밸리에 사는 대략 625,000명의 사람들에게 공급을 한다.
artisan	유럽의 르네상스는 화가, 금속 세공사, 목각사, 보석공을 포함한 많은 유명한 숙련공들을 배출하였다.
bear	Jameson은 그 아이를 역까지 데려다 줘야 한다.
	그 나무는 올해 많은 복숭아를 맺고 있다.
	John이 지탱할 수 있는 가장 무거운 역기는 10킬로그램이다.
bountiful	매년 네브라스카 주에서는 풍부한 밀과 옥수수 작물들이 생산된다.
constituent	구리와 주석은 청동의 구성 물질들이다.

12 dispute**

[dispjúːt]
concede

v. 1. **argue, debate** 논쟁하다

The town's people are **disputing** with the local council over the proposed new road.

n. 2. **argument, disagreement, debate** controversy 논쟁

China and Japan struck a deal to end the trade **dispute** over agricultural products.

13 faculty*

[fǽkəlti]
inability

n. **ability, capacity, aptitude** 능력

Children have the **faculty** to concentrate on what occupies them at the moment.

14 field*

[fíːld]

n. **area** 분야

Northern engineers were experienced in the **field** of iron working.

15 guiltless

[gíltlis]
guilty

adj. **sinless, blameless, innocent** 결백한

A polygraph test can make even **guiltless** people nervous.

16 influx**

[ínflʌ̀ks]
outflow

n. **arrival, inrush, inflow** 유입

Tourism has brought a huge **influx** of wealth into the region.

17 inundate*

[ínʌndèit]

v. **flood, deluge, swamp, submerge** 물에 잠기게 하다

During monsoon season the rice paddies become **inundated** with rain for weeks at a time.

18 lexicon

[léksəkɑ̀n]

n. **vocabulary** 어휘

New words are added to the English **lexicon** each year.

dispute	마을 사람들은 제안된 새 도로에 관해 지방 의회와 논쟁을 벌이고 있다. 중국과 일본은 농산품에 대한 무역 논쟁을 끝내기 위한 거래를 타결했다.
faculty	아이들은 그 순간에 그들을 사로잡는 것에 집중하는 능력을 가지고 있다.
field	북부의 공학자들은 철을 가지고 일하는 분야에서 숙련되어 있다.
guiltless	거짓말 탐지기는 결백한 사람들조차도 긴장하게 만들 수 있다.
influx	여행 산업은 그 지역에 거대한 부의 유입을 가져왔다.
inundate	호우기 동안에 벼 논은 단번에 몇 주씩 물에 잠겨 있게 된다.
lexicon	매년 새로운 단어들이 영어 어휘에 추가된다.

19 lure*
[lúər]
repel

v. **attract, draw, seduce** allure, decoy 유혹하다

Jackson's prey was **lured** into the woods with promises of food and drink.

20 mixture
[míkstʃər]

n. **combination, compound, blend, composite** 혼합(물)

The Philippine language is a **mixture** of Malay and Spanish.

21 mount**
[máunt]
descend

v. 1. **ascend, climb, scale** 오르다

Julie **mounted** the stairs slowly.

decrease

v. 2. **increase, multiply, grow** rise 증가하다

A new scientific report released today says **mounting** evidence links TV viewing to violence.

22 mundane*
[mʌndéin]
exceptional

adj. **ordinary, routine, commonplace** 평범한

Kelly believes that **mundane** activities such as cooking and cleaning are a waste of time.

23 nearly
[níərli]

adv. **almost, approximately, virtually** 거의

Nearly perfect test scores are required to enter elite universities.

24 outstrip*
[àutstríp]
follow

v. **surpass, transcend, exceed** excel 능가하다, 뛰어나다

Mining and business began to **outstrip** agriculture in China.

25 pertinent*
[pə́ːrtənənt]
impertinent

adj. **relevant, germane, applicable** 관련된, 적절한

The detective wanted to know all the **pertinent** details.

lure	Jackson의 사냥감은 먹을 것과 마실 것의 낌새를 채고 숲으로 유인되었다.
mixture	필리핀어는 말레이어와 스페인어가 혼합된 언어다.
mount	Julie는 천천히 계단을 올라갔다.
	오늘 발표된 새로운 과학 보고서에는 점차 늘어가는 증거들이 TV 시청과 폭력을 연관 짓고 있다고 나와 있다.
mundane	Kelly는 요리나 청소와 같은 평범한 활동들이 시간 낭비라고 믿고 있다.
nearly	명문대에 들어가려면 거의 만점에 가까운 점수가 필요하다.
outstrip	중국에서 광업과 상업이 농업을 앞지르기 시작했다.
pertinent	그 탐정은 모든 관련 세부 사항들을 알기를 원했다.

26 **preclude*** | v. **prevent, rule out, forestall, obviate** 그만두게 하다, 막다

[priklú:d]

Age alone will not **preclude** him from running for office.

27 **refrain*** | v. **pause, stop** cease 삼가다, 중단하다

[rifréin]

Many conservative Jews **refrain** from eating foods such as shellfish.

28 **roughly**** | adv. **approximately, nearly** 대략

[rʌ́fli]

The U.S. has spent **roughly** $2 billion a year on AIDS-related issues since 1989.

29 **semblance**** | n. 1. **appearance** 외관

[sémbləns]

The boy has the **semblance** of honesty.

dissemblance | n. 2. **analogy, similarity, likeness, resemblance** 유사함

The election bears some **semblance** to the presidential election between Gore and Bush.

30 **sophisticated*** | adj. **complex, complicated** 복잡한

[səfístəkèitid]
unsophisticated

A more **sophisticated** approach was needed to solve the problem.

31 **stage*** | n. **level, phase, step** 단계

[stéidʒ]

The **stages** of language acquisition are the same for all languages.

32 **thick** | adj. **dense, compact** 빽빽한

[θík]
thin

The jeep was found lying in **thick** bush.

preclude	나이만으로는 그가 선거에 출마하는 것을 막을 수 없을 것이다.
refrain	많은 보수적인 유대인들은 갑각류 같은 음식은 멀리한다.
roughly	미국은 1989년 이래로 AIDS와 관련된 사안들에 일 년에 대략 20억 달러를 써왔다.
semblance	그 소년은 정직한 외모를 가지고 있다.
	그 선거는 Gore와 Bush 사이의 대통령 선거와 유사한 점을 지니고 있다.
sophisticated	그 문제를 푸는 데는 좀 더 정교한 접근법이 필요했다.
stage	언어 습득의 단계들은 모든 언어에 있어서 동일하다.
thick	그 지프차는 울창한 숲 속에 놓인 채로 발견되었다.

33 **thus***
[ðʌ́s]

adv. **consequently, therefore, accordingly** 따라서

New drugs can lower blood pressure, **thus** reducing the risk of stroke.

34 **tiny****
[táini]
huge

adj. **little, minuscule, minute** 작은

Dana used to be a **tiny** girl, but grew up to be a large woman.

35 **verge***
[və́ːrdʒ]

n. **brink, threshold** 경계, 찰나

The city is on the **verge** of becoming prosperous and successful.

Quiz

Choose the synonym.

1. adage	ⓐ relevant, germane, applicable
2. bear	ⓑ maxim, saying, proverb
3. outstrip	ⓒ outrun, excel, surpass
4. verge	ⓓ carry, transport, convey
5. pertinent	ⓔ brink, threshold

Answer 1. ⓑ 2. ⓓ 3. ⓒ 4. ⓔ 5. ⓐ

thus	새로운 약은 혈압을 낮출 수 있고 따라서 뇌졸중의 위험성을 줄인다.
tiny	Dana는 매우 작은 소녀였지만, 몸집이 큰 여자로 성장하였다.
verge	그 도시는 이제 막 번영하고 성공적이 되려는 경계에 있다.

DAY 8 Hackers Voca

1 **abort** [əbɔ́ːrt]

v. **quit, call off** 중단하다

The mission was **aborted** due to a lack of funds.

2 **acquire*** [əkwáiər]
forfeit

v. **obtain, earn, gain, procure** 얻다

The local governments **acquire** land directly from private landowners.

3 **affection** [əfékʃən]
hate

n. **liking, attachment, fondness, love** 애정

Since the death of his wife, Robert's **affections** have centered upon his child.

4 **agree** [əgríː]
deny

v. **assent, accede, consent** 동의하다

The club managers **agreed** to meet later and talk things over.

5 **alert**** [ələ́ːrt]
inattentive

adj. 1. **attentive, vigilant, wakeful, wary** 경계하는

The government officials are **alert** to the menace of communism within their country.

v. 2. **warn, alarm, forewarn** 경고하다

The government of China **alerted** everyone to the danger of floods.

---

abort
acquire
affection
agree
alert

그 임무는 자금이 부족해서 중단되었다.
지방 정부들은 개인 땅 소유주들로부터 직접적으로 땅을 얻는다.
Robert의 아내가 죽은 이래로, 그의 애정은 아이에게 집중되어 왔다.
클럽 매니저들은 나중에 만나 그 문제에 대해 이야기하기로 동의했다.
정부 관료들은 나라 안의 공산주의의 위협을 경계하고 있다.
중국 정부는 홍수의 위험성을 모든 사람들에게 경고했다.

6 **allure***

[əlúər]
repel

v. **appeal, attract, invite** (마음을) 끌다, 유혹하다

The beautiful sirens in Greek mythology **allured** countless men and drove them to their death.

7 **amplify***

[ǽmpləfài]
abbreviate

v. **increase, enlarge, expand, magnify** 늘리다

Scientific farming can **amplify** the production of wheat.

8 **arid***

[ǽrid]
fertile

adj. **dry, barren, waterless** 메마른

To develop the project in the **arid** desert, a great amount of water is needed.

9 **ascribe***

[əskráib]

v. **attribute, impute, refer** ~의 탓으로 돌리다

Some archaeologists **ascribe** the decline of the old city to drought.

10 **barge**

[bá:rdʒ]

n. **a large low boat** 배

In Pittsburgh, many **barges** travel the three rivers transporting coal and other heavy materials to local factories.

11 **compensate****

[kámpənsèit]

v. **atone, recompense; offset, counterbalance** 보상하다 ; 상쇄하다

The bank agreed to **compensate** its customers for their loss of money.

12 **configure***

[kənfígjər]

v. **shape, form, mold** ~의 형체로 만들다

The art teacher instructed her students to **configure** the pile of boards into an archway.

13 **drastic***

[drǽstik]
slight

adj. **extreme, desperate, radical** 과격한, 극단적인

The university took **drastic** measures when it expelled a student for plagiarizing several research papers.

allure	그리스 신화에 등장하는 아름다운 사이렌은 수많은 남자들을 유혹하여 그들을 죽음으로 몰고 갔다.
amplify	과학적 농업은 밀의 생산을 늘릴 수 있다.
arid	메마른 사막에서 그 프로젝트를 수행하기 위해서는 상당한 양의 물이 필요하다.
ascribe	몇몇 고고학자들은 그 오래된 도시의 쇠퇴를 가뭄 탓으로 돌린다.
barge	피츠버그에서는 많은 배들이 석탄과 여타의 무거운 물건들을 지방 공장에 옮기며 세 개의 강을 항해한다.
compensate	은행은 고객들의 손해액을 보상해 주기로 합의했다.
configure	미술 교사는 자신의 학생들에게 여러 개의 판자를 아치 모양으로 만들어 보라고 지시했다.
drastic	대학은 몇 가지 연구 과제에서 남의 것을 그대로 도용한 학생을 퇴학시키는 극단적인 조치를 취했다.

14 embarrass v. **abash, discountenance** 무안케 하다

[imbǽrəs]
relieve

The student's blunt questions **embarrassed** the teacher, making her momentarily tongue-tied.

15 focus v. **concentrate, center, zoom in** 집중하다

[fóukəs]

The investigation **focused** on alleged investment fraud.

16 function n. 1. **purpose, role, use** 기능, 역할

[fʌ́ŋkʃən]

Prosecution of criminals is one of the **functions** of an attorney general.

v. 2. **act, work, operate, go, run** 기능하다

Learning a foreign language **functions** to promote cultural understanding.

17 gathering* n. **amassing, collection; assembly, convocation** 수집 ; 모임

[gǽðəriŋ]

During the Stone Age, hunting was a source of food for early man as was the **gathering** of fruits.

18 haul* v. **pull, tug, drag, heave** 끌어당기다

[hɔ́:l]

The movers had to **haul** the heavy couch two blocks down the street to get it into their truck.

19 immediate* adj. **nearest, close, next** 인접한

[imí:diət]
distant

The **immediate** area was sealed off after the bombing attempt.

20 increase v. **augment, enlarge, escalate** 확대하다

[inkrí:s]
decrease

The new law **increased** fear among the colonists.

---

embarrass	그 학생의 퉁명스런 질문들이 그 교사를 당황하게 해서 잠시 할 말을 잃게 만들었다.
focus	그 수사는 투자 사기 혐의자에 대해 집중하였다.
function	범죄자를 기소하는 것은 법무장관의 역할이다.
	외국어 학습은 문화적 이해를 증진시키는 기능을 한다.
gathering	석기 시대에 원시인들이 과일을 모았던 것처럼 사냥도 원시인들에게는 하나의 식량 획득법이었다.
haul	이사하는 사람들은 그 무거운 소파를 자신들의 트럭에 싣기 위해, 길 아래로 두 블럭이나 끌고 가야 했다.
immediate	그 인접 지역은 폭탄 공격 이후 봉쇄되었다.
increase	그 새 법안은 이주자들 사이에 두려움을 증폭시켰다.

21 **loom****
[lú:m]
disappear

v. **emerge, appear, take shape** 어렴풋이 나타나다

A huge figure **loomed** out of the mist.

22 **overtax***
[òuvərtǽks]

v. **burden heavily** 지나치게 과세하다

The Ministry of Environment can't block pollution by **overtaxing** the companies.

23 **paradox***
[pǽrədɑ̀ks]

n. **contradiction** 모순

It is often said that in love "the **paradox** occurs when two beings become one and yet remain two."

24 **pervasive***
[pə:rvéisiv]
limited

adj. **widespread, prevalent** 퍼지는

It is often argued that the **pervasive** influence of television on today's youth is harming society.

25 **pleasing****
[plí:ziŋ]

adj. **attractive, agreeable** 마음에 드는, 기분 좋은

French wine is especially **pleasing** to the taste buds.

26 **primary***
[práimèri]
secondary

adj. **fundamental, elementary, basic** 근본적인

Karen can't understand the **primary** meaning of this word.

27 **proper****
[prɑ́pər]

adj. **suitable, appropriate** adapted, fitting 적당한

Teenagers are often malnourished because they fail to eat a **proper** diet.

28 **recur**
[rikə́:r]

v. **return, reappear** 재발하다

Studies have shown that cancer can **recur** as long as twenty years after treatment.

loom	거대한 형체가 안개 속에서 어렴풋이 나타났다.
overtax	환경부는 기업체에 지나치게 과세하는 것으로 오염을 막을 수 없다.
paradox	사랑에서 "두 개체가 하나가 되지만 여전히 둘로 남아 있다는 모순이 발생한다"는 사실은 종종 말해지는 것이다.
pervasive	오늘날의 젊은이들에게 미치는 텔레비전의 널리 퍼진 영향력은 사회에 해악을 끼친다는 것이 종종 주장되고 있다.
pleasing	프랑스 와인은 미각을 특별히 즐겁게 한다.
primary	Karen은 이 단어의 근본적인 의미를 이해할 수 없다.
proper	10대들은 종종 적절한 음식을 먹지 못하기 때문에 자주 영양실조에 걸리곤 한다.
recur	암은 치료 후에 20년 동안에 재발할 수 있다는 연구가 나왔다.

29 **save for*****
phr. **except for** ~을 제외하고

The entire report was finished, **save for** the bibliography.

30 **serve***
[sə́:rv]

v. **suit, function (as), suffice** answer 소용이 되다, 도움이 되다

Debris from the ship **served** as lifeboats for the victims.

31 **simulate***
[símjəlèit]

v. **imitate, copy; pretend, feign** 흉내 내다 ; 가장하다

A sheet of metal can be shaken to **simulate** the noise of a thunderclap.

32 **speck****
[spék]

n. 1. **spot, splotch, stain, blot, soil** 얼룩

Michael tried to get rid of the **speck** of blood on his sweater.

n. 2. **particle, atom, bit, grain** 소량

Everything was always in its place, and nowhere could Steve see a **speck** of dust.

33 **strive***
[stráiv]

v. **try, endeavor, struggle** 노력하다

Jerry had been encouraged by his parents to **strive** for success.

34 **suppose**
[səpóuz]

v. **assume, presume** 가정하다

As Steve's wife didn't answer the telephone, he **supposed** that she was out.

35 **surprise***
[sərpráiz]

v. **amaze, astound, startle** astonish 놀라게 하다

The sudden attack of the enemy **surprised** all the people.

save for	참고 문헌을 적는 것을 제외하면 그 보고서는 전부 완성되었다.
serve	그 배의 잔해는 조난자들에게 구명보트 역할을 해주었다.
simulate	금속 한 조각이 진동을 일으켜 뇌성의 소음을 흉내 낼 수도 있다.
speck	Michael은 그의 스웨터에 있는 피 얼룩을 없애려고 애썼다. 모든 것은 제자리에 항상 있었고, Steve는 어느 곳에서도 소량의 먼지를 볼 수 없었다.
strive	Jerry는 성공을 위해 노력하라고 그의 부모님에게서 격려를 받아 왔다.
suppose	Steve의 아내가 전화를 받지 않았기 때문에 그는 그녀가 외출했다고 추측했다.
surprise	적의 갑작스런 공격은 모든 사람들을 놀라게 했다.

36 **treat**	v. **handle, deal with, manage**	다루다, 대하다
[tríːt]	The manager did not like the way his employees **treated** customers.	
37 **undertake****	v. **assume; attempt, set about**	(책임 · 역할을) 맡다 ; 착수하다
[ʌ̀ndərtéik]	Harry must **undertake** full responsibility for the new changes.	
38 **variant***	n. **variation, modification**	변형
[vέəriənt]	A **variant** of tubercle bacillus has been discovered that is more likely to infect Americans.	

Quiz

Choose the synonym.

1. acquire	ⓐ spot, splotch, stain
2. suppose	ⓑ quit, call off
3. pleasing	ⓒ attractive, agreeable
4. speck	ⓓ obtain, procure, earn
5. abort	ⓔ assume, presume

Answer 1. ⓓ 2. ⓔ 3. ⓒ 4. ⓐ 5. ⓑ

treat	매니저는 직원들이 손님을 대접하는 방법이 마음에 들지 않았다.
undertake	Harry는 새로운 변화에 대한 전적인 책임을 떠맡아야 한다.
variant	미국인들을 감염시킬 가능성이 더 많은 결핵 간상균의 변형이 발견되었다.

DAY 9

Hackers TOEFL **Vocabulary**

Hackers Voca

www.goHackers.com

1 **abandon***	v.	**give up, desert, relinquish, forsake**	그만두다, 버리다
[əbǽndən] acquire		The president was accused of **abandoning** his political principles.	
2 **antidote****	n.	**remedy**	치료법
[ǽntidòut]		Rat poison has no known **antidote**.	
3 **at hand**	phr.	**available, accessible, handy**	사용 가능한
		The bank had many cash reserves **at hand**.	
4 **bear in mind**	phr.	**remember, keep in mind**	명심하다
		Please **bear in mind** that children are in the audience.	
5 **boost**	v.	**increase, raise, amplify**	증대시키다
[bú:st]		Taking vitamins can **boost** one's immune system.	
6 **conspicuous****	adj.	**noticeable, obvious, prominent**	뚜렷한
[kənspíkjuəs] hidden		Sharon's addiction to alcohol became **conspicuous** as she lost control of her drinking habit.	

abandon	대통령은 그의 정치적 원칙을 버렸다고 비난받았다.
antidote	쥐약에는 알려진 해독제가 없다.
at hand	그 은행은 사용 가능한 현금 보유량이 많았다.
bear in mind	관객 중에 아이들이 있다는 것을 명심해 주세요.
boost	비타민 섭취는 면역 시스템을 강화시킬 수 있다.
conspicuous	Sharon이 자신의 음주 습관에 대한 자제력을 상실하면서 그녀가 알코올에 중독되었다는 것이 더욱 뚜렷해졌다.

7 **critical*** [krítikəl] insignificant	adj. **1. important, crucial, essential, indispensable**	중요한	Air traffic controllers are under enormous stress because of the **critical** decisions they make in directing air traffic.
	adj. **2. dangerous**	위험한	The patient's adverse reaction to the medicine caused his heart rate to drop to a **critical** level.
8 **discriminate*** [diskrímənèit] confound	v. **distinguish, discern**	식별하다	Most color blind people cannot **discriminate** between red and green.
9 **dorsal*** [dɔ́:rsəl] ventral	adj. **relating to the back, on the back of**	등(부분)의	The **dorsal** fin of the great white shark cut through the water.
10 **eliminate**** [ilímənèit]	v. **remove, get rid of, discard**	제거하다	The government **eliminated** funds for day care centers.
11 **fuse*** [fjú:z] solidify	v. **melt, dissolve**	녹다, 녹이다	The fire caused the machines in the factory to **fuse** together.
12 **hinterland** [híntərlæ̀nd]	n. **bush, boondocks**	배후지, 오지	Behind the Danube River, there is a vast **hinterland**.
13 **in earnest*** facetious	phr. **serious**	진지한	Mary is sure Larry was **in earnest** when he said he wanted to marry Julia.

critical	항공 교통 관제관은 항공 교통을 지휘하며 내리는 중요한 결정들 때문에 엄청난 스트레스를 받는다. 약물에 대한 부작용으로 환자의 심장박동율이 위험한 수준까지 떨어졌다.
discriminate	색맹인 사람들은 대부분 적색과 녹색을 구별하지 못한다.
dorsal	백상어의 등지느러미가 물살을 갈랐다.
eliminate	정부는 탁아소에 대한 기금을 없앴다.
fuse	화재로 공장에 있던 기계들이 모두 녹았다.
hinterland	도나우 강 뒤쪽에는 광대한 배후지가 있다.
in earnest	Mary는 Larry가 Julia와 결혼하고 싶다고 말했을 때, 그가 매우 진지했다는 걸 확신한다.

14 **laden*** adj. **burdened, loaded, weighed down** (짐을) 실은

[léidən]

Washington Ave. always becomes a traffic **laden** street during rush hour.

15 **lumber*** n. **board, timber, wood** 판재, 재목

[lʌ́mbər]

Last year Home Depot was hurt by the deflation in **lumber** and building material prices.

16 **mirror*** v. **reflect, echo** 반영하다

[mírər]

The newspaper aims to **mirror** the opinions of ordinary people.

17 **mutual**** adj. **reciprocal; joint, common** 상호 간의 ; 공동의

[mjúːtʃuəl]

Mutual respect is necessary for a partnership to work.

18 **obtainable** adj. **available, accessible, attainable** 손에 넣을 수 있는

[əbtéinəbl]
unavailable

Most of the ingredients for Chinese cooking are **obtainable** at the supermarket.

19 **patch*** v. 1. **mend, repair, fix** 수선하다

[pǽtʃ]

Dick felt ashamed of his ragged coat and **patched** pants.

n. 2. **area, part, section** 작은 부분, 지역

The car began to skid after hitting a **patch** of ice.

20 **protest** v. **remonstrate, complain, object** 항의하다

[prətést]

Mexico **protested** the admission of Texas into the United States.

laden	Washington Ave.는 출퇴근 시간에 항상 교통이 혼잡한 도로가 된다.
lumber	지난해 Home Depot는 판재와 건축 자재 가격의 하락으로 손실을 입었다.
mirror	그 신문은 평범한 사람들의 의견들을 반영하는 것을 목표로 한다.
mutual	함께 일하기 위해서는 상호 존중이 필수적이다.
obtainable	중국 요리를 위한 대부분의 재료들은 슈퍼마켓에서 구입할 수 있다.
patch	Dick은 너덜너덜한 코트와 기운 바지에 부끄러움을 느꼈다.
	자동차는 도로의 빙판 부분에 닿자 미끄러지기 시작했다.
protest	멕시코는 텍사스가 미국으로 편입되는 것에 항의했다.

21 **recall***	v.	remember, **recollect**	회상하다
[rikɔ́:l]		The Athenians **recalled** that Minos, a great and powerful king, once lived in a large palace.	
22 **reflection****	n.	indication, **expression, manifestation**	반영
[riflékʃən]		A nation's life expectancy is usually a **reflection** of its living standards.	
23 **regain**	v.	restore, **recover, retrieve**	~을 되찾다
[rigéin]		At Cambridge, Eric met John who helped him **regain** his interest in nature.	
24 **reinforce**	v.	strengthen, **fortify**	강화하다
[rì:infɔ́:rs] weaken		A soundboard is a resonator that uses sonic vibrations to **reinforce** the integrity of a sound wave.	
25 **relevant**	adj.	applicable, **pertinent, germane**	관련된, 적절한
[réləvənt] irrelevant		The English teacher told her students the **relevant** chapters they needed to study for the test.	
26 **reminisce****	v.	remember, recollect, **recall, look back**	추억하다
[rèmənís]		Karen and Esther walked through the park as they **reminisced** about their college days.	
27 **route**	n.	path, **course, road, direction**	길
[ru:t]		The trade **route** between China and Europe allowed many other cultures to experience their products.	
28 **secrete****	v.	produce, **discharge**	분비하다
[sikrí:t]		Tears are **secreted** by an organ under the upper eyelid.	

recall	아테네인들은 위대하고 강한 왕인 Minos가 한때 큰 궁전에 살았다고 회상했다.
reflection	한 국가의 평균 수명은 삶의 질의 반영이다.
regain	캠브리지에서 Eric은 그가 자연에 대한 관심을 회복하도록 도와준 John을 만났다.
reinforce	'soundboard'는 음파의 본래 성질을 강화하기 위해 음의 진동을 이용하는 공명판이다.
relevant	그 영어 교사는 그녀의 학생들에게 시험을 위해 그들이 공부해야 할 관련 단원들을 말해 주었다.
reminisce	Karen과 Esther는 자신들의 대학 시절을 회상하면서 공원을 거닐었다.
route	중국과 유럽 간의 교역로는 많은 다른 문화권이 이들의 상품을 경험할 수 있게 해주었다.
secrete	눈물은 윗 눈꺼풀 아래에 있는 기관에 의해 분비된다.

29 semiarid adj. **rather dry** 반건조한

[sèmiǽrid]

Much of Spain is in a **semiarid** climate zone.

30 soothe* v. **allay, mitigate, relieve** 진정시키다, 완화하다

[sú:ð]
excite

The store manager tried to **soothe** the irate customer by offering a refund.

31 stay* v. **remain, reside, sojourn** 머무르다

[stéi]
go

The workers **stayed** in the factories where the heat was shut off.

32 surplus* n. **extra, redundance, excess, excessive quantity** 나머지, 잔여

[sə́:rplʌs]
deficiency

The price of food fell nearly 72% due to a huge **surplus**.

33 toothed* adj. **uneven, jagged, ragged** 들쑥날쑥한

[tú:θt]
even

As William leapt in the air to catch the baseball, he fell into a stretch of **toothed** barbwire.

34 transform* v. **convert, change, alter** 변형시키다

[trænsfɔ́:rm]

The United States was **transformed** by the enormous growth of industry.

35 unbalanced* adj. **asymmetric, lopsided, unequal** 균형을 잃은

[ʌ̀nbǽlənst]
symmetric

Malnutrition can result from an **unbalanced** diet.

36 uniformly adv. **consistently, regularly, evenly** 균일하게

[jú:nəfɔ̀:rmli]

If the paint is not spread **uniformly** over the wall, it will have bumps and drips later.

semiarid	스페인의 대부분은 반건조 지대이다.
soothe	그 가게 주인은 화가 난 손님에게 환불을 해주며 진정시켰다.
stay	노동자들은 난방이 차단된 그 공장 안에 머물렀다.
surplus	엄청난 잉여분 때문에 식품 가격이 거의 72% 떨어졌다.
toothed	William은 야구공을 잡기 위해 공중으로 뛰어올랐다가 쭉 뻗어 있는 울퉁불퉁한 가시 철사 위로 떨어졌다.
transform	미국은 엄청난 산업의 성장에 의해 변형되었다.
unbalanced	영양실조는 균형 잡히지 않은 식단으로 생길 수 있다.
uniformly	페인트가 벽에 고르게 발라지지 않는다면, 나중에 돌기가 생기거나 방울져서 흘러내릴 것이다.

37 **utilitarian***

[juːtìlitέ(:)əriən]

adj. **practical, pragmatic, functional** 실용적인

The factory is very **utilitarian** in design.

38 **variety****

[vəráiəti]

n. 1. **diversity, multiplicity** 다양성

The **variety** of trees is a result of millions of years of evolution.

n. 2. **type, species, sort** 종류

Tropical coral reefs contain a wide **variety** of organisms.

39 **wonderful**

[wʌ́ndərfəl]
lousy

adj. **marvelous, remarkable, awesome** 놀라운

Sunny had the **wonderful** opportunity to help raise an orphaned baby.

Quiz

Choose the synonym.

1. boost	ⓐ distinguish, discern
2. discriminate	ⓑ applicable, pertinent, germane
3. reflection	ⓒ indication, expression, manifestation
4. relevant	ⓓ increase, raise, amplify
5. utilitarian	ⓔ practical, pragmatic, functional

Answer 1. ⓓ 2. ⓐ 3. ⓒ 4. ⓑ 5. ⓔ

utilitarian	그 공장은 디자인 면에서 매우 실용적이다.
variety	수목의 다양성은 수백만 년에 걸친 진화의 결과이다.
	열대 산호초들은 상당히 다양한 유기체들을 포함한다.
wonderful	Sunny는 고아가 된 아기를 기르는 일을 도울 놀라운 기회를 가졌다.

Hackers TOEFL Voca TEST DAY 07-09

Choose the synonym of the highlighted word in the sentence.

1. The soldiers were alert and on the lookout for a spy.
(A) delicate (B) vigilant (C) fierce (D) wily

2. Outbreaks of cholera are pervasive in areas without proper sanitation.
(A) comprising (B) pedestrian (C) prevalent (D) suitable

3. Sociologists have to strive for neutrality with respect to research and policy formation.
(A) ponder (B) endeavor (C) mask (D) alternate

4. It is widely accepted by both geologists and astronomers that the Earth is roughly 4.6 billion years old.
(A) dubiously (B) approximately (C) eagerly (D) painstakingly

5. A big increase in the number of visitors to China has been particularly conspicuous in recent years.
(A) inactive (B) prominent (C) futile (D) apathetic

6. Enron had an embarrassing incident that caused many employees to quit their jobs and file a lawsuit.
(A) assuring (B) abashing (C) looming (D) empowering

7. Cold can be a friend to humans because it limits mosquitoes to seasons and regions where temperatures stay above certain levels.
(A) remain (B) cripple (C) hoist (D) peek

8. The lifelong friends spent the afternoon reminiscing about their childhood.
(A) reliving (B) resuscitating (C) reviewing (D) recollecting

9. In 1864, Lincoln signed the 13th amendment which abolished slavery.
(A) annulled (B) gave off (C) feigned (D) elucidated

10. The wreck of the Titanic looms like a ghost out of the dark.
(A) conceals (B) emerges (C) escapes (D) wallows

정답 p.419

To A SKYLARK 종달새에게

Percy Bysshe Shelley

Hail to thee, blithe Spirit!
Bird thou never wert,
That from Heaven, or near it,
Pourest thy full heart
In profuse strains of unpremeditated art.

Higher still and higher
From the earth thou springest
Like a cloud of fire;
The blue deep thou wingest,
And singing still dost soar, and soaring ever singest.

오 반갑다, 쾌활한 정령(精靈)이여!
너는 결코 새가 아니니라,
하늘에서, 하늘 가까이에서
벅찬 마음을 쏟는 자여
즉흥적 기교의 풍성한 노래로.

더 높이 더욱 더 높이
대지로부터 너는 솟아오른다.
불의 구름마냥
푸른 하늘을 너는 나른다.
그리고 한결같이 노래하고 솟아오르고, 솟아오르며 노래한다.

DAY 10

Hackers TOEFL **Vocabulary**

Hackers Voca

www.goHackers.com

1 **advantage***	n.	**benefit, profit, gain**	이익
[ədvǽntidʒ] drawback		The electric industry gained an undeserved **advantage** in the new marketplace.	
2 **arise from**	phr.	**emerge from, originate from**	~에서 기인하다
		The problem **arose from** a miscommunication between the President and his assistant.	
3 **barrier****	n.	**bar, obstacle, obstruction** barricade	장애물, 장벽
[bǽriər]		The mountains form a natural **barrier** between the two countries.	
4 **betray**	v.	**be disloyal to, be a traitor to**	배신하다
[bitréi]		Bob had heartlessly **betrayed** John's confidence.	
5 **bind***	v.	**tie, fasten**	묶다
[báind] release		Before going on a jungle trek, Mary **bound** up her hair so that it would not get caught in the brush.	
6 **blur**	v.	**make vague, obscure, cloud**	흐리게 하다
[blə́ːr]		The reporter said that the warmer climate is **blurring** British seasons.	

advantage	전기 산업은 새로운 시장에서 부당한 이득을 얻었다.
arise from	그 문제는 대통령과 보좌관들의 의사소통이 잘 이루어지지 않았던 것에서 기인한다.
barrier	산맥은 그 두 나라 사이에 자연적인 장벽을 형성한다.
betray	Bob은 냉정하게 John의 신뢰를 배신했었다.
bind	Mary는 정글 여행을 가기 전에 전에 나뭇가지에 걸리지 않도록 머리를 묶었다.
blur	그 기자는 더욱 따뜻해지는 기온이 영국의 계절 사이의 경계를 모호하게 하고 있다고 말했다.

7 circumvent v. **bypass, detour, go around** 우회하다

[sə̀ːrkəmvént]

Jack and Fred went north in order to **circumvent** the mountains.

8 clumsy adj. **awkward, unskillful, maladroit** 서투른

[klʌ́mzi]
apt

Unlike the grizzly bear, the black bear is timid, **clumsy**, and rarely dangerous.

9 commence v. **begin, start, originate** 시작하다

[kəméns]

The day after the battle of the Alamo had **commenced**, Jim Bowie was deathly sick with pneumonia.

10 conduct** n. 1. **behavior, demeanor, bearing** manner 행동

[kɑ́ndʌkt]

The senator was blamed for his immoral **conduct**.

[kəndʌ́kt] v. 2. **transmit, administer, convey, carry** (빛 · 열 등을) 전도하다

The newly built power lines **conduct** energy from the urban center to rural homes and businesses.

11 conserve** v. **keep, protect, preserve, save** 보존하다

[kənsə́ːrv]
waste

Using the sun's rays to **conserve** energy makes sense to most people.

12 contradiction* n. **paradox, inconsistency** 모순

[kɑ̀ntrədíkʃən]

The prosecution pointed out the **contradictions** in the defendant's testimony.

13 culminate* v. **result, end** ~로 끝나다

[kʌ́lmənèit]
begin

The final game of the Super Bowl **culminated** in a crushing loss for Miami.

circumvent	Jake와 Fred는 산맥을 우회하기 위해서 북으로 향했다.
clumsy	회색곰과는 달리, 흑곰은 소심하고 서투르며 거의 위험하지 않다.
commence	Alamo 전투가 시작된 다음날, Jim Bowie는 폐렴으로 심하게 아팠다.
conduct	그 상원의원은 그의 부도덕한 행동에 대해 비난을 받았다.
	새로 설치된 송전선은 도심지로부터 교외 지역의 주택과 업체들에 에너지를 전달한다.
conserve	에너지 보존을 위해 태양 광선을 이용하는 것은 대부분의 사람들에게 이치에 합당하다.
contradiction	검사는 피고인의 증언에서 모순점을 지적했다.
culminate	수퍼볼의 결승전은 Miami팀의 완전한 패배로 끝이 났다.

14 delineate* v. trace, outline, **describe** 윤곽을 그리다

[dilínièit]

A police artist **delineated** a sketch of the suspect with the help of the victim.

15 donation* n. contribution, **gift, offering** 기부(금), 기증(물)

[dounéiʃən]

It's wonderful to be here helping to raise **donations** for a children's charity.

16 embark on* phr. start, **commence, begin** 시작하다

conclude

After two months of preparation, Bernie **embarked on** her backpacking trip across Europe.

17 foundation** n. basis, underpinning, **base** ground 기초

[faundéiʃən]

The building's **foundation** is made with modern earthquake-resistant concrete.

18 fundamental** adj. basic, essential, **primary, elementary** 근본적인

[fʌ̀ndəméntl]
incidental, trivial

Math and science are **fundamental** to a good education.

19 handful n. **few, smattering** 소량, 소수

[hǽndfùl]
large quantity

Tony grabbed a **handful** of cookies from the cookie jar before leaving for school.

20 height* n. peak, **apex, crest, zenith** 정상, 절정

[háit]
nadir

Looking down from the dizzying **height** of Mount Fuji, the entire hiking party felt tremendous pride at their recent climb.

21 identical* adj. same, indistinguishable, **alike, equal** 동일한

[aidéntikəl]

Friends and even family can often have trouble distinguishing between **identical** twins.

delineate	경찰은 피해자의 도움으로 용의자의 몽타주 윤곽을 그렸다.
donation	아이들을 위한 자선사업의 기부금 모으는 일을 도우면서 여기 있는 것은 참 멋진 일이다.
embark on	두 달간의 준비가 끝난 후, Bernie는 유럽을 가로지르는 배낭여행을 시작했다.
foundation	그 건물의 기초는 지진에 견딜 수 있는 현대적인 콘크리트로 만들어졌다.
fundamental	수학과 과학은 양질의 교육에 있어 근본적인 것이다.
handful	Tony는 학교로 떠나기 전, 쿠키가 든 항아리에서 한 줌의 쿠키를 집어왔다.
height	아찔한 높이의 후지산에서 아래를 내려다 보며, 하이킹을 한 사람들 모두는 자신들의 새로운 등반을 무척이나 자랑스러워하고 있었다.
identical	친구나 심지어 가족조차 일란성 쌍둥이를 구분하는 데 종종 어려움을 겪는다.

22 **impediment***
[impédəmənt]
n. obstacle, **barrier, difficulty, obstruction** 장애
If Ben puts his mind to something, no **impediment** can stop him from reaching his goals.

23 **justify***
[dʒʌ́stəfài]
v. prove, **confirm, verify** (정당성을) 증명하다
Jefferson believed that his triumphant re-election **justified** his toleration of his critics.

24 **lament**
[ləmént]
rejoice, delight
v. grieve, regret, **deplore** bemoan, mourn 슬퍼하다, 애도하다
The young man **lamented** the loss of his true love in the drowning accident.

25 **microorganism***
[màikrouɔ́:rgənìzəm]
n. microbe, **bacterium** 미생물
Biologists have found a new **microorganism** recently.

26 **origin****
[ɔ́:ridʒin]
n. beginning, source 발생, 근원
The book was about the **origin** of the universe.

27 **peculiarity**
[pikjù:liǽrəti]
n. feature, **characteristic, quality** 특성
A need for privacy is a cultural **peculiarity** in western society.

28 **physical**
[fízikəl]
adj. 1. material, **substantial** 물질의
There was little **physical** evidence of the defendant's guilt.

adj. 2. **bodily, corporeal** 육체의
Daily exercise is important to **physical** health.

impediment	Ben이 어떤 일에 집중하면, 어떤 장애물도 그가 자신의 목적을 달성하는 것을 멈추게 할 수 없다.
justify	Jefferson은 그의 성공적인 재선거가 그를 비판하던 사람들을 참아낸 것이 옳았음을 증명한다고 믿었다.
lament	그 젊은 남자는 그가 진정으로 사랑하는 사람을 익사 사고로 잃은 것을 한탄했다.
microorganism	생물학자들은 최근에 새로운 미생물을 발견했다.
origin	그 책은 우주의 기원에 대한 것이었다.
peculiarity	사생활의 필요성은 서구 사회의 문화적 특징이다.
physical	피고인의 죄에 대한 물질적 증거가 거의 없었다.
	매일 운동하는 것은 신체 건강에 있어 중요하다.

29 **predict** [pridíkt]

v. **foretell, prophesy, foresee** 예측하다

Policy makers could have **predicted** the unsuccessful outcomes.

30 **progress**** [prágres]
regression

n. **strides, improvement, advance** development 발전

Machines would bring **progress** as well as profit.

31 **scoop**** [skú:p]

v. **gather up** 긁어모으다

Oliver **scooped** the sand into a bucket with his hands.

32 **score*** [skɔ́:r]
lose

v. 1. **gain, win** 얻다

Ms. Rice has certainly **scored** a success with her latest novel.

n. 2. **musical composition, musical note** 악보, 악곡

Various information will be posted intermittently regarding the musical **score** of the motion picture.

33 **scrap*** [skrǽp]

n. **fraction, piece, portion** 파편

After the party, there was not a single **scrap** of food to be found anywhere.

34 **singularly** [síŋgjulərli]
unexceptionally

adv. **particularly, especially** 각별히

Julia Roberts is a **singularly** beautiful woman.

35 **skilled*** [skíld]
unskilled

adj. **skillful, expert, adept** proficient 숙련된

Skilled tool makers can fashion excellent tools or jewelry.

predict	정책 수립자들은 성공적이지 못한 결과를 예언할 수도 있었다.
progress	기계들은 이익뿐만 아니라 발전을 가져올 것이다.
scoop	Oliver는 손으로 모래를 긁어 모아 양동이에 넣었다.
score	Rice씨는 그녀의 최근 소설로 확실히 성공을 거두었다.
	영화 음악의 악보와 관련하여 다양한 정보가 때때로 게시될 것이다.
scrap	파티가 끝난 후 어느 곳에서든 단 한 조각의 음식 부스러기도 찾아볼 수 없었다.
singularly	Julia Roberts는 뛰어나게 아름다운 여성이다.
skilled	숙련된 도구 제작자들은 멋진 도구와 보석을 만들 수 있다.

36 **stem from****

phr. **arise from, originate from, derive from** ~에서 유래하다

The damage to the environment **stemmed from** the energy crisis of the 1970s.

37 **subsidize***

[sʌ́bsidàiz]

v. **assist, encourage, finance, support, back, fund** 후원하다

During World War I, the federal government **subsidized** farms.

38 **unanimity**

[jù:nənímәti]

n. **total agreement, accord** (만장)일치

Tom was elected as the new class president by the **unanimity** of his classmates.

Quiz

Choose the synonym.

1. circumvent	ⓐ back, finance, fund
2. fundamental	ⓑ bypass, detour, go around
3. lament	ⓒ feature, characteristic, quality
4. subsidize	ⓓ basic, essential, primary
5. peculiarity	ⓔ deplore, grieve, mourn

Answer 1. ⓑ 2. ⓓ 3. ⓔ 4. ⓐ 5. ⓒ

stem from — 환경에 끼친 손실은 1970년대의 에너지 위기에서 유래했다.
subsidize — 제 1차 세계대전 동안, 연방 정부는 농장들을 후원했다.
unanimity — Tom은 반 전체 만장일치로 새 학급 회장에 선출되었다.

DAY Hackers TOEFL **Vocabulary**

11 Hackers Voca

www.goHackers.com

1 **account**	n. **description, narrative, explanation**	기술(記述)
[əkáunt]	John Reed wrote a famous **account** of the Russian Revolution.	
2 **alloy****	v. **mix, blend, fuse** compound	혼합하다
[əlɔ́i] separate	Gold is commonly **alloyed** with other metals to increase durability.	
3 **barely***	adv. **scarcely, hardly**	거의 ~않다
[bɛ́ərli] wholly	Colleen had **barely** sat down before the interviewer started firing questions at her.	
4 **carry on**	phr. **continue**	~을 계속하다
	Those in positions of leadership must be able to encourage their followers to **carry on** despite obstacles.	
5 **cohesion****	n. **bond, unity**	결속
[kouhíːʒən] incohesion	In rural societies, family **cohesion** is customarily strong.	
6 **coincide****	v. 1. **exist at the same time, occur at the same time**	동시에 일어나다
[kòuinsáid]	The Queen's visit has been planned to **coincide** with the school's 200th anniversary.	

account	John Read는 러시아 혁명에 관한 유명한 기술서를 썼다.
alloy	금은 내구성을 증가시키기 위해 흔히 다른 금속과 혼합된다.
barely	Colleen이 자리에 채 앉기도 전에 그 회견자가 그녀에게 질문을 쏟아 부었다.
carry on	지도자의 지위에 있는 이들은 부하들을 격려하여 장애 요소들에도 불구하고 일을 지속할 수 있게 할 수 있어야 한다.
cohesion	시골 마을에서, 가족간의 유대감은 관습적으로 강하다.
coincide	여왕의 방문은 그 학교의 200번째 기념일과 동시에 일어나도록 계획되었다.

differ | v. 2. **agree, concur** 의견이 일치하다

Tom and Cathy did not **coincide** in opinion on the issue.

7 colossal*

[kəlɑ́səl]
undersized

adj. **enormous, monstrous, gigantic** tremendous 거대한

The government paid a **colossal** sum for accidents regardless of the cause.

8 considerable**

[kənsídərəbl]
trivial

adj. 1. **significant, substantial, meaningful** 중요한

The **considerable** issue of education must be addressed by both parties.

adj. 2. **large, big, sizable** 상당한

Plankton is gaining **considerable** interest among marine scientists.

9 converge*

[kənvə́ːrdʒ]
disperse

v. **meet, come together, merge** 한데 모이다

Curious onlookers began to **converge** at the scene of the crime.

10 conviction**

[kənvíkʃən]

n. **strong belief, strong opinion, faith** 신념

Gandhi remained committed to his **convictions**, such as non-violence, his entire life.

11 covet*

[kʌ́vit]
spurn

v. **desire, long for, aspire to, envy, crave** 갈망하다

One of the Ten Commandments states, "Thou shalt not **covet** thy neighbor's wife."

12 defect*

[dífekt]
merit

n. **shortcoming, blemish, fault** flaw 결점

The ship has structural **defects** that make it difficult to handle in high seas.

coincide	Tom과 Cathy는 그 사안에 대한 의견이 일치하지 않았다.
colossal	정부는 원인에 상관없이 사고에 대해 엄청난 총액을 지불했다.
considerable	중요한 교육 문제는 양당 모두에 의해 다뤄져야 한다.
	플랑크톤이 해양 과학자들 사이에서 상당한 관심을 얻고 있다.
converge	호기심 많은 구경꾼들이 범죄 현장으로 한데 모이기 시작했다.
conviction	간디는 일생 동안 변함없이 비폭력주의와 같은 자신의 신념에 충실했다.
covet	십계명 중 한 계명은 "네 이웃의 아내를 탐하지 말라"라고 말하고 있다.
defect	그 배는 높은 파도에서는 그것을 조종하기 어렵게 하는 구조적 결함들을 가지고 있다

13 defection n. **apostasy** 변절, 탈당

[difékʃən]
loyalty

The congressman's **defection** from his political party caused lots of controversy.

14 dull adj. **boring, prosaic, uninteresting** tiresome, tiring 지루한

[dʌ́l]
lively

Edward needed someone who could bring joy and laughter into his **dull** days.

15 endeavor* v. **strive, struggle, attempt** 노력하다, 애쓰다

[indévər]

Although she was exhausted, Corinne **endeavored** to work hard and finish painting the house before nightfall.

16 flock* n. **group, herd, bevy** 무리, 떼

[flɑ́k]

The shepherd drives **flocks** of sheep from pasture to pasture.

17 grant* v. **bestow, confer, award** 주다

[grǽnt]

Leonard willingly **granted** the institute a sum of $10 million.

18 hustle** v. 1. **rush, hurry, hasten** 서두르다

[hʌ́sl]
dawdle

The streets of New York City are filled with people **hustling** to get to work or catch the last subway home.

v. 2. **push, shove** 밀다

The eager young boy **hustled** his way through the line to buy a ticket for the movie.

19 intermediate* adj. **between extremes, mean, median** halfway 중간의

[ìntərmíːdiət]

Neanderthals were **intermediate** between ape and man.

defection	그 의원의 탈당은 상당한 논쟁을 불러일으켰다.
dull	Edward는 그의 지루한 일상에 기쁨과 웃음을 가져다 줄 누군가가 필요했다.
endeavor	Corinne은 비록 기진맥진하긴 했지만 열심히 일하여 해가 지기 전에 집에 페인트 칠하는 것을 끝내려고 애썼다.
flock	그 양치기는 이곳저곳의 목초지로 양 무리들을 몰고 다닌다.
grant	Leonard는 총 천만 달러를 그 기관에 기꺼이 주었다.
hustle	뉴욕 시의 거리는 직장에 가기 위해서 혹은 집으로 가는 마지막 지하철을 타기 위해서 서두르는 사람들로 가득 차 있다.
	그 열성적인 소년은 줄 서 있는 사람들을 밀치며 영화표를 사기 위해 앞으로 나아갔다.
intermediate	네안데르탈인들은 원숭이와 사람 사이의 중간 단계였다.

20 intolerant

[intálərənt]
forbearing

adj. **bigoted, illiberal** 옹졸한, 편협한

Lily is **intolerant** of any opinion that differs from her own.

21 kind*

[káind]
unkind

adj. 1. **benign, humane, compassionate** 친절한, 인정 많은

The professor is uncommonly **kind** to all of his students.

n. 2. **type, sort, variety** 유형, 종류

Many **kinds** of music are popular in the United States.

22 limit**

[límit]

n. 1. **bound, boundary** 경계, 한계

There seems to be absolutely no **limit** to Donald's ambition.

broaden

v. 2. **restrict, confine** 제한하다

The committee **limited** the use of profanity in TV shows.

23 margin*

[mɑ́:rdʒin]

n. **border, edge, rim** verge 가장자리

Brenda scribbled some notes in the **margin**.

24 militia*

[milíʃə]

n. **military, army** 시민군

Che Guevara was a Central American **militia** leader who has become a powerful symbol of revolution.

25 moreover**

[mɔ:róuvər]

adv. **in addition, additionally, as well** besides 게다가

Melanie had gotten thinner with age; **moreover**, her whole image had changed.

---

intolerant — Lily는 자기의 의견과 다른 모든 의견들에 대해서 옹졸하다.
kind — 그 교수는 모든 제자들에게 매우 친절하다.
미국에서는 다양한 종류의 음악이 유행한다.
limit — Donald의 야망에는 결코 한계가 없는 것으로 보인다.
그 위원회는 텔레비전 쇼에서 욕설의 사용을 제한했다.
margin — Brenda는 가장자리에 메모를 휘갈겨 썼다.
militia — 체 게바라는 중앙아메리카 시민군의 지도자였던 인물로, 이후 강력한 혁명의 상징이 되었다.
moreover — Melanie는 나이가 들면서 수척해졌고 게다가, 그녀의 전체적 이미지가 변했다.

26 **necessary**** | adj. **required, indispensable, essential** vital | 필수적인

[nésəsèri]
unnecessary

Public schools were **necessary** to educate children at the time of settlement.

27 **obstruct** | v. **block, bar, hinder, impede** | 막다, 방해하다

[əbstrʌ́kt]

After the earthquake, many roads were **obstructed** by collapsed buildings.

28 **on the spot*** | phr. **instantly, immediately** | 즉시

Completely impressed by her professional manner, the recruiter hired Judy **on the spot**.

29 **partial**** | adj. 1. **biased, prejudiced, unfair** | 편파적인

[pɑ́ːrʃəl]

Sam and Tyler could recognize Gerald from his **partial** remarks about religion.

whole

adj. 2. **incomplete, fractional** | 부분적인

The observer may gain only a restricted and **partial** understanding of the situation.

30 **placid*** | adj. **calm, serene, tranquil, untroubled** | 평온한

[plǽsid]
turbulent

The lake was **placid** under the moonlight.

31 **porosity*** | n. **space, pore; porousness** | 구멍 ; 다공성

[pɔːrɑ́səti]
density

The **porosity** of a sponge allows it to absorb a great amount of liquid.

32 **reform*** | v. **amend, improve, ameliorate** | 개정하다, 개선하다

[riːfɔ́ːrm]

The Cherokee **reformed** their political system by adopting a type of republican government.

necessary	정착 시기에 아이들을 교육하기 위해 공립학교들이 필요했다.
obstruct	지진이 있은 후 많은 길들이 붕괴된 건물들로 막혔다.
on the spot	Judy의 전문가다운 태도에 완전히 감명을 받은 채용자는 즉시 그녀를 고용했다.
partial	Sam과 Tyler는 Gerald의 종교에 대한 편파적인 의견으로부터 그가 어떤 사람인지 알 수 있었다.
	관찰자는 상황에 대한 제한적이고 부분적인 이해만을 가지게 될 것이다.
placid	호수는 달빛 아래에서 고요했다.
porosity	스폰지의 구멍은 그것이 다량의 수분을 흡수할 수 있도록 해준다.
reform	Cherokee족은 공화정치의 한 유형을 채택함으로써 그들의 정치 시스템을 개정했다.

33 **rigid****	adj. 1. **stiff, hard, inflexible**	단단한, 뻣뻣한
[rídʒid] elastic	When Ted heard the news, his whole body went **rigid** with shock.	
indulgent	adj. 2. **strict, severe, rigorous**	엄격한
	Military boot camp is so **rigid** that many drop out on the first day.	
34 **scarcity**	n. **lack, shortage, insufficiency, deficiency**	부족, 결핍
[skέərsəti]	A **scarcity** of fish damaged the seaside town's economy.	

Quiz

Choose the synonym.

1. considerable	ⓐ block, bar, hinder
2. intolerant	ⓑ bigoted, prejudiced
3. obstruct	ⓒ calm, serene, tranquil
4. placid	ⓓ enormous, monstrous, gigantic
5. colossal	ⓔ significant, substantial

Answer 1. ⓔ 2. ⓑ 3. ⓐ 4. ⓒ 5. ⓓ

rigid
Ted가 그 뉴스를 들었을 때, 그의 온몸은 충격으로 경직되었다.
군대 신병 캠프가 매우 엄격하여 많은 사람들이 첫날부터 낙오한다.

scarcity
물고기의 부족으로 해안 마을들의 경제가 피해를 입었다.

DAY 12

Hackers TOEFL **Vocabulary**

Hackers Voca

www.goHackers.com

1 **adaptable**	adj.	**flexible, adjustable, malleable**	융통성 있는, 적응성 있는
[ədǽptəbl]		The comedian's style was **adaptable** to different types of audiences.	
2 **adhesion**	n.	**getting together, sticking together**	달라붙음, 부착
[ædhíːʒən]		Sticky notes are a popular use of technology in **adhesion**.	
3 **blame***	v.	**incriminate, reproach, censure** condemn	비난하다
[bléim] praise		People **blamed** authorities for the food shortages.	
4 **chaotic**	adj.	**disorganized, disordered, anarchic**	무질서한
[keiátik] ordered		Kindergarten classes can become **chaotic** if the children are not constantly engaged in some form of activity.	
5 **comprehend**	v.	**grasp, perceive, apprehend**	이해하다
[kàmprihénd] misunderstand		It took the police officer a few minutes to **comprehend** what the frantic woman was trying to say.	
6 **decided***	adj.	**obvious, definite; resolute, determined**	분명한 ; 단호한
[disáidid] questionable		Analysts thought it was **decided** that the stock market would decline due to poor economic news.	

adaptable	그 코미디언의 스타일은 다양한 관객들을 위한 융통성 있는 것이었다.
adhesion	접착노트는 부착하는데 널리 쓰이는 제품이다.
blame	사람들은 음식 부족 문제로 관련 당국을 비난했다.
chaotic	아동들이 끊임없이 어떤 형태의 활동을 하고 있지 않으면, 유치원 교실은 무질서해지기 쉽다.
comprehend	경찰이 그 극도로 흥분한 여자가 말하고자 하는 것을 이해하는 데는 몇 분이 걸렸다.
decided	분석가들은 나쁜 경제 소식으로 인해 주식시세가 하락할 것이 분명하다고 생각했다.

7 displace*　v. **supplant, replace**　대체하다

[displéis]

The television had **displaced** the radio in American living rooms by 1960.

8 enclose**　v. **surround, circle, encompass**　에워싸다

[inklóuz]
reveal

The cultivated land was **enclosed** by a strong high fence to keep the wild animals out.

9 entail**　v. **involve, require**　~을 수반하다

[intéil]

Farming has always **entailed** the willingness to accept risk and to put in long hours of labor.

10 excel*　v. **be superior to, surpass, outdo**　transcend　능가하다, 빼어나다

[iksél]
be inferior to

Children who **excel** their peers in school are often eligible for special academic programs.

11 expend　v. **use, spend**　(시간 · 노력 등을) 쓰다, 들이다

[ikspénd]

Athletes **expend** more energy in hot and humid weather.

12 facility　n. **aptitude, skill, ability**　재능, 소질

[fəsíləti]

Erika has a natural **facility** for playing the piano.

13 genre*　n. **sort, kind, type, style**　유형

[ʒɑ́:nrə]

Billy's favorite **genre** of movie is Western.

14 illustrate**　v. **represent, picture**　묘사하다

[íləstrèit]

The medical book **illustrates** how the blood circulates through the body.

displace	1960년 미국의 가정에서 텔레비전이 라디오를 대체하였다.
enclose	그 경작지는 야생 동물들이 들어 오지 못하도록 강하고 높은 울타리로 둘러싸여 있었다.
entail	농장 일은 항상 위험을 감수하고 오랜 시간의 노동을 기꺼이 하는 마음을 수반한다.
excel	학교에서 같은 또래 학생들을 능가하는 아이들은 종종 특수 교육 프로그램을 이수할 자격이 있다.
expend	운동선수들은 날씨가 덥고 습할 때 더 많은 에너지를 소모한다.
facility	Erika는 피아노 연주에 타고난 재능을 가지고 있다.
genre	Billy가 가장 좋아하는 영화 장르는 서부 영화이다.
illustrate	그 의학 서적은 혈액이 체내를 어떻게 순환하는지를 보여준다.

15 **infrastructure*** n. foundation, **base, basis, groundwork** 기반, 하부 구조

[ínfrəstrʌ̀ktʃər]
superstructure

Beijing should encourage more investment in agriculture, technology, and **infrastructure**.

16 **inhibit**** v. hinder, limit; **ban, prohibit, forbid** 억제하다 ; 금지하다

[inhíbit]
allow, approve

Some factors in Chinese tradition seriously **inhibited** artistic imagination.

17 **involve*** v. include, **entail** ~을 수반하다

[inválv]

The prime minister decided to **involve** members of the opposition in the decision making process.

18 **lease**** v. rent, hire, charter 임차하다

[lí:s]

Some people prefer to **lease** rather than buy a car.

19 **likewise**** adv. also, **as well**; similarly 또한 ; 마찬가지로

[láikwàiz]
differently

The German government has **likewise** supported research projects for the quantum particle accelerator in Switzerland.

20 **limited**** adj. narrow, confined, restricted 제한된

[límitid]
infinite

Environmental groups have a very **limited** online presence.

21 **lodge in**** phr. **embed, implant** 박다, 꽂아 넣다

A large stone was **lodged in** the wall.

22 **mingle*** v. unite, **mix, blend** 섞이다, 혼합되다

[míŋgl]

John **mingled** among the party guests, meeting new people and socializing with old friends.

infrastructure	베이징은 농업, 기술 그리고 사회 기반에 더 많은 투자를 장려해야 한다.
inhibit	중국의 전통 중 몇몇 요소들은 예술적인 상상력을 심하게 억제했다.
involve	총리는 야당 의원들을 의사 결정 과정에 참여시키기로 결정했다.
lease	몇몇 사람들은 차를 사는 것보다 빌리는 것을 더 선호한다.
likewise	독일 정부 또한 스위스에 있는 양자(量子) 입자 가속기에 대한 연구 계획을 지원해 왔다.
limited	환경 단체들은 온라인상에 매우 제한적으로 등장한다.
lodge in	큰 돌이 벽에 박혀 있었다.
mingle	John은 파티에 초대된 손님들 사이에 섞여 새로운 사람들을 만나고 옛 친구들과 어울렸다.

23 **obligation****

[àbləgéiʃən]

option

n. **requirement, duty, responsibility** 의무

The French Border Police shares the **obligation** of security at all airports in France.

24 **oblige**

[əbláidʒ]

disoblige

v. **require, compel, force** impel 강요하다

The law **obliged** us to pay heavy taxes.

25 **offer**

[ɔ́(:)fər]

receive

v. **present, proffer, tender** 제공하다, 제안하다

The FBI **offered** Harold a bribe to forget that they had met.

26 **on occasion***

frequently

phr. **occasionally, periodically** 가끔

On occasion Miguel's friend Heather calls to have coffee, but usually they rarely see each other.

27 **pare****

[pέər]

v. **peel, skin; reduce, whittle, trim** 껍질을 벗기다 ; 삭감하다

The chef **pared** the carrots and then cut them into cubes.

28 **predominately***

[pridάmənèitli]

adv. **primarily, predominantly, chiefly** 주로

Native Americans have been **predominately** powerless economically and politically.

29 **preordained***

[prì:ɔ:rdéind]

adj. **determined beforehand, predestined** 예정된

People have no free will – everything in our lives has been **preordained**.

30 **render****

[réndər]

v. 1. **make** ~가 되게 하다

Tom's back injury **rendered** him physically unable to work.

obligation	프랑스 국경 경찰대는 프랑스의 모든 공항의 경비의 의무를 분담하고 있다.
oblige	법은 우리에게 무거운 세금을 지불하도록 강요하고 있다.
offer	FBI는 그들이 만났다는 것을 잊게 하려고 Harold에게 뇌물을 제시하였다.
on occasion	때때로 Miguel의 친구 Heather가 커피를 마시자고 연락하긴 하지만 대체로 그들은 서로를 만나는 일이 드물다.
pare	요리사는 당근 껍질을 벗긴 후에 정육면체 모양으로 잘랐다.
predominately	미국 원주민들은 주로 경제적으로나 정치적으로 무기력했다.
preordained	인간은 어떤 자유 의지도 가지고 있지 않다-우리 삶의 모든 것은 예정되어졌다.
render	Tom은 허리를 다쳐 일할 수 없게 되었다.

v. 2. **provide, give, afford, impart** 주다

The government **rendered** the Cuban refugees all necessary assistance.

v. 3. **represent** ~을 표현하다

The New York Poets **rendered** experience as pure phenomenon rather than as representative subject.

31 **renown****

[rináun]
infamy

n. **fame, repute, distinction** reputation 명성

Michael had gained **renown** as a gymnast at Harvard College.

32 **repel****

[ripél]
allure

v. **drive away, repulse, parry** 물리치다

Truman decided to act boldly to **repel** the aggressors.

33 **sanitation***

[sæ̀nətéiʃən]

n. **health, hygiene** 공중위생

Almost four out of every ten takeout food-processing companies violated **sanitation** regulations.

34 **scorching**

[skɔ́:rtʃiŋ]

adj. **exceedingly hot, boiling, broiling** 몹시 뜨거운(더운)

The travelers had a hard time adapting to the **scorching** desert climate.

35 **secluded**

[siklú:did]

adj. **remote, isolated, solitary** 외딴

Tired of crowds, Janice chose to stay on a **secluded** beach.

36 **spare***

[spέər]

v. 1. **save, economize** 절약하다

Ian spent all the time he could **spare** from his duties studying physics.

render	정부는 쿠바 망명자들에게 필요한 모든 도움을 주었다.
	뉴욕 시인들은 경험을 상징적인 주제라기보다는 순수한 현상으로 표현했다.
renown	Michael은 Harvard 대학에서 체조 선수로서 명성을 얻었다.
repel	Truman은 침략자들을 물리치기 위해 용감하게 행동하기로 결정했다.
sanitation	10개 중 거의 4개의 가공 식품 회사들이 공중위생 규칙들을 위반했다.
scorching	그 여행자들은 몹시 뜨거운 사막 기후에 적응하느라 힘든 시간을 보냈다.
secluded	많은 사람들에 싫증이 나서, Janice는 외딴 해변에서 지내기로 결정했다.
spare	Ian은 해야 하는 일들에서 절약할 수 있는 모든 시간을 물리 공부하는 데 썼다.

v. 2. **give, afford, allow** 주다, (시간을) 할애하다

Irene tried to find time to **spare** for The Literacy Project.

37 **stimulating***

[stímjulèitiŋ]
deadening

adj. **restorative, refreshing, inspiring** 활기(자극)를 주는

A cut in interest rates had a **stimulating** effect on the economy.

38 **typify***

[típəfài]

v. **represent, embody, symbolize** 대표하다, 특징을 나타내다

The art of Bali is **typified** by strong colors and dramatic movement.

39 **wholesale***

[hóulsèil]
constricted

adj. **extensive, indiscriminate** 대규모의

1967 was the year of a **wholesale** assault on morality and values.

Quiz

Choose the synonym.

1. chaotic ⓐ disorganized, disordered, anarchic
2. facility ⓑ drive away, repulse, parry
3. mingle ⓒ aptitude, skill, ability
4. repel ⓓ represent, embody, symbolize
5. typify ⓔ unite, mix, blend

Answer 1. ⓐ 2. ⓒ 3. ⓔ 4. ⓑ 5. ⓓ

spare	Irene은 글자 교육 프로젝트에 할애할 시간을 찾으려고 애썼다.
stimulating	이자율 삭감은 경제에 활기를 주는 영향을 미쳤다.
typify	Bali의 예술은 강한 색깔들과 극적인 움직임으로 대표된다.
wholesale	1967년은 도덕과 가치관에 대한 대규모의 공격이 있은 해였다.

Hackers TOEFL Voca TEST DAY 10-12

Choose the synonym of the highlighted word in the sentence.

1. The black bear is timid, clumsy, and rarely dangerous, but if attacked, most can climb trees and cover ground at great speeds.

(A) gallant (B) awkward (C) fluent (D) uninteresting

2. Bush drew sharp distinctions between his plan and the Democrats' plan to reform Medicare and Social Security.

(A) deny (B) contaminate (C) feature (D) improve

3. Costa Ricans have blamed the National Liberation Party's outgoing president for ruining their national economy and putting the country into recession.

(A) incriminated (B) maneuvered (C) absolved (D) qualified

4. The lawyer was compensated by the client for services rendered during the trial.

(A) repelled (B) afforded (C) pared (D) illustrated

5. Particularly important are those cellular proteins called enzymes, which catalyze the chemical reactions necessary for life.

(A) brisk (B) abstract (C) keen (D) essential

6. Because of decreasing elasticity with age, the arteries tend to become rigid tubes.

(A) repulsive (B) lubricious (C) stiff (D) polite

7. Chemistry involves the study of the atomic composition and structural architecture of substances.

(A) includes (B) strikes (C) confirms (D) breaches

8. Meteorology entails a systematic study of short-term variations in temperature, humidity, air pressure, and precipitation, along with their causes.

(A) requires (B) yields (C) fabricates (D) shares

9. Dyslexia can be a serious impediment to learning in young children and adults.

(A) project (B) structure (C) obstacle (D) blockage

10. The antibiotic inhibits an enzyme that controls the way bacterial DNA unravels and rewinds when microbes reproduce.

(A) discloses (B) hinders (C) alloys (D) renders

정답 p.419

제임스타운과 포카혼타스

미국인들이 자신들의 진정한 선조로 생각한다는 Pilgrim Fathers(순례시조)가 메이플라워호를 타고 뉴잉글랜드로 건너온 것은 1620년이지만, 그 이전에도 신대륙을 개척하려는 영국의 노력은 끊이지 않았다. 그 중의 하나가 1607년의 최초 식민도시인 제임스 타운의 건설이다. 국왕으로부터 남부 버지니아에 대한 특허권을 획득한 일단의 개척자들은 힘든 항해를 거쳐 지금의 체사피크만 부근에 자리를 잡게 되는데, 제임스 국왕의 이름을 따서 도시 이름을 제임스타운이라 짓게 된다. 초기에 이곳에 도착한 사람들은 일확천금을 노리거나, 노동을 거부하는 안일한 사고로 인해 출발 시부터 매우 피폐한 삶을 살게 되는데, 이런 그들 사이에서 특이한 경력과 모험정신 그리고 지도력을 갖춘 인물이 등장하니 그가 바로 존 스미스 선장이었다. 그는 이전에도 많은 전장에서 장교로 활동했던 인물인데 특이한 언행과 사고방식으로 인해 기인으로 통했던 모양이다. 신대륙 개척기의 고난기에 혁혁한 공을 세운 그는 이후 작가로도 활동을 하면서 자신의 자서전을 쓰게 되니 그 중의 유명한 이야기가 포카혼타스와의 일화이다. 이미 디즈니사가 만화영화로 제작한 바도 있다. 인어공주에서 뮬란까지 일관되게 그리고 있는 디즈니사의 여성캐릭터가 모두 그렇듯이 이 인디언 부족 추장의 딸 포카혼타스도 자신의 삶의 테두리에 만족하지 않고 더 넓은 세상을 꿈꾸는 자의식 강하고 모험심 강한 여자로 묘사되고 있다. 그는 우연한 계기로 원주민들에게 생포되어 죽음의 위기에 처한 존 스미스 선장을 간언을 통해 구해줄 뿐만 아니라, 개척자와 인디언 사이의 화해를 이끌어내고 담배 제배법을 개척자들에게 소개함으로써 제임스타운 개척의 성공을 담보하게 된다. 만화 영화 내에서는 존 스미스 선장을 사모하는 것으로 표현되고 있으나, 그녀가 결혼한 사람은 이후의 다른 제임스타운 시민 존 롤프라는 사람으로, 그와 함께 영국으로 건너가고 세례를 받기도 한다. 이후 벌어지는 수많은 개척민과 원주민과의 반목과 살육의 역사를 볼 때 아직 생존의 문제로 번지지 않은 동화같은 아름다운 이야기라 하겠다.

TAKE A BREAK

D A Y **13**

Hackers TOEFL **Vocabulary**

Hackers Voca

www.goHackers.com

1 **admire**** | v. **esteem, respect** | 존경하다

[ædmáiər]
despise

The whole world **admired** Amelia Earhart's successful attempt to fly across the Atlantic.

2 **adroit*** | adj. **skillful, dexterous, proficient** | 능숙한

[ədrɔ́it]
incompetent

Hillary Clinton is a good politician because she is **adroit** at gaining people's trust.

3 **ambivalent** | adj. **unsure, mixed, undecided** | 불확실한, 상반된 감정이 공존하는

[æmbívələnt]
certain

Joe has **ambivalent** feelings about getting back into a relationship with his ex-girlfriend.

4 **camouflage*** | v. **hide, disguise, conceal** | 감추다, 위장하다

[kǽməflɑ̀:ʒ]
expose

Captain Stencil ordered his troops to **camouflage** the trenches dug around the battlefields in order to surprise the enemy.

5 **composed**** | adj. 1. **calm, tranquil** | 차분한

[kəmpóuzd]

Kennedy seemed very **composed** in spite of the stress he was under.

adj. 2. **created, written, formed** | 작성된

The newly **composed** Weekly Leading Index is a balance of seven major economic indicators.

admire	전 세계가 Amelia Earhart의 성공적인 대서양 횡단 비행 도전에 경탄했다.
adroit	Hillary Clinton은 뛰어난 정치가이다. 왜냐하면 그녀는 사람들의 신망을 얻는 데 능숙하기 때문이다.
ambivalent	Joe는 그의 과거 여자 친구와 예전의 관계로 되돌아 가는 것에 대해 상반되는 감정을 동시에 느꼈다.
camouflage	Stencil 대령은 적군을 놀라게 하기 위해 교전지 주변에 파인 참호를 감추라고 그의 군대에게 명령했다.
composed	Kennedy는 그가 받는 스트레스에도 불구하고 매우 차분해 보였다.
	그 새로이 작성된 주간 주요 지표는 일곱 개의 주요 경제 지표들의 균형 상태이다.

6 **conceal****

v. **hide, cover, obscure** mask, bury 숨기다

[kənsí:l]
reveal

Police officers found the cocaine **concealed** inside the doll.

7 **deliberate****

adj. 1. **careful, thoughtful, cautious** 신중한

[dilíbərit]

The Parliament reduced funding for many programs in a **deliberate** effort to cut the deficit.

casual

adj. 2. **intentional, designed, planned** voluntary 의도적인

The film's graphic scenes were a **deliberate** attempt to grab the attention of a specific audience.

8 **exhilarate**

v. **excite, thrill, elate** 들뜨게 하다

[igzílərèit]

The student was **exhilarated** when he won a scholarship.

9 **exposure**

n. **disclosure, revelation, uncovering, unveiling** 폭로, 발각

[ikspóuʒər]

The **exposure** of corruption in the government sparked a public outcry.

10 **glow***

v. **shine, radiate, beam** 빛나다

[glóu]

Joey's face **glowed** with happiness when he saw the Statue of Liberty for the first time.

11 **hiatus****

n. **break, interruption, gap** 중단, 단절

[haiéitəs]

After the rebellion, the country had a peaceful **hiatus** before another conflict erupted.

12 **incinerate***

v. **burn** 태우다

[insínərèit]

The rebels would pillage the farmer's villages and **incinerate** them to the ground.

conceal	경관들은 인형 안에 숨겨져 있는 코카인을 발견했다.
deliberate	의회는 재정 적자를 줄이기 위한 신중한 노력의 일환으로 여러 프로그램에 대주던 자금을 삭감했다.
	그 영화의 생생한 장면들은 특정한 관중의 관심을 얻기 위한 의도적인 시도였다.
exhilarate	그 학생은 장학금을 탔을 때 들떴었다.
exposure	정부 부패의 폭로는 대중의 강력한 항의의 도화선이 되었다.
glow	처음으로 자유의 여신상을 보았을 때 Joey의 얼굴은 행복감으로 빛났다.
hiatus	반란이 일어난 후, 그 나라는 다른 분쟁이 일어나기 전까지 긴 평화로운 휴지기를 가졌다.
incinerate	그 반란자들은 농가를 약탈하고, 불태워서 재로 만들곤 했다.

13 ineffectively** — adv. **without any result, inefficiently, unproductively** 비효과적으로

[ìniféktivli]

If professors express themselves **ineffectively**, students can't be expected to excel.

14 inert* — adj. **motionless, inactive, stationary** 자동력(自動力)이 없는, 움직일 수 없는

[inə́:rt]
active

At the end of the day, Joseph spends half an hour lying **inert** on the sofa.

15 luster** — n. **sheen, brightness, brilliance** radiance 광채

[lʌ́stər]

The new cosmetics line will add **luster** to the skin and hair.

16 massive** — adj. **huge, colossal, enormous** bulky, large 거대한, 막대한

[mǽsiv]
puny

Massive ships in the Spanish Armada could easily endure the attack of a huge cannon.

17 occupy* — v. **engross, engage, absorb** (주의 · 마음을) 끌다, 사로잡다

[ɑ́kjəpài]

The school teacher prepared several activities to keep the children **occupied**.

18 precede* — v. **come before, antecede, forerun** 앞서다, 우선하다

[prisí:d]
follow

A recovery in airline stocks typically **precedes** a rebound in the economy.

19 prove** — v. **verify, substantiate, confirm** 입증하다

[prú:v]
refute

Scientists agree that it is impossible to **prove** a theory if it cannot be tested.

20 purchase** — v. **buy, procure** 얻다, 획득하다

[pə́:rtʃəs]
sell

Jerry carefully **purchased** a secondhand car in good condition.

ineffectively	교수들이 자신이 의미하는 바를 효과적으로 표현하지 못하면, 학생들이 잘하기를 기대할 수 없다.
inert	하루를 마칠 때가 되자, Joseph은 소파에 누워서 움직이지 않고 30분을 보냈다.
luster	그 새로운 화장품은 피부와 모발에 광채를 더할 것이다.
massive	스페인의 무적 함대에 속한 대형 선박들은 거대한 대포의 공격을 쉽게 견딜 수 있었다.
occupy	학교 선생님은 아이들을 계속 집중시키게 하려고 몇 가지 활동들을 준비했다.
precede	항공 주식의 주가 회복은 전형적으로 경제가 회복되기 전에 일어난다.
prove	과학자들은 시험할 수 없다면 어떤 이론을 입증하는 것이 불가능하다는 사실에 동의한다.
purchase	Jerry는 양호한 상태의 중고차를 신중하게 구입했다.

21 **restrict****
[ristríkt]
free

v. limit, **confine, restrain** 제한하다

The legislation **restricted** the sale of soft drinks in schools during school hours.

22 **rupture****
[rʌ́ptʃər]

n. 1. breach; **burst** 불화 ; 파열

The **rupture** in Amy and Diana's friendship was never healed.

v. 2. break apart, **burst, split, tear** 찢다, 파열시키다

Patty **ruptured** her eardrum at the loud rock concert.

23 **scrutiny***
[skrú:təni]

n. examination, **investigation, inspection** 정밀 조사

Closer **scrutiny** of the archaeological sites has rendered Orville's hypothesis untenable.

24 **seductive***
[sidʌ́ktiv]
repulsive

adj. tempting, **enticing** 유혹적인

Nothing is more **seductive** than the promise of getting something for nothing.

25 **seep***
[sí:p]

v. go through slowly, pass through slowly, **permeate** 스며들다

The gas **seeped** throughout the entire building before anyone noticed the leaking valve.

26 **segment**
[ségmənt]

n. portion, **division, section, part** 부분

The four-hour television program was separated into **segments**.

27 **shatter****
[ʃǽtər]

v. break, **pulverize, smash** crash 박살 내다

A tornado **shattered** windows of nearby houses last night.

restrict	그 법은 수업이 있는 동안 학교 내에서 청량음료의 판매를 제한했다.
rupture	Amy와 Diana의 우정에 생긴 금은 결코 아물지 않았다.
	Patty는 시끄러운 락 콘서트에서 고막이 파열됐다.
scrutiny	고고학 유적지들을 정밀 조사한 결과 Orville의 가설은 성립되지 않는 것으로 밝혀졌다.
seductive	무언가를 거저 얻게 된다는 약속만큼 매혹적인 것이 없다.
seep	밸브가 새는 것을 누군가 알아채기 전에, 가스가 건물 전체에 스며들었다.
segment	4시간짜리 TV 프로그램은 부분들로 나눠졌다.
shatter	토네이도가 간밤에 근처 주택들의 창문을 박살 냈다.

28 shock* v. **jolt, startle, stun** 충격을 주다, 놀라게 하다

[ʃɑ́k]

The scandal in the White House **shocked** the whole world.

29 significant** adj. **important, essential, considerable, substantial, serious** 중요한

[signífikənt]
unimportant

The dolphin-safe campaign brought **significant** change to the tuna industry.

30 slab n. **single piece of material** 조각

[slǽb]

The patio was made of enormous granite **slabs**.

31 slaughter** v. **massacre, butcher, kill** 학살하다

[slɔ́:tər]

Endangered animals are **slaughtered** for traditional medicines.

32 strife n. **conflict, struggle, fight** 싸움

[stráif]
accord

Selfishness is a major cause of **strife** in modern society.

33 style** n. **mode, manner, technique** 방식

[stail]

The boss employs an abrasive **style** of leadership in his relations with employees.

34 sustained* adj. **continued, constant, prolonged, steady** 지속적인

[səstéind]
intermittent

Running a marathon requires **sustained** physical activity and great endurance.

35 temperance n. **moderation, continence, self-discipline** 자제, 절제

[témpərəns]
intemperance

During her reign, Queen Victoria instilled the virtues of thrift, **temperance**, and hard work into the minds of the British people.

shock	백악관의 그 추문은 전 세계를 경악시켰다.
significant	돌고래 보호 운동은 참치 산업에 중요한 변화를 가져왔다.
slab	그 테라스는 거대한 화강암 석판으로 만들어진 것이었다.
slaughter	멸종 위기에 놓여진 동물들은 전통적인 약제용으로 도살된다.
strife	이기심은 현대 사회에 있는 분쟁의 주원인이다.
style	그 사장은 직원들과의 관계에서 화를 돋우는 방식의 리더쉽을 사용한다.
sustained	마라톤 경주를 하는 것은 지속적인 육체의 활동과 엄청난 인내력을 필요로 한다.
temperance	Victoria 여왕의 집권기 때, 그녀는 영국 국민들의 마음 속에 근검 절약과 절제 그리고 노동의 미덕을 주입시켰다.

36 tremendous** | adj. **huge, great, gigantic** colossal | 엄청난

[triméndəs]
minute

The Arab-Israeli conflict has had a **tremendous** impact on the world economy.

37 vivid* | adj. **bright, brilliant; graphic, pictorial** | 선명한 ; 생생한

[vívid]
lifeless

The Pop Art movement featured the use of **vivid** colors and meaningful cultural themes.

38 wedge | v. **cram, squeeze, crowd** | 억지로 밀어 넣다

[wédʒ]
loosen up

Every morning Cynthia **wedges** herself into the shuffling crowd on the subway.

Quiz

Choose the synonym.

1. adroit	ⓐ huge, gigantic, colossal
2. deliberate	ⓑ skillful, dexterous, proficient
3. restrict	ⓒ careful, thoughtful, cautious
4. tremendous	ⓓ confine, limit, restrain
5. strife	ⓔ conflict, struggle, fight

Answer 1. ⓑ 2. ⓒ 3. ⓓ 4. ⓐ 5. ⓔ

tremendous	아랍과 이스라엘의 충돌은 세계 경제에 엄청난 영향을 끼쳐오고 있다.
vivid	팝아트 운동은 선명한 색상과 의의 있는 문화적 주제들을 특징으로 삼았다.
wedge	매일 아침 Cynthia는 지하철에서 이리저리로 휩쓸리는 사람들 속으로 스스로를 억지로 밀어 넣는다.

DAY 14

Hackers TOEFL **Vocabulary**

Hackers Voca

www.goHackers.com

1 **actually***	adv.	in fact, **as a matter of fact, literally**	실제로
[ǽktʃuəli]		The transmission screen displays the picture that is **actually** being broadcast on the air.	
2 **adorn****	v.	decorate, **beautify, ornament**	장식하다
[ədɔ́ːrn] disfigure		Christine **adorned** herself in her finest jewelry for the party.	
3 **calculate***	v.	figure, determine	추정하다, 어림잡다
[kǽlkjulèit]		Before deciding whether or not he could afford a new jeep, Jason **calculated** his expenses and earnings.	
4 **claim***	v.	call for, declare, **demand, request**	요구하다
[kléim] renounce		Calvin **claimed** a share of the profits from the use of the software he developed.	
5 **commemorate***	v.	celebrate	기념하다
[kəmémərèit]		To **commemorate** the victory, Napoleon awarded everyone in his army a medal.	
6 **conformity***	n.	**agreement, accordance**	일치
[kənfɔ́ːrməti] discord		American colleges and universities must act in **conformity** with immigration laws when accepting international students.	

actually	방송 스크린은 실제로 방송되고 있는 장면을 보여 준다.
adorn	Christine은 파티를 위해 가장 좋은 보석으로 치장했다.
calculate	그가 새로운 지프차를 살 수 있을지 없을지를 결정하기 이전에, Jason은 그의 수입과 지출을 어림잡아 보았다.
claim	Calvin은 그가 개발한 소프트웨어를 사용해서 나온 이익금의 배당을 요구했다.
commemorate	그 승리를 기념하기 위해, Napoleon은 그의 군대의 모든 병사들에게 메달을 수여했다.
conformity	미국의 대학들은 교환 학생을 받아들일 때, 입국 관리법에 따라서 행동해야 한다.

7 **copious**** adj. **plentiful, ample, bountiful** 풍부한

[kóupiəs]

The **copious** rainfall in the winter allowed the farmers to irrigate their crops all year.

8 **desire**** v. **covet, long for; seek, request** 열망하다 ; 요구하다

[dizáiər]

The Islamic Jihad **desires** to protect the Palestinian national interest.

9 **diligently*** adv. **assiduously, carefully, earnestly, industriously** 열심히

[dílidʒəntli]

Students must conduct research **diligently** in doing a term paper or thesis.

10 **enthrall*** v. **fascinate, captivate, enchant** mesmerize 매혹하다

[inθrɔ́:l]
repulse

Chicago has an on-site museum that will **enthrall** visitors.

11 **feast** n. 1. **celebration, festival, fiesta** 축제

[fí:st]

The company held a **feast** to celebrate its profitable new contract.

v. 2. **eat, gorge, indulge** 배불리 먹다

At Thanksgiving, many people get together with their families and **feast** on traditional foods.

12 **gather*** v. **collect, aggregate, assemble** 모으다

[gǽðər]
scatter

Robert **gathered** information on election problems.

13 **gauge** v. **measure, calculate, appraise** 평가하다, 판단하다

[géidʒ]

Researchers disagree as to whether IQ scores accurately **gauge** intelligence.

copious	겨울의 풍부한 강우량은 농부들이 일 년 내내 작물에 물을 댈 수 있게 해주었다.
desire	이슬람교의 성전은 팔레스타인의 국익을 수호하길 갈망한다.
diligently	학생들은 학기말 보고서나 논문을 쓸 때 열심히 연구를 해야만 한다.
enthrall	Chicago에는 방문객들을 매혹시키는 현장 박물관이 있다.
feast	회사는 수익이 좋은 새 계약을 축하하기 위해 만찬을 주최했다.
	추수감사절에는, 많은 사람들이 가족과 함께 모여서 전통 음식을 즐긴다.
gather	Robert는 선거 문제에 관한 정보를 모았다.
gauge	과학자들은 IQ 점수가 지능을 정확히 측정하는지에 대해 엇갈린 주장을 하고 있다.

14 **glue*** | v. **stick, fix, cement, paste** 접착시키다

[glúː]
unfasten

The kindergarten students created a collage by **gluing** numerous magazine photographs and pictures onto one sheet of paper.

15 **grand*** | adj. **imposing, stately, august** 웅장한

[grǽnd]
trivial

Ansel Adams' photographs of the western United States show nature on a **grand** scale.

16 **hearten**** | v. **encourage, inspire, cheer** 격려하다

[hɑ́ːrtn]
dampen

The news will greatly **hearten** the students.

17 **hub**** | n. **center** 중심

[hʌ́b]

New Delhi is not really a traveler's destination, but it is a **hub** city in India.

18 **hybrid** | n. **combination, cross, mixture** 잡종, 혼합물

[háibrid]

Many modern crops are **hybrids** of earlier species.

19 **impetus*** | n. **stimulus** 자극

[ímpitəs]

Einstein's work provided the **impetus** for a major shift in the study of physics.

20 **improvise** | v. **extemporize, ad-lib** (연주 · 연설 등을) 즉흥적으로 하다

[ímprəvàiz]
rehearse

Maurice was impressed by the comedian's ability to **improvise** a comic skit and entertain the audience.

21 **irresistible*** | adj. **attractive, fascinating; overwhelming** 매혹적인 ; 저항할 수 없는

[ìrizístəbl]

The **irresistible** bargains at the store caused patronage to increase dramatically.

glue	그 유치원의 원생들은 여러 장의 잡지 사진과 그림을 한 장의 종이에 붙임으로써 콜라주를 만들었다.
grand	Ansel Adams가 찍은 미국 서부의 사진은 웅장한 규모의 자연을 보여준다.
hearten	그 뉴스는 학생들을 상당히 고무시킬 것이다.
hub	New Delhi는 사실상 여행자의 목적지는 아니지만, 인도의 중심 도시이다.
hybrid	많은 현대 농작물들은 이전 종들을 섞은 잡종이다.
impetus	Einstein의 연구는 물리학에서 큰 전환이 되는 자극을 주었다.
improvise	Maurice는 즉흥적으로 농담을 하고, 방청객들을 즐겁게 해주는 그 코미디언의 능력에 감명받았다.
irresistible	그 상점의 매력적인 특가품으로 인하여 단골 고객이 극적으로 증가했다.

22 **incised***	adj. **carved**	새겨진
[insáizd]	Subtle lighting emphasizes delicately **incised** patterns and surface inflections.	

23 **inherent in*****	phr. **characteristic of, built in**	내재된
	Competition is **inherent** both **in** and between human societies.	

24 **juvenile***	adj. **children's, puerile, young**	어린
[dʒú:vənàil] adult	The most common cause of death for **juvenile** owls was starvation.	

25 **main**	adj. **chief, prime, principal**	주요한
[méin] minor	Religious conflict was the **main** factor contributing to the migration of the Pilgrims.	

26 **negligence***	n. **carelessness**	부주의, 태만
[néglidʒəns]	James would not forgive my **negligence** in failing to contact him sooner.	

27 **outweigh**	v. **preponderate, outbalance, override, prevail over**	~보다 뛰어나다
[àutwéi]	After thinking about it, Meghan decided that the benefits of her new refrigerator **outweighed** the exorbitant cost.	

28 **pigment****	n. **color, dye, tincture**	색소
[pígmənt]	Ancient Romans extracted purple **pigment** from shellfish.	

29 **plausible**	adj. **believable, credible, likely, probable**	그럴듯한
[plɔ́:zəbl]	The story seemed **plausible**, but witnesses said it was untrue.	

incised	섬세한 조명은 정교하게 새겨진 도안들과 표면 굴곡을 강조한다.
inherent in	인간 사회 내에는, 그리고 인간 사회 간에는 경쟁이 내재되어 있다.
juvenile	어린 올빼미들의 가장 흔한 사망 원인은 굶주림이었다.
main	종교적 갈등은 초기 정착민들이 이민을 한 주원인이었다.
negligence	James는 부주의로 더 일찍 그에게 연락하지 못한 나를 용서하지 않을 것이다.
outweigh	그것에 대해 생각해본 후 Meghan은 그녀의 새 냉장고의 이점이 그 어마어마한 가격을 능가한다고 판단했다.
pigment	고대 로마인들은 조개에서 보라색 색소를 추출해냈다.
plausible	그 진술은 그럴듯해 보였지만, 증인들은 그것이 거짓이라고 했다.

30 prudent adj. **cautious, discreet, careful** wary 조심성 있는, 신중한

[prú:dənt]
imprudent

It would have been more **prudent** for Mrs. Baker to read the rental contract before signing it.

31 revise* v. **modify, correct, alter, edit** 수정하다

[riváiz]

Scientists **revised** their earlier claims that the ozone layer would recover by 2050.

32 spirit* n. **mind** 정신

[spírit]

Elaine succeeded in developing a **spirit** of loyalty in her employees.

33 skillful** adj. **deft, skilled, adept** dexterous, adroit, proficient 숙련된

[skílfəl]
maladroit

Kevin is an extremely **skillful** writer.

34 tenet*** n. **principle, doctrine, dogma** 원칙

[ténit]

Evolution is one of the main **tenets** of modern biology.

35 transformation* n. **change, conversion, metamorphosis** 변화

[trænsfərméiʃən]

In recent years, Allen's attitude has undergone a complete **transformation**.

36 traverse* v. **cross, go across, pass** 가로지르다

[trəvə́:rs]

The Moon, planets, and stars **traverse** the night sky from east to west.

37 unbearably* adv. **extremely** 극도로

[ʌnbɛ́(:)ərəbli]

Due to global warming, the summers in the city have become **unbearably** hot.

prudent	Baker 부인이 서명을 하기 전에 임대차 계약서를 읽어 보았다면, 더욱 조심성 있었을 것이다.
revise	과학자들은 오존층이 2050년까지 회복될 것이라는 그들의 초기 주장을 수정했다.
spirit	Elaine은 그녀의 사원들로부터 충성심을 이끌어내는 데 성공했다.
skillful	Kevin은 매우 숙련된 작가이다.
tenet	진화는 현대 생물학의 주요 원칙 중 하나이다.
transformation	최근에, Allen의 태도는 완전히 변했다.
traverse	달, 행성, 별들은 동쪽에서 서쪽으로 밤하늘을 가로지른다.
unbearably	지구 온난화 때문에 도시의 여름은 극도로 더워졌다.

38 **variable***

[vɛ́əriəbl]
uniform

adj. **unstable, changeable, inconstant** fickle 변하기 쉬운

The weather is rather **variable** in South Africa.

39 **while**

[*h*wail]

con. 1. **during the time; as long as** ~동안에 ; ~하는 한

Many students work part-time jobs **while** attending college.

con. 2. **although; whereas** ~할 지라도 ; ~와는 반대로

While the senator was concerned, he did not voice his doubts.

Quiz

Choose the synonym.

1. adorn ⓐ principle, doctrine, dogma
2. prudent ⓑ go across, pass, cross
3. traverse ⓒ cautious, discreet, careful
4. tenet ⓓ plentiful, ample, bountiful
5. copious ⓔ decorate, beautify, ornament

Answer 1. ⓔ 2. ⓒ 3. ⓑ 4. ⓐ 5. ⓓ

variable
while

남아프리카의 날씨는 다소 변덕스럽다.
많은 학생들이 대학에 다니는 동안에 파트타임으로 일한다.
그 상원의원은 염려되긴 했지만, 그의 의심들을 표현하지 않았다.

DAY 15

Hackers TOEFL **Vocabulary**

15 Hackers Voca

www.goHackers.com

1 **affluent** | adj. **wealthy, plentiful, opulent, abundant** | 부유한, 풍족한

[ǽfluənt]
poor

Jackie came from an **affluent** family.

2 **aggravate*** | v. **worsen, exacerbate** | 악화시키다

[ǽgrəvèit]
soothe

Heather's poor health condition was **aggravated** by excessive stress and a lack of sleep.

3 **cling to** | phr. **hold tightly, stick to, adhere to** | 달라붙다, 고수하다

Static electricity can make light objects **cling to** one another.

4 **craft** | v. **skillfully produce, fabricate, make** | 솜씨 있게 만들다

[krǽft]

The artisans **crafted** some elaborately decorated pottery.

5 **crest** | n. **acme, peak, apex, top, crown** | 정상

[krést]

The **crest** of the tidal wave reached ten meters high.

6 **critic*** | n. **reviewer, judge** | 비평가

[krítik]

Today **critics** have begun to understand the importance of Wilson's writings.

affluent	Jackie는 부유한 가정 출신이다.
aggravate	Heather의 나쁜 건강 상태는 과도한 스트레스와 수면 부족으로 인해 악화되었다.
cling to	정전기는 가벼운 물체가 다른 물체에 달라붙게 할 수 있다.
craft	그 장인들은 정교하게 꾸며진 도자기 몇 개를 솜씨 있게 만들었다.
crest	해일의 물마루가 10미터 높이에 달했다.
critic	오늘날 비평가들은 Wilson의 글들의 중요성을 이해하기 시작했다.

7 cross-hatching* — n. shade — 음영

[krɔ́(:) shæ̀tʃiŋ]

Modern art frequently uses **cross-hatching** patterns.

8 decimate* — v. eliminate, wipe out, extinguish, eradicate — 많은 사람을 죽이다

[désəmèit]

The Black Plague **decimated** the population in Europe.

9 disciple* — n. pupil, student, scholar — 제자

[disáipl]

Confucius spent a large part of his life teaching a small group of **disciples**.

10 disclose* — v. reveal, divulge, unveil — (사실 등을) 밝히다

[disklóuz]
conceal

Government officials **disclosed** that they had been negotiating with the rebels.

11 disposition — n. temperament, temper, nature, spirit — 성질, 기질

[dìspəzíʃən]

The **disposition** of some animals makes them impossible to domesticate.

12 dissimilar — adj. different, heterogeneous, unlike — 다른

[dissímələr]

Although identical in appearance, the twin brothers were **dissimilar** in personality.

13 dominant* — adj. supreme, prevailing, ruling — prevalent — 우세한

[dámənənt]
subordinate

Rome was the **dominant** military power on the Italian Peninsula.

14 effect* — n. influence, impact; result, consequence — 영향 ; 결과

[ifékt]
cause

Inflation is having a disastrous **effect** on the economy.

cross-hatching	현대 예술에서는 음영 기법을 자주 사용한다.
decimate	흑사병이 유럽의 많은 사람을 죽였다.
disciple	공자는 많지 않은 학생들을 가르치는 데 그의 생애 상당 부분의 시간을 보냈다.
disclose	정부 관리들은 그들이 반역자들과 협상하고 있었다는 사실을 밝혔다.
disposition	몇몇 동물들의 성질이 그들을 길들일 수 없게 만든다.
dissimilar	그 쌍둥이 형제는 겉모습은 같았지만 성격이 달랐다.
dominant	로마는 이탈리아 반도의 지배적 군사 강국이었다.
effect	인플레이션이 경제에 상당히 심한 피해를 주고 있다.

15 **enhance**

v. **improve, enrich, intensify, upgrade** 향상시키다, 개선하다

[inhǽns]

The invention of the telegraph **enhanced** the speed of communication.

16 **enunciate***

v. **articulate, phonate, pronounce** 분명하게 발음하다

[inʌ́nsièit]

Tom Cruise **enunciated** his French lines precisely in the movie.

17 **eradicate****

v. **root up, extirpate, eliminate, remove** 근절하다

[irǽdəkèit]
implant

The US spends $50 billion per year trying to **eradicate** drugs from its borders.

18 **harsh****

adj. **severe, rigorous, inclement** ruthless 가혹한

[hάːrʃ]
mild

Conditions in the prison camp were unbearably **harsh**.

19 **heritage***

n. **tradition, inheritance, legacy** 전통, 유산

[héritidʒ]

The nation owed its entire **heritage** to its neighboring country.

20 **inappropriate****

adj. **improper, unsuitable** 부적당한

[ìnəpróupriət]

Joking and laughing is completely **inappropriate** behavior at a funeral service.

21 **insolent****

adj. **impudent, impertinent, rude** audacious 무례한

[ínsələnt]
deferential

Dan was coldly **insolent** to those he considered his inferiors.

22 **jeopardy***

n. **danger, venture, peril** risk, hazard 위험

[dʒépərdi]
safety

Deflation in farmland prices placed many farmers in financial **jeopardy**.

enhance	전신의 발명은 통신의 속도를 향상시켰다.
enunciate	Tom Cruise는 그 영화에서 프랑스어 대사들을 정확하게 발음했다.
eradicate	미국은 이 나라에서 마약을 근절하기 위해 일 년에 500억 달러를 쓴다.
harsh	포로 수용소의 환경은 참을 수 없을 정도로 가혹했다.
heritage	그 나라는 인접 국가에 전 유산을 빚지고 있었다.
inappropriate	농담과 웃음은 결코 장례식에서의 적절한 행동이 아니다.
insolent	Dan은 자기보다 능력이 떨어진다고 생각되는 사람들에게는 차갑고 거만했다.
jeopardy	농지 가격 하락은 많은 농부들을 경제적 위험에 빠뜨렸다.

23 **luxury**	n. extravagance, **frill**	사치
[lʌ́kʃəri]	In the 1930s, owning a telephone was a sign of **luxury**.	

24 **manipulate***	v. operate, control, handle, **maneuver**	조종하다, 다루다
[mənípjəlèit]	Astronauts **manipulate** devices like the Canada Arm, a tool used to grab floating objects in space.	

25 **mock***	v. ridicule, make fun of, **deride** jeer	조롱하다
[mák]	Glen deliberately **mocked** the principles I adhered to.	

26 **precious**	adj. valuable, **dear, priceless**	귀중한
[préʃəs] worthless	The colonies were forced into providing **precious** metals to the mother country.	

27 **regard***	n. attention, **notice; affection, respect**	관심 ; 호감, 존경
[rigá:rd] disdain	The professor showed little **regard** for student concerns about the exam's being too difficult.	

28 **return****	v. recur, **revert, come back**	되돌아가다
[ritə́:rn] advance	Memories of his university days **returned** as Donald visited his alma mater.	

29 **set***	v. situate, **place, put** lay, locate	~을 놓다
[sét]	The movers will **set** the furniture inside the house.	

30 **spacious****	adj. roomy, **ample, capacious** extensive	넓은
[spéiʃəs] confined	The president has a **spacious** office on the seventh floor in the building.	

luxury	1930년대에는 전화를 소유하는 것은 호사스러움의 표상이었다.
manipulate	우주 비행사들은 우주에 떠다니는 물체들을 붙잡는 데 사용되는 기구인 'Canada Arm'과 같은 장치들을 다룬다.
mock	Glen은 내가 고수하는 원칙들을 고의로 조롱했다.
precious	식민지들은 귀금속들을 본국으로 보내도록 강요당했다.
regard	교수는 시험이 너무 어렵다는 학생들의 걱정에 별 주의를 보이지 않았다.
return	Donald가 모교를 방문했을 때 그는 대학 시절 추억으로 되돌아갔다.
set	이삿짐 운송업자들은 집 안에 그 가구들을 놓을 것이다.
spacious	사장은 그 건물 7층에 넓은 사무실을 가지고 있다.

31 **spectator*** n. **viewer, observer** 구경꾼

[spékteitər]

The tennis match attracted over 30,000 **spectators**.

32 **strict** adj. **rigid, rigorous, stringent** 엄격한

[stríkt]
lenient

The old woman made sure that the girls lived by **strict** moral standards.

33 **swift*** adj. **quick, speedy, fleet** rapid 빠른

[swíft]
sluggish

With a **swift** movement, Maggie stood upright.

34 **synchronize*** v. **occur at the same time** 동시에 일어나다

[síŋkrənàiz]

The two plane crashes **synchronized**, causing much suspicion about terrorism.

35 **throughout** prep. **in every part of, in all parts of** ~의 도처에

[θru(:)áut]

Every country maintains a network of embassies **throughout** the world.

36 **undermine** v. **attenuate, weaken** 약화시키다

[ʌ̀ndərmáin]
reinforce

Income reductions have **undermined** the foundation of the middle class.

37 **upset** v. 1. **capsize, overthrow, overturn** 뒤엎다, 전복시키다

[ʌpsét]

The underdogs team **upset** the champions in the final soccer match.

v. 2. **disturb, distress, perturb** 당황하게 하다

The mayor's ignorance **upset** the whole city.

spectator	그 테니스 경기는 30,000명 이상의 관객을 동원했다.
strict	그 노파는 그 소녀들이 엄격한 도덕적 기준을 가지고 살았는지를 확인했다.
swift	Maggie는 빠른 움직임으로 똑바로 섰다.
synchronize	비행기 추락사고 두 건이 동시에 발생하여 테러가 아니냐는 의문을 품게 만들었다.
throughout	각 국가들은 전 세계에 널리 퍼진 대사관 네트워크를 보유하고 있다.
undermine	수입 감소는 중산층의 기반을 약화시켜 왔다.
upset	축구 결승 시합에서 약체팀이 우승팀을 이겼다.
	시장의 무지함은 모든 시민을 당황하게 했다.

38 virtuous | adj. **righteous, good, moral** | 덕 있는

[vəː́rtʃuəs]
vicious

Bernard was known as a courageous and **virtuous** man.

39 wrangle* | v. argue, debate; **quarrel, bicker** | 논쟁하다 ; 말다툼하다

[rǽŋgl]
assent

Israel and Palestine have been **wrangling** over the West Bank territory for more than 30 years.

40 withdraw | v. **retire, retreat** | 물러나다

[wiðdrɔ́ː]
advance

Stanton has completely **withdrawn** from public life to devote himself to his books.

41 worship* | v. venerate, **revere, respect** | 숭배하다

[wə́ːrʃip]

The Hittites **worshipped** a sun goddess and a storm god.

Quiz

Choose the synonym.

1. affluent — ⓐ eliminate, wipe out, extinguish
2. decimate — ⓑ roomy, ample, capacious
3. insolent — ⓒ argue, debate
4. spacious — ⓓ wealthy, plentiful, opulent
5. wrangle — ⓔ impudent, impertinent, rude

Answer 1. ⓓ 2. ⓐ 3. ⓔ 4. ⓑ 5. ⓒ

virtuous	Bernard는 용기 있고 덕 있는 남자로 알려졌다.
wrangle	이스라엘과 팔레스타인은 'West Bank' 지역을 놓고 30년 넘게 논쟁을 벌여 오고 있다.
withdraw	Stanton은 책 쓰는 일에 전념하기 위해 공적인 생활에서 완전히 물러났다.
worship	히타이트족은 태양 여신과 폭풍 신을 숭배했다.

Hackers TOEFL Voca TEST DAY 13-15

Choose the synonym of the highlighted word in the sentence.

1. Elements vary from those that are highly active to those that are inert.
(A) animated (B) motionless (C) dynamic (D) basic

2. Weather becomes more extreme and variable with atmospheric heating in part because the warming accelerates the water cycle.
(A) consistent (B) fickle (C) rigid (D) tough

3. Confederate forces in the American Civil War had to withdraw from northern territory after their devastating defeat at Gettysburg in 1863.
(A) retreat (B) remove (C) extract (D) position

4. After years of working twelve hour days, Rachel decided to take a six month hiatus in order to travel and reflect.
(A) session (B) break (C) adventure (D) crest

5. The founding of Rollins College gave impetus to the community's growth.
(A) malice (B) variety (C) stimulus (D) humility

6. The brown dwarfs are not the dominant constituent of the universe's mass.
(A) latent (B) ruling (C) malcontent (D) aggressive

7. There are several plausible theories to explain the disappearance of the dinosaurs.
(A) credible (B) determined (C) proven (D) deliberate

8. Scarcity of food, clothing, and shelter influences Arctic living conditions more than the harsh climate does.
(A) tedious (B) cumbersome (C) severe (D) abstract

9. 'The Birds of America' was a work conceived and executed on a grand scale.
(A) base (B) limited (C) imposing (D) sober

10. The tornado's devastating blasts of wind put human life in the community in jeopardy.
(A) sorrow (B) danger (C) pact (D) intimacy

정답 p.419

TAKE A BREAK

Hope 희망(希望)

Hope is a waking dream. 희망은 백일몽이다.

- Aristotle 아리스토텔레스

While there's life, there's hope. 삶이 있는 한 희망도 있다.

- Cicero 키케로(로마 정치가, 철학자)

All human wisdom is summed up in two words. 모든 인간의 지혜는 두 가지 말로 요약된다,
Wait and hope. 기다림과 희망.

- A. Dumas A. 뒤마(프랑스 소설가)

Hope is the parent of faith. 희망은 신념의 어버이이다.

- C.A. Bartol C. A. 바르톨(미국 목사)

He who has never hoped can never despair. 희망을 가져본 적이 없는 자는 절망할 자격도 없다.

- Bernard Shaw 버나드 쇼(영국 극작가, 평론가)

DAY 16 Hackers Voca

1 **alternative*****
[ɔ:ltə́:rnətiv]

n. 1. **choice, option, substitute** 대안

Survey research provides an **alternative** to the experimental method.

adj. 2. **substitutive** 대용이 되는

The city encouraged people to take **alternative** means of transportation to help reduce traffic congestion.

2 **analogous***
[ənǽləgəs]
dissimilar

adj. **comparable, similar, parallel** 유사한

Archimedes was certain that the wings of an airplane were **analogous** in function to the wings of a hummingbird.

3 **annually**
[ǽnjuəli]

adv. **yearly, per annum** 매년

Interest on the bank loan was calculated **annually**.

4 **awkward**
[ɔ́:kwərd]
deft

adj. **clumsy, unskillful** 서투른

Adams lost votes because of his **awkward** efforts to resolve the Texas issue.

5 **capability****
[kèipəbíləti]
inability, incapability

n. **flair, talent, ability**, aptitude 재능

The school's theater department is confident of its **capability** to put on a wonderful performance of *Romeo & Juliet*.

alternative	질의 응답 연구는 실험적인 방법에 하나의 대안을 제공한다. 그 도시에서는 교통 혼잡을 줄이기 위해 대용이 되는 교통수단을 이용할 것을 권장했다.
analogous	아르키메데스는 비행기의 날개가 벌새의 날개와 그 기능 면에서 유사하다고 확신했다.
annually	은행 부채에 대한 이자는 매년 계산되었다.
awkward	Adams는 텍사스에 관한 문제를 해결하려는 서투른 노력으로 선거에 패했다.
capability	그 학교의 연극과는 멋진 로미오와 줄리엣 공연을 상연할 수 있는 능력을 가지고 있다고 확신한다.

6 **cleanse*** — v. purify, **clean** — 깨끗이 하다

[klénz]

Clean-Rite air filters are guaranteed to **cleanse** the air inside offices.

7 **collide*** — v. hit each other, **smash, clash** bump — 충돌하다

[kəláid]

A train **collided** with a pickup truck late Monday morning in Waukesha County.

8 **congested**** — adj. overcrowded, crowded — 혼잡한

[kəndʒéstid]
sparse

Downtown was becoming increasingly **congested**, so another alternative was needed.

9 **contemporary**** — adj. current, modern; coexisting, **simultaneous** — 현대의 ; 동시대의

[kəntémpərèri]
antecedent

The film festival featured movies by three **contemporary** American filmmakers.

10 **cover**** — v. include, **contain, encompass** — 포함하다

[kʌ́vər]

No law can be provided which **covers** every possible crime.

11 **deceitful*** — adj. misleading, **dishonest, deceptive** — 허위의

[disí:tfəl]
truthful

Matthew often uses **deceitful** promises to keep his girlfriends from leaving him.

12 **exception*** — n. exclusion — 제외

[iksépʃən]

With the **exception** of the U.S. and Canada, most nations limit the flow of capital across borders.

13 **feature*** — n. characteristic — 특징

[fí:tʃər]

The building contains many novel architectural **features**.

cleanse	Clean-Rite 공기 청정기는 사무실 내의 공기를 깨끗하게 해줄 것이다.
collide	기차가 Waukesha 지역에서 지난 월요일 아침에 작은 화물 트럭과 충돌했다.
congested	시내는 점차 혼잡해지고 있어서 다른 대안이 필요했다.
contemporary	영화제에서는 세 명의 미국인 현대 영화제작자들의 영화가 상영되었다.
cover	발생 가능한 모든 범죄를 포함하는 법은 없다.
deceitful	Matthew는 그의 여자 친구가 자신을 떠나지 않도록 하기 위해 종종 허위 약속을 하곤 한다.
exception	미국과 캐나다를 제외한, 대부분의 나라들은 국경 밖으로 자본이 유출되는 것을 제한한다.
feature	그 건물은 여러가지의 새로운 건축적 특징들을 갖고 있다.

14 **fractious**	adj. **irritable, petulant, tetchy** fretful		성미가 까다로운

[frǽkʃəs]
good-humored

Great diplomacy is required at UN Council meetings in order to keep the peace amongst so many **fractious** nations.

15 **incorporate****	v. **combine, include, integrate**	통합하다

[inkɔ́ːrpərèit]

Louise traced how Americans **incorporate** nature into their urban and suburban lives.

16 **intimate****	adj. **close, familiar**	친숙한

[íntəmit]
remote

Monroe was **intimate** with many of the greatest minds of her day.

17 **invariably**	adv. **without exception**	예외 없이, 반드시

[invɛ́(ː)əriəbli]

When forced to make decisions, people **invariably** act in their own interest.

18 **inveigle***	v. **entice, lure, coax**	꾀다, 유혹하다

[invéigl]

Advertising for fatty foods has **inveigled** millions of Americans into poor dietary choices.

19 **lead***	n. 1. **clue, hint, indication**	단서

[líːd]

As soon as the detective heard about a new **lead** on the murder case, he raced out of the office to follow it up.

v. 2. **cause**	야기하다

Amy's desire to help people **led** her to pursue a career in social work.

20 **loop***	v. **knot**	묶다

[lúːp]

Houdini **looped** the rope around the leg of the chair.

fractious	UN 이사회 회의에서는 성미가 까다로운 여러 국가들 사이에서 평화를 유지하기 위해 뛰어난 외교 능력이 요구된다.
incorporate	Louise는 어떻게 미국인들이 그들의 도시와 시골 생활에 자연을 통합했는지를 추적했다.
intimate	Monroe는 당대의 위대한 지성들 중 상당수와 친밀했다.
invariably	결정을 내리도록 강요당하면, 인간은 예외 없이 자신의 이익을 위해서 행동한다.
inveigle	지방이 많은 음식들에 대한 광고는 수백만의 미국인들을 나쁜 식습관으로 몰고 갔다.
lead	그 탐정은 새로운 단서에 대한 이야기를 듣자마자 이를 추적하기 위해 사무실을 달려 나갔다. Amy는 다른 사람들을 돕고자 하는 소망 때문에 복지사업 쪽 일을 하게 되었다.
loop	Houdini는 의자 다리에 밧줄을 감았다.

21 **lucid****
adj. **clear, obvious, distinct** 명료한, 명쾌한
[lú:sid]
obscure
The teacher's explanation was **lucid** enough for a child to understand.

22 **master***
v. **learn thoroughly, pick up, grasp** 정통하다
[mǽstər]
The student has **mastered** the highest level of study.

23 **option***
n. **choice, selection** 선택
[ápʃən]
John had an **option** between learning German and French.

24 **paradoxical***
adj. **seemingly contradictory** 역설적인
[pæ̀rədáksikəl]
It's **paradoxical** that winters in Korea occur when the Earth is closer to the sun.

25 **plumage***
n. **feather** 깃털
[plú:midʒ]
As Tom was passing through the aviary, the parrot's brilliant blue **plumage** caught his eye.

26 **prevent***
v. **preclude, avoid, impede, avert** deter ~을 방해하다, 막다
[privént]
allow
Eating fruits and vegetables regularly may help in **preventing** cancer.

27 **profuse***
adj. **abundant, plentiful, copious, lavish** 풍부한
[prəfjú:s]
meager
The Old English sheepdog has a **profuse** shaggy coat that must be brushed every day to keep it from tangling.

28 **revolve****
v. **rotate, circulate, circle** turn 회전하다
[riválv]
The metal disk **revolves** at high speed.

lucid	그 교사의 설명은 아이가 이해하기에 충분할 정도로 명료했다.
master	그 학생은 가장 높은 수준의 학습에 정통했다.
option	John은 독일어와 프랑스어 중 배울 것을 선택할 수 있었다.
paradoxical	지구가 태양에서 가장 가까울 때 한국에 겨울이 온다는 것은 역설적이다.
plumage	Tom이 새장을 지나쳐 가고 있을 때, 앵무새의 선명한 파란색 깃털이 그의 시선을 사로잡았다.
prevent	과일과 채소를 규칙적으로 먹는 것은 암을 예방하는 데 도움이 될 것이다.
profuse	Old English 목양견은 엉키지 않도록 하기 위해 매일 같이 솔질을 해줘야 하는 풍성한 털을 지니고 있다.
revolve	금속 디스크는 빠른 속도로 회전한다.

29 **scale****

[skéil]

v. 1. **climb, mount, ascend** (기어)오르다

The bear saw the little squirrels **scaling** the tree.

n. 2. **extent** 정도, 단계

Farmers must be able to produce food on the **scale** needed to meet the demands of consumers.

30 **scant***

[skǽnt]
amplify

v. **minimize, reduce, decrease** 줄이다

Rick's free time was **scanted** by a full courseload and a part-time job.

31 **sensational****

[senséiʃənl]

adj. **exciting, stimulating** 세상을 들끓게 하는

The **sensational** murder trial drew a large crowd outside the courthouse.

32 **shallow***

[ʃǽlou]

adj. **not deep, shoal** 얕은

Diving into **shallow** water is a common cause of neck injuries.

33 **sort***

[sɔ́ːrt]
merge

v. 1. **classify, class, assort** 분류하다

Anna got a job **sorting** letters at the Post Office.

n. 2. **type, kind** 종류

Compatibility tests can help determine what **sort** of person would be right for the company.

34 **stylus***

[stáiləs]

n. **pen, pencil** 첨필

A **stylus** is used for navigation and input for personal digital assistants.

scale	그 곰은 작은 다람쥐들이 나무를 기어오르는 것을 보았다.
	농부들은 소비자의 수요를 맞출 정도의 식량을 생산할 수 있어야 한다.
scant	Rick은 많은 학업량과 아르바이트 때문에 여가 시간이 줄어들었다.
sensational	세상을 들끓게 한 그 살인 사건의 재판으로 많은 인파가 재판소 밖에 몰려들었다.
shallow	얕은 물에서 하는 다이빙은 목 부상의 일반적인 원인 중 하나이다.
sort	Anna는 우체국에서 편지들을 분류하는 직업을 얻었다.
	적합성 테스트는 그 회사에 어떤 부류의 사람이 잘 맞는지를 결정할 수 있게 도와준다.
stylus	첨필은 네비게이션과 PDA의 입력을 위해 사용된다.

35 **typically****	adv. **usually, normally, ordinarily**	일반적으로
[típikəli]	Pain relief tablets **typically** take ten to thirty minutes to start working.	
36 **vary***	v. **differ, be unlike, be diverse**	다르다
[vέəri]	Sue and Susan **vary** in some ways though they are twin sisters.	
37 **voracious***	adj. **insatiable, greedy, gluttonous**	만족할 줄 모르는, 탐욕적인
[vɔːréiʃəs]	Growing children can have **voracious** appetites.	

Quiz

Choose the synonym.

1. awkward	ⓐ climb, mount, ascend
2. deceitful	ⓑ distinct, obvious, clear
3. lucid	ⓒ include, contain, encompass
4. scale	ⓓ misleading, deceptive, dishonest
5. cover	ⓔ clumsy, unskillful

Answer 1. ⓔ 2. ⓓ 3. ⓑ 4. ⓐ 5. ⓒ

typically	진통제는 일반적으로 효과가 생기기까지 10분에서 30분 정도 걸린다.
vary	Sue와 Susan은 쌍둥이이지만 몇 가지 점에서 서로 다르다.
voracious	자라는 아이들은 왕성한 식욕을 가지게 마련이다.

DAY Hackers TOEFL Vocabulary

17 Hackers Voca

www.goHackers.com

1 **absolute**** adj. **unqualified, complete, utter** 완전한

[ǽbsəlùːt]
incomplete

Jones is an **absolute** expert in his field of study.

2 **adapted*** adj. **modified, altered** 개조된

[ədǽptid]
unaltered

Early prototypes of the spinning wheel were **adapted** to include a manual foot pedal, which made the work much easier.

3 **chamber*** n. **compartment** (작은) 방

[tʃéimbər]

Five of the allegedly watertight **chambers** of the Titanic were pierced by an iceberg, causing the ship to sink.

4 **compact*** v. 1. **compress** 압축하다

[kəmpǽkt]
loose

Paper is made by **compacting** pulp firmly.

adj. 2. **dense, thick, compressed** 조밀한, 밀집한

The gardener dug a hole in the **compact** soil.

5 **complacency*** n. **satisfaction** 만족

[kəmpléisənsi]
discomfort

Graduating from college and immediately finding a job gave Siobhan a sense of **complacency**.

absolute	Jones는 그의 학문 분야에서 절대적인 전문가이다.
adapted	물레의 초기 원형은 수동 발 페달을 포함하도록 개조되었는데, 이는 작업을 한결 쉽게 해주었다.
chamber	타이타닉 호의 방수 구획실이라고 알려진 5군데가 빙산에 의해 구멍이 뚫려 배가 가라앉았다.
compact	종이는 펄프를 단단히 압축해서 만들어진다. 그 정원사가 단단한 흙에 구멍을 팠다.
complacency	대학을 졸업한 후 즉시 직업을 구한 것은 Siobhan에게 만족감을 가져다 주었다.

6 **compulsory*****
[kəmpʌ́lsəri]
adj. **obligatory, forced, necessary, compelled** 강제적인
In Britain, education is **compulsory** between the ages of 5 and 16.

7 **concomitant***
[kankámitənt]
adj. **concurrent, simultaneous, synchronous** 동시에 일어나는
Mr. Baker's sudden bankruptcy, and the **concomitant** stress it produced, plunged his whole family into despair.

8 **condense***
[kəndéns]
amplify
v. **concentrate, compress** 압축(응축)하다
The gaseous metal is **condensed** by cold into a liquid.

9 **conform**
[kənfɔ́:rm]
diverge
v. **comply, follow** 순응하다, 따르다
Hoover **conformed** to the mainstream of progressive social thought.

10 **consistent***
[kənsístənt]
adj. **compatible, harmonious, coherent** 모순이 없는, 일관된
All the general's principles were **consistent** with virtue and honor.

11 **constrain****
[kənstréin]
release
v. **bind, inhibit, restrain** 억제하다
The country's economic growth was **constrained** by a high level of inflation.

12 **contagious***
[kəntéidʒəs]
adj. **infectious, communicable** 전염성 있는
A flu is a sort of virus highly **contagious** through the air.

13 **counterpart****
[káuntərpà:rt]
n. **complement, equivalent, parallel** (동등한 자격의) 대응물
Russian president Vladimir Putin toasted his South Korean **counterpart** leader Kim Dae-Jung during a dinner meeting in Moscow.

compulsory	영국에서는 5세에서 16세까지의 교육이 의무적이다.
concomitant	Baker씨의 갑작스런 파산과 그것이 함께 가져오는 스트레스는 그의 가족 모두를 절망에 잠기게 했다.
condense	기체화된 금속은 냉각되어 액체로 응축된다.
conform	Hoover는 진보적 사회주의라는 대세에 순응했다.
consistent	그 장군의 모든 원칙들은 미덕과 신의에 있어 일관되어 있었다.
constrain	높은 수준의 인플레이션으로 인해 그 국가의 경제 성장이 억제되었다.
contagious	유행성 감기는 공기를 통한 전염성이 상당히 높은 일종의 바이러스이다.
counterpart	러시아의 대통령 Vladimir Putin은 모스크바에서 있었던 저녁 만찬에서 자신의 상대자인 남한의 지도자 김대중에 대통령에게 축배를 들었다.

14 **debris****

[dəbríː]

n. **dregs, wreckage, remains** 잔해

The shipwreck left **debris** floating near the shore, which was picked up by local beachcombers as it drifted to the coast.

15 **decisive***

[disáisiv]
hesitant

adj. **definite, definitive, conclusive** 결정적인

A **decisive** victory for the North, the Battle of Gettysburg led to the end of the Civil War.

16 **disdain**

[disdéin]
respect

v. **despise, scorn** 경멸하다

Winston worships strength and **disdains** weakness.

17 **element****

[éləmənt]

n. **component, part, feature, constituent** ingredient 구성 요소

Hydrogen is the most common **element** on Earth.

18 **erratic**

[irǽtik]
consistent

adj. **irregular, inconsistent** 불규칙적인, 변덕스러운

The doctor was concerned because Mr. Ascot's heartbeat was **erratic** and unstable.

19 **exhaust****

[igzɔ́ːst]
conserve

v. 1. **use up, deplete, run out of** expend, consume 다 써버리다

The world has **exhausted** much of its natural resources.

v. 2. **tire, weary, fatigue** 지치게 하다

Running the marathon **exhausted** Linda so much that she could not get up for two days.

20 **expand****

[ikspǽnd]
contract

v. **increase, bloat, swell** enlarge, extend 확장하다

Dunaway tried to **expand** his great idea into a worldwide program.

debris	난파선은 해변 가를 떠다니는 잔해들을 남겼는데, 이것이 해안가로 떠내려 오자 그 지역 해안에서 물건을 줍는 사람들이 이것을 주웠다.
decisive	Gettysburg 전투에서 북부의 결정적인 승리로 남북 전쟁이 종식되었다.
disdain	Winston은 힘을 숭배하고 약한 것을 경멸한다.
element	수소는 지구상에서 가장 흔한 원소이다.
erratic	의사는 Ascot씨의 심장 박동이 불규칙적이고 불안정했기 때문에 걱정이 되었다.
exhaust	지구 천연 자원의 상당량이 고갈되었다.
	Linda는 마라톤으로 너무 지쳤기 때문에 이틀 동안 일어날 수가 없었다.
expand	Dunaway는 그의 위대한 생각을 세계적인 프로그램으로 확장시키려 노력했다.

21 **flattering***
[flǽtəriŋ]
adj. **complimentary** 아부하는
Dicken's manner to Hemmings was full of **flattering** courtesy.

22 **full-blown***
[fúl-blóun]
adj. **complete, matured** 성숙한
Everyone was surprised at Marie's **full-blown** musical talent.

23 **henceforth***
[hénsfɔ̀:rθ]
adv. **from now on, forward** 앞으로, 차후
The court ruled that the man is **henceforth** only allowed to buy the chassis from the car dealer.

24 **inadvertently**
[ìnədvə́:rtəntli]
adv. **unintentionally, accidentally** 뜻하지 않게, 우연히
Grace **inadvertently** deleted the files by clicking the wrong button.

25 **intricate****
[íntrəkit]
adj. **complex, complicated, elaborate** 복잡한
Not many students understand the **intricate** functioning of the cyber university.

26 **mammoth***
[mǽməθ]
diminutive
adj. **huge, gigantic, colossal, large** 거대한
The government limited foreign ownership of the **mammoth** electric company.

27 **merely***
[míərli]
adv. **simply, just, purely** 단지
The student **merely** wanted to ask the professor a question, but Doctor Schmidt was too busy with his research to even notice.

28 **ordinary****
[ɔ́:rdənèri]
extraordinary
adj. **unexceptional, mundane, routine, common** 보통의, 평범한
Lincoln learned how **ordinary** citizens felt about their government.

flattering	Dicken이 Hemmings를 대하는 태도는 아부하는 공손함으로 가득 차 있었다.
full-blown	모든 사람이 Marie의 성숙한 음악적 재능에 놀랐다.
henceforth	법원은 앞으로 남자가 차대를 그 자동차 판매상으로부터만 구매할 수 있다는 판결을 내렸다.
inadvertently	Grace는 버튼을 잘못 눌러서 뜻하지 않게 파일을 지워 버렸다.
intricate	소수의 학생들만이 가상 대학의 복잡한 기능을 이해한다.
mammoth	정부는 거대한 전기 회사의 외국인 소유권을 제한했다.
merely	그 학생은 단지 교수님에게 한 가지만 질문하기를 원했으나, Schmidt 교수는 그의 연구 때문에 너무 바빠 눈을 돌릴 겨를도 없었다.
ordinary	링컨은 보통 시민들이 그들의 정부에 대해 어떻게 느끼는지를 알았다.

29 **plain***

adj. 1. **clear, distinct, obvious** 분명한

[pléin]
abstruse

It is quite **plain** that Jack will break off their engagement.

adorned

adj. 2. **unadorned, undecorated, simple** 꾸밈없는, 간소한

Lee's paintings, which feature **plain** objects, tell the stories of normal people.

30 **popular***

adj. **widespread, common, current** general 대중적인

[pάpjulər]
unpopular

Marriage between members of the same sex is quickly becoming a **popular** issue among the press.

31 **reconcile**

v. **conciliate, settle, resolve** 화해시키다, 조정하다

[rékənsàil]
estrange

Clint found it hard to **reconcile** him with his family after 20 years of silence.

32 **reexamine***

v. **review, reassess** 재검토하다

[rì:igzǽmin]

The police **reexamined** the scene of the crime for additional clues in the hopes of finding a lead.

33 **requirement***

n. **stipulation, condition, provision** 조건, 조항

[rikwáiərmənt]

Senator Robert Byrd asked Powell to be mindful of the constitutional **requirement**.

34 **revolutionize****

v. **completely change** ~에 혁명을 일으키다

[rèvəlú:ʃənàiz]

The invention of the light bulb **revolutionized** world civilization.

35 **rival***

n. 1. **competitor, antagonist, opponent** 경쟁자

[ráivəl]

Unlike Washington, Adams had **rivals** for the presidency.

plain	Jack이 그들의 약혼을 깰 것이라는 것은 꽤 확실하다. 꾸밈이 없는 물체들을 그린 Lee의 그림들은 평범한 사람들에 대해 이야기한다.
popular	동성끼리의 결혼이 언론에서 빠르게 대중적인 이슈가 되고 있다.
reconcile	Clint는 20년간의 침묵을 깨고 가족들과 화해한다는 게 어렵다는 것을 알았다.
reexamine	경찰은 단서를 찾을 수 있기를 바라며 좀 더 많은 실마리를 얻기 위해 범죄 현장을 재조사했다.
requirement	Robert Byrd 상원 의원은 Powell에게 헌법상의 필요 조건들에 신경을 쓸 것을 요구했다.
revolutionize	백열전구의 발명은 세계 문명에 혁명을 일으켰다.
rival	Washington과 달리, Adams에게는 대통령직을 놓고 다투는 경쟁자들이 있었다.

v. **2. compete with** 경쟁하다

Heavy investment ensured that the new publication could **rival** its established competitors.

36 shovel*

[ʃʌ́vəl]

v. **excavate, dig, scoop** (삽으로) 파다

An archeologist and his team must **shovel** earth carefully when conducting an excavation.

37 succinct*

[səksíŋkt]
discursive

adj. **concise, brief, terse** 간결한

The general offered a **succinct** summation of the situation.

38 tie**

[tai]

n. **relationship, bond, connection** 관계

Through his travels, James developed **ties** all over the world.

Quiz

Choose the synonym.

1. conform	ⓐ terse, concise, brief
2. disdain	ⓑ conciliate, settle, resolve
3. ordinary	ⓒ comply, agree, assent
4. succinct	ⓓ despise, scorn
5. reconcile	ⓔ common, routine, mundane

Answer 1. ⓒ 2. ⓓ 3. ⓔ 4. ⓐ 5. ⓑ

rival	많은 투자로 인해 새로운 출판물이 기존의 것들과 경쟁할 수 있음이 보장되었다.
shovel	고고학자와 그의 팀은 발굴 작업을 수행할 때 땅을 조심스럽게 파야만 한다.
succinct	그 장군은 상황에 대한 간결한 요약을 제공했다.
tie	James는 여행을 통해서 세계 각지의 사람들과 관계를 맺었다.

DAY 18

Hackers TOEFL **Vocabulary**

Hackers Voca

www.goHackers.com

1 **ability***	n.	**faculty, capacity, competence**	능력
[əbíləti] impotence		Computers have a prodigious **ability** to store and process information.	
2 **accessible**	adj.	**available, obtainable, reachable**	이용 가능한, 접근하기 쉬운
[əksésəbl] inaccessible		Luckily, Tina's school was **accessible** by bus and subway, since she lived too far away to walk.	
3 **accord***	v.	**grant, give, bestow; agree, assent**	주다, 수여하다 ; 일치하다
[əkɔ́ːrd]		The economist was **accorded** the highest honor in his field for this paper on choice theory.	
4 **appear**	v.	**seem, look**	~인 듯하다, ~인 것 같이 보인다
[əpíər]		Fake diamonds can **appear** much like real ones.	
5 **be rooted in****	phr.	**be based on, originate from**	~에 근거를 두다, ~에서 유래하다
		The invention of the electric bulb **was rooted in** Edison's curiosity.	
6 **bog***	n.	**marsh, swamp, fen**	습지
[bάg]		The elk attracted tourists, but they also caused damage to the **bogs**.	

ability	컴퓨터는 정보를 저장하고 처리하는 놀라운 능력을 가지고 있다.
accessible	다행히도 Tina의 학교는 버스와 지하철로 쉽게 갈 수 있었다. 그녀가 걸어가기에는 너무나 먼 거리에 살고 있었기 때문이다.
accord	경제학자는 선택 이론에 대한 논문으로 경제 분야에서 가장 명예로운 상을 받게 되었다.
appear	가짜 다이아몬드들은 진짜 다이아몬드와 매우 유사한 듯 보일 수 있다.
be rooted in	전구의 발명은 Edison의 호기심에 기인한 것이었다.
bog	고라니가 관광객을 끌어들이기도 하겠지만, 습지에 피해를 입히기도 한다.

7 **collaborate***

[kəlǽbərèit]

v. **effort together, cooperate** 협력하다

The high school **collaborated** with the public library to make the fair a great success.

8 **crucible**

[krú:səbl]

n. **container** 도가니, 용광로

The intense heat of the fire melted the gold in the **crucible**.

9 **curb***

[kə́:rb]

incite

v. **control, repress, suppress** restrain 제한(억제)하다

The industrialist took measures to **curb** pollution generated by his factories.

10 **cycle***

[sáikl]

n. **sequence** 주기

The study of the human life **cycle** shows that its main stages are birth, puberty, reproduction, and death.

11 **deem***

[dí:m]

v. **consider, believe, regard** ~라고 여기다

Mrs. Watson bluntly told her daughter that she **deemed** it unwise for young ladies to be out on their own at night.

12 **devout***

[diváut]

impious

adj. **pious, reverent, religious** 독실한

The shrine is a proper place for a **devout** Buddhist to pray and meditate.

13 **disperse***

[dispə́:rs]

assemble

v. **spread out, scatter, disseminate, dissipate** 흩어지게 하다

The smell was rapidly **dispersed** by the strong winds.

14 **economical**

[ì:kənámikəl]

extravagant

adj. **saving, thrifty, frugal** 절약하는

It is often necessary to adapt more **economical** spending habits during tough economic times.

collaborate	그 고등학교는 전시회를 성공적으로 이끌기 위해 공공 도서관과 협력했다.
crucible	용광로의 강한 열로 금이 녹았다.
curb	제조업자는 자신의 공장에 의한 오염을 줄이기 위한 조치를 취했다.
cycle	인간의 일생 주기에 대한 연구는 그 주요 단계가 탄생, 사춘기, 자녀 생산, 그리고 죽음이라는 것을 보여 준다.
deem	Watson 부인은 젊은 아가씨들이 밤에 혼자서 나다니는 것은 현명하지 못하다고 생각한다며 그녀의 딸에게 퉁명스레 말했다.
devout	그 성지는 독실한 불교 신자들이 기도하고 명상을 하는 데 적절한 장소이다.
disperse	그 냄새는 강한 바람에 의해 빠르게 흩어졌다.
economical	경제적으로 어려운 시기에는 더욱 절약하는 소비 습관을 기를 필요가 있다.

15 **eventually****

adv. **in time, finally, ultimately, in due time, in the long run** 결국

[ivéntʃuəli]

The U.S.A. **eventually** recognized the Filipinos' desire for independence.

16 **faint****

adj. **indistinct, dim, feeble** 희미한

[féint]
clear

Red giant stars appear **faint** even though they are quite luminous.

17 **financial**

adj. **monetary, pecuniary** 재정상의

[fainǽnʃəl]

Financial problems forced Randy to sell his business.

18 **frighten**

v. **scare, terrify, alarm** 두렵게 하다

[fráitn]
embolden

The young children were **frightened** by the loud thunder.

19 **geognosy***

n. **geology (study of the makeup of the earth)** 지질학

[dʒiágnəsi]

Werner defined the new science **geognosy** as the study of the layers of minerals.

20 **give way to***

phr. **retreat, withdraw** 물러가다, 양보하다

The citizens **gave way to** the President's motorcade.

21 **immense***

adj. **enormous, huge, tremendous** 거대한, 막대한

[iméns]
tiny

The **immense** statue of the Greek goddess Athena attracted many tourists to the Acropolis.

22 **impact**

n. **influence, effect** 영향

[ímpækt]

The printing press had a major **impact** on history.

eventually	미국은 마침내 독립을 향한 필리핀인들의 열망을 인식했다.
faint	적색 거성들은 빛나기는 하지만 희미해 보인다.
financial	재정적 문제는 Randy가 회사를 매각하도록 만들었다.
frighten	어린아이들은 큰 천둥소리에 두려웠다.
geognosy	Werner는 새로운 과학인 지질학을 광물층들에 관한 연구로 정의했다.
give way to	시민들은 대통령의 자동차 행렬에 길을 터 주었다.
immense	그리스 여신인 Athena의 거대한 조각상은 많은 관광객들을 Acropolice로 끌어들였다.
impact	인쇄술은 역사에 큰 영향을 미쳤다.

23 **ingenuity** | n. **creativeness, inventiveness** 독창성, 창의력
[ìndʒənjúːəti]
Thomas Edison was a man of extraordinary **ingenuity**.

24 **in keeping with*** | phr. **in agreement with, consistent with, in conformity with** ~와 일치하여
All Linda's remarks were **in keeping with** the seriousness of the occasion.

25 **job** | n. **project, assignment, task, undertaking** 일, 직무
[dʒáb]
The committee did an excellent **job** with its report.

26 **lethargic** | adj. **sluggish, drowsy, listless, slow** 무기력한
[ləθáːrdʒik]
Reptiles become **lethargic** when the temperature drops.

27 **meager*** | adj. **scarce, scanty, deficient** 부족한
[míːgər]
ample
Lincoln's **meager** education aroused his desire to learn.

28 **parody***** | n. **lampoon, mockery, spoof, takeoff, travesty** 풍자적 변형
[pǽrədi]
The new theater company produced a **parody** of Shakespeare's *Hamlet* that had the audience rolling in the aisles.

29 **refuge** | n. **shelter, sanctuary** 피난처, 은신처
[réfjuːdʒ]
exposure
Sandra tried to find **refuge** from oppression in a foreign country.

30 **rural*** | adj. **country, rustic, pastoral** 시골의
[rúːərəl]
urban
The economic development has enormously affected life in **rural** communities.

ingenuity	Thomas Edison은 비범한 창의력을 가진 사람이었다.
in keeping with	모든 Linda의 발언은 그 행사의 진지한 분위기에 어긋남이 없었다.
job	그 위원회는 그 보고에 관한 일을 훌륭하게 해냈다.
lethargic	파충류는 기온이 떨어지면 무기력해진다.
meager	Lincoln의 부족한 학교 교육은 배우고자 하는 그의 열망을 부추겼다.
parody	그 새로운 극단은 관객들을 포복절도하게 만든 셰익스피어의 '햄릿'의 패러디 작품을 상연했다.
refuge	Sandra는 외국에서 억압을 피해 은신처를 찾으려고 애썼다.
rural	경제적 발전은 시골 지역의 삶에 큰 영향을 끼쳤다.

31 **scrub****

[skrʌ́b]

v. **scour, rub** 북북 문지르다

The maid **scrubbed** the tiles of the kitchen floor.

32 **secure****

[sikjúər]

v. 1. **acquire, obtain, procure** get 확보하다

The manager approved Foster's plan to **secure** necessary information.

adj. 2. **safe** 안전한

The invading army ensured that the oil fields were **secure** before moving into the capital.

33 **skepticism***

[sképtisìzəm]
belief

n. **doubt, suspicion, uncertainty** 회의(론)

Though some expressed **skepticism** about the project, the chief went forward with it.

34 **so far***

phr. **until now, up to present** 지금까지

The large-scale application of geothermal energy has **so far** gone unexplored.

35 **spark***

[spɑ́:rk]

v. **bring about, trigger, stimulate** 야기하다

The government council proposed tax reforms in order to **spark** activity in the stagnant economy.

36 **speculation***

[spèkjuléiʃən]

n. **conjecture, supposition, surmise** 추측

There was much **speculation** in the office as to who the new employee would be.

37 **terrain***

[təréin]

n. **land, territory, area** 지역

Under Sipiera's direction, crew members will search the **terrain** for meteorites.

scrub	그 하녀는 부엌 바닥의 타일을 문질러 닦았다.
secure	담당자는 필요한 정보를 확보하자는 Foster의 계획에 동의했다.
	그 침략군은 수도로 쳐들어 오기 전에 석유 매장 지역이 안전하다는 것을 확실히 하였다.
skepticism	그 프로젝트에 대한 몇몇 회의론에도 불구하고, 팀장은 그것을 추진해 나갔다.
so far	지열 에너지의 광범위한 응용은 지금까지는 연구되고 있지 않은 상태이다.
spark	정부 협의회는 정체된 경제에 활력을 불러일으키기 위해 세제 개혁을 제안했다.
speculation	누가 새로운 사원이 될 것인가에 관해 사무실에 추측이 난무했다.
terrain	Sipiera의 지도하에, 팀원들은 운석을 찾기 위해 그 지역을 조사할 것이다.

38 **tumult***	n.	**chaos, disturbance, turbulence**	혼란, 소란
[tjú:mʌlt] calm		Many lost faith in the **tumult** of revolution and war.	
39 **unlimited**	adj.	**infinite, limitless, boundless, endless**	무한한
[ʌnlímitid]		The service provider offered **unlimited** access to the Internet.	
40 **vagarious**	adj.	**changeable, whimsical, capricious, arbitrary**	변덕스러운
[vəgέ(:)əriəs]		**Vagarious** weather conditions in Bangladesh worsen during the monsoon season.	
41 **volume**	n.	**book, tome**	책
[válju:m]		Professor Martin's history of trade and industry took up three **volumes**.	

Quiz

Choose the synonym.

1. collaborate	ⓐ scarce, scanty, deficient
2. curb	ⓑ chaos, disturbance, turbulence
3. ingenuity	ⓒ control, repress, suppress
4. meager	ⓓ creativeness, inventiveness
5. tumult	ⓔ effort together, cooperate

Answer 1. ⓔ 2. ⓒ 3. ⓓ 4. ⓐ 5. ⓑ

tumult	많은 사람들이 혁명과 전쟁의 소란 속에서 신념을 잃었다.
unlimited	그 서비스 공급자는 인터넷의 무한한 이용을 제공했다.
vagarious	방글라데시의 변덕스러운 날씨 상태는 몬순 기후 동안에 더 악화된다.
volume	Martin 교수가 쓴 무역산업사는 3권 분량이다.

Hackers TOEFL Voca TEST DAY 16-18

Choose the synonym of the highlighted word in the sentence.

1. Organic architecture incorporates built-in architectural features such as benches and storage areas.
(A) combines (B) strains (C) accuses (D) urges

2. Disaster struck when two planes collided in midair as the result of a mistake in air traffic control.
(A) met briefly (B) narrowly missed (C) hit each other (D) took off

3. Regardless of the circumstances, Alec's behavior was always consistent with his principles.
(A) effective (B) grateful (C) compatible (D) huge

4. Geognosy is a scientific discipline concerned with the structure of the earth's surface and interior.
(A) chemistry (B) geography (C) anthropology (D) geology

5. The function of a car engine is analogous to the human heart.
(A) similar (B) contradictory (C) opposite (D) mixed

6. To a large extent, the recession has scanted traditional economic activities but has not affected the information technology industry.
(A) reduced (B) completed (C) increased (D) strengthened

7. There is a profuse variety of plant and animal species in tropical rain forests.
(A) narrow (B) liberal (C) abundant (D) positive

8. Due largely to draining their habitat to make way for development, many animal species that live in bogs are in danger of extinction.
(A) plains (B) marshes (C) forests (D) prairies

9. Although the crime rate had fallen dramatically in the past year, the police chief cautioned against complacency.
(A) satisfaction (B) conceit (C) egoism (D) damage

10. People with a mental illness often have erratic behavior.
(A) inconsistent (B) full-blown (C) uncertain (D) status

정답 p.419

스터디 시작 10분 전 : 피 말리는 점심시간

D A Y **19**

Hackers TOEFL **Vocabulary**

Hackers Voca

www.goHackers.com

1 **advent****	n. arrival, **appearance**	출현
[ǽdvent] exit	The **advent** of the computer has revolutionized modern people's lives dramatically.	
2 **article****	n. item, object, **thing**	(개개의) 물품
[ɑ́:rtikl]	The **article** of clothing was manufactured in China.	
3 **assembly***	n. congress, **legislature, parliament**	의회
[əsémbli]	All the citizens were hoping that the mayor would run for election to the National **Assembly**.	
4 **associated****	adj. connected, **correlated, linked**	연관된
[əsóuʃièitid] divided	Changes in the upper ocean temperature are **associated** with global warming.	
5 **aware***	adj. conscious	~을 알고 있는
[əwέər] ignorant	The government made people **aware** of the results of population explosion.	
6 **bank***	n. edge, **brink, margin, shore**	물가, 기슭
[bǽŋk]	Since they weren't very good at canoeing, Tracy and Bill rowed along the **bank** of the river just to be safe.	

advent	컴퓨터의 출현은 현대인의 삶을 극적으로 변화시켰다.
article	그 옷들은 중국에서 만들어졌다.
assembly	모든 시민들은 그 시장이 국회의원으로 입후보하기를 바라고 있었다.
associated	바다 상층부의 온도 변화는 지구 온난화와 연관되어 있다.
aware	정부는 사람들이 인구 폭발의 결과에 대해 인식하도록 만들었다.
bank	Tracy와 Bill은 카누를 젓는 데 능숙하지 않았기 때문에, 그냥 안전하게 강기슭을 따라 노를 저어 갔다.

7 **by and large***

phr. **on the whole** 전반적으로, 대체로

By and large, the members of Jinny's team agreed on the terms of the contract.

8 **challenge***

[tʃǽlindʒ]

n. 1. **difficulty, problem** 난제

The main **challenge** that early gold miners faced in Alaska was the constantly freezing weather.

v. 2. **defy** 도전하다

Galileo **challenged** the widely-held belief that the world was flat.

9 **compress**

[kəmprés]
spread

v. **compact, condense, contract, squeeze** 압축하다

The machine **compresses** old cars into blocks of scrap metal.

10 **consort***

[kansɔ́ːrt]

v. **associate, fraternize** 교제하다

To succeed in business one needs to **consort** with financial experts.

11 **construe***

[kənstrúː]
misconstrue

v. **interpret** 해석하다

Newspaper reporters wrongly **construed** the writer's comments about her forthcoming book.

12 **correct**

[kərékt]
spoil

v. **remedy, amend, rectify** 고치다, 바로잡다

Only Theo's new plan can **correct** the problem without serious side effects.

13 **curious***

[kjú(ː)əriəs]
indifferent

adj. **inquisitive, nosy, inquiring** 호기심이 강한

Bert was **curious** as to why his business partner was taking so many days off and rarely coming into the office.

by and large	대체로, Jinny 팀의 구성원들은 그 계약의 조건들에 동의했다.
challenge	Alaska의 초기 금광 인부들이 겪었던 주된 난제는 끊임없이 지속되는 추위였다.
	Galileo는 지구가 평평하다는 널리 퍼져 있던 믿음에 도전하였다.
compress	그 기계는 낡은 차들을 압축하여 고철 덩어리로 만든다.
consort	사업에서 성공하기 위해서는 금융 전문가와 제휴할 필요가 있다.
construe	신문 기자들은 자신의 신작에 대한 작가의 의견을 잘못 해석했다.
correct	Theo의 새 계획만이 심각한 부작용이 없이 그 문제를 수정할 수 있다.
curious	Bert는 그의 사업 동료가 왜 그렇게 자주 회사를 쉬면서 드물게 출근하는 지에 대해 무척 호기심이 생겼다.

14 **deadly***	adj.	**fatal, lethal, mortal**	치명적인
[dédli] harmless		It is possible for mosquitoes to carry a **deadly** virus.	
15 **defeated***	adj.	**conquered**	패배한
[difí:tid]		There were **defeated** soldiers in the area of the north mountains.	
16 **deplete***	v.	**exhaust, empty, use up**	고갈시키다
[diplí:t] replenish		The family **depleted** their savings to renovate the house.	
17 **edge****	n.	**periphery, border, margin** boundary, rim	가장자리
[édʒ]		People are moving to the **edges** of cities and suburban areas.	
18 **elude****	v.	**evade, dodge, avoid**	피하다
[ilú:d] face		The prey managed to **elude** the hunter by hiding in the thick bush.	
19 **endow**	v.	**dower, endue**	부여하다
[endáu]		From his first public performance, critics realized that the young pianist was **endowed** with an incredible gift.	
20 **exceedingly**	adv.	**extremely, excessively, surpassingly**	지나칠 정도로
[iksí:diŋli]		It was obvious from the woman's diamond necklace and fancy car that she was **exceedingly** rich.	
21 **far-reaching***	adj.	**broad, extensive, widespread**	방대한
[fá:rrí:tʃiŋ]		Arab leaders unanimously agreed on a **far-reaching** Saudi proposal for peace with Israel.	

deadly	모기들은 치명적인 바이러스를 옮길 수 있다.
defeated	북쪽 산등성이 지역에 패배한 군인들이 있었다.
deplete	그 가족은 집을 개조하는 데 저축한 돈을 모두 썼다.
edge	사람들은 도시 외곽 지역으로 이동하고 있다.
elude	그 사냥감은 무성한 덤불 안에 숨어 가까스로 사냥꾼을 피했다.
endow	비평가들은 그의 첫 대중 공연을 통해서 젊은 피아니스트에게 엄청난 재능이 주어졌다는 것을 알게 되었다.
exceedingly	그 여자의 다이아몬드 목걸이와 고급 승용차를 보면 그녀는 엄청난 부자임에 틀림없다.
far-reaching	아랍 지도자들은 만장일치로 이스라엘과의 평화를 위한 사우디의 방대한 제안에 동의했다.

22 **fluster****

[flʌ́stər]
calm

v. **confuse, addle, befuddle** 혼란시키다

Bob became **flustered** during the job interview by the difficult questions.

23 **guess***

[gés]

v. **conjecture, suppose, fancy** 추측하다

A good chess player can **guess** what kind of move his opponent will make next.

24 **importance***

[impɔ́ːrtəns]
inconsequence

n. **significance, consequence, moment** 중요함

Wilson agrees with the **importance** of high-level Israeli support.

25 **interfere****

[ìntərfíər]

v. **disrupt, intervene, intrude, meddle** 방해하다, 간섭하다

Sally didn't mean to **interfere** with the game as she walked through the field.

26 **irksome**

[ə́ːrksəm]

adj. **tedious, boring** 지루한

Many students find homework **irksome** and generally a waste of time.

27 **last****

[lǽst]
initial

adj. 1. **final, ultimate, conclusive** 마지막의

The **last** survivor of the Titanic died in her home.

v. 2. **continue, persist** 지속하다

The stormy weather **lasted** for ten days.

28 **manage***

[mǽnidʒ]

v. **control, conduct, direct** administer 관리하다

The producer **manages** all programs that have an entertainment focus.

fluster	Bob은 면접을 보는 동안 어려운 질문들 때문에 머리가 혼란해졌다
guess	훌륭한 체스 선수는 상대방이 다음에 어떤 수를 둘 것인지 추측할 수 있다.
importance	Wilson은 고위급 이스라엘인들의 지지의 중요성에 대해 동의한다.
interfere	Sally는 경기장을 가로질러 걸어갔지만 경기를 방해하려는 의도는 없었다.
irksome	많은 학생들이 숙제를 귀찮게 여기고, 대부분 시간 낭비라고 생각한다.
last	타이타닉 호의 마지막 생존자는 그녀의 집에서 사망했다.
	폭풍이 부는 날씨는 열흘간 지속됐다.
manage	그 제작자는 오락에 초점을 맞춘 모든 프로그램을 관리하고 있다.

29 mastery* n. **expertise** 전문 기술, 숙달

[mǽstəri]

Marcus Tullius Cicero was a Roman statesman and orator who is remembered for his **mastery** of Latin prose.

30 monopolize** v. **dominate, occupy** 독점하다

[mənάpəlàiz]
share

John D. Rockefeller once **monopolized** the oil industry in the U.S.

31 overcome v. **defeat, conquer** 이기다, 정복하다

[òuvərkʌ́m]
submit

Invaders from northern and central Europe **overcame** the Roman Empire.

32 ratify* v. **endorse, confirm, sanction** validate 승인하다

[rǽtəfài]
reject

The peace treaty was **ratified** by Congress.

33 replica* n. **copy, duplicate, reproduction** 복제

[répləkə]
original

A **replica** of Leonardo da Vinci's Mona Lisa was stolen from the Metropolitan Museum of Art.

34 shift** v. **move, transfer; switch, change** 옮기다 ; 바꾸다

[ʃíft]

The chief executive decided to **shift** production to another area.

35 stride* n. **progress** 진보, 발전

[stráid]

Doctors have made many great **strides** forward in medical technology during the past century.

36 subject to* phr. **susceptible to** (영향을) 받기 쉬운

The latest skiing conditions are **subject to** change due to weather, skier traffic and other factors.

mastery	Marcus Tullius Cicero는 라틴어 산문에 대한 그의 정통함으로 기억되는 로마의 정치인이자 웅변가이다.
monopolize	John D. Rockefeller는 미국에서 한때 모든 석유 산업을 독점했었다.
overcome	북부와 중앙 유럽에서 온 침략자들은 로마 제국을 정복했다.
ratify	그 평화 협정은 국회에 의해 승인되었다.
replica	레오나르도 다빈치의 작품인 모나리자의 복제품이 뉴욕 메트로폴리탄 미술관에서 도난당했다.
shift	사장은 생산을 다른 분야로 옮기기로 결정했다.
stride	의사들은 지난 세기 동안 의학 기술에 있어서 많은 진보를 이루어냈다.
subject to	최근의 스키를 하기 위한 조건들은 날씨, 사람들이 붐비는 정도, 그리고 다른 요소들에 따라 변하기 쉽다.

37 **successive**	adj. **consecutive, sequential, serial**	연속적인
[səksésiv]	The Labor Party suffered its third **successive** election defeat.	
38 **transition***	n. change, **alteration, shift**	변화
[trænzíʃən] uniformity	The biologist studied the caterpillar's metamorphosis, or physical **transition** into a butterfly.	
39 **undertaking***	n. enterprise, **project, task**	사업, 과제
[ʌ̀ndərtéikiŋ]	Starting a new business can be a risky **undertaking**.	

Quiz

Choose the synonym.

1. correct — ⓐ tedious, boring
2. elude — ⓑ change, switch, move
3. fluster — ⓒ addle, confuse, befuddle
4. shift — ⓓ amend, remedy, rectify
5. irksome — ⓔ avoid, evade, dodge

Answer 1. ⓓ 2. ⓔ 3. ⓒ 4. ⓑ 5. ⓐ

successive	노동당은 세 번 연속 선거의 패배를 겪었다.
transition	생물학자들은 애벌레의 변태, 즉 몸이 나비로 변형되는 것에 대해 연구했다.
undertaking	새로운 사업을 시작하는 것은 위험 요소가 많은 과제일 수 있다.

DAY 20 Hackers Voca

www.goHackers.com

1 **accurate****	adj.	**precise, true, exact, correct**	정확한

[ǽkjurit]
lax

The movie was praised for giving an **accurate** depiction of what happens in a war.

2 **advisor****	n.	**consultant**	고문

[ædváizər]

Katie McGinty was a senior environmental **advisor** to President Clinton.

3 **antagonize***	v.	**counteract**	대항하다

[æntǽgənàiz]

The author **antagonized** her critics with a lengthy and detailed rebuttal.

4 **architecture****	n.	**structure, framework**	구조

[á:rkitèktʃər]

The building's **architecture** was unique in that it used a combination of styles.

5 **assure****	v.	**convince, persuade, satisfy**	확신시키다

[əʃúər]
discomfit

Jefferson Davis **assured** the South that he would protect slavery.

6 **bond***	n.	**tie, connection, link**	유대, 결속

[bánd]

The couple's 50th wedding anniversary signified the strong **bond** they had.

accurate	그 영화는 전쟁에서 일어난 일들을 정확하게 묘사한 것에 대해 격찬받았다.
advisor	Katie McGinty는 클린턴 대통령의 수석 환경 고문이었다.
antagonize	저자는 길고 자세한 반론으로 그녀의 비평가들에 대항했다.
architecture	그 건물의 건축 양식은 여러 양식을 조합해서 사용했다는 점에서 특이하다.
assure	Jefferson Davis는 그가 노예 제도를 보호할 것이라는 사실을 남부에 확신시켰다.
bond	그 부부의 50번째 결혼기념일은 그 동안의 그들의 견고한 결합을 증명했다.

7 **brave*** adj. courageous, gallant, dauntless 대담한

[bréiv]
craven

Being **brave** doesn't mean looking for trouble.

8 **crucial***** adj. essential, important, acute, deciding, vital 중대한

[krúːʃəl]

Public opinion was the **crucial** factor in entering the war.

9 **complement*** n. supplement 보충, 보완

[kámpləmənt]

A fine white wine is a perfect **complement** to any salmon dinner.

10 **comprise**** v. consist of, be made up of 구성되다

[kəmpráiz]
exclude

The Dow Jones Industrial Average **comprises** thirty of largest companies in the U.S.

11 **counter to*** phr. in opposition to ~와 정반대로

The chief's decision to publicize the misogynist film runs **counter to** the standards of the newspaper.

12 **daring*** adj. bold, courageous, brave 용감한

[dέəriŋ]

As a result of his **daring** confrontations, Kennedy had to face numerous threats.

13 **devise*** v. create, design, contrive, invent 고안하다

[diváiz]

The government is carefully **devising** new trade rules.

14 **duplicate**** v. copy, imitate, reproduce 복사(복제)하다

[djúːpləkèit]

It is considered stealing to illegally **duplicate** a copyrighted work without permission.

brave	용감한 것이 문제를 찾아 다니는 것을 의미하지는 않는다.
crucial	전쟁에 참가하는 데 대중의 의견은 중요한 요소였다.
complement	좋은 백포도주는 저녁 식사의 모든 연어 요리에 완벽한 보완물이 된다.
comprise	다우존스 공업지수는 미국의 30개 우량기업들로 구성된다.
counter to	여자를 싫어하는 사람들에 대한 영화를 광고하기로 한 팀장의 결정은 그 신문의 규정에 반하는 것이다.
daring	그의 용감한 대결의 결과, Kennedy는 수많은 위협에 직면해야만 했다.
devise	정부는 조심스럽게 새로운 교역 규칙들을 고안하고 있다.
duplicate	저작권이 있는 작품을 허가 없이 불법적으로 복사하는 것은 절도 행위로 간주된다.

15 dwindle v. decrease, **diminish** 줄다, 감소시키다

[dwíndl]
increase

The crowd of Koreans celebrating their World Cup victory didn't start to **dwindle** until the early hours of the morning.

16 embody* v. 1. incarnate, **exemplify, represent** 구현하다

[imbádi]

Literature often **embodies** the social ideals of either the author or the author's culture.

v. 2. contain ~을 포함하다

The composition **embodied** several musical styles, including jazz, funk and reggae.

17 etch* v. cut, **carve, engrave** 식각하다, 새기다

[étʃ]

The Holocaust was a terrible event that will be forever **etched** in Jewish history.

18 flash* v. flame, **flare, glare** 번쩍이다

[flǽʃ]

The fireworks **flashed** so brightly that they hurt the eyes of some onlookers.

19 imaginable* adj. conceivable, **thinkable, supposable** 상상할 수 있는

[imǽdʒənəbl]
unbelievable

Exploring outer space was not an **imaginable** idea in the late 19th century.

20 infectious* adj. contagious, **communicable** 전염성의

[infékʃəs]

Vaccines have accomplished near miracles in the fight against **infectious** disease.

21 innumerable* adj. countless, **numberless, numerous** 무수한

[injú:mərəbl]
numerable

Jim Henson produced **innumerable** films and TV shows.

dwindle	월드컵에서의 승리를 축하하는 한국인들의 무리는 이른 아침 시간까지도 줄어들 줄 몰랐다.
embody	문학은 종종 작가, 혹은 작가의 문화가 지니는 특수한 사회적 이상을 구현하곤 한다.
	그 악곡은 재즈, 펑크, 레게를 포함한 여러 가지 음악적 양식들을 포함했다.
etch	유대인 대학살은 유대인들의 역사에 영원히 새겨질 끔찍한 사건이었다.
flash	불꽃이 너무 밝게 타올라 구경꾼 몇 명의 눈을 다치게 했다.
imaginable	우주 공간을 탐험하는 것은 19세기 후반에는 상상도 할 수 없는 일이었다.
infectious	백신은 전염성 질병에 대한 싸움에 있어서 기적에 가까운 일을 해냈다.
innumerable	Jim Henson은 수없이 많은 영화와 TV쇼를 만들어냈다.

22 invariable*
[invέəriəbl]
varying

adj. **constant, consistent, unchanging** 불변의

There has been **invariable** struggle for justice in Cuba since the 1950s.

23 meditate**
[médətèit]

v. **think deeply, ponder, contemplate** reflect 숙고하다

Plato **meditated** about the question for some time before answering.

24 opposite*
[ápəzit]

adj. 1. **counter** (성질 · 의미 등이) 정반대의

Cars in England drive on the **opposite** side of the road than the ones in the U.S.

n. 2. **contrast** 정반대

Joe and his brother were very much **opposites**, one outgoing and the other introverted.

25 outdo
[àutdú:]

v. **surpass, excel, exceed, outmatch** ~을 능가하다

Thomas **outdid** the rest of his classmates on the test.

26 outline*
[áutlàin]

n. **summary; contour, silhouette** 개요 ; 윤곽

Since the report was 700 pages long, most committee members just read the **outline**.

27 parallel*
[pǽrəlèl]
unparalleled

adj. 1. **corresponding, comparable, analogous** ~와 유사한

Rosa's addiction to overeating is almost **parallel** to her father's addiction to alcohol.

surpass

v. 2. **match, compare, equate** ~에 필적하다

The high jumper **paralleled** the world record, but he could not break it.

---

invariable 1950년대 이래로, 쿠바에서는 정의를 위한 계속적인 투쟁이 있어 왔다.
meditate Plato는 대답하기 전에 잠시 동안 그 질문에 대해 깊이 생각했다.
opposite 영국에서 자동차는 미국의 자동차들이 운행하는 도로의 반대편으로 운행한다.
Joe와 그의 동생은 성격이 정반대로 한 명은 외향적이고 한 명은 내성적이다.
outdo Thomas는 시험에서 급우들을 능가했다.
outline 보고서가 700페이지 분량이라 대부분의 위원회 구성원들은 개요만을 읽었다.
parallel Rosa의 과식 중독은 거의 그녀의 아버지의 알코올 중독과 유사하다.
그 높이뛰기 선수의 기록은 세계 기록에 필적했으나, 기록을 갱신하지는 못했다.

28 **preeminent** | adj. **outstanding, foremost, distinguished** 탁월한

[priːémənənt]

Some **preeminent** women became teachers and poets in the town.

29 **reassuring** | adj. **encouraging, refreshing, revitalizing** 용기를 북돋는

[riːəʃúəriŋ]

The teacher's **reassuring** comments made Jeff feel much better prior to taking his final exam.

30 **regulate** | v. **control, adjust** 조절하다

[régjulèit]

Mammals differ from other animals in the way they **regulate** body temperature.

31 **respectful** | adj. **courteous, polite, well-mannered** civil 공손한

[rispéktfəl]
insolent

The younger generation has to be **respectful** of the elderly.

32 **shrink** | v. **shrivel, decrease, diminish** 줄어들다

[ʃríŋk]
swell

Italy's population is expected to **shrink** from 57 million today to 41 million by 2050.

33 **skill**** | n. **expertise, know-how, craft** technique 기술

[skíl]

The Airline Recareerment Project provides **skill** training and job placement assistance.

34 **steadily**** | adv. **constantly, continuously** 지속적으로

[stédili]

Lawn and garden chemical usage has been dropping **steadily** for the last two decades.

35 **struggle*** | v. **contend, fight, battle** 싸우다

[strʌ́gl]

The abolitionist **struggled** for women's suffrage.

preeminent	그 마을에서는 탁월한 여자들은 교사나 시인이 되었다.
reassuring	그 선생님의 격려가 기말고사 전에 Jeff의 기분을 훨씬 좋게 해주었다.
regulate	포유동물은 체온을 조절하는 방식에 있어 다른 동물들과 다르다.
respectful	젊은 세대들은 어른들에게 공손해야 한다.
shrink	이탈리아의 인구는 2050년경 지금의 오천 칠백만에서 사천 백만으로 줄어들 것으로 예상된다.
skill	항공사의 재취업 프로젝트는 기술 훈련과 직업 소개 지원을 제공한다.
steadily	잔디와 정원용 화학 물질의 사용은 지난 20년간 꾸준히 감소하고 있다.
struggle	그 폐지론자는 여성의 참정권을 위해 싸웠다.

36 **subsequence***	n. **next in a series, succession, sequel** 이어서 일어나는 것
[sʌ́bsəkwəns]	Brandy had the misfortune of performing in **subsequence** to an unusually gifted singer.

37 **warrant***	v. **justify, deserve, merit** 정당화하다
[wɔ́ːrənt]	Although organic produce is supposedly healthier, it still doesn't **warrant** such high prices.

38 **ware***	n. **product** 제품
[wɛ́ər]	It was common in medieval times for craftsmen to go about the towns and villages selling their **wares**.

39 **yet***	adv. **nevertheless, however** 그럼에도 불구하고
[jét]	Harrison was very pressed for time, and **yet** he was not late for class.

Quiz

Choose the synonym.

1. outdo	ⓐ contend, contest, strive
2. flash	ⓑ encouraging, refreshing, revitalizing
3. invariable	ⓒ constant, consistent, unchanging
4. struggle	ⓓ flame, flare, glare
5. reassuring	ⓔ surpass, excel, exceed

Answer 1. ⓔ 2. ⓓ 3. ⓒ 4. ⓐ 5. ⓑ

subsequence	불행히도 Brandy는 대단히 재능 있는 가수에 이어 공연을 해야 했다.
warrant	유기농산물이 아마도 더 건강에 좋긴 하겠지만, 그래도 그만큼 높은 가격의 가치는 없다.
ware	중세 시대에는 장인들이 마을과 촌락을 돌아다니면서 그들의 제품을 파는 것이 흔한 일이었다.
yet	Harrison은 시간에 쫓겼지만 그럼에도 불구하고 수업에는 늦지 않았다.

DAY 21 | Hackers TOEFL **Vocabulary**

Hackers Voca

www.goHackers.com

1 **abundance****	n.	**large number, profusion, plenty** bounty	풍부함
[əbʌ́ndəns] lack		There was an **abundance** of wild animals in the dense forests.	
2 **adaptability**	n.	**ability to change, changeability, flexibility**	적응성, 융통성
[ədæ̀ptəbíləti] rigidity		It was James' **adaptability** that allowed him to constantly travel and move to new countries.	
3 **arrest**	v.	**seize, apprehend, capture**	체포하다
[ərést] liberate		Demonstrators at the protest were **arrested** for disorderly conduct.	
4 **assigned***	adj.	**specified, designated, appointed**	정해진
[əsáind]		In June of 1942, J. Robert Oppenheimer was given the **assigned** task of designing the atomic bomb.	
5 **be at odds with****	phr.	**disagree with**	~와 불화하다
		Alice **is at odds with** her teacher over her grade on the paper.	
6 **curiously**	adv.	**surprisingly**	신기하게도
[kjú(:)əriəsli]		**Curiously**, the dictator denounced human rights violations in a developing nation.	

abundance	나무들이 빽빽한 숲 속에 야생 동물들이 많았다.
adaptability	James가 계속해서 새로운 나라들을 여행하며 옮겨 다닐 수 있게 해준 것은 그의 적응력이었다.
arrest	항의를 하던 시위자들은 난폭한 행동으로 인해 체포되었다.
assigned	1942년 6월 J. Robert Oppenheimer는 핵 폭탄을 만드는 임무를 부여받았다.
be at odds with	Alice는 보고서 점수를 놓고 선생님과 다투고 있다.
curiously	그 독재자는 신기하게도 개발국에서의 기본권 침해를 비난했다.

7 **dense** adj. **thick, heavy** 짙은

[déns]
porous

The solitary lighthouse shone its beacon through the **dense** fog as ships passed slowly in the gathering night.

8 **deploy** v. **set up, distribute, position, arrange** (전략적으로) 배치하다

[diplɔ́i]

Military forces are currently **deployed** on the India-Pakistan border.

9 **discreet** adj. **judicious, prudent, sensible** regardful 분별력 있는

[diskríːt]
foolhardy, irrational

After Hal and Tom exchanged greetings, Hal made a **discreet** inquiry about Tom's journey.

10 **entire**** adj. **whole, complete, total** 전체의

[intáiər]
partial

Fire destroyed the **entire** factory, but the owner vowed to rebuild.

11 **evident**** adj. **obvious, apparent, manifest** plain, clear 분명한

[évidənt]
vague

The presence of cycles in history is **evident** when studying later Mesopotamia.

12 **extensive**** adj. **wide, far-reaching, broad** commodious 넓은

[iksténsiv]
restrained

The new park covers an **extensive** area.

13 **extinguish** v. 1. **put out, quench** (불을) 끄다

[ikstíŋgwiʃ]

Special chemicals have been designed to **extinguish** forest fires.

v. 2. **abolish, destroy** 소멸시키다

Scientists believe that a giant meteor once **extinguished** almost all life on Earth.

dense	홀로 서있는 등대는 어스름한 밤에 배들이 지나다닐 때 짙은 안개 사이로 불빛을 비추었다.
deploy	군인들이 현재 인도-파키스탄 국경지대에 배치되었다.
discreet	Hal과 Tom이 서로 인사를 나눈 뒤, Hal은 Tom의 여행에 대해서 조심스럽게 물어봤다.
entire	화재는 공장 전체를 파괴했지만 사장은 공장을 다시 짓겠다고 결심했다.
evident	후기 메소포타미아를 공부하면 역사에 주기가 존재한다는 것이 명백해진다.
extensive	그 새로운 공원은 넓은 지역에 걸쳐 있다.
extinguish	산불을 끄기 위해 특별한 화학 물질들이 만들어졌다.
	과학자들은 거대한 운석이 한때 지구상의 거의 모든 생명체를 멸종시켰다고 믿는다.

14 **feeble*** adj. **weak, delicate, fragile** frail, unsubstantial 연약한

[fí:bl]
robust

Wanda was in **feeble** health and totally unfit for active service.

15 **flavor** n. 1. **nature, character** 특징

[fléivər]

Settled by immigrant groups, the neighborhood had an ethnic **flavor**.

n. 2. **savor, taste, relish** 맛, 풍미

A dash of soy sauce will add **flavor** to the dish.

16 **fragmentary** adj. **incomplete, partial, fractional** 단편적인

[frǽgməntèri]

The trauma victim had only **fragmentary** memories of the accident.

17 **in charge of** phr. **responsible for** ~에 책임이 있는

Allison was left **in charge of** her younger siblings whenever her mother and father went out to dinner alone.

18 **minor*** adj. **less important, secondary, subordinate** 중요치 않은

[máinər]
major

The photographer made some **minor** adjustments in the settings of his camera before taking the picture.

19 **parcel out***** phr. **administer, deal out, distribute, divide** 분할(분배)하다

It is always Terri's father's job to **parcel out** the gifts to her family on Christmas morning.

20 **perceive*** v. **see, discern, notice** apprehend, recognize 알아차리다

[pərsí:v]

Despite the heavy fog, Max could **perceive** the outline of the building in front of him.

---

feeble Wanda는 몸이 연약해 현역 근무에는 부적합했다.
flavor 그 동네는 이민자들이 정착을 해서 이국적인 특징을 가지고 있다.
소량의 간장은 그 음식에 맛을 더할 것이다
fragmentary 그 외상 피해자는 사고의 단편적인 기억들만 떠올릴 수 있었다.
in charge of Allison은 그녀의 어머니와 아버지가 저녁 식사를 하러 외출할 때면 항상 남겨져 어린 동생들을 책임지게 되었다.
minor 사진을 찍기 전 사진작가는 카메라 설정에 사소한 몇 부분을 조정했다.
parcel out 크리스마스 아침에 Terri의 가족에게 온 선물을 나누어 주는 것은 언제나 아버지의 몫이었다.
perceive 짙은 안개에도 불구하고, Max는 정면에 있는 건물의 윤곽을 알아볼 수 있었다.

21 **piece*** [pí:s]

n. 1. **fragment, shard, segment** shred, scrap 조각

Sherie picked up the **pieces** of broken glass.

v. 2. **join, combine, unite** 잇다, 접합하다

Alex slowly **pieced** the broken vase back together.

22 **pledge** [plédʒ]

n. **promise, oath, vow, swear** 맹세

Before the start of the school day, children all across America make a **pledge** of allegiance to the flag.

23 **portray*** [pɔ:rtréi]

v. **depict, picture, describe** represent 묘사하다

Early American writers often **portrayed** Indians as brutal savages.

24 **project**** [prádʒekt]

n. 1. **plan, scheme** 계획

The new housing **project** failed to get federal funding.

[prədʒékt]

v. 2. **protrude, extend, jut** 돌출하다

The sailors found something strange **projecting** from the surface of Lake Michigan.

25 **region**** [rí:dʒən]

n. **area, domain, tract, expanse** 지역

The central **region** of the country is notorious for its strong winds.

26 **safe*** [séif]

dangerous, unsafe

adj. **secure, protected** 안전한

The government should provide us the right to live in a **safe** environment.

piece	Sherie는 깨진 유리 조각들을 주웠다.
	Alex는 깨진 화병 조각을 천천히 맞추어 붙였다.
pledge	미국 전역의 모든 어린이들은 수업이 시작하기 전에 국기에 대한 맹세를 한다.
portray	초기 미국 작가들은 종종 인디언들을 난폭한 야만인들로 묘사하였다.
project	새로운 주택 공급 프로젝트는 연방 기금을 얻어내는 데 실패했다.
	선원들은 미시간 호의 수면 위로 튀어나온 이상한 무언가를 발견했다.
region	그 나라의 중부 지역은 바람이 강한 것으로 악명 높다.
safe	정부는 안전한 환경에서 살 권리를 우리에게 주어야 한다.

27 **search**** | v. **comb, scour, seek** explore | 탐색하다, 조사하다

[sə́:rtʃ]

Scientists are constantly **searching** for new sources of power.

28 **seethe*** | v. **boil, fume, rage** | (화가 나서) 속이 끓다

[síːð]

The Israeli government is **seething** with anger towards Palestine due to recent events.

29 **shortcoming*** | n. **disadvantage, defect, failing** | 결점

[ʃɔ́:rtkʌ̀miŋ]
merit

The inspection revealed some serious **shortcomings** in our safety procedures.

30 **special*** | adj. **express, particular, especial** specific | 특별한

[spéʃəl]
common

Because of the **special** occasion of Halloween, John's parents allowed him to stay up past midnight.

31 **survey*** | v. **examine, inspect, scrutinize** view | 조사하다

[səːrvéi]

The Sumerians developed mathematics and **surveying** techniques.

32 **temperament*** | n. **disposition, temper, nature** make-up | 성질

[témpərəmənt]

Football players often have excitable **temperaments**.

33 **tool*** | n. **implement, instrument, utensil** | 도구

[tú:l]

Standardized testing is a widely used **tool** for measuring educational achievement.

34 **uninitiated*** | adj. **inexperienced, unfamiliar** | 미숙한

[ʌ̀niníʃièitid]

To the **uninitiated** spectator, rugby can look just like a lot of overweight men wrestling in the mud.

search	과학자들은 대체 에너지원을 끊임없이 찾고 있다.
seethe	이스라엘 정부는 근래의 사건들 때문에 팔레스타인에게 화가 나서 속이 끓고 있다.
shortcoming	조사는 우리의 안전 절차에 몇 가지 심각한 결점이 있다는 것을 드러냈다.
special	John의 부모님은 할로윈이라는 특별한 행사 때문에 12시 넘어서까지 깨어 있어도 된다고 허락했다.
survey	수메르인들은 수학과 측량술을 개발했다.
temperament	미식축구 선수들은 종종 쉽게 흥분하는 기질들을 가지고 있다.
tool	표준화된 시험은 학업 성취도를 평가하는 데 널리 쓰이는 도구이다.
uninitiated	초보 관객들에게 럭비는 단지 다수의 덩치 좋은 남자들이 진흙에서 싸움을 하는 것으로 보일 수도 있다.

35 vanish** v. **disappear, fade** 사라지다

[vǽniʃ]

Like a ghost, the magician **vanished** into thin air.

36 vile** adj. **wicked** 사악한

[váil]

Claude Frollo is a man of **vile** character.

37 worldly* adj. **mundane, earthly, secular** 세속적인

[wə́ːrldli]
naive

The composition portrays the harmony of **worldly** beauty and religious spirit.

38 wreck* v. **destroy, devastate, ruin** shatter, crush 파괴하다

[rék]

The ship was almost **wrecked** by the heavy storm.

Quiz

Choose the synonym.

1. dense ⓐ disappear, fade
2. discreet ⓑ judicious, prudent, sensible
3. pledge ⓒ thick, heavy
4. seethe ⓓ promise, oath, vow
5. vanish ⓔ boil, fume, rage

Answer 1. ⓒ 2. ⓑ 3. ⓓ 4. ⓔ 5. ⓐ

vanish	유령처럼, 그 마술사는 완전히 자취를 감췄다.
vile	Claude Frollo는 사악한 성격의 남자이다.
worldly	그 글은 세속적인 아름다움과 종교적인 영혼의 조화를 그리고 있다.
wreck	그 배는 엄청난 폭풍으로 거의 파괴되었다.

Hackers TOEFL Voca TEST DAY 19-21

Choose the synonym of the highlighted word in the sentence.

1. The country's foreign currency reserves began to dwindle as a result of the global financial crisis.
(A) hinder (B) dissipate (C) diminish (D) dampen

2. The bite of a garter snake, unlike that of the deadly cobra, is benign.
(A) amiable (B) fatal (C) intimate (D) scenic

3. Those who are attempting to overcome their addiction to nicotine have found the most common cures ineffective.
(A) amaze (B) shudder (C) defeat (D) mold

4. The estimate was very accurate compared to the actual numbers.
(A) intense (B) amiable (C) precise (D) forceful

5. Fine pottery has an enameled surface decorated with elaborate designs, the outlines of which are formed by small bands of metal.
(A) merits (B) contours (C) attributes (D) traps

6. The researcher spent hours trying to piece the ancient pot together.
(A) construe (B) join (C) conjecture (D) scrutinize

7. After a war, a country's extensive growth will eventually slow.
(A) delicate (B) constant (C) wide (D) subordinate

8. If the United States, a major declared possessor of chemical weapons, does not ratify the treaty, it is difficult for one to imagine that the organization can move forward.
(A) prophesy (B) last (C) escort (D) endorse

9. The president became flustered in response to tough questioning from reporters.
(A) confused (B) organized (C) lapsed (D) hounded

10. Out of the four biggest industrialized countries at the time (U.S., Germany, U.K., and France), France was the last to be hit by the Depression.
(A) severe (B) conscious (C) final (D) courageous

정답 p.419

A RED, RED ROSE 새빨간 장미

Robert Burns

O My luve's like a red, red rose,
That's newly sprung in June;
O My Luve's like the melodie
That's sweetly played in tune.

As fair art thou, my bonnie lass,
So deep in luve am I;
And I will luve thee still, my dear,
Till a'the seas gang dry.

오 나의 님은 유월에 새로이 피어난
새빨간 장미
오 나의 님은 곡조맞춰 감미롭게
연주된 멜로디.

이처럼 너는 예뻐, 사랑스런 소녀야,
이처럼 깊이 나는 너를 사랑해
언제까지나 나는 너를 사랑하리, 내 님이여,
온 바다가 말라 버릴 때까지.

DAY 22

Hackers TOEFL **Vocabulary**

Hackers Voca

www.goHackers.com

1 **accustomed***	adj.	**used to, customary, habitual** wont	익숙한
[əkʌ́stəmd]		Vanessa was **accustomed** to getting up late.	
2 **allege***	v.	**assert, claim, affirm** declare	주장하다, 우기다
[əlédʒ] gainsay		Prosecutors **alleged** that Robert set the fire to collect insurance money.	
3 **at the expense of***	phr.	**at the cost of**	~의 비용(대가)으로
		Tom's successful career has come **at the expense of** his family life.	
4 **breed****	v.	**raise, rear, nurture** nourish	기르다
[brí:d]		To **breed** rabbits was cheaper than to buy rabbits at the time.	
5 **chisel***	v.	**carve, engrave**	조각하다
[tʃízəl]		The masonry worker **chiseled** pieces of stone in order to make them fit together.	
6 **conclusive***	adj.	**definite, decisive**	결정적인
[kənklú:siv]		The experiment failed to provide any **conclusive** evidence of the theory's validity.	

accustomed	Vanessa는 늦게 일어나는 것에 익숙했다.
allege	검사들은 Robert가 보험금을 타내기 위해 방화를 저질렀다고 주장했다.
at the expense of	가족 생활의 희생으로 Tom은 성공적인 업적을 이룰 수 있었다.
breed	그 당시에는 토끼를 기르는 것이 사는 것보다 비용이 적게 들었다.
chisel	석수는 돌들이 서로 알맞게 들어가도록 돌들을 조각했다.
conclusive	그 실험은 그 이론의 정당성에 대한 어떠한 결정적인 증거도 제공하지 못했다.

7 **costly***

adj. **expensive, high-priced** 비싼

[kɔ́(:)stli]

The sisters' trip to Ireland was rather **costly**, but they both agreed it was well worth the money.

8 **crack down***

phr. **enforce laws** ~을 엄히 단속하다

In December, Israeli forces began confining Arafat, in an effort to **crack down** on militants who attack Israelis.

9 **degree***

n. **measure, extent, scale** 정도

[digríː]

It takes a high **degree** of patience to work with children all day long.

10 **delicate**

adj. **dainty, exquisite, fine** 섬세한

[délikət]
gross

The tea cups were so **delicate** that Sheila used them only for decoration.

11 **devote****

v. **dedicate, commit** 헌신하다

[divóut]

Evangeline **devoted** her lifetime to the search for Gabriel.

12 **die**

v. **decease, perish, pass away** 죽다

[dái]
live

On September 25, 1866 Connelly **died** suddenly in Charleston at age 42.

13 **distribute***

v. **parcel out, allot, apportion** divide 분배하다

[distríbjuːt]
amass

The company decided to **distribute** the bonus fund based on employee performance.

14 **emergency***

n. **crisis, exigency** 위기, 위급

[imə́ːrdʒənsi]

Poor crops have created a national **emergency**.

costly	그 자매의 아일랜드 여행에는 다소 많은 돈이 들긴 했지만, 그것이 그만한 돈의 가치가 충분히 있었다는 데 두 사람 모두 동의했다.
crack down	이스라엘군은 이스라엘을 공격하는 무장 세력을 엄중히 다스리기 위해 12월부터 Arafat의 행동을 제한하기 시작했다.
degree	하루 종일 아이들을 다루는 것은 고도의 인내력을 요한다.
delicate	찻잔이 너무 섬세해서 Sheila는 그것을 장식용으로만 사용했다.
devote	Evangeline은 Gabriel을 찾는 데 그녀의 전 생애를 바쳤다.
die	1866년 9월 25일 Connelly는 42세의 나이로 Charleston에서 갑자기 죽었다.
distribute	회사는 직원의 성과에 근거한 보너스를 배분하기로 결정했다.
emergency	흉작으로 국가적인 위기가 초래되었다.

15 fatal* | adj. **deadly, mortal, lethal** | 치명적인

[féitl]
benign

It would be **fatal** for the nation to overlook the urgency in the moment.

16 guilty | adj. **criminal, culpable** | 유죄의

[gílti]
innocent

The Rosenbergs were found **guilty** of giving information to the Soviets.

17 hazard* | n. **danger, peril, jeopardy** | 위험

[hǽzərd]

Reduced regulation created **hazards** to public health and safety.

18 in any case | phr. **regardless** | 여하간에, 여하튼

Applications should be sent as soon as possible but **in any case** before the deadline.

19 incite | v. **provoke, inflame, spur** | 자극하다

[insáit]

The love poem **incited** Todd to such a passion that he impetuously asked for his girlfriend's hand in marriage.

20 moist* | adj. **damp, humid, wet** | 축축한

[mɔ́ist]

The palms of Janet's hands were **moist**.

21 ornament* | v. **decorate, adorn, embellish** | 장식하다

[ɔ́:rnəmənt]

Timothy's house was **ornamented** with various flowers.

22 peripheral | adj. **outer, exterior, external** | 주변의

[pərífərəl]

Houses on the **peripheral** side of the city are the most vulnerable to flooding.

fatal	국가가 현재의 급박함을 간과하는 것은 치명적인 일일 것이다.
guilty	Rosenbergs가 소련 연방에 정보를 준 혐의가 유죄로 판결되었다.
hazard	규제 완화는 공공 건강과 안전에 위험을 초래했다.
in any case	신청서는 되도록이면 빨리, 그러나 어쨌든 마감일 전까지는 보내져야 한다.
incite	그 사랑의 시가 Todd의 강한 정열을 자극하여, 그는 즉흥적으로 자신의 여자 친구에게 청혼했다.
moist	Janet의 손바닥은 축축했다.
ornament	Timothy의 집은 다양한 꽃으로 장식되어 있었다.
peripheral	그 도시의 변두리 지역에 있는 집들은 홍수에 가장 취약하다.

23 **precipitous***	adj. **sudden, hasty, rash**	성급한
[prisípitəs] deliberate	Ginny always regretted her **precipitous** decision to drop out of high school.	
24 **primarily**	adv. 1. **mostly, mainly, chiefly**	주로
[praimérəli]	Members of the country club were **primarily** wealthy old men.	
	adv. 2. **originally, at first**	본래, 처음에
	The Republican Party was **primarily** created to stop the spread of slavery.	
25 **primeval**	adj. **ancient, primitive, pristine**	원시의
[praimí:vəl]	The monitor lizard reflects some of the **primeval** characteristics of the early reptiles.	
26 **raw***	adj. **unprocessed, crude, rude** uncooked	가공하지 않은
[rɔ́:] matured	**Raw** materials were almost entirely concentrated in Northern mines.	
27 **reject***	v. **renounce, refuse, decline** deny	거절하다
[ridʒékt] accept	The nation's highest court has **rejected** a request for the immediate release of a prominent human rights activist.	
28 **replenish*****	v. **restore, renew, refill**	보충하다
[ripléniʃ]	Mike worked hard to **replenish** his bank account, empty after his big shopping trip.	
29 **rot***	v. **decay, corrupt, degenerate**	부패하다
[rɑ́t]	Fruits and vegetables will **rot** quickly unless refrigerated.	

precipitous	Ginny는 항상 고등학교를 중퇴하기로 한 그녀의 성급한 결정을 후회했다.
primarily	컨트리클럽의 회원들은 주로 부유한 노인들이었다.
	공화당은 처음에 노예 제도 확산을 막기 위해 만들어졌다.
primeval	왕도마뱀은 초기 파충류의 특징을 일부 나타낸다.
raw	천연 자원들은 거의 대부분이 북부 광산에 집중되어 있었다.
reject	그 나라의 대법원은 저명한 인권 운동가를 즉각적으로 석방하라는 요구를 거절했다.
replenish	Mike는 대대적인 쇼핑 여행 후에 탕진된 은행 잔고를 다시 채우기 위해서 열심히 일했다.
rot	과일과 야채는 냉장시키지 않는 한 금방 부패한다.

30 ruin*
[rú:in]

v. **devastate, destroy, wreck** 파괴하다

Members of the Temperance Movement feared alcohol would **ruin** the American way of life.

31 runoff
[rʌ́nɔ̀(:)f]

n. **overflow, overspill** 범람, 넘쳐흐름

The main force of the tsunami's impact hit the shore, but a substantial **runoff** made its way into downtown Tokyo.

32 shorten
[ʃɔ́:rtn]
elongate

v. **abbreviate, abridge, lessen** curtail, reduce 줄이다

Working hours were **shortened** to give people more time for leisure activities.

33 spoil*
[spɔ́il]
benefit

v. **mar, hurt, damage** impair, harm 망치다, 손상시키다

Violence from a few members of the crowd **spoiled** the soccer game.

34 standard**
[stǽndərd]

n. 1. **criterion, gauge** 기준

Steuben set a **standard** that became universal in the army.

exceptional

adj. 2. **unexceptional, usual, average** mean 보통의

Critics contended that the book was too **standard** to merit attention from the reading public.

35 stipulation*
[stìpjəléiʃən]

n. **requirement, qualification, proviso** 조건

The business partners signed the contract with the **stipulation** that they would share the profits equally.

36 strikingly*
[stráikiŋli]
unremarkably

adv. **remarkably** 두드러지게

Marilyn Monroe was a **strikingly** beautiful woman with her bleached blond hair, full lips, and shapely figure.

ruin	금주회의 회원들은 술이 미국인들의 생활양식을 파괴할까봐 두려웠다.
runoff	해일의 충돌에 의한 대부분의 힘은 해변을 강타했지만, 엄청난 양의 범람한 물은 도쿄 시내로 흘러갔다.
shorten	사람들에게 더 많은 여가 활동 시간을 주기 위해 근무시간이 단축되었다.
spoil	몇몇 관중의 난폭한 행동이 축구 경기를 망쳐 놓았다.
standard	Steuben은 군대에서 보편적이 된 기준을 세웠다.
	비평가들은 그 책이 너무나 평범해서 독자들로부터 관심을 끌 수 없다고 주장했다.
stipulation	그 사업의 동업자들은 그들이 이윤을 균등하게 나눠 갖는다는 조건을 포함한 계약서에 서명했다.
strikingly	Marilyn Monroe는 그녀의 탈색된 금발 머리와 도톰한 입술 그리고 맵시 있는 모습으로 인해 두드러지게 아름다운 여성이었다.

37 subtract*

[səbtrǽkt]
add

v. **deduct, discount** 빼다

The company **subtracted** the cost of environmental degradation from the total cost.

38 thaw**

[θɔ́ː]

v. **defrost** 녹다

The ice doesn't **thaw** until June in Siberia.

39 unpin*

[ʌnpín]
pin

v. **to remove a pin or pinned object from** 핀(핀 종류의 것)을 빼다

After the parade, the officer **unpinned** the badge from his shirt.

Quiz

Choose the synonym.

1. accustomed	ⓐ decay, corrupt, degenerate
2. incite	ⓑ customary, habitual, wont
3. replenish	ⓒ restore, renew, refill
4. rot	ⓓ provoke, inflame, spur
5. peripheral	ⓔ outer, exterior, external

Answer 1. ⓑ 2. ⓓ 3. ⓒ 4. ⓐ 5. ⓔ

subtract 회사는 전체 비용에서 환경 악화에 대한 비용을 뺐다.
thaw 시베리아의 얼음은 6월까지 녹지 않는다.
unpin 퍼레이드 후에, 그 경관은 그의 셔츠에서 배지를 떼어냈다.

DAY | Hackers TOEFL **Vocabulary**

23 Hackers Voca

www.goHackers.com

1 **akin to**	phr. **similar to**	~와 유사한, ~에 가까운

Ukrainians are culturally and linguistically **akin to** Russians.

2 **appealing**	adj. **desirable, attractive, charming, winsome**	매력적인

[əpíːliŋ]

Advertising firms try to create **appealing** brand images.

3 **approach****	n. 1. **method, way**	접근법, 방법

[əpróutʃ]

A psychodynamic **approach** to the guidance of children has infused North American popular culture.

retreat

	v. 2. **move toward, come toward, reach**	접근하다

Parents should teach their children what to do if **approached** by a stranger.

4 **argue****	v. **dispute, debate, claim, discuss**	논쟁하다

[áːrgjuː]

After **arguing** with the child, Susan tried to soothe him.

5 **assert****	v. **claim, declare, maintain**	주장하다

[əsə́ːrt]

Most antivirus experts **asserted** that no computer worm is a good worm.

akin to	우크라이나 사람들은 문화적, 언어학적으로 러시아 사람들과 유사하다.
appealing	광고 회사들은 매력적인 브랜드 이미지를 창조하려고 노력한다.
approach	아이들의 지도에 대한 정신 역학적 접근은 북미 대중문화를 고취시켰다.
	부모들을 자식들에게 낯선 사람이 접근했을 때 어떻게 해야 하는지를 가르쳐 주어야 한다.
argue	Susan은 그 아이와 말다툼을 벌이고 나서 그를 달래려고 애썼다.
assert	대부분의 항바이러스 소프트웨어 전문가들은 어떤 컴퓨터 버그도 좋지 않다고 주장했다.

6 **brace*** v. support, **buttress, reinforce** 받치다, 보강하다

[bréis]

The walls of the newly constructed building were **braced** by metal beams dug deep into the ground.

7 **catastrophic*** adj. disastrous, **tragic** 비참한, 비극적인

[kæ̀təstrάfik]

The attack on Pearl Harbor was a **catastrophic** event in American history.

8 **clarify*** v. elucidate, **clear up** 명료하게 하다

[klǽrəfài]
obfuscate

Homer sought to **clarify** his argument in favor of the death penalty using contemporary analogies and references.

9 **constantly*** adv. continually, continuously, always, perpetually 지속적으로

[kάnstəntli]
temporarily

As Priscilla walked through the village for the first time in 20 years, she was **constantly** reminded of her childhood.

10 **deception*** n. fraud, **cheating, trickery** 속임수, 사기

[disépʃən]
candidness

Margaret's **deception** in providing false testimony to the police earned her ten years in prison.

11 **distinct**** adj. 1. separate, different, **discrete** 별개의

[distíŋkt]
indistinguishable

Each region of Italy maintains its own **distinct** traditions and flavors of Italy.

nebulous adj. 2. definite, **apparent, clear** 뚜렷한

The onion has a **distinct** flavor.

12 **edition***** n. version, volume (간행물)판

[idíʃən]

The newest **edition** of the encyclopedia includes more diagrams.

brace	새로 지은 건물의 벽은 땅속 깊이 박힌 금속 들보로 지탱되고 있다.
catastrophic	진주만 공습은 미국 역사에 있어 매우 비극적인 사건이다.
clarify	Homer는 사형 제도에 찬성하는 그의 주장을 현대의 유사 사건과 참조 사건을 이용하여 명료하게 하려 했다.
constantly	Priscilla가 20년 만에 처음으로 마을로 걸어 들어왔을 때, 그녀는 끊임없이 자신의 어린 시절이 떠올랐다.
deception	Magaret은 경찰에게 위증을 한 사기 행위로 10년의 감옥형을 선고받았다.
distinct	이탈리아는 각 지역마다 이탈리아의 독특한 전통과 맛을 갖고 있다.
	양파는 뚜렷한 향을 지니고 있다.
edition	그 백과사전의 신판에는 도표가 많이 포함되어 있다.

13 **elaborate**** adj. **detailed, intricate, complicated, complex** 복잡한, 정교한

[ilǽbərət]
simple

Youths in some African tribes go through an **elaborate** initiation rite to prepare themselves for adult life.

14 **flaw**** n. **defect, blemish, fault** failing, shortcoming 결점

[flɔ́ː]

In the play Cyrano De Bergerac, the protagonist's most obvious **flaw** is his grotesque nose.

15 **flood*** v. **inundate, deluge, overflow** 범람시키다

[flʌ́d]
trickle

The town was **flooded** with water after the levee broke.

16 **floods of*** phr. **great number of** 다수의, 쇄도하는

Authorities concerned about **floods of** immigrants failed to persuade the Chinese government to assist them.

17 **habitat**** n. **home, dwelling, living quarter** 거주지

[hǽbitæ̀t]

Efforts to protect lynx **habitats** are under way in 57 forests in 16 states.

18 **hint*** n. **indication, implication** 암시

[hint]

When the host of the party began getting ready for bed, her guests took the **hint** to go home.

19 **intensify** v. **strengthen, reinforce, deepen** 강화하다

[inténsəfài]
abate

The Kansas Nebraska Act **intensified** the sectional quarrel over the extension of slavery.

20 **intentional** adj. **deliberate, designed, planned** purposeful 고의적인

[inténʃənl]
accidental

Increased oil prices were the **intentional** result of the decision to cut back production.

elaborate	몇몇 아프리카 부족들의 젊은이들은 성인으로서의 삶을 준비하기 위해 복잡한 절차의 성인식을 행한다.
flaw	연극 Cyrano De Bergerac에서 그 주인공의 가장 두드러진 결점은 그의 기괴한 코이다.
flood	제방이 부서지고 난 뒤 그 도시로 물이 범람했다.
floods of	몰려드는 이민자들을 우려하는 관계당국은 중국 정부를 설득하여 그들을 돕도록 하는 데 실패했다.
habitat	스라소니 거주지를 보호하려는 노력이 16개 주 57개 숲에서 진행 중에 있다.
hint	파티의 주최자가 잠잘 준비를 하기 시작하자, 그녀의 손님들은 이를 집에 돌아가라는 암시로 받아들였다.
intensify	Kansas Nebraska 법령은 노예 제도 확장에 대한 파벌적인 논쟁을 강화시켰다.
intentional	유가 상승은 생산을 줄인다는 결정에 따른 의도된 결과였다.

21 **kin*** n. relative, 친척

[kín]

Seamus traveled to Ireland to visit his **kin**, whom he had only seen before in photographs.

22 **make one's way*** phr. travel, **journey, trek** 나아가다

The first explorers used canoes to **make their way** down the country's many rivers.

23 **measure*** v. gauge, **calculate, estimate** 측정하다

[méʒər]

Religion cannot be **measured** by human standards, since it is of divine origin.

24 **minute*** adj. tiny, **diminutive; detailed, precise** 미세한 ; 정밀한

[mainjúːt]
general

Many microchips are so **minute** that a microscope is needed to see them fully.

25 **notwithstanding*** prep. despite, in spite of, nevertheless ~에도 불구하고

[nὰtwiðstǽndiŋ]

The proposal for a pay cut was approved, **notwithstanding** our objection.

26 **profound**** adj. deep, **abysmal** 심오한

[prəfáund]

Carson has a **profound** sense of responsibility for the zoo animals' welfare.

27 **protect*** v. shield, **defend, guard** harbor 보호하다

[prətékt]
attack

The chief was the leader that the people counted on to **protect** them.

28 **receive*** v. obtain, **accept, acquire, get** 받다, 얻다

[risíːv]

Once an international student **receives** a letter of acceptance from an American university, he or she can apply for a student visa.

kin	Seamus는 아일랜드로 그의 친척을 방문하러 갔는데, 그 친척은 그가 이전에 사진에서만 본 적이 있는 사람이었다.
make one's way	최초의 탐험가들은 그 나라의 많은 강들을 따라 내려가는 데 카누를 이용했다.
measure	종교는 신성함을 기원으로 하기 때문에 인간의 기준에 의해 측정될 수 없다.
minute	많은 마이크로 칩들은 너무나 미세해서 제대로 보려면 현미경이 필요하다.
notwithstanding	우리의 반대에도 불구하고, 임금 인하 제안이 승인되었다.
profound	Carson은 동물원의 동물들을 돌보는 데 있어서 깊은 책임감을 가지고 있다.
protect	그 추장은 사람들이 그들을 보호하기 위해 의지한 지도자였다.
receive	일단 교환 학생이 미국 대학으로부터 허가 편지를 받기만 하면 그 또는 그녀는 학생 비자를 신청할 수 있다.

29 relevance* n. germaneness, **pertinence** 적절, 타당성

[réləvəns]
irrelevance

The 30-page research paper lacks **relevance** because it cites only two sources.

30 reliance** n. dependence 의존

[riláiəns]

The country's **reliance** on imported oil is becoming larger.

31 represent** v. 1. depict, portray, **express** 묘사하다, 표현하다

[rèprizént]

The report **represents** the current situation in our schools.

v. 2. stand for 대표하다

Bill Cosby's comedy **represents** a common form of humor popular during the 1980s.

32 require* v. demand, entail, call for enjoin 요구하다

[rikwáiər]

The book publishers **required** Mahfouz to be present.

33 resemble* v. be similar to, be like, **take after** 닮다

[rizémbl]

The bar is designed to **resemble** a hotel lobby desk.

34 resolve* v. 1. **determine, decide** 결정하다

[rizálv]

After losing thousands of dollars in the stock market, Peter **resolved** never to dabble in stocks again.

unsettle

v. 2. find a solution for, **solve** 해결하다

The American newcomers **resolved** some of their conflicts.

relevance	그 30페이지 분량의 연구 논문은 타당성이 부족한데, 그 이유는 이것이 오직 두 개의 출처만을 언급했기 때문이다.
reliance	그 나라의 수입 석유에 대한 의존은 더 커지고 있다.
represent	그 보고서는 우리 학교들의 현 상황을 나타낸다.
	Bill Cosby의 코미디는 1980년대에 유행했던 유머의 일반적인 형태를 보여 준다.
require	그 출판업자들은 Mahfouz에게 출석을 요구했다.
resemble	그 술집은 호텔의 로비 책상과 비슷하게 디자인되어 있다.
resolve	주식 시장에서 수천 달러를 잃고 난 후, Peter는 다시는 주식에 절대 손대지 않기로 결정했다.
	미국에 새로 온 사람들은 자신들이 갖고 있던 갈등을 일부 해소했다.

35 retard** | v. **delay** | 지체시키다

[ritɑ́:rd]
accelerate

Failing to obtain the necessary inputs on time can **retard** the production of the final product.

36 roster* | n. **list, register, rota** | 명부

[rɑ́stər]

The baseball coach read the final **roster** of names listing all players who made the cut.

37 scenic | adj. **beautiful, picturesque** | 풍경이 아름다운

[sí:nik]

Many of Switzerland's tourists are attracted by the **scenic** views of the Alps.

Quiz

Choose the synonym.

1. catastrophic	ⓐ beautiful, picturesque
2. edition	ⓑ version, volume
3. intentional	ⓒ deliberate, designed, planned
4. hint	ⓓ indication, implication
5. scenic	ⓔ disastrous, tragic

Answer 1. ⓔ 2. ⓑ 3. ⓒ 4. ⓓ 5. ⓐ

retard	필요한 정보를 제때 얻지 못하면, 최종 제품의 생산이 늦추어질 수 있다.
roster	그 야구 코치는 방출되는 모든 선수들의 이름이 기록되어 있는 최종 명단을 읽었다.
scenic	스위스를 방문하는 관광객의 대다수가 알프스의 아름다운 경관에 매료된다.

24 Hackers Voca

1 **absurd***

[əbsə́ːrd]
rational

adj. 1. **illogical, irrational, unreasonable** inconsistent 불합리한

The **absurd** law that requires all people with colds to stay indoors should be revoked.

smart

adj. 2. **preposterous, ridiculous, foolish** stupid 어리석은

It is **absurd** to believe in ghosts.

2 **activity***

[æktívəti]
inactivity

n. **liveliness, sprightliness, vivacity** 활기

Being nocturnal creatures, bats display the most **activity** at night.

3 **assort****

[əsɔ́ːrt]
disarrange

v. **categorize, classify, codify** separate, sort 분류하다

Emma found her friend engaged in **assorting** the clothes.

4 **beam***

[bíːm]

v. **ray, shine, gleam** glitter, radiate 빛나다

When Joseph received Harriet's letter, his face instantly **beamed** with joy.

5 **break***

[bréik]

v. 1. **shatter, destroy, batter** 부수다

The windows of neighborhood homes were **broken** by vandals.

absurd	감기에 걸린 사람들은 모두 실내에 있을 것을 강요하는 어처구니없는 법은 철폐되어야 한다. 유령을 믿는 것은 어리석다.
activity	박쥐는 야생 동물이기 때문에, 밤에 가장 활기를 띤다.
assort	Emma는 그녀의 친구가 옷을 분류하고 있는 것을 발견했다.
beam	Joseph이 Harriet의 편지를 받았을 때, 그의 얼굴은 즉시 기쁨으로 빛났다.
break	이웃집의 창문들이 기물 파손자들에 의해 깨졌다.

n. 2. rest, **pause, respite** (짧은) 휴식

House Speaker Dennis Hastert urged Bush to call on Congress to cut short its **break**.

6 bromide

[bróumaid]

n. dull remark, commonplace, **cliché** 진부한 말(생각)

Although Samuel was trying to be original, his statement was only a **bromide**.

7 common*

[kámən]
rare

adj. **shared, joint** 공통의

People having diverse backgrounds work together towards a **common** objective.

8 consciously**

[kánʃəsli]

adv. intentionally 의도적으로

After the war, the Americans **consciously** forced most Mexicans out of Texas.

9 context*

[kántekst]

n. setting 배경

Garrett is judged in the historical **context** as an advanced liberalist.

10 damage

[dǽmidʒ]
advantage

n. **harm, impairment, detriment** injury 손상, 손해

Unfortunately, the earthquake caused tremendous **damage** throughout the city.

11 detach**

[ditǽtʃ]
affix

v. separate, **disconnect, disengage** 분리하다

The inner lining of the coat can be **detached** to make the coat less bulky.

12 dormant*

[dɔ́:rmənt]
active, dynamic

adj. inactive, **latent, stagnant** inert 활동하지 않는

In many horror movies, a monster lies **dormant** until roused by an unwitting human.

break	하원 의장인 Dennis Hastert는 Bush가 의회에 휴식기간을 단축하도록 요청할 것을 촉구했다.
bromide	Samuel은 독창적인 사람이 되려 노력하지만 그가 하는 말은 진부한 말일 뿐이다.
common	다양한 배경을 가진 사람들이 공통의 목표를 향해 함께 일한다.
consciously	미국은 전쟁 후 멕시코인들을 의도적으로 텍사스에서 내쫓았다.
context	Garrett은 시대적 상황이 고려되어 진보적인 자유주의자로 평가된다.
damage	불행히도 지진은 전 도시에 거대한 손해를 야기했다.
detach	외투의 부피가 너무 크지 않도록 하기 위해 안감은 분리될 수도 있다.
dormant	많은 공포 영화에서, 어떤 부주의한 사람이 깨우기 전까지 괴물은 활동하지 않은 상태로 있다.

13 **environment**** n. **setting, ecology** 환경

[inváiərənmənt]

The Fertile Crescent had an ideal **environment** to give rise to the first world civilization.

14 **essential**** adj. **vital, prerequisite, fundamental, indispensable** 필수적인

[isénʃəl]
accidental

The earth itself is the most **essential** natural resource.

15 **heighten*** v. **increase** 늘리다

[háitn]
diminish

Meredith's awkward excuse **heightened** her father's anxiety.

16 **hinder*** v. **stunt, hamper, interfere with, impede** 방해하다

[híndər]
help

Terrance's frequent absences from the lab **hindered** his research.

17 **impose*** v. **force, pressure, enforce** 강요하다

[impóuz]

Karen managed to **impose** her will upon the rest of the group, as usual, and they all ended up at the karaoke bar.

18 **ingenious*** adj. **inventive, creative, innovative, clever, original** 독창적인

[indʒíːnjəs]

An **ingenious** system of water pumps has been built to protect the city from flooding.

19 **insignificant*** adj. **trivial, slight, trifling, negligible** 사소한

[ìnsignífikənt]
important

Kathy's new book was a disappointment, as it contained many **insignificant** details that merely slowed down the reader.

20 **keen** adj. **sharp, bright** intelligent 예리한

[kíːn]
impassive

Duddy was a very **keen** and intuitive young man.

environment	비옥한 초승달 지대(나일 강과 티그리스, 페루시아만을 연결하는 지대)는 최초의 세계 문명을 불러 일으키기에 이상적인 환경을 가지고 있었다.
essential	지구 그 자체가 가장 필수적인 천연 자원이다.
heighten	Meredith의 서투른 변명이 그녀의 아버지를 더 걱정시켰다.
hinder	Terrance가 연구실에 자주 안 나온 것은 그의 연구 진행을 방해했다.
impose	Karen은 늘 그렇듯이 자신의 뜻을 나머지 사람들에게 강요하고야 말았으며, 그들 모두는 결국 노래방으로 향하게 되었다.
ingenious	도시를 홍수로부터 보호하기 위해 독창적인 양수기 시스템이 설치되었다.
insignificant	Kathy의 새 책은 단지 독자를 지루하게 할 뿐인 별로 중요치 않은 내용을 너무 많이 포함하고 있어 실망스러웠다.
keen	Duddy는 매우 예리하고 직관적인 청년이었다.

21 lodge*

[ládʒ]

v. 1. **shelter, harbor, house** 거처(피난처)를 제공하다

The family **lodged** an escaped convict.

v. 2. **quarter, house** 숙박하다

The travelers **lodged** at a hotel.

22 power*

[páuər]

n. **strong effect, strength** 영향력, 힘

The U.S. government has come to **power** in Afganistan since Bush sent military forces there.

23 prominent

[prámənənt]

adj. **conspicuous, remarkable, outstanding** 탁월한

Bismarck is one of the most **prominent** figures in German history.

24 provided*

[prəváidid]

conj. **if, on condition that** 만약 ~이라면

Life is good, even in a heap of rubble, **provided** there is someone who has a warm heart.

25 put together

phr. **combine, connect** 결합시키다

Researchers **put together** a report from many pages of documents.

26 reflect

[riflékt]

v. 1. **meditate, think, consider, ponder** 숙고하다

Casey needed some time to **reflect** before making his decision.

v. 2. **demonstrate, display, show** 반영하다, 나타내다

Chants of "encore!" **reflected** the crowd's enjoyment of the performance.

lodge	그 가족은 탈출한 죄수에게 피난처를 제공했다. 그 여행객들은 호텔에서 숙박했다.
power	미국 정부는 Bush가 군사력을 아프가니스탄에 보낸 이후로 그곳에서 정권을 잡았다.
prominent	Bismarck는 독일 역사에서 가장 저명한 인물 중 하나이다.
provided	온정을 가진 누군가가 있다면 파편 더미 속의 삶조차 즐겁다.
put together	연구원들은 문서들 여러 장에서 보고서를 종합했다.
reflect	Casey는 결정을 내리기 전에 숙고할 시간이 필요했다. "앙코르!"라는 외침은 공연에 대한 관객들의 기쁨을 반영했다.

27 **relinquish** | v. give up, **surrender, abandon, resign** 포기하다, 버리다

[rilíŋkwiʃ]

The king **relinquished** his throne because of the revolution.

28 **representative*** | adj. typical, **characteristic, exemplary** 전형적인

[rèprizéntətiv]
atypical

The newly employed man was in no way **representative** of dog-trainers in general.

29 **scan*** | v. examine, **scrutinize, investigate** 조사하다

[skǽn]

To find the cause of the problem, the researchers **scanned** the sky of the southern hemisphere.

30 **sever*** | v. cut, **separate, divide, part** cleave 절단하다, 분리하다

[sévər]

Noah's right leg was **severed** from his body in the accident.

31 **shortly*** | adv. soon, **presently, before long** 곧

[ʃɔ́:rtli]

Mr. Jones will be back **shortly** as his lunchtime is almost over.

32 **showcase*** | v. display, **exhibit** 전시하다

[ʃóukèis]

The company **showcased** its new car at the auto convention.

33 **succession*** | n. series, **sequence** 연속

[səkséʃən]

Melody is the **succession** of sounds.

34 **summit**** | n. peak, **acme, zenith** apex, pinnacle 정상

[sʌ́mit]

At the **summit** of the mountain, the climber could see unthawed snow.

relinquish	그 왕은 혁명 때문에 왕위를 포기했다.
representative	새로 채용된 그 사람은 어떤 면으로도 일반적인 개 조련사의 전형은 아니었다.
scan	그 문제의 원인을 발견하기 위해, 그 연구원들은 남반구의 하늘을 조사했다.
sever	Noah의 오른쪽 다리는 그 사고로 절단되었다.
shortly	Jones씨는 점심 시간이 거의 끝나가니까 금세 돌아올 것이다.
showcase	그 회사는 자동차 컨벤션에서 새 차를 전시했다.
succession	멜로디는 소리의 연속이다.
summit	그 산의 정상에서, 그 등산객은 녹지 않은 눈을 볼 수 있었다.

35 **token**	n. **symbol, mark, sign**	상징, 표시
[tóukən]	Wedding rings are given as a **token** of love and commitment.	
36 **transmit**	v. **communicate, send, convey**	전달하다
[trænsmít] receive	Samuel Morse first **transmitted** a message by telegraph in 1844.	
37 **useful****	adj. **profitable, advantageous** serviceable	유익한, 도움이 되는
[jú:sfəl] useless	The manager regarded mandatory attendance records as a **useful** way of reducing absenteeism.	
38 **vestige***	n. **remnant, trace, shadow**	흔적
[véstidʒ]	The new law removed the last **vestiges** of royal power.	

Quiz

Choose the synonym.

1. assort	ⓐ harm, impairment, detriment
2. damage	ⓑ stunt, hamper, impede
3. hinder	ⓒ remnant, trace, shadow
4. relinquish	ⓓ categorize, classify, codify
5. vestige	ⓔ give up, surrender, abandon

Answer 1. ⓓ 2. ⓐ 3. ⓑ 4. ⓔ 5. ⓒ

token	결혼반지는 사랑과 약속의 상징으로 받는다.
transmit	Samuel Morse는 1844년 처음으로 전신으로 메시지를 보냈다.
useful	경영자는 출석 기록의 의무화는 장기 결석을 줄이는 유용한 방법이라고 생각했다.
vestige	새로운 법은 왕권의 마지막 흔적을 제거했다.

Hackers TOEFL Voca TEST DAY 22-24

Choose the synonym of the highlighted word in the sentence.

1. The United States forced Mexico to relinquish large amounts of territory after victory in the Mexican War.

(A) cede (B) indemnify (C) request (D) negotiate

2. The protestors were completely devoted to furthering their cause.

(A) devised (B) declined (C) dedicated (D) degraded

3. Smallpox remained a dreaded, often fatal illness until very recently.

(A) mortal (B) latent (C) acute (D) artful

4. Several weeks of heavy rainfall retarded progress on the road construction project.

(A) hastened (B) delayed (C) reschedule (D) altered

5. Later writers took the tales and made them their own, sometimes adding or subtracting parts, but the core remained the same.

(A) conducting (B) deducting (C) obstructing (D) deliberating

6. Egyptian peasants did not need the elaborate irrigation system of their neighbors to the north, for it required little labor to tap into the pools.

(A) steadfast (B) skillful (C) deliberate (D) intricate

7. Her heavy reliance on her notes made her speech appear unrehearsed.

(A) deterioration (B) criterion (C) dependence (D) custom

8. Deciduous plants protect themselves by dropping their leaves and resting dormant until growth starts again in spring.

(A) inactive (B) sharp (C) resolved (D) profitable

9. Friends and family alike were surprised by Charles's precipitous decision to move a new city.

(A) mundane (B) categorical (C) declarative (D) sudden

10. The defense attorney considered the witness insignificant and did not cross-examine.

(A) senseless (B) trivial (C) intelligent (D) pragmatic

정답 p.419

Trail of Tears

미국의 개척민들과 원주민들과의 관계에 있어서 포카혼타스의 일화가 초기 동화적 측면을 상징한다면, 그 반대편에 참혹한 현실의 상징으로서 Trail of Tears(눈물의 길)가 존재한다. 초기 백인이 소수파이던 시절에 유지되었던 원주민과의 우호관계는 백인의 수적인 팽창과 영국으로부터의 독립, 서부개척 등과 맞물리며 결국 인디언들이 그들의 땅에서 이방인의 신세로 전락하는 것으로 마감한다. 1820년대 미연방정부는 동남부 인디언들에 대한 이주정책을 본격적으로 추진하며 원주민들을 위협하기 시작했다. 이에 대한 원주민들의 반응은 크게 세 종류였는데, 크리크, 체로키 그리고 세미놀 이렇게 대표적인 세 종족이 각각 그 예이다. 우선 크리크 족은 강압을 이기지 못하고 자진하여 백인들의 뜻대로 오클라호마로 떠나게 되는데, 이 지역은 인디언 보류지 즉 Reservation이라 불리게 된다. 이 명칭은 이전에 인디언이 조약에 의해 토지를 버려두고 돌보지 않았을 때 그 일부를 그들 자신들이 사용하기 위해서 보류(reserving)하면서 생긴 이름이다. 비교적 국가체계를 갖추고 있던 체로키 족은 미국의 주정부 및 연방정부에 대해 그들의 권리승인을 위한 소송을 제기하는 방식을 선택하였는데, 이를 묵살하는 백인들에 밀려 결국은 크리크 족과 같이 오클라호마로 향하게 된다. 이러한 이주의 험로 위에서 수 많은 원주민들이 죽고 병들어 갔는데, 이주지에 도착했을 때 전체 14,000명 중 겨우 1,200명만이 살아 남았다고 한다. 이 죽음의 길을 그들은 'Trail of Tears(눈물의 길)' 라 불렀던 것이다. 또 다른 부족인 세미놀 족은 무력을 통한 백인과의 항전을 택했지만, 7년간의 싸움 끝에 수많은 인원이 사상을 당하고 결국 살아남은 자들은 앞서의 두 부족과 같은 처지가 될 수 밖에 없었다. 이 과정에 대한 기록들은 참혹하기 이를 데 없는 것이니, 이는 인디언들에게는 아픔의 역사요, 백인들에게는 지울 수 없는 죄의식의 역사로 영원히 남게 되었다.

DAY 25

Hackers TOEFL **Vocabulary**

Hackers Voca

www.goHackers.com

1 **aim****	v.	1. **attempt, aspire, point** intend	목표하다
[éim]		The soccer team **aimed** to make it to the semifinals.	
	n.	2. **goal, objective, target**	목적
		The prime minister began a three-day visit to India with the **aim** of enlisting support for peace efforts.	
2 **allocate***	v.	**designate, earmark; distribute, allot**	책정하다 ; 배분하다
[ǽləkèit] collect		The plan **allocates** $24 million to City Opera for a new theater downtown.	
3 **attributed to**	phr.	**explained by**	~에서 기인한, ~로 설명되는
		Tidal patterns have been **attributed to** the gravity of the moon.	
4 **authenticate**	v.	**verify, substantiate, prove**	입증하다, 증명하다
[ɔːθéntəkèit]		Computer security programs are used to **authenticate** a user's identification.	
5 **confuse***	v.	**disturb, disconcert, confound**	혼란시키다
[kənfjúːz] clarify		The new operating system **confused** Tom at first.	

aim	그 축구 팀은 준결승까지 가는 것을 목표로 했다.
	그 국무총리는 평화 활동을 위한 지지를 얻을 목적을 가지고 3일간의 인도 방문을 시작했다.
allocate	그 계획은 시내에 새로운 극장을 짓는 데 City Opera에 2천4백만 달러를 책정한다.
attributed to	조수간만의 형태는 달의 중력으로 설명되어져 왔다.
authenticate	컴퓨터 보안 프로그램들은 사용자의 신분을 증명하기 위해 이용된다.
confuse	처음에는 그 새로운 작동 시스템이 Tom을 혼란스럽게 했다.

6 **debate**** | n. **discussion, argument, controversy** dispute | 논쟁

[dibéit]

Debate over immigration policy is not new to the nation's history.

7 **detractor*** | n. **critic** | 험담하는 사람

[ditrǽktər]
advocate

The President's **detractors** expressed their usual skepticism about her policies.

8 **disguise*** | v. **conceal, hide, camouflage, cloak** | 속이다, 감추다

[disgáiz]
unmask

In order to **disguise** their secret hideout, the children placed leafy tree branches all over the roof.

9 **dissent** | v. **differ, disagree** | 의견을 달리하다

[disént]
assent

Scientists **dissent** about the role of instinct in human behavior.

10 **distinguish**** | v. **differentiate, tell apart, separate** | 구별하다

[distíŋgwiʃ]
confound

Its overall design **distinguishes** Chinese architecture from that of Japan.

11 **draw***** | v. **attract, haul, pull** tug, drag | 끌다

[drɔ́ː]

The migration pattern of whales has **drawn** the curiosity of naturalists and researchers.

12 **drawback*** | n. **disadvantage, defect, shortcoming** fault | 결점

[drɔ́ːbæ̀k]

One **drawback** of the book is that it does not contain any English translations.

13 **dye*** | n. **pigment, stain** | 염료, 물감

[dái]

To make red yarn, a crimson **dye** such as cranberry juice or brazilwood is used.

debate	이민 정책에 관한 논쟁이 그 나라의 역사상 처음 있는 일은 아니었다.
detractor	대통령을 험담하는 사람들은 그녀의 정책에 대해 그들이 평소에 갖고 있던 회의적인 입장을 표명했다.
disguise	그들의 비밀 은신처를 숨기기 위해, 아이들은 지붕 전체에 잎이 무성한 나뭇가지를 덮어두었다.
dissent	과학자들은 인간의 행동에 있어 본능의 역할에 대해 의견을 달리한다.
distinguish	그것의 전반적인 디자인이 중국 건축과 일본의 건축을 구별하게 한다.
draw	고래 떼 이동의 형태가 생태학자들과 연구가들의 호기심을 끌었다.
drawback	그 책의 한가지 결점은 영어 번역을 포함하고 있지 않다는 사실이다.
dye	빨간색 방사를 만들기 위해서는 덩굴월귤의 즙이나 브라질 소방목과 같은 진홍색 염료가 사용된다.

14 emit**

[imít]

v. **give off, exhale, release** shed, radiate 발산하다

In the fireplace was a red-hot fire which **emitted** a small amount of smoke.

15 expose**

[ikspóuz]
cover

v. **exhibit, subject, uncover, reveal** 드러내다

Hemingway did not want to **expose** his life to everyone.

16 flawless*

[flɔ́:lis]
imperfect

adj. **perfect, impeccable, faultless** 흠 없는

The Star of India is the world's largest and most **flawless** sapphire.

17 frustrate

[frʌ́streit]

v. **disappoint, thwart** 좌절시키다

The student's poor grades **frustrated** his parents.

18 full*

[fúl]
incomplete

adj. 1. **complete, whole, perfect** 완전한

Court TV broadcasted every minute of the trial for two **full** days.

adj. 2. **thorough, minute, detailed** 상세한

Notes on the debates afford the only **full** record of the proceedings.

19 indicate*

[índəkèit]

v. **suggest, imply, signal** 넌지시 비추다

Recent economic markers **indicate** that the Euro is undervalued.

20 initially

[iníʃəli]

adv. **at first, originally, primarily, in the beginning** 처음에

The board was **initially** surprised about the investigaton.

emit	벽난로에는 약간의 연기를 피워내는 빨갛게 달은 뜨거운 불이 있었다.
expose	Hemingway는 그의 삶이 모든 사람에게 드러나기를 원하지 않았다.
flawless	'Star of India'는 세계에서 가장 크고 완전한 사파이어이다.
frustrate	그 학생의 나쁜 성적이 부모님을 실망시켰다.
full	법정 TV는 이틀에 걸쳐 재판의 매 순간을 방영했다.
	토론에 대한 메모만이 진행 과정을 빠짐없이 기록하고 있다.
indicate	최근의 경제 지표들은 유로화가 평가 절하되고 있음을 암시하고 있다.
initially	그 위원회는 처음에 그 조사에 대해 놀랐다.

21 **innovative**
[ínəvèitiv]

adj. original, **inventive, creative, ingenious** 기발한, 혁신적인

Herbal remedies are an **innovative** approach to medicine.

22 **landslide***
[lǽndslàid]

n. rockfall, **landslip** 산사태

The sudden **landslide** swept into the little village at the base of the mountain and completely buried everything under solid rock.

23 **malady**
[mǽlədi]

n. disease, ailment, **illness** 병

There's no simple cure to the smog-induced **malady**.

24 **minimize***
[mínəmàiz]
increase

v. 1. decrease, reduce, **discount** 줄이다

The environmentalists fought to **minimize** usage of nuclear power.

v. 2. **underestimate** 과소평가하다

Eisenhower **minimized** the importance of racial tensions.

25 **order***
[ɔ́ːrdər]

n. 1. **direction, mandate, command** 명령

Orders are expected to be followed in the military.

confusion

n. 2. peace 질서, 조화

The police are responsible for keeping **order** in society.

26 **prohibit***
[prouhíbit]
permit

v. forbid, **proscribe** 금지하다

In most Muslim countries, women are strictly **prohibited** from wearing revealing clothes or leaving their heads bare.

innovative	한약치료들은 의술의 혁신적인 접근법이었다.
landslide	갑작스런 산사태는 산 아래 있는 작은 마을을 휩쓸어, 단단한 바위 아래로 모든 것을 완전히 묻어 버렸다.
malady	스모그로부터 야기되는 질병에는 간단한 치료책이 없다.
minimize	환경학자들은 핵전력의 사용을 줄이기 위해 투쟁했다.
	Eisenhower는 인종적 대립의 심각성을 과소평가했다.
order	군대에서는 명령을 따르도록 요구된다.
	경찰은 사회 질서를 유지시키는 책임이 있다.
prohibit	대부분의 회교 국가에서 여성들은 노출이 심한 옷을 입거나 머리를 드러내 놓는 것이 엄격하게 금지되어 있다.

27 reduce**

v. **diminish, decrease** curtail, lessen 감소시키다

[ridjúːs]
increase

The poor tobacco crops of 1755 greatly **reduced** the amount of tobacco exports.

28 reveal**

v. **show, unveil, uncover, expose** divulge 드러내다

[rivíːl]
cover, conceal

Merill **revealed** that the company will concentrate on sales of its digital video cameras.

29 shed light on*

phr. **clarify, elucidate** ~을 명백히 하다

obfuscate

New discoveries in cancer research may **shed light on** the mysteries of this deadly disease.

30 sink*

v. **descend, drop to the bottom, submerge** 가라앉다

[síŋk]
rise

The Titanic **sank** into the sea after scraping against an iceberg.

31 size**

n. **dimensions, proportions, volume** magnitude 크기

[sáiz]

Another $1 billion will be invested in coming years to double the amusement park's **size**.

32 slope*

n. **declivity, inclination, slant** 경사

[slóup]
flat

The south **slope** of the Acropolis played a significant role in the religious activity of ancient Athens.

33 subside

v. **abate, die down** 진정되다

[səbsáid]

John's headache gradually began to **subside** after taking some medicine.

34 take place

phr. **occur, happen, befall** 발생하다

The crime **took place** in an area where there were many witnesses.

reduce	1755년에는 담배 수확이 저조해서 담배 수출량이 감소되었다.
reveal	Merill은 회사가 디지털 비디오 카메라 사업에 중점을 둘 것이라고 공표했다.
shed light on	암 연구에서의 새로운 발견은 이 치명적인 질병에 대한 수수께끼들을 명백히 밝혀 줄 것이다.
sink	타이타닉 호는 빙산에 스친 후에 바다 속으로 가라앉았다.
size	그 놀이공원의 크기를 두 배로 늘리기 위해 앞으로 또 다른 10억 달러가 투자될 것이다.
slope	아크로폴리스의 남쪽 사면은 고대 아테네의 종교 활동에 있어 중요한 역할을 했다.
subside	약을 먹은 후 John의 두통이 점차 진정되기 시작했다.
take place	목격자들이 많은 장소에서 범죄가 발생했다.

35 though
[ðóu]

adv. 1. **however, nevertheless, still, yet** 그러나

The actress was nominated for an Oscar. She probably won't win, **though**.

conj. 2. **although** ~이지만, 비록 ~일지라도

Paul admitted to making mistakes, **though** he claims never to have lied.

36 underground
[ʌ̀ndərgráund]

adj. **secret, clandestine, covert** 비밀의

Al-Qaeda is an **underground** terrorist organization.

Quiz

Choose the synonym.

1. confuse	ⓐ camouflage, conceal, cloak, hide
2. disguise	ⓑ forbid, proscribe
3. innovative	ⓒ unveil, uncover, expose
4. reveal	ⓓ disturb, confound, disconcert
5. prohibit	ⓔ inventive, original, creative, ingenious

Answer 1. ⓓ 2. ⓐ 3. ⓔ 4. ⓒ 5. ⓑ

though	그 여배우는 오스카상 후보에 올랐다. 그러나 아마도 상을 받지는 못할 것이다. Paul은 거짓말한 적이 결코 없다고 주장했지만, 실수한 것들은 인정했다.
underground	Al-Qaeda는 비밀스런 테러 조직이다.

DAY 26 Hackers Voca

1 antipathy n. **dislike, disgust, hatred** 반감

[æntípəθi]
attachment

His campaign tactics earned Nixon the **antipathy** of a number of independents.

2 applicable* adj. **capable of being applied, appropriate** 적용 가능한, 적절한

[ǽplikəbl]

Gravitational rules are not **applicable** in space and zero gravity environments.

3 blot out** phr. **cover, hide, screen, veil** 가리다

The dark clouds **blotted out** the sun.

expose

4 bold** adj. **brave, daring, courageous** valiant 대담한

[bóuld]
cowardly

Despite Nancy's **bold** words, there was a cold terror in her eyes.

5 boom** v. **flourish, thrive, prosper** 번성하다

[bú:m]

During the Civil War, the American economy was **booming**.

6 characteristic** adj. 1. **distinctive, special, peculiar** 독특한

[kæ̀riktərístik]
general

The ostrich's **characteristic** size and speed set it apart from other birds.

antipathy	그의 선거 전략으로 인해 Nixon은 많은 무소속자들의 반감을 샀다.
applicable	중력의 법칙은 우주와 무중력 상황에서는 적용이 안 된다.
blot out	먹구름들이 태양을 가렸다.
bold	Nancy는 대담하게 말했음에도 불구하고, 눈에 차가운 공포가 서려 있었다.
boom	남북 전쟁 기간 동안, 미국 경제는 번성하고 있었다.
characteristic	타조의 특징적인 몸집과 속력은 타조를 다른 조류와 구별짓는 요소이다.

n. 2. **feature, element, trait, quality** 특성

Freedom of expression is a fundamental **characteristic** of democracy.

7 clear*

[klíər]
obscure

adj. **lucid, apparent, obvious** 명쾌한

The GNP lawmaker expressed **clear** opposition to the revision of the security law.

8 coarse*

[kɔ́:rs]
courteous

adj. **rough, crude, vulgar** 거친, 천한

Henry's **coarse** language at the dinner party offended many of the guests.

9 concentrate*

[kánsəntrèit]
dissipate

v. 1. **focus** 집중하다

The company will **concentrate** on the domestic market.

v. 2. **center, cluster** 모으다

A quarter of Japan's population is **concentrated** in the city of Tokyo.

10 contemplate*

[kántəmplèit]

v. **consider, ponder, brood** dwell on 심사숙고하다

John accepted a teaching position in Vancouver while he **contemplated** the future.

11 cripple*

[krípl]

v. **maim, disable, ruin** injure, impair 손상시키다

The Trojan virus **crippled** the software company's operations.

12 demanding*

[dimǽndiŋ]
effortless

adj. **difficult, exacting** 힘든, 큰 노력을 요하는

Although her career at the World Health Organization is **demanding**, Heather enjoys the people she works with.

characteristic	표현의 자유는 민주주의의 가장 근본적인 특성이다.
clear	한나라당의 그 국회 의원은 보안법의 개정에 대해 분명한 반대의사를 표시했다.
coarse	만찬회에서의 Henry의 버릇없는 말은 많은 손님들을 화나게 했다.
concentrate	그 회사는 국내 시장에 전력을 기울일 것이다.
	일본 인구의 1/4은 도쿄에 집중되어 있다.
contemplate	John은 미래에 대해 심사숙고하는 동안 벤쿠버에 있는 강사 자리를 받아들였다.
cripple	Trojan 바이러스는 그 소프트웨어 회사의 업무를 마비시켰다.
demanding	비록 세계 보건 기구에서의 그녀의 직업은 힘들었지만 Heather는 함께 일하는 사람들과 즐겁게 지냈다.

13 **deviate** [dí:vièit]

v. **diverge, wander, stray** 벗어나다

Ancient sailors looked at the stars so that they would not **deviate** from their course.

14 **discover*** [diskʌ́vər]

assume

v. ascertain, **determine, find out** 확인하다, 찾아내다

Galileo **discovered** that the concentration of neon is a tenth of its solar value.

15 **discrete**** [diskrí:t]

blended

adj. distinct 구별되는

In Weber's mind, the **discrete** elements were tied together into a coherent totality.

16 **encompass*** [inkʌ́mpəs]

exclude

v. include, **embrace, contain** 포함하다

The company's new strategic plan **encompasses** many different goals and ideals.

17 **entertain** [èntərtéin]

v. **divert, amuse, please** 즐겁게 하다

The audience was **entertained** by various local bands.

18 **far-sighted**** [fá:rsáitid]

adj. wise, **judicious** 현명한

The investor was successful because he was more **far-sighted** than other investors.

19 **fluctuate*** [flʌ́ktʃuèit]

remain

v. change, vary, **vacillate, sway** 변동하다

Because the temperature **fluctuates** so much in Wisconsin, many people carry warm clothes and umbrellas in their cars.

20 **halt*** [hɔ́:lt]

v. stop, **cease, stand still** 멈추다

The traffic guard **halted** Susan and her friends at the crosswalk until the light turned green.

deviate	고대의 선원들은 항로에서 벗어나지 않기 위해 별을 보았다.
discover	Galileo는 네온의 농축 정도가 태양에서 그것의 농축 정도의 10분의 일이라는 사실을 발견했다.
discrete	Weber의 마음 속에서, 구별되는 요소들은 일관된 전체성 안에 묶여졌다.
encompass	그 회사의 새로운 전략적 계획은 여러 가지 다양한 목적과 이상들을 포함하고 있다.
entertain	청중은 다양한 지역 악단 덕에 즐거웠다.
far-sighted	그 투자가는 다른 투자가들보다 장기적인 안목을 가졌기 때문에 성공했다.
fluctuate	Wisconsin 주의 날씨는 매우 변동이 심하기 때문에, 많은 사람들이 따뜻한 옷과 우산을 차에 넣어 다닌다.
halt	교통 순경은 파란 불이 될 때까지 Susan과 그녀의 친구들을 횡단보도에서 정지시켰다.

21 **incessantly**** | adv. constantly, **continuously** | 끊임없이

[insésəntli]
intermittently

Patton had to **incessantly** plead with Congress for equipment for his army.

22 **leading*** | adj. dominant, **chief, foremost, primary** | 우세한, 주된

[lí:diŋ]

The **leading** cause of cancer in the United States is smoking, while the second is skin damage from UV-ray exposure.

23 **modify**** | v. change, alter, adapt vary | 변경하다

[mádəfài]

The lifestyle of the American people is being **modified**.

24 **mutation*** | n. change, **alteration, modification** | 변이, 변화

[mju(:)téiʃən]
fixity

The Centers for Disease Control and Prevention monitors infectious viruses that are likely to undergo **mutation** such as the SARS virus.

25 **obelisk*** | n. obelus, **stone pillar** | 방첨탑, 오벨리스크

[ábəlisk]

The movement to promote the return of the Aksum **Obelisk** from Rome to Ethiopia was a success.

26 **pastime**** | n. entertainment, **diversion, recreation** | 기분 전환

[pǽstàim]

Gambling is an addictive **pastime** that has ruined many people's lives.

27 **rather than*** | phr. instead of | ~대신에

Jinny signed up for the 8 o'clock class **rather than** the 9 o'clock one.

28 **receptacle**** | n. container, vessel, reservoir, **holder** | 그릇, 용기

[riséptəkl]

The cook put the ingredients into a **receptacle**.

incessantly
leading
modify
mutation
obelisk
pastime
rather than
receptacle

Patton은 그의 군대에 장비를 마련해달라고 국회에 끊임없이 청원해야만 했다.
미국에서의 주된 암의 원인은 흡연이며 그 두 번째 원인은 자외선 노출로부터 온 피부 손상이다.
미국인들의 생활방식은 변하고 있다.
질병 관리 통제 센터는 SARS 바이러스와 같이 변이를 일으킬 수 있는 전염성 바이러스들을 관찰한다.
로마로부터 에티오피아로 Aksum 오벨리스크를 귀환시키려는 운동은 성공적이었다.
도박은 많은 이들의 삶을 파괴시켜온 중독성 있는 기분 전환법이다.
Jinny는 9시 수업 대신에 8시 수업에 등록했다.
그 요리사는 용기에 재료들을 넣었다.

29 rely [rilái]

v. **depend** 의지하다

Children **rely** on adults for life's necessities.

30 remote* [rimóut]

adjacent

adj. **secluded, distant, removed** 외딴, 멀리 떨어진

While Watson was smoking, Gertrude would sit in a **remote** corner of the garden.

31 rotten [rátn]

adj. **decayed, decomposed, corrupt** 썩은, 부패한

The cook would not accept diseased cattle, **rotten** flour and wormy corn.

32 rove [rouv]

v. **roam, wander** 배회하다

With no destination in mind, Harry and Sally **roved** about the countryside.

33 shoddy [ʃádi]

adj. **inferior, poor, base** 조악한, (질이) 떨어지는

The professor was upset by the **shoddy** quality of his students' writing.

34 shred [ʃréd]

v. **tear apart, cut, tatter** (갈기갈기) 찢다

The documents were **shredded** to protect the client's confidentiality.

35 simply [símpli]

adv. **only, just, merely** 단지

Meteorologists thought that the radar image was **simply** a tropical storm, but it was actually a large hurricane.

36 span* [spǽn]

n. 1. **duration, period, length** 기간

The paper briefly summarizes the vast problems during the war's eleven year **span**.

rely	아이들은 생활 필수품을 어른에게 의지한다.
remote	Watson이 담배를 피우고 있는 동안, Gertrude는 정원의 멀리 떨어진 구석에 앉아 있고는 했다.
rotten	그 요리사는 병든 소나 썩은 밀가루, 벌레 먹은 옥수수는 받아들이지 않을 것이다.
rove	어느 방향으로 갈지 아무런 생각 없이 Harry와 Sally는 시골길을 헤맸다.
shoddy	그 교수님은 제자들의 조악한 글쓰기 실력에 화가 났다.
shred	그 문서들은 고객의 비밀 유지를 위해 찢겨졌다.
simply	기상학자들은 그 레이더 상이 단지 열대성 태풍일 것이라 생각했으나 사실 그것은 거대한 규모의 허리케인이었다.
span	그 신문은 11년간의 전쟁 기간에 생긴 방대한 문제들을 요약하고 있다.

v. **2. extend across, cover, cross** ~에 걸치다, 이르다

The Golden Gate Bridge **spans** over 1.2 miles in length and is nearly 800 feet high.

37 **stun***

[stʌ́n]

v. **amaze, astound, daze** astonish, stupefy 놀라게 하다

Many readers were **stunned** by the tragic end of the novel.

38 **tranquil**

[trǽŋkwil]

adj. **peaceful, calm, placid** serene, restful 평온한, 차분한

The father and son spent a **tranquil** day fishing on the lake.

Quiz

Choose the synonym.

1. antipathy	ⓐ astound, daze, stupefy
2. deviate	ⓑ distant, removed, secluded
3. remote	ⓒ roam, wander
4. stun	ⓓ dislike, disgust, hatred
5. rove	ⓔ diverge, wander, stray

Answer 1. ⓓ 2. ⓔ 3. ⓑ 4. ⓐ 5. ⓒ

span 금문교는 길이 1.2마일에 높이 800피트에 이른다.
stun 많은 독자들이 그 소설의 비극적인 결말에 놀랐다.
tranquil 그 아버지와 아들은 호수에서 낚시를 하며 평온한 하루를 보냈다.

DAY 27 Hackers Voca

1 **assistance**** | n. **aid, help, support** | 원조

[əsístəns]

Due to the **assistance** of volunteers, many victims of the hurricane were rescued.

2 **avoid**** | v. **eschew, shun, prevent** evade, escape | ~을 피하다

[əvɔ́id]
face, confront

Brian wants to **avoid** saying anything that would change his relationship.

3 **best-suited** | adj. **most appropriate** | 가장 적절한

[béstsú:tid]
unsuitable

The council was assigned the task of finding the **best-suited** person for the job.

4 **bridle** | n. **harness, halter** | 굴레

[bráidl]

Annie got her favorite horse Bandito ready for the trail ride, and put on the **bridle** before lifting the saddle into place.

5 **classify**** | v. **categorize, arrange, assort** | 분류하다

[klǽsəfài]
disorder

It is the job of scientists to **classify** all living organisms into groups that can be applied universally.

6 **collectively*** | adv. **together, unitedly** | 공동으로

[kəléktivli]
singly

The two families **collectively** decided to pitch in money for a new lake cabin to share.

assistance	자원봉사자들의 도움으로 많은 수의 허리케인 피해자들이 구조되었다.
avoid	Brian은 관계를 변화시킬 수 있는 어떤 것도 말하기를 피하고 싶어한다.
best-suited	위원회는 그 일에 가장 적합한 사람을 찾는 업무를 부여받았다.
bridle	Annie는 그녀의 애마인 Bandito가 오솔길을 달릴 수 있도록 준비시키면서, 안장을 올려 놓기 전에 말굴레를 씌웠다.
classify	살아 있는 모든 유기체를 여러 그룹으로 분류하여 보편적으로 적용될 수 있게끔 하는 것은 과학자들의 일이다.
collectively	그 두 가족들은 새로 지은 호숫가 근처의 오두막을 공유하기 위해 돈을 모을 것을 공동으로 결정했다.

7 **comparable****

[kάmpərəbl]
disparate

adj. similar, **like, analogous** uniform 유사한

There were clay figures that are **comparable** to those found in China.

8 **cultivator***

[kΛ́ltəvèitər]

n. farmer, **grower** 경작자

The mushroom **cultivator** decided to grow mushrooms at home.

9 **designated***

[dézignéitid]
unspecified

adj. specified, **assigned, appointed** 지정된

Unlike the National League, the American Baseball League selects a **designated** hitter to bat for the pitcher.

10 **detrimental***

[dètrəméntəl]
beneficial

adj. harmful, **damaging, prejudicial** 해로운, 불리한

Drinking and smoking have been proven to be **detrimental** to health.

11 **differentiate**

[dìfərénʃièit]

v. distinguish 구별하다

Only one expert could **differentiate** between the two artists' work.

12 **display****

[displéi]
hide

v. show, **exhibit** 보여 주다

Mr. Wheeler **displayed** the farm to Claude as if he were a stranger.

13 **emissary***

[émisèri]

n. messenger, **carrier, agent** 사절

The pharmaceutical companies are sending **emissaries** to tell doctors about the safeness of the low-cost generic drugs.

14 **enact****

[inǽkt]
repeal

v. pass, adopt, make into law legislate 제정하다

The movement pressured Congress to **enact** the 1964 Civil Rights Act.

comparable	중국에서 발견되는 것과 유사한 점토 인물상들이 있었다.
cultivator	버섯 재배업자가 집에서 버섯을 기르기로 결정했다.
designated	내셔널 리그와 달리 아메리칸 리그에서는 투수 대신에 타석에 나서는 지명타자를 지정한다.
detrimental	음주와 흡연은 건강에 해로운 것으로 증명되어 왔다.
differentiate	오직 한 사람의 전문가만이 두 예술가의 작품을 구별할 수 있었다.
display	Wheeler씨는 Claude가 마치 낯선 사람인 양 그에게 농장을 보여 주었다.
emissary	그 제약회사는 의사들에게 저가의 상표 등록이 안된 약들의 안전성에 대해 말하도록 사절을 보내고 있다.
enact	그 운동은 국회가 1964년 민권법을 제정하도록 압력을 가했다.

15 evenly**

adv. **equally, uniformly** 고르게, 일관되게

[í:vənli]

The general employees are split almost **evenly** down the gender line, with 46% women and 54% men.

16 expedience*

n. **advantage, convenience** 편의

[ikspí:diəns]
inexpedience

What Park has done is to sacrifice long-term effectiveness for short-term **expedience**.

17 genuinely

adv. **actually, truly, really** 정말로

[dʒénjuinli]

Unlike most politicians, Smith was **genuinely** concerned about the poor.

18 immediately

adv. **straight away, instantly, directly, promptly** 즉시, 당장

[imí:diətli]

A cocktail reception was held **immediately** after the ceremony.

19 important*

adj. **significant, critical, consequential** remarkable 중요한

[impɔ́:rtənt]
trivial

One of Cro-Magnon's truly **important** discoveries was how to make a fire.

20 inconceivable

adj. **unimaginable, unthinkable** 상상도 못할

[ìnkənsí:vəbl]

Exploring outer space was once considered **inconceivable**.

21 in progress

phr. **unfinished, ongoing** 진행 중인

Policemen came to the bank as a robbery was **in progress**.

22 it followed that ~

phr. **it was logical that ~** 그 결과로서 ~가 되었다

After the criminal confessed, **it followed that** he would testify.

evenly	일반 직원들은 여자가 46%, 남자가 54%로 거의 고르게 성별에 있어서 나누어져 있다.
expedience	Park가 한 것은 단기간의 편의를 위해 장기간의 효율성을 희생한 것이다.
genuinely	다른 대다수의 정치인들과는 달리, Smith씨는 정말로 가난한 사람들을 걱정했다.
immediately	식이 끝나고 나서 즉시 칵테일 파티가 열렸다.
important	크로마뇽인이 발견한 것 중 정말 중요한 한가지는 불을 만드는 방법이었다.
inconceivable	우주 공간을 탐사하는 것은 한때 상상도 못할 일로 여겨졌었다.
in progress	강도 행각이 진행 중일 때 경찰들이 은행에 도착했다.
it followed that~	그 범인은 자백을 하고 난 뒤, 증언을 하게 될 것이다.

23 **keep in touch** — phr. **communicate** 연락을 유지하다

be out of contact

A person who travels all the time must work hard to **keep in touch** with family and friends by writing letters, telephoning, and e-mailing.

24 **massacre*** — n. **slaughter, annihilation, murder** 대량학살

[mǽsəkər]

The **massacre** of political opponents was followed by confiscation of their property.

25 **mean** — v. 1. **signify, imply, express** ~을 의미하다

[mí:n]

Harold's remark **meant** that he would resign from the presidency soon.

honorable

adj. 2. **contemptible, despicable, ignoble** 비열한

Janie told her other friends Marcus was **mean**.

26 **mute*** — adj. **quiet, silent, dumb** speechless 무언의

[mjú:t]
articulate

Deaf and **mute** people are often able to communicate through sign language.

27 **participate**** — v. **share, partake** 함께 하다

[pɑ:rtísəpèit]

After the young man won the lottery, he wanted his family and friends to **participate** in his good fortune.

28 **pit*** — v. 1. **set into opposition** (사람 · 기술 등을) ~와 대항시키다

[pít]

The war **pitted** brother against brother.

n. 2. **hole, cavity** 구멍

Drake dug a **pit** and buried the rubbish in it.

---

keep in touch — 늘 여행을 하는 사람은 편지를 쓰거나, 전화를 하거나 이메일을 씀으로써 가족이나 친구들과 연락이 지속되도록 애써야 한다.
massacre — 정치적 반대파들의 대량학살이 있은 후에 그들의 재산 몰수가 이어졌다.
mean — Harold의 말은 그가 곧 회장에서 물러날 것임을 의미했다.
Janie는 다른 친구들에게 Marcus가 비열하다고 말했다.
mute — 청각과 언어장애인들은 종종 수화를 통해 의사소통을 할 수 있다.
participate — 그 젊은이는 복권에 당첨된 후에, 자기 가족들과 친구들이 모두 자기 재산을 함께 나누길 바랬다.
pit — 그 전쟁은 형제끼리 싸우게 했다.
Drake는 구멍을 파서 쓰레기를 그 안에 묻었다.

29 raise* | v. **boost, lift, elevate** hoist 올리다

[réiz]
lower

Any organizing of workers to **raise** wages was an illegal act in 1806.

30 rare** | adj. **scarce, unusual, infrequent** extraordinary, exceptional 드문

[rɛ́ər]
usual

Huck and Jim shared a friendship that was **rare** between a servant and his master.

31 respectively | adv. **particularly, individually** 각각

[rispéktivli]

Third quarter earnings in machine tool exports and vehicle imports are 51.4 million and 29.6 million, **respectively**.

32 seemingly* | adv. **apparently** 보기에

[síːmiŋli]

The country road was dusty and **seemingly** endless.

33 sporadically | adv. **occasionally, at intervals, infrequently** 때때로, 간헐적으로

[spərǽdikəli]

Taking his medication **sporadically**, John did not recover from his illness.

34 stringent* | adj. **strict, austere, tight** 엄한

[stríndʒənt]
lenient

The Spartan's way of rearing their children was very **stringent**.

35 superficial** | adj. **external, outward** 외면의

[sùːpərfíʃəl]
in-depth

John had a **superficial** appearance of being happy, but he was actually quite upset.

36 timid** | adj. **shy** 소심한

[tímid]
audacious

Sarah overcame her **timid** nature to become an influential woman during the Civil War.

raise	임금을 인상하기 위한 노동자들의 어떠한 조직도 1806년에는 불법 행위였다.
rare	Huck과 Jim은 하인과 주인 사이에 흔치 않은 우정을 나누었다.
respectively	세 번째 분기의 기계 장비 수출과 자동차 수입에서의 소득은 각각 5140만 달러와 2960만 달러이다.
seemingly	그 시골길은 먼지투성이었고 끝이 없어 보였다.
sporadically	약물치료를 때때로 받았지만, John은 병이 낫지 않았다.
stringent	스파르타 인들의 아이들을 교육하는 방법은 매우 엄하다.
superficial	John은 겉으로는 행복한 모습이었지만, 사실 그는 매우 화가 나 있었다.
timid	Sarah는 그녀의 소심한 성격을 극복하고 남북 전쟁 기간 동안 영향력 있는 여성이 되었다.

37 transport — v. carry, **convey, transfer, bear** — 운송하다

[trænspɔ́ːrt]

Tankers were used to **transport** oil from the Middle East.

38 unavoidable — adj. inevitable, inescapable, **ineluctable** — 불가피한

[ʌ̀nəvɔ́idəbl]

The accident was **unavoidable**, so the driver was not charged with a crime.

39 uniform** — adj. consistent, even, **invariable** unchangeable — 일관성 있는

[júːnəfɔ̀ːrm]
various

Foster formed a **uniform** system of discipline that catered to the revolutionary beliefs.

40 unsubstantial — adj. **unreal, dreamlike, ethereal** — 비현실적인

[ʌ̀nsəbstǽnʃəl]
concrete

Most scientists doubt extra sensory perception because it is **unsubstantial** and cannot be tested objectively.

Quiz

Choose the synonym.

1. avoid — ⓐ specified, assigned, appointed
2. designated — ⓑ slaughter, annihilation, murder
3. massacre — ⓒ eschew, shun, prevent
4. participate — ⓓ share, partake
5. superficial — ⓔ external, outward

Answer 1. ⓒ 2. ⓐ 3. ⓑ 4. ⓓ 5. ⓔ

transport — 유조선은 중동에서 석유를 운송하기 위해 사용되었다.
unavoidable — 그 사고는 불가피했었기 때문에 운전사에게 죄가 씌워지지 않았다.
uniform — Foster는 혁명적 믿음에 영합한 일관성 있는 훈련 체계를 만들었다.
unsubstantial — 대부분의 과학자들은 초감각적 인지가 비현실적이고 객관적으로 증명될 수 없기 때문에 이에 대해 의혹을 품는다.

Hackers TOEFL Voca TEST DAY 25-27

Choose the synonym of the highlighted word in the sentence.

1. The professor was very disappointed at the shoddy quality of his students' writing.
(A) livid (B) marvelous (C) poor (D) ridiculous

2. High rent and taxation are two of the drawbacks of living in major metropolitan areas.
(A) disadvantages (B) issues (C) dilemma (D) benefits

3. Photography enabled astronomers to measure the quantity of light emitted by stars.
(A) disregarded (B) diverged (C) altered (D) radiated

4. The general received word from an enemy emissary that his counterpart wanted to negotiate a ceasefire.
(A) order (B) engagemen (C) fortune (D) messenger

5. The temperature in August held steady, fluctuating only a few degrees.
(A) changing (B) undulating (C) mending (D) transferring

6. Defense industries boomed in the 1940's, and millions of men entered the armed forces.
(A) blotted out (B) crippled (C) flourished (D) extracted

7. The middle class is composed of a number of discrete segments.
(A) ruthless (B) distinct (C) dissatisfied (D) daring

8. Several board members dissented when the board decided to layoff workers.
(A) corroborated (B) disagreed (C) discerned (D) proposed

9. The responsibilities of Ted's job encompassed both writing and researching for a university sociology department.
(A) transpired (B) proposed (C) included (D) halted

10. The students were always trying to avoid the mean bully because he would always pick on them.
(A) contemptible (B) wily (C) mute (D) timid

정답 p.419

TAKE A BREAK

Honesty 정직(正直)

No legacy is so rich as honesty.

정직만큼 훌륭한 유산은 없다. - Shakespeare 셰익스피어

The great consolation in life is to say what one thinks.

인생에서 가장 큰 위안은 자신의 생각을 말하는 것이다. - Voltaire 볼테르

Honesty is the first chapter of the book of wisdom.

정직은 지혜라는 책의 제1장(第一章)이다. - T. Jefferson T. 제퍼슨

To make your children capable of honesty is the beginningof education.

교육의 시작은 자녀가 정직할 수 있도록 키우는 것이다. - J. Ruskin J. 러스킨

We must make the world honest before we can honestly say to our children that honesty is the best policy.

우리의 자녀들에게 '정직이 최상의 방책이다' 라고 정직하게 말하려면 먼저 우리는 세상을 정직하게 만들어야 한다. - Bernard Shaw 버나드 쇼

28 Hackers Voca

1 **aptly***	adv. **appropriately, suitably, relevantly**	적절히
[ǽptli]	The region was **aptly** named the 'Iron Triangle' because steel rails connected the cities.	
2 **attract****	v. **appeal, draw, charm, allure**	(마음을) 끌다
[ətrǽkt] repel	Many students were **attracted** to their teacher.	
3 **beverage***	n. **drink**	음료수
[bévəridʒ]	The dormitory bans students from drinking any kind of alcoholic **beverages**.	
4 **blunt***	adj. **dull, obtuse**	무딘
[blʌ́nt] sharp	All the cook could find was a **blunt** knife.	
5 **bustling***	adj. **busy, active, energetic**	부산한
[bʌ́sliŋ] stagnant	The sidewalks and shops are **bustling** with people.	
6 **control***	v. **manage, dominate, govern** rule	지배하다
[kəntróul]	The governor's policies were a means of **controlling** the economy of the colonies.	

aptly	그 지역은 철로가 도시들을 연결했기 때문에 'Iron Triangle'이라고 적절히 이름 지어졌다.
attract	많은 학생들이 그들의 선생님에게 마음이 끌렸다.
beverage	그 기숙사는 학생들이 어떤 종류의 알코올 음료도 마시지 못하도록 한다.
blunt	그 요리사가 찾을 수 있었던 것은 무딘 칼뿐이었다.
bustling	인도와 가게들은 사람들로 붐비고 있다.
control	그 총독의 정책들은 식민지의 경제를 통제하는 수단이었다.

7 **controversy*****

[kántrəvə̀:rsi]

n. dispute, debate, disagreement, **argument** 논쟁

Brown had been abroad during most of the **controversy**.

8 **dichotomy***

[daikátəmi]

n. division 양분, 이분

Jane planned the concert to break the **dichotomy** of pure and popular art.

9 **disruption**

[disrʌ́pʃən]

n. interruption 중단

Protesters caused a major **disruption** at the conference.

10 **enthusiasm***

[inθú:ziæzəm]

apathy

n. eagerness, **zeal, passion** fervor, ardor 열정

Warren showed no marked **enthusiasm** for doing his chores.

11 **episode**

[épisòud]

n. event, occurrence, **incident, happening** 하나의 사건

Watergate was an embarrassing **episode** in the history of the U.S.

12 **equivalent**

[ikwívələnt]

adj. equal, **even, commensurate** 동등한

Although much international aid goes to help the masses, an **equivalent** amount is lost due to corruption and inefficiency.

13 **evoke***

[ivóuk]

v. draw, arouse, **elicit, educe** 일깨우다, 자아내다

The sudden accident has **evoked** social disorder.

14 **exotic****

[igzátik]

adj. unusual, **strange, weird** odd 기묘한, 못 보던

People can go to zoos to see rare and **exotic** animals on exhibition.

controversy	Brown은 그 논쟁이 있던 대부분의 기간 동안 해외에 나가 있었다.
dichotomy	Jane은 순수예술과 대중예술의 구분을 없애기 위해 그 콘서트를 계획했다.
disruption	시위자들이 그 회의를 전면 중단시켰다.
enthusiasm	Warren은 자신의 허드렛일에 대한 어떤 두드러진 열정도 보이지 않았다.
episode	워터게이트는 미국 역사상에서 곤혹스러운 사건이었다.
equivalent	국제 협력기금 중 많은 부분이 민중을 돕는 데 쓰이지만, 이와 비슷한 양이 부패와 비효율성으로 인해 상실된다.
evoke	그 갑작스런 사고가 사회적 분란을 일으켰다.
exotic	사람들은 전시된 진귀하고 이상한 동물들을 보기 위해 동물원에 갈 수 있다.

15 flair* n. **talent, aptitude, knack** 재주, 재능

[fléər]

Bach developed a reputation because of his **flair** for composing music.

16 flight n. **escape, breakout, getaway** 탈출

[flait]

Although the driver did not participate in the robbery, he was put in jail for aiding in the robber's **flight** from police.

17 formidable* adj. **dreadful, threatening, fearful** frightful 무서운

[fɔ́:rmidəbl]
comforting

The prospect of an outbreak of disease was so **formidable** that the authorities ordered victims to be quarantined.

18 frugal adj. **economical, thrifty** 절약하는

[frú:gəl]
wasteful

Patrick has been very **frugal** with money since losing his job.

19 fuel* v. **encourage, stimulate** 지지하다, 자극하다

[fjú(:)əl]

The government's attempt to stop the protest only **fuelled** the demonstrators' resentment.

20 game* n. **wild animals (hunted for food or sport)** 사냥감

[géim]

French cookbooks often have a section for recipes involving **game** meat such as wild boars, rabbits and deer.

21 hand in hand* phr. **together** 협력하여, 동반하여

The boys should solve the problem **hand in hand**.

22 intermittent adj. **sporadic, periodic, occasional** 간헐적인

[ìntərmítənt]

Intermittent service caused Michael to change cell phone carriers.

flair	Bach는 음악을 작곡하는 그의 재주 덕분에 명성을 쌓았다.
flight	그 운전기사는 강도질에 참여하지는 않았지만, 강도가 경찰한테서 도망치는 것을 도운 죄로 감옥에 갇혔다.
formidable	질병이 발생할 것이라는 전망은 너무 두려운 것이어서 당국은 피해자들을 격리하라고 명했다.
frugal	Patrick은 실직한 이후로 돈을 매우 아껴 써왔다.
fuel	정부의 시위를 멈추려는 시도는 단지 시위대의 분노만 자극했을 뿐이었다.
game	프랑스의 요리책들은 종종 멧돼지, 토끼, 사슴과 같은 사냥감 고기와 관련된 조리법에 해당하는 난을 포함하고 있다.
hand in hand	소년들은 그 문제를 협력해서 풀어야 한다.
intermittent	Michael은 때때로 중단되는 서비스 때문에 통신회사를 바꾸기로 했다.

23 **intersect** v. cross, **intercross** 교차하다, 가로지르다

[ìntərsékt]

Traffic lights are built where city streets **intersect**.

24 **make sense** phr. be logical 이치에 맞다

nonsense

The roommates drew up a cleaning schedule that **made sense**, so that no one person always had to wash the dishes.

25 **movement*** n. **drive, crusade** (정치 · 사회적) 운동

[mú:vmənt]

The anti-slavery **movement** became a formidable force in northern politics.

26 **pass through*** phr. penetrate 꿰뚫다

It is easier for a camel to **pass through** the eye of a needle than it is for a rich man to enter the Kingdom of God.

27 **precise**** adj. accurate, exact, **definite, strict** correct 정확한

[prisáis]

loose

The investigators will look into the **precise** details of the accident.

28 **publish*** v. declare, **announce, proclaim** 발표하다

[pʌ́bliʃ]

New procedures to reduce the time it takes to resolve disputes between telecoms companies were **published** by the communications agency.

29 **readily*** adv. easily, **effortlessly; willingly, without reluctance** 쉽게 ; 기꺼이

[rédəli]

Claire can't **readily** make a decision about her future.

30 **record**** n. document, evidence 기록

[rékərd]

Fossil **records** do not give any information on the origin of insects.

intersect	신호등은 도로가 교차하는 곳에 세워진다.
make sense	그 동거인들은 합리적인 청소 계획을 짜서 한 사람이 항상 설거지를 하는 일이 없도록 했다.
movement	노예 제도 폐지 운동은 북부 정치의 강력한 힘이 되었다.
pass through	낙타가 바늘 구멍을 뚫고 들어가는 것이 부자가 천국에 들어가는 것 보다 더 쉽다.
precise	조사관들은 그 사건의 정확한 세부 사항들을 살펴볼 것이다.
publish	전자통신통신 업체들간의 분쟁을 신속히 해결할 수 있는 새로운 절차가 통신부에 의해 발표되었다.
readily	Claire는 그녀의 장래 희망에 대해 쉽게 결정하지 못한다.
record	화석 기록은 곤충의 기원에 대한 어떠한 정보도 제공하지 않는다.

31 relieve | v. **reduce, ease, alleviate, assuage** 경감하다

[rilíːv]
aggravate

Drugs are used to **relieve** pain.

32 settle down | phr. **calm down, pacify** 진정시키다

The doctors were finally able to **settle down** the violent patient with a sedative.

33 shun | v. **elude, avoid, evade** escape 피하다

[ʃʌ́n]
accept, adopt

Due to the scandal, Regina has been **shunned** by her neighbors.

34 spectacular* | adj. **splendid, impressive, sensational** 멋진, 장엄한

[spektǽkjulər]

Each room had a **spectacular** view of the ocean.

35 steady | adj. **stable, solid, firm, fixed** 안정된

[stédi]
unsteady

After years of unemployment, Ben finally found a **steady** job.

36 store | v. **reserve, keep, save** 따로 떼어두다, 비축하다

[stɔ́ːr]

Students are provided a locker to **store** their books and personal belongings.

37 stupid | adj. **fatuous, dull, silly** senseless 어리석은

[stjúːpid]
intelligent, smart

It was **stupid** of Travis to lose his temper.

38 success | n. **achievement, accomplishment, triumph** 성공, 달성

[səksés]

Bill Gates has achieved great **success** in the computer business.

relieve	마취제는 고통을 완화하는 데 사용된다.
settle down	의사들은 마침내 그 격렬한 환자를 진정제로 진정시켰다.
shun	그 소문 때문에 Regina는 이웃들에게 외면당해 왔다.
spectacular	각각의 방에서 바다의 인상적인 모습을 볼 수 있었다.
steady	몇 년 동안의 실업 뒤에, Ben은 마침내 안정된 직장을 찾았다.
store	학생들은 책과 소지품을 보관할 수 있도록 락커를 제공받았다.
stupid	Travis가 화를 낸 것은 어리석었다.
success	Bill Gates는 컴퓨터 사업에서 크게 성공했다.

39 tend*

[tend]

v. **look after, care for, foster** 돌보다

Alice asked her neighbors to **tend** her garden when she went away on vacation.

40 wattle*

[wátl]

n. **stick** 가는 막대기

Mr. Johnson used **wattle** and cedar logs to make a fence around his home.

41 wrath*

[rǽθ]

tolerance

n. **anger, fury, resentment** indignation 분노

Zeus looked back at Hera with **wrath** in his eyes.

Quiz

Choose the synonym.

1. bustling	ⓐ aptitude, talent, knack
2. flair	ⓑ splendid, sensational, impressive
3. spectacular	ⓒ teeming, busy, crowded
4. tend	ⓓ equal, even, commensurate
5. equivalent	ⓔ look after, care for, foster

Answer 1. ⓒ 2. ⓐ 3. ⓑ 4. ⓔ 5. ⓓ

tend Alice는 그녀가 휴가를 간 동안 이웃들에게 자신의 정원을 돌봐줄 것을 부탁했다.
wattle Johnson씨는 그의 집 주변에 울타리를 만들기 위해 가는 막대기와 삼나무 목재를 이용했다.
wrath Zeus는 분노에 찬 눈으로 Hera를 돌아보았다.

DAY 29 | Hackers TOEFL **Vocabulary**

Hackers Voca

www.goHackers.com

1 **acid**	adj. **biting, acrid**	신랄한
[ǽsid] agreeable	Mary and Fran's voices sounded a little **acid**, as if they had been quarrelling.	
2 **amass***	v. **accumulate, collect, gather**	모으다
[əmǽs] distribute	The clever speculator **amassed** a fortune shortly before the market collapsed.	
3 **breakthrough***	n. **advance, progress**	약진, 큰 발전
[bréikθrùː] loggerhead	The discovery of a cure for AIDS would be a huge **breakthrough** for modern science.	
4 **cause****	v. **trigger, result in, bring about, produce, elicit**	야기시키다, 초래하다
[kɔ́ːz]	Cooling or net evaporation **causes** surface water to become dense enough to sink.	
5 **certain***	adj. **specific, definite**	일정한
[sə́ːrtn] indefinite	Every element in the periodic table has a **certain** arrangement of molecules.	
6 **component*****	n. **element, ingredient, constituent**	성분
[kəmpóunənt]	Nitrogen is one of the major **components** of the air humans breathe.	

acid	Mary와 Fran의 목소리는 마치 그들이 말다툼을 했었던 듯 다소 날카롭게 들렸다.
amass	영리한 투기꾼은 주식 시장이 폭락하기 직전에 재산을 모아 놓았다.
breakthrough	AIDS에 대한 치료법의 발견은 현대 과학의 약진이 될 것이다.
cause	냉각이나 순수 증발량은 물의 표면이 밀도가 높아져 가라앉을 정도가 되게 한다.
certain	원소주기표에 있는 모든 원소들은 분자의 일정한 배열을 갖고 있다.
component	질소는 인간이 숨을 쉬는 공기를 구성하는 주요 성분 중 하나이다.

7 conditional*

adj. **dependent, contingent** 조건부의, ~여하에 달린

[kəndíʃənəl]
unrestricted

The sale of the company was **conditional** upon the approval of the share holders.

8 confront*

v. **face, affront, encounter** meet 직면하다

[kənfrʌ́nt]
avoid

With great courage, the soldiers **confronted** the enemy.

9 consequence*

n. **ramification, result, effect, aftermath** outcome 결과

[kánsikwèns]

The economic depression in the U.S. was unique in its **consequences**.

10 crack*

v. **break, snap, slit** split 쪼개다, 깨뜨리다

[krǽk]

The workers **cracked** the stone by using hammers.

11 crude*

adj. **rough, raw, unrefined** 천연 그대로의, 가공하지 않은

[krú:d]
refined

Since 1869 US **crude** oil prices adjusted for inflation have averaged $18.63 per barrel.

12 drought*

n. **a prolonged lack of moisture, aridity** 가뭄

[dráut]

The country has depended on international food aid in recent years after a series of **droughts**.

13 effort*

n. **attempt, endeavor, exertion** striving 노력

[éfərt]
ease

The **effort** to increase wages brought about hundreds of strikes in the 1850s.

14 emerge**

v. **appear, loom, spring up, come out** 나타나다

[imə́:rdʒ]
disappear

On the ninth ballot Polk **emerged** as the first nominee.

conditional	그 회사의 매각은 주주들의 승인 여하에 달려 있었다.
confront	대단한 용기를 가지고 군인들은 적을 마주했다.
consequence	미국의 경제 불황은 그 결과에 있어서 독특했다.
crack	노동자들은 망치를 사용해 그 돌을 깨뜨렸다.
crude	1869년 이후 물가 상승을 감안한 미국의 원유 가격은 배럴당 18.63달러였다.
drought	그 나라는 연이어 발생한 가뭄으로 인해 최근 몇 년간 국제적 식량 원조에 의존해 왔다.
effort	임금을 인상하려는 노력은 1850년대에 수백 건의 파업을 가져왔다.
emerge	9번째 비밀투표에서 Polk는 첫 번째 지명자로 나타났다.

15 endurance**

[indjúərəns]

n. stamina, **patience;** durability, **lastingness** 인내 ; 내구력

The TV show 'Survivor' tests contestants' mental prowess and physical **endurance**.

16 euphoria

[ju (:) fɔ́:riə]

n. extreme happiness, **ecstasy, rapture** 행복감

The **euphoria** Noah felt as his daughter was born was greater than any joy he had previously experienced.

17 exacerbate*

[igzǽsərbèit]

mitigate

v. intensify, worsen, **aggravate** 더욱 심하게 하다

Salty water **exacerbated** the pain of the cut on Timothy's foot.

18 explain*

[ikspléin]

confuse

v. account for, **elucidate, explicate** clarify 설명하다

Lincoln **explained** in his speech why the war was going on.

19 finish**

[fíniʃ]

v. complete, terminate, **end** conclude 끝내다

As soon as Jody **finished** training her replacement, she resigned her position.

20 hollow*

[hálou]

adj. empty 텅 빈

The trees look very solid, but in fact they are **hollow**.

21 lash**

[lǽʃ]

v. tie, **bind** 묶다, 매다

The soldier **lashed** a letter to a military carrier pigeon for delivery.

22 leisurely

[lí:ʒərli]

adj. relaxed, slow, **easy, unhurried** 느긋한

The couple took a **leisurely** walk in the park on Sunday.

endurance	TV 쇼 'Survivor'은 경쟁자들의 정신적인 용맹성과 육체적 인내를 시험한다.
euphoria	Noah가 그의 딸이 태어났을 때 느꼈던 행복감은 그가 이전에 경험했던 어떤 즐거움보다 컸다.
exacerbate	소금기가 있는 물은 Timothy의 발에 난 베인 상처를 심화시켰다.
explain	Lincoln은 그의 연설에서 왜 전쟁이 계속되고 있는지를 설명했다.
finish	Jody는 그녀의 후임자 교육을 끝내자마자, 직장을 그만두었다.
hollow	그 나무들은 매우 단단해 보이지만, 사실상 텅 비어 있다.
lash	그 군인은 편지를 보내기 위해 군대의 전송용 비둘기에게 편지를 묶었다.
leisurely	그 부부는 일요일에 공원에서 느긋한 산책을 했다.

23 manageable*
[mǽnidʒəbl]
uncontrollable

adj. **controllable, affordable** 관리할 수 있는, 감당할 수 있는

Due to its small and **manageable** space, Delaware is a great place to develop an international free-trade city.

24 note*
[nóut]
disrepute

n. **eminence, repute, celebrity** 명성

The Three Tenors are singers of international **note**.

25 periphery**
[pərífəri]
center

n. **edge, border, fringe** margin, verge 주변부

The outer **periphery** of the hurricane is generally made up of rain bands.

26 practical**
[prǽktikəl]
academic

adj. **pragmatic, effective, practicable** useful 실용적인

The blacksmith would make a blade so thin that it had no **practical** purpose.

27 prerequisite***
[prì(:)rékwizit]

n. **necessary condition, qualification, requirement** 필요조건

Basic science is a **prerequisite** for the advanced class.

28 relatively*
[rélətivli]

adv. **comparatively, by comparison** 비교적으로

Women like flowers **relatively** more than men do.

29 rudimentary**
[rù:dəméntəri]

adj. **basic, primitive, undeveloped, elementary** 기본적인, 기초적인

Joy has only a **rudimentary** understanding of art.

30 selected
[siléktəd]

adj. **chosen** 선택된

The student panel was composed of randomly **selected** seniors.

manageable	그 작고 통제하기 쉬운 공간 때문에, Delaware는 국제적인 자유 무역 도시를 개발하기에 좋은 장소이다.
note	그 세 명의 테너는 국제적 명성을 지닌 성악가들이다.
periphery	허리케인의 바깥 주변부는 일반적으로 비의 띠들로 구성된다.
practical	그 대장장이는 칼날을 너무나 얇게 만들곤 했기 때문에 그것은 실용적인 용도로 쓰일 수 없었다.
prerequisite	기초 과학은 고급 과정 수강을 위한 선수과목이다.
relatively	여성들은 남성들보다 비교적 꽃을 더 많이 좋아한다.
rudimentary	Joy는 예술에 대해 기초적인 이해만을 하고 있다.
selected	그 학생 심사위원단은 무작위로 선택된 상급생들로 구성되었다.

31 shed*

[ʃéd]

v. 1. **discard, cast off, molt** 탈피하다

A snake will **shed** its skin several times in its lifetime.

v. 2. **radiate** (빛 등을) 비추다

The lamp **shed** its light into every corner of the room.

32 spotty

[spáti]

adj. **intermittent, uneven, irregular** 고르지 않은

Those traveling by rail should know that train service can be **spotty** and should have a back-up plan.

33 spread

[spréd]

v. **extend, stretch, reach** 퍼지다, ~에 이르다

The computer virus **spread** through attached files in email.

34 staunch

[stɔ́ːntʃ]

adj. **strong, firm, faithful** stalwart, loyal 확고한, 충실한

The politician thanked his campaign workers for their **staunch** support.

35 stress*

[strés]

n. 1. **emphasis, accent** 강조

Hippocrates laid more **stress** upon the expected outcome of a disease than upon its diagnosis.

v. 2. **emphasize** 강조하다

All his life, Michael's parents had **stressed** the importance of education.

36 stunted*

[stʌ́ntid]

adj. **hindered** (성장이) 멎은

John suffered from polio during his childhood, and is now permanently **stunted** in his ability to walk normally.

---

shed	뱀은 살아있는 동안 여러 번 껍질을 벗을 것이다. 그 램프는 방의 구석구석에 빛을 비추었다.
spotty	기차로 여행하는 이들은 열차 운행이 고르지 않을 수 있다는 것을 알고 있어야 하며 비상시에 이를 대체할 수 있는 수단을 가지고 있어야 한다.
spread	컴퓨터 바이러스는 이메일에 첨부된 파일을 통해 퍼진다.
staunch	그 정치인들은 그의 선거운동원들의 확고한 지지에 감사를 표했다.
stress	히포크라테스는 진단보다는 질병의 예측되는 결과에 더 강조점을 두었다. Michael의 일생 동안 그의 부모님들은 교육의 중요성을 강조해왔다.
stunted	John은 어린 시절 소아마비로 고통받았으며, 지금은 정상적으로 걸을 수 있는 능력이 영구히 정지되었다.

37 trespass**

[tréspæs]

v. **invade, encroach, infringe** intrude 침해하다

Tom and Sally were **trespassing** on privately owned land.

38 trumpet

[trʌ́mpit]

v. **proclaim, announce, broadcast, declare** 공표하다

The United Nations **trumpeted** the eradication of polio as the first step to a healthier world.

39 via

[viːə]

prep. **by way of, by, through** ~을 경유하여

Online journals allow people to keep up with advances **via** the Internet.

Quiz

Choose the synonym.

1. amass	ⓐ elucidate, explicate, clarify
2. explain	ⓑ necessary condition, qualification
3. prerequisite	ⓒ collect, gather, accumulate
4. trespass	ⓓ encroach, infringe, intrude
5. trumpet	ⓔ proclaim, announce, broadcast

Answer 1. ⓒ 2. ⓐ 3. ⓑ 4. ⓓ 5. ⓔ

trespass	Tom과 Sally는 사유지를 침범하고 있었다.
trumpet	UN은 보다 건강한 세계로의 첫걸음으로 소아마비의 근절을 공표했다.
via	온라인 간행물은 사람들이 인터넷을 통해서 기사들의 정보를 얻을 수 있게 해준다.

DAY Hackers TOEFL Vocabulary

30 Hackers Voca

www.goHackers.com

1 accumulate**

v. collect, compile, build up, **pile up** amass 모으다

[əkjúːmjəlèit]
dissipate

Trump **accumulated** much of his wealth in real estate.

2 antithesis*

n. opposite, **contrary, converse** 정반대

[æntíθisis]

Julia Roberts is the **antithesis** of this actress's style.

3 astute

adj. clever, **shrewd, canny, sharp** 기민한

[əstjúːt]

Daniel's **astute** and well-researched presentation impressed his classmates.

4 be up to*

phr. rest with ~에 달려 있다

The success of Mary's novel **is up to** the readers.

5 being

n. creature 생물

[bíːiŋ]

Scientists know little about the **beings** living at the depths of the ocean.

6 bring about

phr. cause, **produce, make happen** 초래하다

High inflation can **bring about** crippling economic problems.

accumulate	Trump는 재산의 상당량을 부동산을 통해 모았다.
antithesis	Julia Roberts는 이 여배우의 스타일과 정반대이다.
astute	Daniel의 예리하고 잘 구성된 발표는 그의 동료들에게 깊은 인상을 주었다.
be up to	Mary의 소설의 성공은 독자들에게 달려 있다.
being	과학자들은 심해 생물들에 대해서 거의 알지 못한다.
bring about	높은 인플레이션은 심각한 경제적 문제들을 초래한다.

7 cache [kǽʃ]

n. **hidden place** 은닉처

Occupation soldiers failed to find the guerillas' weapons **cache**.

8 celebratory* [séləbrətɔ̀ːri]

adj. **congratulatory, honoring** 축하의, 축하하는

Hank's boss sent him a **celebratory** message about winning the award.

9 close* [klóus]

inattentive

adj. 1. **careful, minute, rigorous** 면밀한

The babysitter kept a **close** eye on the kids at the park.

[klóuz]

open up

v. 2. **restrict, shut** 차단하다

The Mission theater was **closed** down by the government for putting on anarchist performances.

10 cognitive* [kɑ́gnitiv]

adj. **mental, thinking, perceiving** 정신적인, 인식의

Prolonged alcohol abuse has been shown to lead to permanent **cognitive** damage.

11 create*** [kriéit]

v. **invent, devise, produce** 만들어내다

Thomas Edison **created** the first incandescent light.

12 destroy** [distrɔ́i]

establish

v. **ruin, demolish, smash** maim, spoil 파괴하다, 망치다

On their route, the army **destroyed** anything and everything.

13 diminutive* [dimínjutiv]

adj. **small** 작은

Despite his **diminutive** stature, Diego Maradona was one of the greatest ever soccer players.

cache	점령군은 게릴라의 무기 은닉처를 찾지 못했다.
celebratory	Hank의 상사는 그에게 상을 수상한 것에 대해 축하하는 메시지를 보냈다.
close	그 유모는 공원에 있는 아이에게 주의를 놓치지 않았다.
	Mission 극장은 무정부주의적인 공연을 상연했다는 이유로 정부에 의해 폐쇄되었다.
cognitive	장기적인 알코올 남용은 영구적인 정신적 손상을 가져온다는 것이 증명되어 왔다.
create	토마스 에디슨이 최초의 백열등을 발명했다.
destroy	그 군대는 그들이 가는 행로에 있는 어떤 것이든 모조리 파괴했다.
diminutive	작은 신장에도 불구하고, Diego Maradona는 지금까지의 가장 위대한 축구 선수 중 한 명이다.

14 **endangered** adj. **jeopardized, imperiled** 멸종위기에 처한, 위험에 처한

[indéindʒərd]

Stricter laws are needed to protect **endangered** species.

15 **formative*** adj. **shaping, developmental** 형성되는, 발달의

[fɔ́:rmətiv]

Talks with the Tokyo exchange were still at a **formative** stage.

16 **founder*** v. **fail** 실패하다

[fáundər]

Ted's plans for college **foundered** when he didn't receive the scholarship he had anticipated.

17 **glean**** v. **gather, collect, reap** 모으다

[gli:n]

The students **gleaned** a lot of information about sociology by listening to the professor's speech.

18 **govern***** v. 1. **dominate, rule, reign** 지배하다

[gʌ́vərn]

The entire activity of the organization is **governed** by definite laws.

neglect

v. 2. **regulate, monitor, control** 통제하다

All of the community felt that Mayor Walter Gray **governed** with a firm but loving hand.

19 **indigenous*** adj. **native, aboriginal, inherited** 토착의

[indídʒənəs]

The government regulatory agency rejected environmental complaints by **indigenous** groups.

20 **integrate**** v. **unify, synthesize, consolidate** 통합하다

[íntəgrèit]
disintegrate

Kirin and Takeda would first **integrate** their food operations by establishing a joint venture next spring.

endangered	멸종 위기에 처한 동물들을 보호하기 위해 좀 더 엄격한 법이 요구된다.
formative	동경 주식 거래소와의 협상은 아직 초기 단계에 있었다.
founder	Ted의 대학에 대한 계획은 그가 예상했던 장학금을 받지 못해 실패하였다.
glean	그 학생들은 그 교수의 강연을 경청하여 사회학에 대해 많은 정보를 얻었다.
govern	그 조직체의 전체 활동은 명백한 법에 의해 지배된다.
	모든 지역 단체들은 Walter Gray 시장이 엄하지만 애정 어린 자세를 지니고 통제한다는 것을 느꼈다.
indigenous	그 정부 규제 위원회는 토착 단체들에 의한 환경 관련 불만 사항들을 받아들이지 않았다.
integrate	Kirin과 Takeda는 내년 봄에 합작 벤처 회사를 설립함으로써 그들의 식품 사업을 먼저 통합할 것이다.

21 **interval*** n. **space, distance, period** (시간 · 거리의) 간격

[íntərvəl]

After an **interval** of studying medicine, Harrison decided on a military career.

22 **largely** adv. **generally, mostly** 대개

[lá:rdʒli]
hardly

The citizens of Korea are **largely** of Korean descent, although there are a few other ethnic groups that call the country home.

23 **magnificent*** adj. **gorgeous, beautiful, splendid** 굉장히 멋진

[mægnífiəsənt]
modest

Malaysia has sun drenched beaches, enchanting islands, and **magnificent** mountains.

24 **overshadow*** v. **dim, eclipse** 가리다, 어둡게하다

[òuvərʃǽdou]
illuminate

The mighty oak tree **overshadowed** the tiny house.

25 **particular**** adj. **specialized, specific, special** individual, especial 특별한

[pərtíkjulər]
general

Galileo tried to disprove one **particular** statement of Aristotle's.

26 **ramification*** n. **consequence, effect, result** 결과

[ræ̀məfəkéiʃən]

The environmental **ramifications** of the road-building program had not been considered fully.

27 **rather*** adv. **somewhat, fairly** 약간, 다소

[rǽðər]

The result of Lucas' plan would be **rather** interesting.

28 **realm*** n. **area, sphere, field, domain** province 범위, 영역

[rélm]

Dr. Wright used the telescope to discover many undiscovered **realms** of space.

interval	의학을 잠시 공부한 후에, Harrison은 군인의 길을 가기로 결정했다.
largely	한국 국민들은 대부분 한민족이지만 한국을 고향으로 여기는 몇몇의 다른 민족도 있다.
magnificent	Malaysia에는 태양에 흠뻑 젖은 해안, 매력적인 섬, 아름다운 산들이 있다.
overshadow	그 거대한 참나무는 작은 집을 가렸다.
particular	Galileo는 Aristotle의 한 가지 특정 진술이 사실이 아니라는 것을 보여 주려고 애썼다.
ramification	도로 건설 계획이 환경에 미칠 영향이 충분히 검토되지 않았다.
rather	Lucas의 계획의 결과는 다소 흥미로울 것이다.
realm	Wright박사는 우주의 많은 발견되지 않은 영역들을 발견하기 위해 망원경을 사용했다.

29 rivalry [ráivəlri]

n. **competition, contention, contest** 경쟁

The intense **rivalry** between the two teams made the game exciting.

30 silent* [sáilənt]

talkative

adj. **speechless, dumb, mute** taciturn 말이 없는

Charlie Chaplin was a **silent** movie star.

31 situate** [sítʃuèit]

v. **place, locate** 위치시키다

The VIPs **situated** themselves in the front row, blocking everyone else's view.

32 sphere** [sfiər]

n. **area, field** 분야

The 20th century has seen many developments in the **sphere** of transportation.

33 stealthily** [stélθili]

adv. **silently, sneakily, secretly** 은밀히, 몰래

The robber **stealthily** crawled into the warehouse.

34 superb [su(:)pə́:rb]

adj. **outstanding, excellent, magnificent** 뛰어난, 훌륭한

Fans cheered wildly at the athlete's **superb** performance.

35 swell [swél]

v. **enlarge, expand, grow larger, increase** (크기 · 수량 등이) 증가하다

California's population **swelled** during the Gold Rush.

36 tender* [téndər]

rough

adj. 1. **soft, delicate, mild** 부드러운

Julia kept cooking the meat until it was **tender**.

rivaly	두 팀 사이의 팽팽한 긴장감 때문에 게임이 더 흥미진진했다.
silent	Charlie Chaplin은 무성 영화 스타였다.
situate	VIP 입장객들은 앞줄에 앉아서 다른 사람들 모두의 시야를 가렸다.
sphere	20세기에는 교통 분야에서의 많은 발전이 있었다.
stealthily	그 도둑은 몰래 창고로 기어들어왔다.
superb	팬들은 그 선수의 뛰어난 솜씨에 격렬하게 환호했다.
swell	캘리포니아의 인구는 골드러시 때 증가했다.
tender	Julia는 고기가 부드러워질 때까지 계속해서 요리를 했다.

n. 2. **money, payment** 변상금

Legal **tender** is any type of money that must be accepted by law in payment of a debt.

37 **velocity****

[vəlάsəti]

n. **speed, rapidity, celerity** pace 속도, 신속함

Hurricanes are classified according to wind **velocity**, the strongest, with winds above 155 mph, being Category 5.

38 **wild***

[wáild]

cultivated

adj. 1. **uncultivated, untamed, undomesticated** 야생의

There are many **wild** beasts in the jungle.

relaxed

adj. 2. **unruly, uncontrollable, frantic** violent 난폭한

Victor was almost run down by a **wild** motorist.

Quiz

Choose the synonym.

1. astute — ⓐ consequence, effect, result
2. endangered — ⓑ gather, collect, reap
3. glean — ⓒ enlarge, expand, increase
4. ramification — ⓓ jeopardized, imperiled
5. swell — ⓔ clever, shrewd, canny

Answer 1. ⓔ 2. ⓓ 3. ⓑ 4. ⓐ 5. ⓒ

tender
velocity
wild

법적 변상금은 빚을 지불하는 데 있어서 법으로 받아들여져야만 하는 모든 종류의 돈이다.
허리케인은 풍속에 따라 구분되는데, 전체 5종류 중 가장 강력한 것은 시속 155마일 이상이다.
밀림에는 사나운 짐승들이 많다.
Victor는 난폭한 운전자에 의해 하마터면 치일 뻔했다.

Hackers TOEFL Voca TEST DAY 28-30

Choose the synonym of the highlighted word in the sentence.

1. We may attempt to predict weather but we cannot control it.

(A) elicit (B) separate (C) govern (D) accumulate

2. Jane's frugal ways often led to arguments with her friends, who accused her of being a miser.

(A) thrifty (B) salubrious (C) cautious (D) peremptory

3. Revenues collected by exporting countries swelled as a result of the worldwide increase in oil prices.

(A) functioned (B) increased (C) relinquished (D) altered

4. A diamond is known for its sparkling quality and its reputation as a girl's best friend.

(A) trespassing (B) glittering (C) sweeping (D) comforting

5. The movement to establish a college began during the American Revolutionary War.

(A) avenging (B) distinction (C) drive (D) constitutive

6. The major components of musical sound include tone, timbre, and texture.

(A) debates (B) periods (C) divisions (D) elements

7. The columnist's astute and witty observations on the issues of the day brought him a loyal readership.

(A) shrewd (B) considerable (C) measurable (D) vacuous

8. After being stuck on the mountain for a few days, the victim could see the diminutive forms of a rescue team approaching.

(A) tender (B) vigilant (C) rapid (D) small

9. Pollution in the atmosphere exacerbates the highlightedhouse effect.

(A) influence (B) provoke (C) terminates (D) intensifies

10. The prime minister faced the wrath of voters due to the country's poor economy.

(A) restitution (B) fury (C) jealousy (D) generosity

정답 p.419

TAKE A BREAK

해커스보카 스터디중 : 단어는 곧 돈이다.

D A Y **31**

Hackers TOEFL **Vocabulary**

Hackers Voca

www.goHackers.com

1 **accompany***	v.	**escort, companion, attend**	동반하다
[əkʌ́mpəni]		Jinny volunteered to **accompany** her mother.	
leave			
2 **adverse***	adj.	**negative, not favorable, opposed**	적대적인
[ædvə́:rs]		President Bush's speech received an **adverse** reaction from most European leaders.	
favorable			
3 **appeal***	n.	1. **entreaty, request, petition**	탄원, 청원
[əpí:l]		An **appeal** to a higher court resulted in a victory for labor unions.	
	n.	2. **attraction, charm, fascination**	매력
		Medical quackery has a powerful **appeal** even to the well-educated individuals.	
4 **arouse****	v.	**stimulate, awaken, provoke, incite**	자극하다, 유발시키다
[əráuz]		The strange sight **aroused** Watson's curiosity.	
calm			
5 **boundary***	n.	**dividing line, border, limit**	경계(선)
[báundəri]		Slaves were purchased from beyond the **boundaries** of the empire.	

accompany	Jinny는 자진하여 그녀의 어머니와 동행했다.
adverse	Bush 대통령의 연설은 대부분의 유럽 지도자들로부터 적대적인 반응을 얻었다.
appeal	상급 법원으로의 항소가 노동조합에 승리를 가져다 주었다.
	비과학적 의술은 상당한 교육을 받은 사람들에게조차도 굉장한 매력을 지니고 있다.
arouse	그 이상한 광경이 Watson의 호기심을 유발했다.
boundary	노예들은 그 제국의 경계선 밖에서 매입되었다.

6 **bury***

[béri]
disclose

v. **cover, hide, conceal** veil 가리다

Helen **buried** her face in her hands.

7 **collective***

[kəléktiv]

adj. **accumulated, assembled** 집합된, 축적된

By using our **collective** power as voters and consumers, we can reduce pollution.

8 **confine****

[kənfáin]

v. **limit, cramp, restrict** 제한하다

Charles, a very tall man, felt **confined** in his friend's compact car.

9 **cumbersome****

[kʌ́mbərsəm]

adj. **burdensome, awkward, bulky** clumsy 성가신, 다루기 힘든

Although the machine looks **cumbersome**, it is actually easy to use.

10 **dispensable**

[dispénsəbl]

adj. **unnecessary, needless, nonessential** 없어도 되는

The editor removed information he considered **dispensable** from the article.

11 **distribution**

[dìstrəbjú:ʃən]

n. **dispersion, apportionment, allocation, allotment** 분배

Food **distribution** efforts prevented a massive hunger crisis in Afghanistan.

12 **eat**

[i:t]

v. **consume, devour, ingest, take in** 먹다

The koala bear can only **eat** one species of plant.

13 **entirely**

[intáiərli]

adv. **wholly, totally, thoroughly, utterly** 완전히

The membership of the committee was composed **entirely** of former business executives.

bury	Helen은 손에 그녀의 얼굴을 파묻었다.
collective	투표자와 소비자로서의 우리의 집합된 힘을 이용함으로써, 우리는 오염을 줄일 수 있다.
confine	매우 키가 큰 Charles가 친구의 소형 자동차를 타니 갇힌 느낌이 들었다.
cumbersome	그 기계는 다루기 힘들어 보이지만, 사실은 사용하기 쉽다.
dispensable	그 편집장은 기사에서 없어도 된다고 생각되는 정보를 삭제하였다.
distribution	식량 분배 노력들이 아프가니스탄의 대규모 기아 사태를 막았다.
eat	코알라는 한가지 종류의 식물만을 먹을 수 있다.
entirely	위원회의 구성원들은 모두 회사 경영진 출신들이었다.

14 **equal****

[íːkwəl]
disparate

adj. **equivalent, tantamount** 동등한

Congress passed an order declaring that black and white troops were **equal**.

15 **evaluate**

[ivǽljuèit]

v. **judge, assess, gauge, appraise** 평가하다

Judges use several criteria to **evaluate** Olympic gymnasts' performances.

16 **false***

[fɔ́ːls]
veracious

adj. **erroneous, wrong, incorrect** 잘못된

John had also heard **false** rumors about young Harrison's character.

17 **focal point***

phr. **central area, focus** 중심(지)

Abkhazia, a separatist region of Georgia, has been a **focal point** of tensions between the Caucasus country and Russia.

18 **gallant***

[gǽlənt]
coward

adj. **brave, valiant, daring** valorous 용감한

Although his opponent was clearly stronger, the boxer made a **gallant** effort to win the match.

19 **hence***

[héns]

adv. **consequently, therefore, thus** 그러므로

The eggs were freshly laid, and **hence** satisfactory to Cosmo's epicurean tastes.

20 **integral****

[íntəgrəl]
unessential

adj. **essential, crucial, indispensable** 필수적인

With its syncopations, ragtime played an **integral** part in the jazz legacy.

21 **lay down**

phr. **establish, ordain** (규칙 · 원칙 등을) 정하다

The teacher **laid down** the rules of her classroom on the first day of school.

---

equal	국회는 흑인과 백인 병력이 동등함을 선언하는 명령을 통과시켰다.
evaluate	심판관들은 올림픽 체조 선수들의 연기를 평가하기 위해 여러가지 평가 기준들을 사용한다.
false	John 역시 어린 Harrison의 성격에 관한 잘못된 소문들을 들었다.
focal point	Georgia로부터 독립을 요구하고 있는 Abkhazia 지역은 러시아와 코카서스 간 긴장의 중심지이다.
gallant	상대편이 분명히 더 강함에도 불구하고, 그 권투 선수는 경기에 이기기 위해 용감하게 노력을 다했다.
hence	그 달걀은 금방 나온 것이었으므로 Cosmo의 미식가적 식성에 만족스러웠다.
integral	당김음과 더불어, 래그타임은 재즈 유산에서 필수적인 역할을 했다.
lay down	그 교사는 개학 첫날에 그녀의 학급의 규칙을 정했다.

22 launch* — v. **begin, initiate, commence** — 착수하다

[lɔ́:ntʃ]

The government is **launching** a major forestry campaign.

23 magnify** — v. **amplify, intensify, enlarge, increase** — 확대하다, 증대하다

[mǽgnəfài]
belittle

Microscopes are used to **magnify** objects that are not visible to the naked eye.

24 match* — v. **equal, peer, mate** — 필적하다

[mǽtʃ]

The Australian stock market was unable to **match** China's.

25 more or less — phr. **fairly, approximately, roughly** — 어느 정도, 다소

conclusively

Gretchen decided to go to bed once she was **more or less** prepared for the exam.

26 nature** — n. **tendency, characteristic, attribute, character** — 특징, 성향

[néitʃər]

It is in the inherent **nature** of dogs to want to please their owners.

27 operative — adj. **effective, efficient, effectual** — 효과적인

[ápərətiv]
ineffective

The telephone banking service was no longer **operative**.

28 pragmatic — adj. **practical** — 실용적인

[prægmǽtik]
unrealistic

Very few politicians take a **pragmatic** approach to politics; they usually follow party ideologies.

29 proliferate** — v. **multiply, increase in number** — 증식하다

[prəlífərèit]
decrease

Mosquitoes **proliferate** faster and bite more as the air becomes warmer.

launch	정부는 중요한 삼림 관리 캠페인을 시작하고 있다.
magnify	현미경은 육안으로는 보이지 않는 물체를 확대하는 데 사용된다.
match	호주 주식 시장은 중국의 그것에 필적할 수 없었다.
more or less	Gretchen은 어느 정도 시험 준비를 하고 나면 잠을 자기로 했다.
nature	개가 그들의 주인에게 사랑받고 싶어하는 것은 개들의 타고난 특성이다.
operative	텔레뱅킹 서비스는 더 이상 효과적이지 않다.
pragmatic	정치학에 대해 실용적인 접근을 하는 정치인들은 거의 없다. 그들은 대개 정당의 사상들을 따른다.
proliferate	모기들은 대기가 따뜻해짐에 따라 더 빨리 증식하고 더 많이 문다.

30 **proven*** adj. **established, verified** 증명된

[prú:vən]

The new employee was a man of **proven** ability.

31 **provoke*** v. **incite, irritate, vex** enrage 자극하다, 화나게 하다

[prəvóuk]
relax

Betty's rude attitude **provoked** Sam's anger.

32 **register*** v. 1. **sign up, enroll** 등록하다, 기록하다

[rédʒistər]

A student who **registers** for twelve credit hours is classified as a full-time student.

n. 2. **list, catalogue** 목록

Guests write their names in the hotel **register**.

33 **respectable** adj. **estimable, honorable, reputable** 존경할만한

[rispéktəbl]
disreputable

Webster is an eminently **respectable** lawyer.

34 **rig*** v. **equip, furnish** 장비를 갖추다

[ríg]

Jude **rigged** up a simple shower at the back of the cabin.

35 **sterile*** adj. **barren, unproductive, fruitless** 불모의

[stéril]
fertile, fecund

The loss of the rain forests led to droughts, floods, and **sterile** soil.

36 **sufficient**** adj. **enough, adequate, ample** 충분한

[səfíʃənt]
deficient

The government can only prosecute if there is **sufficient** evidence.

---

proven	그 새로운 직원은 능력이 증명된 사람이었다.
provoke	Betty의 무례한 태도가 Sam의 화를 돋구었다.
register	12학점을 등록한 학생은 전일제 학생으로 분류된다.
	손님들은 호텔 숙박부에 그들의 이름을 쓴다.
respectable	Webster는 매우 존경할만한 변호사이다.
rig	Jude는 그 오두막의 뒤에 간단한 샤워 장비를 갖추었다.
sterile	우림의 손실은 가뭄, 홍수, 그리고 황폐한 토양을 가져왔다.
sufficient	정부는 충분한 증거가 있을 때에만 기소할 수 있다.

37 transparent* | adj. **clear, obvious, lucid, limpid** 명백한

[trænspέərənt]
opaque

The conglomerate makes its financial records as **transparent** as possible.

38 uneasy** | adj. **apprehensive, unstable, disturbed, ill at ease** 불안한

[ʌní:zi]

The Chilean people were **uneasy** when General Pinochet took power following a bloody coup.

39 unpretentious | adj. **simple, humble, plain** 수수한

[ʌ̀npriténʃəs]

The Johnson's home was classically decorated and **unpretentious**.

Quiz

Choose the synonym.

1. cumbersome ⓐ simple, humble, plain
2. confine ⓑ clear, lucid, limpid
3. sterile ⓒ barren, unproductive, fruitless
4. transparent ⓓ awkward, burdensome, clumsy
5. unpretentious ⓔ limit, cramp, restrict

Answer 1. ⓓ 2. ⓔ 3. ⓒ 4. ⓑ 5. ⓐ

transparent 대기업은 재정 기록을 최대한 투명하게 만든다.
uneasy 칠레 국민들은 Pinochet 장군이 유혈 쿠데타 이후에 권력을 잡았을 때 불안해 했다.
unpretentious Johnson가의 집은 고전적으로 장식되어 있었고 수수했다.

DAY 32 Hackers TOEFL **Vocabulary**

Hackers Voca

www.goHackers.com

1 **appreciably*** | adv. **significantly, noticeably, considerably** | 뚜렷하게, 상당히

[əpríːʃiəbli]
inappreciably

The temperature dropped **appreciably** this morning.

2 **assess**** | v. **evaluate, estimate, judge** appraise | 평가하다

[əsés]

With the help of her counselors, Helen began to **assess** her life.

3 **banish**** | v. **expel, exile, deport, oust** | 추방하다

[bǽniʃ]
admit

Sue's father was **banished** from the family because of his alcoholism.

4 **choice*** | n. **option, alternative** | 선택권, 대안

[tʃɔ́is]

The new restaurant offers a variety of main course **choices**, including dishes of Mediterranean origin.

5 **comparatively*** | adv. **relatively** | 비교적, 꽤

[kəmpǽrətivli]
precisely

The outbreak of SARS was a **comparatively** harmless development, unlike the AIDS epidemic.

6 **consume*** | v. **expend, use up, exhaust** | 소비(소모)하다

[kənsúːm]
produce

The people next door **consume** a lot more than they earn.

appreciably	기온이 오늘 아침 상당히 떨어졌다.
assess	그녀의 카운슬러들의 도움으로 Helen은 그녀의 삶을 평가하기 시작했다.
banish	Sue의 아버지는 알코올 중독으로 가족으로부터 쫓겨났다.
choice	새 레스토랑은 지중해산 요리들을 포함하여 다채로운 주요리의 선택권을 제공한다.
comparatively	SARS의 발병은 AIDS의 전염과는 달리 비교적 피해가 없었다.
consume	옆집 사람들은 그들이 버는 것보다 훨씬 많이 소비한다.

7 **excavate**** v. **dig out, unearth, disinter, quarry** 발굴하다

[ékskəvèit]
cover

In search of ancient ruins, an archaeology team **excavated** possible sites on the island of Patras.

8 **exclude*** v. **expel, leave out** 배제하다

[iksklú:d]
admit

The new tax law **excludes** families whose incomes fall within the poverty range.

9 **exert**** v. **apply, exercise, employ, wield** (힘 · 능력 등을) 발휘하다

[igzə́:rt]

Andre Agassi won the match without even seeming to **exert** himself.

10 **extraordinary*** adj. **exceptional, unusual, remarkable** uncommon 비범한

[ikstrɔ́:rdənèri]
normal

Grant had an **extraordinary** ability to understand others.

11 **forage*** v. **search, rummage, hunt** 찾아다니다

[fɔ́(:)ridʒ]

Steve was surprised to find a raccoon **foraging** in his garbage can.

12 **fragile** adj. **easily broken, breakable; delicate, weak** 깨지기 쉬운 ; 연약한

[frǽdʒəl]

Newspaper was added to the **fragile** package to prevent items from breaking.

13 **have nothing to do with** phr. **be not related to** ~와 관계가 없다

It was once believed that smoking **had nothing to do with** the likelihood of cancer.

14 **interpret*** v. **construe, explain, explicate** elucidate 설명하다, 해석하다

[intə́:rprit]
misconstrue

Roosevelt's later political activities have been variously **interpreted**.

excavate	고대 유적을 찾는 중에 한 고고학 연구팀이 Patras섬에서 그럴듯한 유적지를 발굴했다.
exclude	그 새로운 세법은 수입이 빈곤층에 속하는 가계를 제외시킨다.
exert	Andre Agassi는 힘을 발휘하는 것으로조차 보이지 않았는데도 그 시합에서 이겼다.
extraordinary	Grant는 다른 사람들을 이해하는 데 있어서 비상한 능력을 가졌다.
forage	Steve는 너구리가 그의 쓰레기통에서 먹이를 찾고 있는 것을 보고 놀랐다.
fragile	내용물 손상을 방지하기 위해 그 깨지기 쉬운 소포에 신문들을 넣었다.
have nothing to do with	한때 흡연이 암 발생 가능성과는 아무런 관계가 없다고 여겨졌었다.
interpret	Roosevelt의 후기 정치 활동들은 다양하게 설명되었다.

15 lavish*

[lǽviʃ]
scant

v. 1. **expend, waste, squander** 낭비하다

Dog lovers will **lavish** time, effort, and huge sums of money on their pets.

humble

adj. 2. **deluxe, luxurious, splendid** 사치스런

The hotel had extremely **lavish** suites.

16 lucrative**

[lú:krətiv]
unproductive

adj. **gainful, profitable, advantageous, fruitful** 이익이 되는

Barbara was offered a **lucrative** three-year contract with the Walt Disney animation crew.

17 mainly*

[méinli]

adv. **generally, largely, chiefly, primarily** 주로

Jacqueline doesn't go out much, **mainly** because she has her hands full raising three boisterous children.

18 manifest*

[mǽnəfèst]
implicit

adj. 1. **obvious, definite, clear, evident** 명백한

It is **manifest** that Paolo does not know what it is to be an artist.

v. 2. **demonstrate evidence, reveal, show** 증명하다

Heart disease **manifests** itself with a variety of symptoms, the most common being chest pain and shortness of breath.

19 material*

[mətí(:)əriəl]
ethereal

adj. **physical, bodily, corporeal, tangible** 물질적인

In the Bible, Jesus tells a rich man that he cannot enter the Kingdom of Heaven without giving up his **material** possessions.

20 meticulously**

[mətíkjələsli]
indiscreetly

adv. **carefully** 주의 깊게

The project needs to be **meticulously** planned since the team only has four weeks to complete it.

lavish	개 애호가들은 그들의 애완동물들에게 시간, 노력, 상당한 돈을 쓸 것이다.
	그 호텔에는 굉장히 사치스러운 스위트룸들이 있었다.
lucrative	Barbara는 Walt Disney사의 애니메이션 제작팀과 이득이 되는 3년 간의 계약을 제의받았다.
mainly	Jacqueline이 좀처럼 외출을 하지 못하는 주된 이유는 세 명의 떠들썩한 아이들을 키우느라 바쁘기 때문이다.
manifest	예술가가 되는 것이 어떤 것인지 Paolo가 모른다는 사실은 명백하다.
	심장병은 다양한 증상들로 자신을 드러내는데 가장 흔한 증상은 가슴 통증과 호흡 곤란이다.
material	성경에서 예수님은 한 부자에게 그가 가진 물질적 소유물을 버리지 않고는 천국에 들어갈 수 없다고 말한다.
meticulously	그 팀은 그 프로젝트를 완성할 오직 4주만의 시간을 가지고 있기 때문에 그것은 신중히 계획되어야 한다.

21 **nervous***

[nə́:rvəs]
calm

adj. on edge, **excitable, uneasy** 신경질적인

Quincy is a quiet, **nervous** man who doesn't like meeting new people.

22 **obstinate***

[ɑ́bstənit]
complaisant, pliable

adj. unyielding, **stubborn, determined, headstrong** 완고한

Tina's father is **obstinate** in his views regarding politics, so he is not always an easy person to talk to.

23 **overstate****

[òuvərstéit]
understate

v. exaggerate, play up 과장하다

Newspaper stories usually **overstated** the strength of the current regime.

24 **pack together***

phr. cluster, **group, gather** 모이다

Cells **pack together** in different ways depending on their functions.

25 **perform****

[pərfɔ́:rm]

v. carry out, execute, **accomplish** achieve 수행하다

In spite of her youth, Debbie **performed** her White House duties well.

26 **perishable***

[périʃəbl]

adj. spoilable, likely to decay, likely to spoil 상하기 쉬운

Butter, milk, fruit, and fish are **perishable** goods that must be refrigerated or they will spoil.

27 **pound***

[páund]

v. beat, **thrash, batter** strike 마구 치다

Steve **pounded** the door with his fists.

28 **prolific***

[proulífik]
unfruitful, sterile

adj. **productive, fertile, fruitful** 결실이 많은, 다작의

Over the last four decades, Harris has proven himself to be a **prolific** director.

nervous	Quincy는 새로운 사람들을 만나는 것을 좋아하지 않는 조용하고 신경질적인 사람이다.
obstinate	Tina의 아버지는 정치관이 완고하기 때문에 언제나 대화하기 쉬운 상대는 아니다.
overstate	뉴스 기사들은 보통 현정권의 강점을 과장했다.
pack together	세포는 그들의 기능에 따라 다른 방식으로 모인다.
perform	나이가 어림에도 불구하고, Debbie는 그녀의 백악관 업무를 잘 수행하였다.
perishable	버터, 우유, 과일 그리고 생선은 상하기 쉬운 상품들이기 때문에 냉장 보관되지 않으면 상할 것이다.
pound	Steve는 주먹으로 문을 마구 쳤다.
prolific	지난 40여 년에 걸쳐, Harris는 자신이 다작을 하는 감독임을 입증해왔다.

29 **proof***

[prú:f]

n. **evidence, testimony** 증거

The scientists have no direct **proof** of Mikhail's hypothesis.

30 **serene****

[sərí:n]
agitated

adj. **calm, peaceful, tranquil** undisturbed 고요한

Paine's painting shows a **serene** summer night in the woods.

31 **spawn***

[spɔ́:n]

v. **create, give rise to, produce, generate** 야기하다

Authorities feared that the terrorist act would **spawn** another terrorist act.

32 **substitute****

[sʌ́bstitjù:t]

v. 1. **exchange, replace** 대체하다

People who lived during the war **substituted** saccharin for sugar.

n. 2. **alternative** 대안

Substitutes for fossil fuels must be developed as the world's supply dwindles.

33 **surpass****

[sərpǽs]

v. **exceed, outrun, excel** beat 능가하다

The Egyptians far **surpassed** all other ancient civilizations.

34 **survival****

[sərváivəl]

n. **existence** 생존

People's disregard for the environment threatens the long-term **survival** of the planet.

35 **ubiquitous****

[ju:bíkwitəs]
nonexistent

adj. **omnipresent, existing everywhere** 어디에나 존재하는

The **ubiquitous** mosquito is especially bothersome during camping trips.

---

proof	과학자들은 Mikhail의 가설의 어떤 직접적인 증거도 가지고 있지 않다
serene	Paine의 그림은 숲 속에서의 조용한 여름 밤을 보여 준다.
spawn	당국은 테러리스트 활동이 또 다른 테러리스트 활동을 야기할 것을 우려했다.
substitute	전쟁 기간 동안 살았던 사람들은 사카린을 설탕 대신 사용했다.
	세계적으로 연료 공급량이 감소함에 따라 화석 연료에 대한 대안이 마련되어야 한다.
surpass	이집트 문명은 모든 다른 고대 문명을 훨씬 능가했다.
survival	사람들의 환경에 대한 무관심은 지구의 장기간의 생존을 위협한다.
ubiquitous	어디에나 있는 모기는 캠핑 여행을 할 때 특히 성가신 존재다.

36 **undergo**** v. **experience, suffer** (어려운 일을) 겪다

[ʌ̀ndərgóu]

The United States has **undergone** many recessions.

37 **weed out*** phr. **remove, eliminate** 제거하다

propagate

The first month of FBI training is made especially difficult in an attempt to **weed out** any unsuitable candidates.

38 **worn-out** adj. **exhausted** 지친

[wɔ́:rnaut]

Peter was so **worn-out** after work that he fell asleep without having dinner.

Quiz

Choose the synonym.

1. appreciably	ⓐ calm, peaceful, tranquil
2. manifest	ⓑ evident, obvious, definite
3. obstinate	ⓒ significantly, considerably, perceptibly
4. serene	ⓓ productive, fertile, fruitful
5. prolific	ⓔ unyielding, stubborn, determined

Answer 1. ⓒ 2. ⓑ 3. ⓔ 4. ⓐ 5. ⓓ

undergo	미국은 많은 경제 불황을 겪었다.
weed out	FBI의 첫 달 훈련은 부적합한 지원자들을 제거하려는 의도에서 특히 어렵게 짜여져 있다.
worn-out	Peter는 너무 지쳐서 퇴근 후에 저녁도 거른 채 잠이 들었다.

DAY Hackers TOEFL Vocabulary

33 Hackers Voca

www.goHackers.com

1 **adhere**** | v. **stick, cleave, cling** | ~에 달라붙다, 고수하다

[ædhíər]
disjoin

Some tiles are not properly **adhered** to the wall.

2 **assertion** | n. **strong statement, declaration** | 주장, 단언

[əsə́ːrʃən]

The lawsuit was dismissed after the plaintiff's **assertions** were proven to be false.

3 **barren**** | adj. **sterile, lifeless, infertile** unproductive | 불모의

[bǽrən]
fertile

The **barren** soil of the Rocky Mountains provides few nutrients to the grasses.

4 **budding*** | adj. **emerging, nascent, not yet fully developed** | 신진의

[bʌ́diŋ]
fully developed

Students at MIT are **budding** scientists and engineers.

5 **central** | adj. **essential, principal, main, chief** | 주요한

[séntrəl]

Most audience members were unable to understand the speaker's **central** argument.

6 **comprehensible**** | adj. **understandable, knowable, apprehensible** | 알기 쉬운

[kɑ̀mprihénsəbl]
incomprehensible

Experience taught Rachel that life could be predictable and **comprehensible.**

adhere	어떤 타일들은 벽에 제대로 붙지 않는다.
assertion	원고의 주장이 거짓으로 입증된 후 그 소송은 기각되었다.
barren	록키 산맥의 황폐한 토양은 풀에 영양소를 거의 공급하지 않는다
budding	MIT 학생들은 막 피어나는 과학자와 공학자들이다.
central	청중들 대다수는 그 연설자의 주장의 핵심을 이해하지 못했다.
comprehensible	경험은 Rachel에게 삶이 예측될 수 있고 이해될 수 있다는 사실을 가르쳤다.

7 concern

[kənsə́ːrn]

n. **interest, regard, care, attention** 관심

Parents should have great **concern** regarding their children's education.

8 configuration

[kənfìgjəréiʃən]

n. **arrangement, conformation** 배치, 배열

The internal combustion engine is made up of a complex **configuration** of parts.

9 deserved*

[dizə́ːrvd]
undue

adj. **due, earned** 당연히 받아야 할

The entire company agreed that the president's vacation was much **deserved**.

10 detect**

[ditékt]

v. **find, discover, recognize, sense, spot** 발견하다, 인지하다

The scientists **detected** a trace of toxic chemicals in the city's water supply.

11 diffuse**

[difjúːz]
concentrate

v. **spread, distribute** 퍼뜨리다

The kitchen stove **diffused** its warmth all over the house.

12 exaggerate

[igzǽdʒərèit]

v. **enlarge, overstate, embroider, hyperbolize** 과장하다

The applicant **exaggerated** his accomplishments on his resume to land the job.

13 fetter

[fétər]

v. **hamper, shackle, manacle, restrain** 구속하다, 제한하다

An ankle injury seriously **fettered** the soccer player's mobility.

14 float**

[flóut]
sink

v. **stay on the top** 뜨다

Tracy **floated** down the river on a raft.

---

concern	부모들은 자식들의 교육에 관해서 많은 관심을 가져야 한다.
configuration	내연 기관은 부품들의 복잡한 배열로 구성되어 있다.
deserved	회사 전체는 회장의 휴가가 매우 정당했다는 데 동의했다.
detect	과학자들은 그 도시의 물 공급지에서 유독한 화학 물질들의 흔적을 발견했다.
diffuse	그 부엌 난로는 집 전체로 온기를 퍼뜨렸다.
exaggerate	그 응시자는 그 직업을 얻기 위해 그의 이력서에 실적들을 과장해 놓았다.
fetter	발목 부상은 축구 선수의 기동성을 상당히 제한한다.
float	Tracy는 뗏목을 타고 강을 떠내려갔다.

15 frequent*

[fríːkwənt]
occasional

adj. **regular, common, customary, recurrent** 빈번한

Because she is a **frequent** customer at the bakery, the owners often give Sheila a discount.

16 groundless***

[gráundlis]

adj. **unfounded, baseless, bottomless** 근거 없는

Although Sarah knew her fear of the dark was **groundless**, she still used a nightlight.

17 hindrance*

[híndrəns]
boost

n. **deterrent, obstacle, barrier** impediment 방해, 장애(물)

Lack of funding was a serious **hindrance** to the progress of the research.

18 maneuver*

[mənúːvər]

n. 1. **scheme, plot, design** 계획, 책략

Hopkin's **maneuver** failed in its major purpose because of lack of cooperation.

v. 2. **move** 움직이다

The researchers were testing the way the car **maneuvered** in wet conditions.

19 mar**

[mɑ́ːr]
adorn

v. **spoil, mangle, ruin** damage 망쳐 놓다

The bad weather **marred** the pleasure of the trip.

20 mighty

[máiti]

adj. **powerful, potent, strong, forceful** 강력한

The **mighty** army of Napoleon was destroyed by the Russian winter.

21 opaque

[oupéik]

adj. 1. **impenetrable, cloudy, filmy** 불투명한

Worried about privacy, Martha had **opaque** windows placed in her office.

frequent	그녀는 제과점에 자주 오는 손님이었기 때문에 주인은 Sheila에게 종종 할인을 해주곤 한다.
groundless	Sarah는 자신의 어둠에 대한 공포가 근거 없는 것이었다는 것을 알게 되었음에도 불구하고 아직도 야간등을 사용한다.
hindrance	자금이 부족한 것은 그 연구의 진전에 있어서 심각한 장애이다.
maneuver	Hopkin의 계획은 협조를 얻지 못해 주목적을 달성하지 못했다.
	연구원들은 자동차가 땅이 젖은 환경에서 어떻게 움직이는지를 실험하고 있다.
mar	좋지 않은 날씨가 여행의 기쁨을 망쳐 놓았다.
mighty	Napoleon의 강력한 군대는 러시아의 추위에 의해 궤멸당했다.
opaque	사생활이 걱정되어, Martha는 그녀의 사무실에 불투명한 창문들을 놓았다.

adj. 2. **obscure, unclear, vague** 불명료한

The man's **opaque** answers aroused the suspicion of the detective.

22 **originate****
[əridʒənèit]
end

v. be grown, **spring, emanate, initiate** 일어나다, 생기다

The philosophy of stoicism **originated** in Greece.

23 **pace***
[péis]

n. 1. **step, gait** 걸음(걸이)

When Kelly thought she heard someone following her, she quickened her **pace.**

n. 2. speed, **bat, velocity** 속력

The **pace** of the car slowed as road conditions worsened.

v. 3. **walk, step** 걷다

Luke **paced** nervously in the waiting room while his wife underwent emergency surgery.

24 **perceptibly**
[pərséptəbli]
intangibly

adv. noticeably, **appreciably, sensibly** 알아차릴 정도로

Over the course of a single afternoon, the position of a plant will change **perceptibly** as it follows the sun across the sky.

25 **promising***
[prάmisiŋ]
unpromising

adj. likely, **encouraging, hopeful** 유망한

Solar and wind power as energy sources don't look **promising** for the future.

26 **punctuality***
[pʌ̀ŋktʃuǽləti]
tardiness

n. promptness, **promptitude** 시간 엄수

Punctuality is very important in a job where many deadlines must be met.

opaque	그 남자의 불명료한 대답은 탐정에게 의심을 불러일으켰다.
originate	금욕주의 철학은 그리스에서 시작되었다.
pace	Kelly는 누군가 자기를 따라오는 소리를 들은 것 같아 걸음을 재촉했다.
	도로 상태가 나빠지면서 자동차의 속력은 느려졌다.
	Luke는 그의 부인이 응급실에서 치료를 받는 동안 대기실에서 초조하게 걷고 있었다.
perceptibly	단지 한나절의 시간만 지나도 식물이 하늘을 넘어가는 태양을 쫓기 때문에 식물의 자세는 눈에 띌 정도로 변할 것이다.
promising	에너지원으로의 태양열 에너지와 풍력은 미래에 유망해 보이지 않는다.
punctuality	지켜져야만 하는 마감 기한이 많은 직종에서는 시간 엄수가 매우 중요하다.

27 rotate** | v. **turn, spin, wheel, swivel** 회전하다

[róuteit]

Tropical cyclones **rotate** clockwise in the Southern Hemisphere.

28 scatter** | v. **disperse, widely spread, dissipate, spread out** 퍼뜨리다

[skǽtər]
gather

The man **scattered** grass seed all over the lawn.

29 sedentary* | adj. **stationary** 움직이지 않는

[sédəntèri]
moving

Rosa's obesity is partly due to her **sedentary** occupation.

30 site* | n. **place, location, position** 장소, 위치

[sáit]

Water is delivered to the **site** via aqueducts and special channels.

31 soak** | v. **drench, saturate, steep, wet** 적시다

[sóuk]

Mother told me to **soak** the beans for two hours in water.

32 subsist** | v. **survive, endure, exist** 존속하다

[səbsíst]
perish

The hostages had to **subsist** on what little bread and water their captors gave them.

33 supremacy | n. **predominance, primacy, sovereignty** 우월, 우위

[suprémәsi]

In the 1920's, Henry Ford lost the battle for **supremacy** in the automobile industry to General Motors.

34 trigger** | v. **activate, cause, generate, start, initiate, stimulate** 일으키다

[trígər]

News of the court decision **triggered** rioting and fires in L.A.

rotate	열대 사이클론은 남반구에서 시계 방향으로 회전한다.
scatter	남자는 잔디밭 전체에 잔디 씨앗을 흩뿌렸다.
sedentary	Rosa의 비만은 부분적으로 그녀의 앉아서 일하는 직업에서 기인한 것이다.
site	물은 수도관과 특별한 수로를 통해 그 장소로 운반된다.
soak	어머니가 물에 두 시간 동안 콩을 담가두라고 나에게 말했다.
subsist	그 인질들은 그들의 생포자가 주는 소량의 빵과 물에 의지하여 생활해야만 했다.
supremacy	1920년대에, Henry Ford는 자동차 시장에서 우위를 차지하기 위한 경쟁에서 General Motors에게 졌다.
trigger	그 법정 판결 소식은 LA에서 폭동과 방화를 일으켰다.

35 **tumultuous****

[tʃu(:)mʌ́ltʃuəs]

adj. **chaotic, anarchic; wild, riotous, boisterous** 무질서한 ; 떠들썩한

Many of the Serbian cultural institutions fell into disrepair during the **tumultuous** revolutionary period.

36 **veritable**

[véritəbl]

adj. **genuine, authentic, believable** 실제의

The male parakeet is a **veritable** rainbow of colors.

37 **waste**

[wéist]

save

v. **squander, dissipate, lavish** 낭비하다

Many young people today **waste** a lot of money and time on recreational activities.

38 **weaken**

[wí:kən]

strengthen

v. **lessen, decrease, undermine, impair** 약화시키다

Julia was **weakened** by her long illness.

Quiz

Choose the synonym.

1. adhere — ⓐ arrangement, conformation
2. configuration — ⓑ noticeably, appreciably, sensibly
3. hindrance — ⓒ stick, cleave, cling
4. perceptibly — ⓓ drench, saturate, steep
5. soak — ⓔ deterrent, obstacle, barrier

Answer 1. ⓒ 2. ⓐ 3. ⓔ 4. ⓑ 5. ⓓ

tumultuous	많은 세르비아의 문화 기관들이 무질서한 혁명 기간 동안 훼손되었다.
veritable	수컷 앵무새는 실제로 무지개와 같은 색깔을 하고 있다.
waste	오늘날 많은 젊은이들이 오락 활동에 많은 돈과 시간을 낭비한다.
weaken	Julia는 오랜 병고로 쇠약해졌다.

Hackers TOEFL Voca TEST DAY 31-33

Choose the synonym of the highlighted word in the sentence.

1. The general's gallant appearance on the front line inspired his troops to victory.
(A) brave (B) detrimental (C) loyal (D) daunted

2. Found in all living things, hydrogen is the most ubiquitous element on Earth.
(A) salubrious (B) omnipresent (C) transcendental (D) minor

3. High rates of inflation and a growing trade deficit fettered the president's efforts to spur an economic recovery.
(A) continued (B) persuaded (C) hampered (D) promoted

4. Some animals are very active when young and only become sedentary when they mature.
(A) neglectful (B) stationary (C) fortunate (D) useless

5. Given the right climate and environmental conditions, non-native species can proliferate in new habitats.
(A) multiply (B) harbor (C) prevaricate (D) decrease

6. The cessation of the Cold War provoked a revival of nationalism, especially in eastern Europe.
(A) crashed (B) alleviated (C) noticed (D) incited

7. The prickly pear anchors itself on rocky, barren slopes and grows to about 3 meters high.
(A) infertile (B) ghastly (C) brazen (D) naive

8. News of the killings triggered rioting and fires in the Pittsburgh rail yards.
(A) caused (B) elevated (C) attacked (D) entombed

9. The professor's argument seemed groundless considering that much of his supporting evidence had been recently disproved by a group of scientists.
(A) dispensable (B) tantamount (C) unfounded (D) lucrative

10. The lowest strata of the caste system are referred to as 'untouchables', because they are excluded from the performance of rituals which confer religious purity.
(A) lifted (B) expelled (C) bowed (D) concurred

정답 p.419

Westward Movement

미국사회는 동부 13주를 모체로 해서 점차 서쪽으로 확대해가는 형태로 발전해 왔는데, 이 서점운동에 따라 프런티어도 당초의 애팔래치아 산맥 지대로부터 미시시피강 유역, 나아가서는 그레이트 플레인스로 통하는 서쪽으로 이동하였다. 이 단계에서는 북부의 자영농민과 남부의 플랜터의 땅을 찾아가는 움직임이 그 주된 원동력이었는데, 19세기 중엽에 미국이 태평양연안의 영토를 획득하고, 캘리포니아에서 금광이 발견되어 골드 러시가 일어나자 서점운동은 급속도로 진행되었다. 1849년 캘리포니아로 금을 캐러 온 사람들을 '포티나이너스(forty niners)' 라고 하였는데, 이들은 금이 처음 발견된 1848년부터 1858년까지 약 5억 5,000만 달러에 이르는 금을 채굴하였다. 1850년 9월 캘리포니아는 정식으로 미국의 한 주가 되었는데, 이처럼 단시간에 인구가 늘어서 주(州)로 승인된 예는 미국 역사상 드문 일이다. 골드 러시 이후 태평양연안을 거점으로 동진(東進)하는 프런티어도 생겨 광물자원의 채굴이 그 추진력이 되었다. 그리하여 19세기 말에는 로키산맥 지대를 최후로 거의 전지역에 이주가 끝났으며, 프런티어 라인(미개척 영역)의 소멸과 더불어 한 시대의 흐름으로서 서부 개척 운동도 종결되었다.

광대한 개척작업은 땅의 입수를 용이하게 하여 농업발달에 기여함과 동시에, 공업제품에도 충분한 국내시장을 제공하였다. 그리고 여기에는 자립의 기회가 열려 있었기 때문에 동부의 과잉노동인구를 흡수하는 안전판의 기능을 다함과 동시에, 미국사회의 유동성(流動性)을 높여 그 중산계급화를 촉진하는 한 원인이 되었다. 정치면에서도 기존의 사회적 제약이 적은 프런티어는 자유 · 평화라고 하는 이념에 제대로 들어맞아 보통선거운동 등에 무시할 수 없는 영향을 끼쳤고, 자치의식도 높였다. 그리고 대자연에 맞서 살아 나가야 하는 냉혹한 상황 속에서 '프런티어 스피릿' 이라 부르는 개척정신의 기풍이 배양되어 미국 국민의 국민성의 일부가 되기도 하였으며, 그들의 개인주의 · 현실주의 · 합리주의 혹은 개개의 독창성을 존중하는 성향을 강화해 주었다.

이와 같이 프런티어는 미국사회에 중요한 의미를 지니며, 특히 그 경제적 발전에서 불가결의 것이라는 생각이 널리 퍼져 있었는데, 그런 만큼 프런티어가 소멸하였다는 의식(意識)은 미국인들 사이에 심각한 위기감을 불러일으켜 새로운 프런티어를 찾아 해외진출로 나서게 하는 하나의 계기가 되었다.

34 Hackers Voca

1 **accretion*** | n. **accumulation** | 축적(물)

[əkríːʃən]

Neptune was formed by the **accretion** of icy planetesimals.

2 **agriculture*** | n. **farming** | 농업

[ǽgrəkʌ̀ltʃər]

Agriculture composes only a small part of Korea's gross domestic product.

3 **attach**** | v. **stick, fasten, affix** | 붙이다

[ətǽtʃ]
detach

Kenneth needs to **attach** his photograph to the application.

4 **counter** | v. **oppose, retort** | 대항하다, 반박하다

[káuntər]

The two scientists used different interpretations of the data to **counter** each other's conclusions.

5 **crop up**** | phr. **appear, arise, come out, emerge** | 나타나다

Problems should be dealt with as soon as they **crop up**.

6 **dimly**** | adv. **faintly** | 희미하게

[dímli]
distinctly

The heavily sedated patient was only **dimly** aware of his surroundings.

accretion	해왕성은 얼음으로 된 미소행성체들의 축적에 의해 형성되어졌다.
agriculture	농업은 한국의 국내 총생산의 작은 부분만을 구성하고 있다.
attach	Kenneth는 그의 사진을 그 지원서에 붙일 필요가 있다.
counter	그 두 과학자들은 서로의 결론들에 맞서기 위해 그 자료를 다르게 해석했다.
crop up	문제는 생기자마자 해결해야 한다.
dimly	강한 진정제를 맞은 그 환자는 그의 주변만을 희미하게 알아보았다.

7 distract v. **divert, sidetrack** 산만하게 하다

[distrǽkt]
focus

Carrie was **distracted** from her studies by the loud music blaring from her roommate's stereo.

8 drain* v. remove water, **draw off, empty** 배수하다

[dréin]

The sink should be **drained** after use.

9 emergent adj. **emerging, nascent** 떠오르는, 신흥의

[imə́:rdʒənt]
declining

The **emergent** ideas of postmodernism have caused a major shift in intellectual discourse and critical theory.

10 enlarge* v. amplify, **extend, augment** magnify 확대시키다

[enlá:rdʒ]
compress

Rosenthal refused to join the liberals who hoped to **enlarge** the New Deal.

11 excessive* adj. extreme, **undue, exorbitant** extravagant 지나친

[iksésiv]
meager

Many congressmen considered Joseph McCarthy's claims of communist infiltration **excessive.**

12 exploit* n. 1. **feat, accomplishment** 위업

[éksplɔit]

The risk he undertook for his latest **exploit** made John feel like a real hero.

[iksplɔ́it] v. 2. use 이용하다

Human rights activists have led boycotts and protests against companies that **exploit** child labor.

13 extract** v. derive, draw, **extort** 이끌어 내다

[ikstrǽkt]

Slaves were put to work on plantations to **extract** maximum harvests from the cotton fields.

---

distract Carrie는 룸메이트의 축음기에서 울려 퍼지는 시끄러운 음악으로 인해 공부에 집중할 수가 없었다.
drain 사용 후 그 싱크대의 물을 빼내야 한다.
emergent 새로이 떠오른 포스트모더니즘 사상은 지적 담론과 비평 이론에 주요한 변화를 유발하였다.
enlarge Rosenthal은 뉴딜 정책을 확대하기를 희망하는 자유 당원들과 함께 하는 것을 거절했다.
excessive 많은 국회 의원들이 Joseph McCarthy의 공산주의자 침투에 관한 주장을 지나친 것으로 생각했다.
exploit John이 최근에 맡은 위업에서 그가 감수한 위험 부담은 그로 하여금 정말 영웅심을 느끼게 했다.
인권 운동가들은 아동 노동력을 착취하는 회사들에 대항하여 불매 운동과 항의를 이끌어 왔다.
extract 노예들은 면화 밭에서 최대한의 수확물을 이끌어 내기 위해 대규모 농원에서 일하도록 배치되었다.

14 **fierce****

adj. **furious, vicious, aggressive, ferocious** 사나운

[fíərs]
mild

The Chickisaw Indians were known as **fierce** warriors.

15 **fiery***

adj. **passionate, fervent, impetuous** 불같은

[fáiəri]
frigid

Andrew Jackson was known for his iron will and **fiery** personality.

16 **first and foremost***

phr. **above all, primarily, to begin with** 무엇보다도 먼저

First and foremost, the scientific method requires a hypothesis.

17 **fluctuation**

n. **variance, variation** • 변동

[flʌ̀ktʃuéiʃən]

Even minor temperature **fluctuations** can be dangerous to tropical fish.

18 **gradually****

adv. **little by little, slowly, steadily, progressively** 점차적으로

[grǽdʒuəli]

The scars from the accident are **gradually** disappearing, but there will always be a small mark on Kevin's forehead.

19 **languid***

adj. **listless, faint, feeble** weak 기운 없는

[lǽŋgwid]
vivacious

Fran was startled to see her friend so **languid.**

20 **location***

n. **site, position, place** 장소, 위치

[loukéiʃən]

The Harry Potter movies were shot on **location** in the United Kingdom.

21 **lengthen***

v. **prolong, extend, stretch** protract 연장하다

[léŋkθən]
abbreviate

Primary school education has now been **lengthened** to six years in America.

fierce	Chickisaw 인디언들은 사나운 전사들로 알려져 있었다.
fiery	Andrew Jackson은 그의 강철 같은 의지와 불 같은 성격으로 유명하다.
first and foremost	과학적인 방법은 무엇보다도 우선적으로 가설을 필요로 한다.
fluctuation	작은 온도의 변동들조차도 열대어에게 위험할 수 있다.
gradually	사고로 인한 상처는 점점 사라져갔지만 Kevin의 이마에는 언제까지나 작은 흉터가 남아 있을 것이다.
languid	Fran은 그녀의 친구가 너무나 기운이 없는 것을 보고 놀랐다.
location	영화 Harry Potter는 영국에서 촬영되었다.
lengthen	초등학교 교육은 현재 미국에서 6년으로 연장되었다.

22 **mandatory**	adj.	**required, compulsory, obligatory, requisite**	필수의
[mǽndətɔ̀ːri]		Military service was once **mandatory** in France, but the draft has now been abolished.	
23 **narrate***	v.	**recount, describe, relate** tell	이야기하다
[nǽreit]		The storyteller **narrated** a tale about a beautiful princess to the young children.	
24 **noxious****	adj.	**harmful, noisome**	유해한
[nɑ́kʃəs] innocuous		The industrial plant released **noxious** chemicals into the river.	
25 **once***	con.	**when**	일단 ~하면
[wʌ́ns]		Coastal populations can prepare for a hurricane **once** it is detected on radar.	
26 **pierce****	v.	**puncture, perforate, penetrate**	관통하다
[píərs]		Gary looked up into the sunlight **piercing** through the branches.	
27 **positive***	adj.	1. **sure, certain**	확신하는
[pɑ́zitiv] irresolute		Shelly was **positive** that her answer was correct.	
negative	adj.	2. **affirmative, helpful**	긍정적인
		Soybeans have many **positive** health benefits.	
28 **pretend**	v.	**feign, affect, assume**	~인 체하다
[priténd]		Rachel **pretended** to be sick to avoid going to school.	

mandatory	프랑스에서 병역은 한때 의무였으나, 지금은 징병제가 폐지되었다.
narrate	그 만담가는 어린 아이들에게 예쁜 공주에 관한 이야기를 해주었다.
noxious	그 생산 공장은 강으로 유독 화학 물질들을 방출했다.
once	해안가의 주민들은 일단 허리케인이 레이더에 탐지되면 대피할 수 있다.
pierce	Gary는 고개를 들어 나뭇가지들을 통과하는 햇빛을 바라보았다.
positive	Shelly는 그녀의 대답이 옳다는 것을 확신했다.
	콩은 건강에 이로운 점이 많다.
pretend	Rachel은 학교에 가기 싫어서 아픈 척을 했다.

29 **range*** | n. 1. **spectrum, extent, scope** compass | 범위

[réindʒ]

Galileo learned the wide intellectual **range** of mathematical reasoning from Archimedes.

v. 2. **vary, go, run, fluctuate** | 변화하다

Temperatures in the Sahara Desert can **range** from scorching hot during the day to freezing at night.

30 **rudiment*** | n. **basic, element, essential** | 기초, 기본

[rú:dəmənt]

George mastered the **rudiments** of Russian grammar in one year.

31 **signify*** | v. **denote, express, indicate** mean | 표명하다, 나타내다

[sígnəfài]

The chairman **signified** his agreement with a nod.

32 **simultaneously**** | adv. **concurrently, at the same time** | 동시에

[sàiməltéiniəsli]
separately

The two pictures were taken **simultaneously** from different camera angles.

33 **symmetrical*** | adj. **proportionally balanced, commensurable** | 균형이 잡힌, 대칭적인

[simétrikəl]
asymmetrical

Rorschach inkblots are **symmetrical** abstract designs that are used in personality analysis.

34 **testify*** | v. **provide evidence, prove** | 증명하다, 입증하다

[téstəfài]

Defense attorneys are locating witnesses who could **testify** on Swan's behalf.

35 **vast**** | adj. **immense, huge, enormous** large | 거대한

[vǽst]
narrow

The continent the pilgrims had begun settling upon was enormously **vast**.

range	Galileo는 Archimedes로부터 넓고 지적인 범위의 수학적 추론을 배웠다. 사하라 사막의 온도는 낮 동안에는 찌는 듯 덥고 밤에는 매우 춥게 변화한다.
rudiment	George는 러시아어 문법의 기초를 1년 안에 터득했다.
signify	의장은 고개를 끄덕임으로써 동의를 나타냈다.
simultaneously	그 두 사진은 서로 다른 카메라 각도에서 동시에 찍혔다.
symmetrical	Rorschach의 잉크 반점은 성격 분석에 사용되는 좌우 대칭의 추상 도안이다.
testify	변호사들은 Swan을 위해 증명할 수 있는 목격자들을 찾아내려 하고 있다.
vast	순례자들이 정착하기 시작한 대륙은 상당히 광대했다.

36 **visionary** | adj. **fanciful, imaginary, illusory** 환상의

[vízənèri]
realistic

Many people think that Chris' ideas are **visionary.**

37 **vogue*** | n. **mode, fashion, style** 유행

[vóug]

Short skirts are very much in **vogue.**

38 **weariness**** | n. **fatigue** 피로

[wíərinis]

The hard work at the construction site led to a great deal of **weariness.**

Quiz

Choose the synonym.

1. drain — ⓐ faint, weak, listless
2. symmetrical — ⓑ accumulation
3. languid — ⓒ basic, element, essential
4. accretion — ⓓ commensurable, proportionally balanced
5. rudiment — ⓔ remove water, draw off

Answer 1. ⓔ 2. ⓓ 3. ⓐ 4. ⓑ 5. ⓒ

visionary	많은 사람들은 Chris의 생각이 환상이라고 생각한다.
vogue	짧은 치마가 굉장히 유행하고 있다.
weariness	공사장에서의 힘든 일이 상당한 피로를 가져왔다.

D A Y | Hackers TOEFL **Vocabulary**

35 Hackers Voca

www.goHackers.com

1 **accelerate*** | v. **speed up, expedite, hasten** quicken | 촉진시키다

[æksélərèit]
decelerate

The tariff act **accelerated** the rise of American trade.

2 **adjust*** | v. **fit, adapt** suit | 맞추다, 조절하다

[ədʒʌ́st]
disarrange

Nancy **adjusted** the steering wheel and rearview mirror in the car to her size.

3 **a great deal of*** | phr. **a lot of** | 다량의

The company earned **a great deal of** money in 2001.

4 **alleviate** | v. **relieve, ease, lessen, abate** | 완화하다

[əlí:vièit]
augment

The president's economic reforms have **alleviated** the crushing poverty to some degree.

5 **aromatic*** | adj. **fragrant** | 향기로운

[æ̀rəmǽtik]
acrid

Aromatic herbs are often used in foods.

6 **celebrated**** | adj. **renowned, famous, well-known** distinguished | 유명한

[séləbrèitid]
unknown

General Sherman's march to the sea was probably the most **celebrated** military campaign in U.S. history.

accelerate	그 관세법은 미국 무역의 부흥을 가속화했다.
adjust	Nancy는 핸들과 백미러를 자신의 사이즈에 맞게 맞추었다.
a great deal of	그 회사는 2001년에 많은 돈을 벌었다.
alleviate	대통령의 경제 개혁은 엄청난 빈곤을 어느 정도 완화시켰다.
aromatic	향기로운 허브는 음식에 종종 사용된다.
celebrated	Sherman 장군의 바다로의 진군은 아마도 미국 역사에서 가장 유명한 군사 작전이었다.

7 characterize* v. **distinguish** 특징 지우다

[kǽriktəràiz]

The loss of physical strength and great difficulty in breathing **characterized** the deadly Spanish flu of 1918.

8 certainly* adv. **surely, assuredly** 확실히

[sə́ːrtənli]
uncertainly

Biliana protested the accusation, saying that she most **certainly** did not eat her brother's food.

9 compliment* n. **commendation, honor, tribute** 칭찬, 경의

[kámpləmənt]
insult

Tommy paid Lily a **compliment** by saying that her dress was very beautiful.

10 decrease** v. **diminish, minimize, dwindle** abate 줄이다

[dikríːs]
increase

Factory owners began to **decrease** wages in order to lower costs.

11 definite* adj. **decisive, unambiguous, unequivocal** fixed 명확한

[défənit]
equivocal

There was a **definite** improvement in Mary's math scores after she got a tutor.

12 dictate** v. **require, prescribe, determine** (조건 · 방침 등을) 지시하다

[díkteit]

The referee **dictated** the rules of the game.

13 distinction** n. **difference, divergence** 차이

[distíŋkʃən]
analogy

Dickinson makes an important **distinction** between rights and duties.

14 embed** v. **fix, fasten, root** 고정시키다, 새겨 넣다

[imbéd]
extract

The story of the American Dream has been **embedded** deeply in American culture.

characterize	체력의 감소와 극심한 호흡 곤란은 1918년의 치명적인 스페인 독감의 특징이다.
certainly	Biliana는 그녀가 남동생의 음식을 먹지 않은 것이 확실하다며 비난에 항의했다.
compliment	Tommy는 Lily에게 그녀의 옷이 아주 예쁘다고 말하며 칭찬을 했다.
decrease	공장 소유주들은 비용을 낮추기 위해 임금을 삭감하기 시작했다.
definite	Mary는 가정교사가 생긴 후, 수학 점수가 명확하게 높아졌다.
dictate	심판은 경기의 규칙들을 지시했다.
distinction	Dickinson은 권리와 의무를 확실히 구별한다.
embed	아메리칸 드림에 대한 이야기는 미국 문화에 깊이 새겨져 왔다.

15 escape**

[iskéip]
abide

v. 1. **flee, evade, avoid** 피하다

The Pilgrims came to America to **escape** religious persecution.

n. 2. **flight, freedom** 도피

Danny Almonte gunned down a police officer during an **escape** that lasted 42 days.

16 essentially*

[əsénʃəli]

adv. **basically, primarily, originally, by nature** 본래, 본질적으로

Although Kelly is **essentially** content with her career, she does occasionally consider starting a family.

17 forge**

[fɔ́:rdʒ]

v. 1. **drive, advance** ~로 나아가다

The Germans **forged** ahead toward Honsfeld.

v. 2. **create, make, fabricate** fashion 만들다

Fairfax **forged** an army with good soldiers who were well-trained.

18 identity*

[aidéntəti]

n. **similitude, uniformity** 동일성

The common bond of ethnic **identity** is a powerful unifying force in the Jewish kibbutz, or communal farms of Israel.

19 illuminate*

[ilú:mənèit]
darken

v. **clarify, elucidate; light up, brighten** 명확히 하다 ; 밝게 하다

The professor's lecture did much to **illuminate** an otherwise complex subject.

20 in a short space of time

phr. **very quickly** 단시간에, 빨리

It is possible to learn another language **in a short space of time**.

escape	그 초기 정착자들은 종교적인 박해를 피하기 위해 미국에 왔다. Danny Almonte는 42일간 지속된 탈출 기간 동안 한 경관에게 총을 쏘았다.
essentially	Kelly는 본질적으로 그녀의 직업에 만족하고 있음에도 불구하고 가끔 가족을 이루는 것에 대해 생각하곤 한다.
forge	독일인들은 Honsfeld를 향해 나아갔다. Fairfax는 잘 훈련된 훌륭한 병사들로 군대를 만들었다.
identity	인종적 동일성이라는 공통된 유대는 유대인의 키부츠, 혹은 이스라엘 공유 농장에서의 강력한 단합의 힘이다.
illuminate	그 교수는 복잡할 수 있는 주제를 매우 명확하게 강의했다.
in a short space of time	단기간 내에 다른 언어를 배우는 것이 가능하다.

21 **inconstant****

adj. **volatile, unstable, fickle** variable 변하기 쉬운

[inkánstənt]
resolute

Weather becomes **inconstant** with atmospheric heating.

22 **initial****

adj. **original, first, beginning** inceptive 처음의

[iníʃəl]
final

The chief designer approved the **initial** design of the satellite.

23 **lay off***

phr. **fire, discharge, dismiss** (일시적으로) 해고하다

employ

The employer plans to **lay off** some of his workers next week.

24 **motif****

[moutí:f]

n. 1. **theme, subject, topic** 주제

Death is a common **motif** in Emily Dickinson's poetry.

n. 2. **design, device, pattern** 문양

Thelma's new quilt has a repetitive floral **motif**.

25 **patience**

n. **endurance, fortitude, perseverance, tolerance** 인내

[péiʃəns]
restiveness

Raising children demands **patience**.

26 **perilous**

adj. **dangerous, hazardous, risky, precarious** 위험한

[pérələs]

Before the Suez Canal, ships had to make the **perilous** trip around the Cape of Good Hope.

27 **personnel**

n. **staff, employees, work force** 직원

[pə̀:rsənél]

The company began a program to change its **personnel** hiring policies.

inconstant	날씨는 대기의 가열 때문에 불안정해진다.
initial	디자인 팀장은 그 인공위성의 최초의 디자인을 승인했다.
lay off	그 고용주는 다음 주에 노동자들 몇 명을 해고할 계획이다.
motif	죽음은 Emily Dickinson의 시에서 공통적인 주제이다.
	Thelma의 새로운 담요에는 반복되는 꽃 문양이 있다.
patience	아이를 키우는 일은 인내를 요구한다.
perilous	수에즈 운하가 생기기 전에는, 배들은 희망봉 주변에서 위험한 항해를 해야만 했다.
personnel	그 회사는 직원 고용 정책을 바꾸기 위한 프로그램을 시작했다.

28 **ready** [rédi]

adj. **organized, prepared, arranged, set** 준비된

A **ready** source of campaign funds is crucial in contemporary politics.

29 **refuse** [rifjú:z]

v. 1. **reject, decline, deny** 거절하다

Some employees **refused** to take part in the strike.

[réfju:s]

n. 2. **garbage, waste, rubbish, trash** 쓰레기

Millions of tons of **refuse** are added to landfills each year.

30 **revival** [riváivəl]

n. **restoration, renewal, resurgence, rebirth** 재생, 부활

Classical architecture saw a **revival** in Renaissance Europe.

31 **sorrow** [sárou]
joy

n. **distress, anguish, grief** sadness, woe 슬픔

The news of Teresa's death brought **sorrow** to many hearts.

32 **spend** [spénd]
save

v. **expend, squander, waste, consume** 소비하다

The teenage girl **spent** her allowance on a new outfit from the mall.

33 **spot**** [spát]

v. **see, detect, find** locate, recognize 발견하다

Almost instinctively, Luis **spotted** the lack of conviction in Ellen's tone.

34 **steadfast*** [stédfæ̀st]
vacillating

adj. **unwavering, firm, resolute, resolved, decided** 확고한

It is the prime minister's **steadfast** belief that more women should be in Parliament.

ready	준비된 선거 자금원은 현대 정치에서 필수적이다.
refuse	몇몇 직원들은 파업에 참여하길 거부했다.
	매년 수백만의 쓰레기가 매립지에 더해진다.
revival	고전 양식의 건축이 르네상스 시대에 유럽에서 부활했다.
sorrow	Teresa의 사망 소식은 많은 사람들에게 슬픔을 가져다 주었다.
spend	그 십대 소녀는 상점에서 새 옷을 사는데 용돈을 썼다.
spot	거의 본능적으로, Luis는 Ellen의 목소리 톤에서 확신이 결여되어 있음을 발견했다.
steadfast	더 많은 여성이 국회에 있어야 한다는 것이 수상의 확고한 믿음이다.

35 **tension** | n. **pressure, strain** | 긴장, 팽팽함

[ténʃən]

If too much **tension** is placed on the rope, it will snap.

36 **ultimate*** | adj. **final, supreme, utmost** | 궁극적인

[ʌ́ltəmit]

The **ultimate** objective of Hinkley's research is to expand the Earth's natural resources.

37 **with respect to*** | phr. **in reference to, in terms of, with regard to** | ~에 대하여

There are no excuses **with respect to** drunk driving.

Quiz

Choose the synonym.

1. compliment ⓐ fickle, variable, volatile
2. dictate ⓑ determine, require, prescribe
3. inconstant ⓒ expend, squander, waste
4. spend ⓓ commendatin, honor, tribute
5. tension ⓔ pressure, strain

Answer 1. ⓓ 2. ⓑ 3. ⓐ 4. ⓒ 5. ⓔ

tension	밧줄에 지나친 장력이 걸리게 되면 끊어질 것이다.
ultimate	Hinkley의 연구의 궁극적인 목적은 지구의 천연자원을 늘리는 것이다.
with respect to	음주 운전에 대해서는 어떤 변명도 있을 수 없다.

DAY 36

Hackers TOEFL **Vocabulary**

Hackers Voca

www.goHackers.com

1 **anger***	v.	**provoke, aggravate, enrage**	화나게 하다
[ǽŋgər] pacify		It was apparent in David's face that he was **angered** by his friend's sarcastic and accusatory comments.	
2 **auxiliary**	adj.	**subsidiary, subordinate, additional**	보조적인
[ɔːgzíljəri] leading		During the blackout, the doctors used an **auxiliary** power generator.	
3 **bizarre****	adj.	**odd, erratic, strange, exotic, irregular**	기괴한
[bizɑ́ːr] ordinary		The dress the young woman wore was so **bizarre** that people stared at her as she walked past.	
4 **broaden***	v.	**enlarge, expand, develop**	확장하다
[brɔ́ːdən] narrow		Deciding it was time for personal growth, Timmy left home to travel the world for a year and **broaden** his horizons.	
5 **check***	v.	1. **monitor, examine, inspect**	조사하다
[tʃék]		The FBI ordered airlines to **check** passengers' shoes.	
expedite	v.	2. **stop**	막다
		The health organization tried to **check** the spread of cholera.	

anger
auxiliary
bizarre
broaden
check

David의 표정에서 그가 친구의 빈정대는 그리고 힐책하는 말에 화가 났다는 것이 명백하게 나타났다.
정전 기간 동안 의사들은 보조 발전기를 이용했다.
젊은 여자가 입은 드레스가 너무 기괴해서 사람들은 그녀가 지나간 후에 뒤에서 빤히 쳐다보았다.
개인적인 성장을 위한 시간이 필요하다고 결정을 한 후, Timmy는 1년 동안 전 세계를 여행하며 시야를 넓혔다.
FBI는 항공사에 승객들의 신발을 조사하도록 명령했다.
보건 기구는 콜레라의 확산을 막으려고 애썼다.

6 **cite****

[sáit]

v. **mention, refer to, specify** 언급하다

The police department **cited** several dangerous areas downtown.

7 **consensus***

[kənsénsəs]
discord

n. **agreement, unanimity** 합의

After a long meeting, the two sides were finally able to reach a **consensus**.

8 **cope with***

phr. **deal with** ~에 잘 대처하다

The soccer players **coped with** heavy rain and a muddy field as they played the game.

9 **ebb***

[éb]

v. 1. **subside, abate, recede** retire 쇠퇴하다, 약해지다

After 15 years of fame, the singer's popularity began to **ebb**.

flow

n. 2. **reflux** 간조, 썰물

The **ebb** and flow of ocean tides are caused by the moon's revolving around the earth.

10 **elementary****

[èləméntəri]
advanced

adj. **rudimentary, basic** fundamental, primary 기초적인

Carl did not even have an **elementary** understanding of physics.

11 **fashion***

[fǽʃən]

n. 1. **style, vogue, mode, fad** 유행

Donna always follows the latest **fashions**.

v. 2. **shape, create, make** fabricate 만들다

Colin Powell's masterful diplomacy **fashioned** a broad international coalition against Iraq.

---

cite — 그 경찰서는 시내의 몇몇 위험 지대를 언급했다.
consensus — 오랜 회의 끝에, 양측은 드디어 합의에 도달할 수 있었다.
cope with — 축구 선수들은 경기하는 동안 폭우와 진흙이 된 경기장 바닥에 잘 대처했다.
ebb — 15년간의 명성을 누린 후에, 그 가수의 인기는 시들기 시작했다.
지구 주위를 공전하는 달에 의해 바다에서 밀물과 썰물이 생긴다.
elementary — Carl은 물리학에 대한 기본적인 이해도 하지 못했다.
fashion — Donna는 항상 최신 유행을 따른다.
Colin Powell의 훌륭한 외교술이 이라크에 대항하는 폭넓은 국제적 동맹을 만들어냈다.

v. 3. **fit, adjust, suit** adapt 맞추다

Companies **fashion** their advertisements to the changing times.

12 **finance***

[fáinæns]

v. **pay for** 자금을 조달하다

Catherine's parents decided that they would **finance** her education as long as she received good grades.

13 **force***

[fɔ́:rs]
impotence

n. **strength, power, might** energy 힘

The Liberal Party is a strong **force** in British politics.

14 **legendary***

[lédʒəndəri]
historical

adj. **mythological, fabulous, mythical** 전설적인

Molly Pitcher was a **legendary** heroine of the battle of Monmouth in the Revolutionary War.

15 **markedly****

[mɑ́:rkidli]

adv. **significantly, noticeably, substantially** 현저하게

The moon's density is **markedly** less than the earth's.

16 **obvious****

[ɑ́bviəs]
obscure

adj. **apparent, conspicuous, clear** manifest 명백한

It was **obvious** that Fred didn't understand what Wilma meant.

17 **output***

[áutpùt]
input

n. **production** 결과물

The factory has doubled its **output** in recent months.

18 **overwhelmingly***

[òuvərhwélmiŋli]

adv. **primarily, predominantly** 압도적으로

Parliament **overwhelmingly** approved the anti-terrorism bill.

fashion	회사들은 변화하는 시대에 그들의 광고를 맞춘다.
finance	Catherine의 부모님은 그녀가 좋은 학점을 받는 한 그녀의 교육비를 계속 조달해 주기로 결정했다.
force	자유당은 영국 정치에서 강한 세력을 가진 정당이다.
legendary	Molly Pitcher는 미국 독립 전쟁 때 있었던 Monmouth 전투의 전설적인 여장부이다.
markedly	달의 밀도는 지구의 밀도보다 현저하게 작다.
obvious	Wilma가 의미한 사실을 Fred가 이해하지 못했다는 사실은 명백했다.
output	그 공장은 최근 몇 달 동안 생산량을 두 배로 늘렸다.
overwhelmingly	국회는 압도적으로 반테러리즘 법안을 승인했다.

19 **pension***

[pénʃən]

n. **subsidy, allowance** 연금

Herbert retired with a small **pension** despite having worked at the same company for many years.

20 **pioneer**

[pàiəníər]

v. **first develop, start, introduce, initiate** 개척하다

Alexander Graham Bell **pioneered** telecommunications.

21 **potent**

[póutənt]
impotent

adj. **powerful, mighty, influential** 강력한

Jackson remained a **potent** member of the Democratic party.

22 **probe***

[próub]

v. 1. **search, examine, explore, investigate** 정밀 조사하다

Detectives questioned the suspect for hours, **probing** for any inconsistencies in his story.

n. 2. **exploration, inquiry, quest** 조사

Both Britain and France launched a **probe** into how Reid had slipped through their security net.

23 **quaint****

[kwéint]

adj. **bizarre, odd, weird** extraordinary, eccentric 기이한

The respected customs of yesterday now seem merely **quaint**.

24 **react**

[riǽkt]

v. **respond, answer, reply** 반응하다

The doctors waited to see how the patient would **react** to the medication.

25 **reap****

[rí:p]

v. **harvest, gather; obtain** 수확하다 ; 획득하다

The slaves **reaped** the wheat in the field all day.

pension	Herbert는 여러 해 동안 같은 회사에서 일했는데도 적은 액수의 연금만을 받고 퇴직했다.
pioneer	Alexander Graham Bell은 전자 통신 분야를 개척하였다.
potent	Jackson은 민주당 내에 강력한 멤버로 남아 있었다.
probe	형사들은 용의자의 진술에 모순이 있는지 조사하면서 여러 시간 동안 그에게 질문을 했다. 영국과 프랑스 둘 다 어떻게 Reid가 그들의 보호망을 뚫고 빠져나갔는지에 대한 조사를 시작했다.
quaint	그 과거에 존중받던 관습들은 이제는 단지 기이하게 보인다.
react	의사들은 환자가 약물에 어떻게 반응하는지를 보기 위해 기다렸다.
reap	그 노예들은 하루 종일 들판에서 밀을 수확했다.

26 spectrum* [spéktrəm]

n. range, **extent, scope** 범위

Jay Leno introduced his two guests as social critics from opposite ends of the political **spectrum**.

27 stock** [sták]

n. reserve, inventory, **hoard** store 비축(물)

The supermarket keeps a **stock** of imported canned goods on its shelves.

28 strain* [stréin]

v. 1. **stretch, tighten** 잡아당기다

Supplies will be further **strained** by the high demands of consumers.

n. 2. tension 팽팽함, 긴장

Dennis could not take the **strain** of working as a stock broker on Wall Street.

29 stroke* [stróuk]

n. hit, striking, **blow** beat 일격

The player up at bat thwacked the ball with such a powerful **stroke** that it flew clear across the stadium.

30 sturdy* [stə́:rdi] decrepit

adj. strong, **robust, stalwart** muscular, stout 튼튼한

The school purchased **sturdy** desks and chairs that are expected to last several years.

31 tactic(s) [tǽktiks]

n. strategy, **maneuver** 전술, 책략

Prohibitionists achieved their goals because of their group **tactics**.

32 tapered [téipərd]

adj. narrow, **tapering** 좁아진

Tapered table legs are a popular furniture design.

spectrum	Jay Leno는 두 초대 손님을 각각 진보와 보수의 대표적인 사회 비평가로 소개했다.
stock	슈퍼마켓에서는 수입 통조림 제품의 재고품을 선반에 보관하고 있다.
strain	공급은 소비자들의 높아진 수요 때문에 더욱 부족해질 것이다.
	Dennis는 월스트리트에서 주식 중매인으로 일하면서 받는 긴장감을 감당할 수 없었다.
stroke	타석에 나선 선수가 공에 힘찬 일격을 가하자, 공이 경기장을 훌쩍 넘어 날라갔다.
sturdy	학교는 수 년 동안 지탱할 만한 튼튼한 책상과 의자들을 구입했다.
tactic(s)	주류 제조 판매 금지론자들은 집단으로 행동하는 그들의 전술 덕분에 목표를 달성했다.
tapered	끝이 좁아지는 탁자 다리는 인기 있는 가구 디자인이다.

33 **upsurge***

[ʌpsə́ːrdʒ]
decline

n. **increase, rise** 급증

Adolescence is marked by an **upsurge** of sexual feelings.

34 **utility**

[juːtíləti]

n. **practicality, usefulness** 실용성

The engineer based his design on **utility** rather than appearance.

35 **whereas**

[*h*wεərǽz]

conj. **while, on the contrary** ~에 반하여

Dorian prefers curling up with a book, **whereas** his roommate enjoys watching ball games on television.

36 **widespread****

[wáidsprèd]
uncommon

adj. **prevalent, broadly accepted, sweeping** 널리 퍼진, 광범위한

The campaign to keep local parks clean has received **widespread** support.

Quiz

Choose the synonym.

1. bizarre	ⓐ practicality, usefulness
2. consensus	ⓑ odd, erratic, exotic
3. pension	ⓒ agreement, unanimity
4. spectrum	ⓓ subsidy, allowance
5. utility	ⓔ range, extent, scope

Answer 1. ⓑ 2. ⓒ 3. ⓓ 4. ⓔ 5. ⓐ

upsurge	사춘기는 성적인 감각의 급증으로 특징 지어진다.
utility	그 기술자는 자신의 설계를 외형보다는 실용성에 기초했다.
whereas	Dorian은 구부려 앉아 책읽는 것을 좋아하는 반면, 그의 룸메이트는 TV로 야구 경기 보는 것을 즐긴다.
widespread	공원을 깨끗하게 보존하기 위한 캠페인이 지역사회에서 널리 지지를 받아 왔다.

Choose the synonym of the highlighted word in the sentence.

1. Despite strong opposition form the public, real estate developers remained steadfast in their plan to tear down the historic building.
(A) uncanny (B) stern (C) unwavering (D) declarative

2. At the dawn of the space age, its scope and possibilities could then be only dimly perceived.
(A) faintly (B) notably (C) influentially (D) clearly

3. During the expansion era of American History, writers began to look across their enlarged continental homeland for their subjects and themes.
(A) qualified (B) extended (C) plunged (D) struggled

4. Soil formation is extremely slow, especially in its initial stages.
(A) definite (B) beginning (C) productive (D) skeptical

5. Three thousand years ago, settlers in central Italy forged a civilization that became the Roman Empire.
(A) contrived (B) created (C) manufactured (D) envisioned

6. Soil erosion has accelerated due to new demands placed on the land.
(A) flourished (B) captivated (C) tightened (D) speeded up

7. Smallpox was the first widespread disease to be eliminated by human intervention.
(A) stationary (B) definite (C) fickle (D) prevalent

8. The flood waters began to ebb just as it appeared that there would be major damage to the city.
(A) dissipate (B) recede (C) relinquish (D) partition

9. The scene of the assassination remained embedded in the minds of witnesses for quite some time.
(A) fixed (B) located (C) ordered (D) purposed

10. The abstract algebra used today evolved out of the fundamentals of elementary algebra.
(A) stained (B) advanced (C) flexible (D) rudimentary

정답 p.419

Perseverance 끈기

Perseverance is more prevailing than violence.
끈기는 폭력보다 더 낫다. - Plutarch 풀루타르크(그리스 전기작가)

The finest edge is made with the blunt whetstone.
아무리 잘 드는 칼날도 뭉툭한 숫돌로 만들어진다. - J. Lyly J. 릴리(영국 극작가)

The difference between perseverance and obstinacy is that one often comes from a strong will, and the other from a strong won't.
끈기와 고집의 차이는 끈기는 강한 의지력에서 나오고, 고집은 강하게 바라지는 않는 것에서 나오는 것이다.
- H. W. Beecher H. W. 비처(미국목사)

All that you do, do with your might, things done by halves are never done right.
무슨 일이든 전력을 다해서 하라.하다가 마는 것은 제대로 하는 것이 아니다.
- R. H. Stoddard R. H. 스토다드(미국시인)

Perseverance is falling nineteen times and succeeding the twentieth.
끈기란 열아홉 번 실패해도 스무 번째 성공하는 것이다. - S. Anderson S. 앤더슨(미국작가)

37 Hackers Voca

1 **accomplish**** | v. **achieve, work out, execute, put through** 성취하다

[əkɑ́mpliʃ]

Nothing could keep David from **accomplishing** his goal.

2 **accordingly**** | adv. **for that reason, consequently** 따라서

[əkɔ́ːrdiŋli]

Sam was told to speak briefly; **accordingly**, he cut short his speech.

3 **alarm*** | n. 1. **fear, fright, terror, dismay** horror 공포, 놀람

[əlɑ́ːrm]
composure

Jane felt **alarm** at the sight of the snake.

v. 2. **upset, surprise, startle** 놀라게 하다

The result of Taiwan's presidential election is certain to **alarm** Beijing.

4 **apparatus** | n. **device, equipment** 기구

[æ̀pərǽtəs]

The word SCUBA is an acronym for Self-Contained Underwater Breathing **Apparatus**.

5 **backbone**** | n. **foundation; spine** 중추 ; 척추

[bǽkbòun]

Agriculture has formed the **backbone** of the country's economy.

accomplish	어떤 것도 그의 목적을 달성하려고 노력하는 David를 막을 수 없었다.
accordingly	Sam은 간단히 연설하라고 들었기 때문에 그는 그의 연설을 짧게 끝냈다.
alarm	Jane은 뱀을 보자 공포를 느꼈다.
	대만의 대통령 선거 결과가 중국 정부를 놀라게 할 것이 확실하다.
apparatus	SCUBA는 '자가 수중 호흡 기구'의 약자이다.
backbone	농업은 그 나라 경제의 중추를 형성했다.

6 **bode***

[bóud]

v. **foretell, presage** 징조가 되다

The early sales figures **bode** well for the success of the book.

7 **cargo***

[káːrgou]

n. **load, freight, shipment, burden** 화물

The sailors unloaded the **cargo** from the ship.

8 **composition***

[kàmpəzíʃən]

n. **make-up, formation, organization** 구성(물), 조직

The **composition** of ordinary table salt is a mixture of chloride and sodium.

9 **conduit***

[kándjuit]

n. **pipe, channel** 도관, 선

Cable networks are a crucial **conduit** for delivering information.

10 **consider****

[kənsídər]
ignore

v. **contemplate, muse; deem** 깊이 생각하다 ; 간주하다

One must carefully **consider** what to do first.

11 **dual***

[djú(ː)əl]

adj. **double** 이중의

After the addition of the camera feature, many cellular phones began to serve a **dual** purpose.

12 **encroach***

[inkróutʃ]
keep off

v. **invade, trespass, intrude** 침입하다

The hunters were fined heavily for **encroaching** on the farmer's property.

13 **ensue***

[insúː]
antecede

v. **follow, result, succeed** 뒤따라 일어나다

The two students began arguing and a fight **ensued**.

bode	초기 판매량은 책의 성공을 위한 좋은 징조이다.
cargo	선원들은 배에서 화물을 내렸다.
composition	일반적인 식탁용 소금의 구성은 염화물과 나트륨의 혼합물로 이루어져 있다.
conduit	케이블 회로망들은 정보를 전달하기 위한 중요한 선이다.
consider	사람은 무엇을 먼저 할 것인지 조심스럽게 깊이 생각해야만 한다.
dual	카메라 기능이 더해진 후에, 많은 휴대폰이 이중적인 용도로 쓰이기 시작했다.
encroach	그 사냥꾼들은 농부의 사유지를 침범했기 때문에 중한 벌금형을 받았다.
ensue	그 두 학생은 논쟁을 하기 시작했고 싸움이 뒤이어 일어났다.

14 equip* | v. **furnish, provide** (필요한 것을) 갖추어 주다

[ikwíp]

The laboratory is **equipped** for atomic research.

15 establish** | v. **organize, constitute, set up, institute** found 설립하다

[istǽbliʃ]
abrogate

Washington's first concern was to **establish** the executive departments.

16 exorbitant** | adj. **expensive, excessive, extravagant, immoderate** 과도한

[igzɔ́ːrbitənt]
reasonable

The restaurant is excellent, but its prices are **exorbitant**.

17 explicit* | adj. **clear, obvious, unambiguous, definite** 명백한

[iksplísit]
ambiguous

The secretary was given **explicit** instructions not to give callers the manager's private phone number.

18 frantic* | adj. **hectic, desperate, frenzied** 미친 (광란의)

[frǽntik]

There was a **frantic** rush to get the last available tickets before the game.

19 hectic* | adj. **full of excitement, feverish, fervid** 매우 흥분한

[héktik]
tranquil

The child had a pretty **hectic** day at school.

20 inaugurate | v. **begin, commence, install** 개시하다

[inɔ́ːgjərèit]
complete

Following every federal election year in America, a ceremony is held to **inaugurate** the new president's term of office.

21 incise** | v. **carve, cut, engrave** 새기다

[insáiz]

A stone **incised** with decorative symbols was recently purchased by the museum.

---

equip	그 실험실은 원자 연구를 위한 장비를 갖추고 있다.
establish	Washington의 첫 번째 관심은 행정 부서를 설립하는 것이었다.
exorbitant	그곳은 멋진 레스토랑이지만 가격이 너무 비싸다.
explicit	비서는 전화를 거는 사람들에게 부장의 개인 전화번호를 주지 말라는 명백한 지시를 받았다.
frantic	그 경기 전에, 마지막으로 남은 티켓들을 얻으려고 사람들이 미친 듯이 쇄도했다.
hectic	그 아이는 학교에서 상당히 흥분된 하루를 보냈다.
inaugurate	미국에서 연방 선거가 있는 그 다음 해가 되면 새로운 대통령의 재임 기간을 개시하기 위한 행사가 열린다.
incise	장식적인 기호들이 새겨져 있는 돌을 최근에 그 박물관이 구입했다.

22 **jubilant*** | adj. **exulting, joyful** | 환희에 찬

[dʒúːbələnt]
mournful

Michelle seemed to be **jubilant** at her success.

23 **mode*** | n. **form, fashion, method, style** | 양식, 형태

[móud]

The North Americans showed a desire for an effective **mode** of transportation.

24 **ominous**** | adj. **foreboding, threatening, doomful** | 불길한

[ámənəs]
auspicious

The Oregon crisis was **ominous** because it coincided with a threat of war with Mexico.

25 **own** | v. **acknowledge, admit, allow** | 인정하다

[óun]
disallow

Nancy **owned** that the pioneering environmental writer influenced her work.

26 **perpetual***** | adj. **constant, ceaseless, enduring** | 끊임없는

[pərpétʃuəl]

Mike moved because of the **perpetual** noise from the apartment next door.

27 **praiseworthy** | adj. **admirable, commendable, laudable, praisable** | 칭찬할 만한

[préizwə̀ːrði]

The students were recognized for their **praiseworthy** efforts in helping the elderly.

28 **progressive*** | adj. **advanced, liberal** | 진보적인

[prəgrésiv]
reactionary

The candidate touted his **progressive** views as being in touch with the electorate.

29 **provide**** | v. **supply, afford, furnish** | 제공하다

[prəváid]

The hotel **provides** a shoe-cleaning service for guests.

jubilant	Michelle은 그녀의 성공으로 인해 환희에 찬 것처럼 보였다.
mode	북미인들은 효과적인 교통 형태에 대한 열망을 보였다.
ominous	Oregon 위기는 멕시코와의 전쟁의 위협과 동시에 일어났기 때문에 불길했다.
own	Nancy는 선구적인 환경 보호 작가가 그녀의 작품에 영향을 주었다고 인정했다.
perpetual	Mike는 옆집으로부터 끊임없이 흘러나오는 소음 때문에 이사했다.
praiseworthy	그 학생들은 노인을 도운 기특한 노력들을 인정받았다.
progressive	그 후보자는 유권자들과 접촉하면서 그의 진보적인 견해를 알렸다.
provide	그 호텔은 손님들을 위해 신발을 닦아 주는 서비스를 제공한다.

30 provision n. **supply, food** 식량

[prəvíʒən]

The students made an investigation of the cause of the present high price of **provisions**.

31 puzzle over phr. **wonder about** 쩔쩔매다, 이리저리 생각하다

The students spent much of the class time **puzzling over** a difficult geometry problem the teacher gave them.

32 ruinous* adj. **destructive, catastrophic** 파괴적인

[rú(:)inəs]

The protracted war had a **ruinous** effect on the invaded nation.

33 solicitation n. **invitation, entreaty, request** 권유, 간청

[səlìsitéiʃən]

College students often receive **solicitations** from credit card companies.

34 solicitude n. **concern, anxiety, care, worry** 근심, 염려

[səlísitjùːd]

The president expressed deep **solicitude** for the victims of the bombing.

35 stray v. **wander, deviate, straggle, swerve** 벗어나다, 이탈하다

[stréi]

Lions will often hunt animals that have **strayed** from the herd.

36 troublesome** adj. **onerous, difficult, annoying** burdensome 힘든 (성가신)

[trʌ́blsəm]
innocuous

The job of amending incorrect land titles was **troublesome** for Thomas Lincoln.

37 unqualified* adj. **complete, absolute, utter, thorough** 절대적인

[ʌnkwɑ́ləfàid]
circumscribed

Martha was an exceptional woman who will be remembered with **unqualified** affection.

provision	그 학생들은 현재 식료품의 높은 가격의 원인에 대한 연구를 수행했다.
puzzle over	학생들은 수업 시간 대부분을 선생님이 주신 어려운 기하 문제에 쩔쩔매면서 보냈다.
ruinous	장기화된 전쟁은 피침략국에게 파괴적인 결과를 가져왔다.
solicitation	대학생들은 종종 신용 카드 회사들로부터 (카드 발급) 권유를 받는다.
solicitude	대통령들은 폭격의 희생자들에게 깊은 애도를 표했다.
stray	사자들은 종종 무리에서 이탈한 동물들을 사냥하곤 한다.
troublesome	잘못된 토지 소유 증서를 정정하는 일은 Thomas Lincoln에게 힘든 일이었다.
unqualified	Martha는 절대적인 애정과 함께 기억될 특별한 여성이다.

38 **weak** | adj. **infirm, fragile, frail, delicate** feeble | 약한

[wí:k]
strong

The cold made Lisa feel tired and **weak**.

39 **witness***

[wítnis]

v. 1. **observe, watch, notice** | 목격하다

Young adults are **witnessing** the worsening of global conditions.

n. 2. **testimony, evidence** | 증거

If there weren't **witnesses** to the event, Mary wouldn't believe Bruce's remark.

Quiz

Choose the synonym.

1. consider
2. exorbitant
3. troublesome
4. weak
5. perpetual

ⓐ excessive, expensive, extravagant
ⓑ annoying, difficult, onerous
ⓒ contemplate, meditate, ponder
ⓓ constant, ceaseless, enduring
ⓔ fragile, frail, delicate

Answer 1. ⓒ 2. ⓐ 3. ⓑ 4. ⓔ 5. ⓓ

weak
witness

추위 때문에 Lisa는 피곤하고 허약하다고 느꼈다.
젊은이들은 지구 환경이 악화되는 것을 목격하고 있다.
그 사건에 대한 증거가 없다면, Mary는 Bruce가 한 말을 믿지 않을 것이다.

DAY 38

Hackers TOEFL **Vocabulary**

Hackers Voca

www.goHackers.com

1 **abhor***	v.	**loathe, hate, detest**	혐오하다
[əbhɔ́:r] admire		Some people genuinely **abhorred** slavery.	
2 **ambition****	n.	**goal, desire**	야망
[æmbíʃən]		Bruce's **ambition** was to be a great scientist.	
3 **bulk****	n.	**great quantity; main part**	거대함(대량) ; 대부분
[bʌ́lk]		Buying its supplies in **bulk**, the department store chain was able to sell for less than its competitors.	
4 **charitable**	adj.	**broad-minded, tolerant, benign, generous**	관대한, 자비로운
[tʃǽritəbl] narrow-minded, stingy		Grandmother was always **charitable** towards strangers.	
5 **conclusively***	adv.	**decisively, definitely, absolutely**	결정적으로, 확실히
[kənklú:sivli] questionably		Even though it is popular with the scientists, the Big Bang theory has not yet been **conclusively** proven.	
6 **confer**	v.	**give, bestow, grant**	수여하다
[kənfə́:r] refuse		An honorary degree was **conferred** on the senator.	

abhor	몇몇 사람들은 노예 제도를 진심으로 혐오했다.
ambition	Bruce의 야망은 위대한 과학자가 되는 것이었다.
bulk	대량으로 물건을 구매해서 그 체인점 매장은 경쟁 업체보다 더 싸게 팔 수 있었다.
charitable	할머니는 언제나 낯선 사람들에게 관대하셨다.
conclusively	대폭발 우주론이 과학자들에게는 널리 알려졌지만 아직 명백히 증명되지는 않았다.
confer	명예 학위가 그 상원 의원에게 수여되었다.

7 deny v. **negate, gainsay, contradict** 부인하다

[dinái]
confirm

Carter **denied** that he was a communist.

8 echo v. 1. **reflect, mirror; resonate, resound** 반영하다 ; 반향하다

[ékou]

Newspaper editorials often **echo** the views of the readers.

v. 2. **repeat, reiterate, parrot, copy** 반복하다

The ballet students **echoed** the movements of their instructor.

9 eerie adj. **strange, mysterious, weird, unearthly** 기묘한

[í(:)əri]

The book 1984 was an **eerie** prediction of the future.

10 emulate v. **imitate, copy, follow, mimic** 모방하다

[émjəlèit]

Children often **emulate** the behavior of their parents.

11 forestall* v. **prevent, hinder** 미리 막다, 미리 손쓰다

[fɔːrstɔ́ːl]
expedite

The union leader **forestalled** a riot by telling the strikers to disperse.

12 generally** adv. **largely, chiefly, mainly** mostly 대부분, 주로

[dʒénərəli]

Generally speaking, women enjoy shopping more than men do.

13 glance n. **glimpse, a brief look, a cursory look** 흘긋 봄

[glǽns]
focus

Francis gave a quick **glance** around the room before leaving.

deny	Carter는 자신이 공산주의자라는 것을 부인했다.
echo	신문 사설은 종종 독자들의 의견을 반영한다.
	그 발레하는 학생들은 선생님의 동작들을 따라 하였다.
eerie	'1984년'이란 그 책은 미래의 기묘한 예언을 담은 책이었다.
emulate	아이들은 종종 부모들의 행동을 모방한다.
forestall	노동조합장은 파업 노동자들이 흩어지라고 말해 폭동을 미리 막았다.
generally	일반적으로 말해서, 여성들은 남성들보다 쇼핑을 더 즐긴다.
glance	Francis는 떠나기 전에 방을 잠깐 둘러 보았다.

14 implement* n. **tool, appliance, device** 도구

[ímpləmənt]

The dentist's **implements** were placed in arm's reach on a tray near the patient.

15 in terms of* phr. **with regard to, with respect to, in relation to** ~에 관하여

Lego toys are unparalleled **in terms of** quality.

16 inveigh against* phr. **rail, object, criticize strongly** 통렬히 비판하다

agree with

The Democrat senator could not agree with further tax cuts, and **inveighed** strongly **against** the Republican party's position.

17 look* v. **gaze, glance, watch, view** 보다

[lúk]

Anxious to go home, Fred would **look** at the clock every few minutes.

18 monetary adj. **financial, pecuniary, capital** 재정(금전)상의

[mániteri]

For **monetary** reasons, the family had to sell their house and move into an apartment.

19 motion* n. **movement, move, gesture** 움직임, 동작

[móuʃən]
inertia

The rocking **motion** of the boat made Julia feel sick.

20 obtain** v. **gain, earn, achieve, acquire** 얻다

[əbtéin]

Despite a difficult childhood, Charles managed to **obtain** a good education.

21 outspoken adj. **frank, open, candid** 솔직한

[àutspóukən]
reserved

Christine's **outspoken** nature sometimes offends people.

implement	치과 의사의 도구는 팔이 닿는 곳에 있는 환자 근처의 접시 위에 놓여져 있었다.
in terms of	레고 장난감들은 질에 있어서 견줄만한 것이 없다.
inveigh against	그 민주당 상원 의원은 더 이상의 세금 인하에 동의할 수 없었으며 공화당의 입장에 대해 통렬하게 비판했다.
look	집에 가고 싶어 안절부절 못하며 Fred는 몇 분마다 시계를 바라보았다.
monetary	금전상의 이유로 그 가족은 집을 팔고 아파트로 이사를 가야만 했다.
motion	그 보트의 흔들리는 움직임 때문에 Julia는 속이 안 좋았다.
obtain	불우했던 유년 시절에도 불구하고, Charles는 양질의 교육을 받았다.
outspoken	Christine의 솔직한 성격이 때로는 사람들을 화나게 한다.

22 **pant***
[pǽnt]

v. 1. **gasp** 숨을 헐떡이다
Unable to sweat, dogs **pant** to regulate their body heat and keep cool.

n. 2. **trouser** 바지
Capri **pants** are a popular trend in women's fashion.

23 **patchy****
[pǽtʃi]

adj. **irregular, uneven, erratic** 고르지 않은
Patchy skin color may be a symptom of a serious condition.

24 **precipitation***
[prisìpitéiʃən]

n. **acceleration, haste, impetuosity** 촉진, 성급함
Political factors contributed to the **precipitation** of the Great Depression.

25 **promote****
[prəmóut]
check

v. **advance, further, encourage** 촉진하다
There was a meeting to **promote** trade between China and the United States.

26 **purified***
[pjúərəfàid]
defiled, sullied, tarnished

adj. **cleansed, refined, clarified, distilled** 정화된
The water must be **purified** before people drink it.

27 **recreational***
[rèkriéiʃənəl]

adj. **as a hobby** 오락의, 휴양의
Recreational activities add to the quality of life.

28 **recruit***
[rikrúːt]

v. **obtain, enlist** 얻다, 모집하다
Countries with labor shortages often **recruit** workers from overseas.

pant	땀을 흘리지 못하기 때문에, 개들은 몸의 열을 조절하고 시원하게 유지시키기 위해 숨을 헐떡인다. 카프리 바지는 여자들 사이에서 인기 있는 패션 경향이다.
patchy	고르지 않은 피부색은 심각한 건강 상태의 증상이다.
precipitation	정치적인 요소들이 대공황을 촉진시키는 한 요인이 되었다.
promote	중국과 미국 사이의 무역을 촉진하기 위한 회의가 있었다.
purified	물은 사람들이 마시기 전에 정화되어야 한다.
recreational	여가 활동들은 삶의 질을 높여 준다.
recruit	노동력 부족을 겪는 나라들은 종종 해외에서 노동자들을 구한다.

29 **seize**** | v. grip, take, **clasp, grasp** grab | 움켜잡다

[síːz]
loose

Robert **seized** Theresa's hand suddenly and dragged her away from the window.

30 **structure**** | n. 1. system, **frame, organization** | 구조

[strʌ́ktʃər]

The industrial **structure** in Italy is made up of mostly small and medium-sized businesses.

v. 2. arrange in definite pattern | 조직화하다

The Bill of Rights was **structured** to protect the individual rights of all citizens.

31 **surreal**** | adj. having a strange dream-like quality | 초현실적인

[sərí:əl]

Surreal artists like Dali became hugely popular in the 1980's.

32 **synthesis**** | n. unit, union, combination, **mixture** | 통합체, 통합

[sínθəsis]

The sect's beliefs are a **synthesis** of Eastern and Western religions.

33 **textile**** | n. cloth, fabric | 직물

[tékstail]

One of the earliest forms of printing was **textile** printing.

34 **thereby*** | adv. by that means, **as a result of that** | 그것에 의하여

[ðɛ̀ərbái]

The tanker ran aground, **thereby** causing a massive oil spill.

35 **title** | n. ownership | 권리

[táitl]

Scientists working at research universities often have no **title** to their own inventions.

seize	Robert는 Theresa의 손을 갑자기 움켜잡고 그녀를 창가로부터 끌어당겼다.
structure	이탈리아의 산업 구조는 대부분 작거나 중간 규모의 사업체들로 구성되어 있다.
	권리 장전은 모든 시민의 권리를 보호하기 위해 조직화되었다.
surreal	Dali와 같은 초현실적인 예술가들이 1980년대에 매우 인기를 얻게 되었다.
synthesis	그 종파의 믿음은 서양과 동양 종교의 통합이다.
textile	인쇄술의 초기 형태들 중 한가지는 직물 인쇄였다.
thereby	그 유조선은 좌초하였고, 그 결과 거대한 기름 유출이 발생했다.
title	연구 중심 대학에서 일하는 과학자들은 자신의 발명에 대해서 아무런 권리를 갖지 못하는 경우가 많다.

36 **transcend**** [trænsénd]
v. **go beyond** 초월하다
The size of the universe **transcends** our understanding.

37 **twig*** [twíg]
n. **branch, stick, offshoot, sprig** 가지
Schoolteachers used to punish children by hitting them with **twigs**.

38 **vulnerable*** [vʌ́lnərəbl]
adj. **easily damaged, susceptible, weak** (영향을) 받기 쉬운
Babies are **vulnerable** to attack from influenza.

39 **wholly*** [hóulli]
partially
adv. **completely, fully, in every respect, thoroughly** 완전히
The team has prepared a **wholly** convincing argument for their debate.

Quiz

Choose the synonym.

1. charitable	ⓐ prevent, hinder, anticipate
2. forestall	ⓑ grasp, grab, grip
3. precipitation	ⓒ generous, benign, kind
4. seize	ⓓ haste, impetuosity, acceleration
5. textile	ⓔ cloth, fabric

Answer 1. ⓒ 2. ⓐ 3. ⓓ 4. ⓑ 5. ⓔ

transcend	우주의 크기는 우리의 이해를 초월한다.
twig	학교 교사들은 아이들을 나뭇가지로 때림으로써 벌주곤 했다.
vulnerable	아기들은 유행성 감기의 공격에 취약하다.
wholly	그 팀은 토론을 위해, 전적으로 수긍이 가는 주장을 준비했다.

DAY Hackers TOEFL Vocabulary

39 Hackers Voca

www.goHackers.com

1 abrupt**

[əbrʌ́pt]
dilatory

adj. **sharp, sudden, hasty** hurried 급한, 갑작스러운

The airbag was released when the car came to an **abrupt** stop.

2 adequate

[ǽdəkwit]
inadequate

adj. **sufficient, satisfactory** 충분한

Richard's research cannot be completed without **adequate** funding.

3 advocate**

[ǽdvəkèit]
impugn

v. 1. **urge, support** 주장하다, 지지하다

The lobbyist is **advocating** the new bill to a senator.

opponent

n. 2. **proponent, supporter, upholder** 지지자

Rep. Norman Sisisky was a strong **advocate** for defense spending during nine terms in Congress.

4 appendix*

[əpéndiks]

n. **supplement, adjunct** 부록, 부가물

The **appendix** to the report provides current figures on the use of modem and broadband connections by region.

5 appropriate

[əpróuprieit]
inappropriate

adj. **suitable, proper, applicable** 적절한

Brittany's clothes were not **appropriate** for a job interview.

abrupt 그 차가 갑자기 멈추자 에어백이 터졌다.
adequate Richard의 연구는 충분한 자금 지원 없이는 완성될 수 없다.
advocate 그 로비스트는 상원의원에게 그 새 법안을 주장하고 있다.
공화당원인 Norman Sisisky는 국회에서의 아홉 번의 임기 동안 국방비 지출을 열렬히 지지했다.
appendix 보고서의 부록은 모뎀 및 광대역 통신망 사용의 지역별 최근 수치들을 제공하고 있다.
appropriate Brittany의 옷은 면접에 적절하지 않았다.

6 **assumption****

[əsʌ́mpʃən]

n. **supposition** 가정

The result of the experiment shook the basic **assumptions** of Steven's theory.

7 **bestow**

[bistóu]

v. **give, grant, confer, award** 주다, 수여하다

Merit financial scholarships are **bestowed** to high-achieving students.

8 **boldly**

[bóuldli]

adv. **bravely, daringly, courageously** 용감하게

Russian settlers **boldly** traveled to Siberia in the eighteenth century.

9 **choicest**

[tʃɔ́isist]

adj. **best, matchless** 엄선된, 가장 좋은

Gourmet foods are made of only the **choicest** ingredients.

10 **classic**

[klǽsik]

adj. **typical, exemplary, model, standard** 전형적인, 대표적인

The Beatles are **classic** examples of British popular musicians.

11 **constitute**

[kánstitjùːt]

v. **make up, comprise, compose** 구성하다

Several different ethnic groups **constitute** the population of Malaysia.

12 **deposit****

[dipázit]

v. **lay, place; save, store** 두다 ; 비축하다

Letters must be **deposited** in the box marked 'To send.'

13 **dogma***

[dɔ́(ː)gmə]

n. **belief, credo, creed** 신념, 신조

The **dogma** that the end justifies the means is not true.

assumption	그 실험의 결과는 Steven의 이론의 기본적인 가정들을 흔들었다.
bestow	성적 우수 장학금은 뛰어난 성적의 학생들에게 수여된다.
boldly	러시아인 개척자들은 18세기에 용감하게 시베리아로 갔었다.
choicest	특별 요리들은 엄선된 재료만으로 만들어진다.
classic	비틀즈는 영국 대중 음악가의 대표적인 예이다.
constitute	몇몇의 다양한 소수 민족들이 말레이시아 인구를 구성한다.
deposit	편지들은 '발송'이라고 표시된 그 상자에 두어야 한다.
dogma	결과가 수단을 정당화한다는 그 신조는 사실이 아니다.

14 **employ****

[implɔ́i]

v. **use, utilize, exploit** 이용하다

High-frequency signals are **employed** for radio transmission.

15 **endorse***

[indɔ́:rs]
disapprove

v. 1. **support, back, approve, advocate** 보증하다, 지지하다

A slim majority of British politicians **endorsed** the prime minister's controversial decision to go to war.

v. 2. **sign, subscribe** 배서(서명)하다

The bank refused to accept Kelly's check until she **endorsed** it.

16 **exponential***

[èkspounénʃəl]

adj. **explosive, incremental** 급격한

Analysts predicted the pharmaceutical company would continue to grow at an **exponential** rate.

17 **foremost***

[fɔ́:rmòust]

adj. **most respected, preeminent, supreme** 으뜸가는

Colin Powell is considered by many to be the **foremost** African-American government official in U.S. history.

18 **fragrance***

[fréigrəns]
malodor

n. **scent** 향기

Jane's room was full of the sweet **fragrance** of roses.

19 **furthermore****

[fə́:rðərmɔ̀:r]

adv. **moreover, in addition** 더욱이

Furthermore, it should be stated that not everyone who gets married early will eventually divorce.

20 **genetic***

[dʒənétik]
acquired

adj. **hereditary, inborn, inheritable** 유전(학)적인

Scientists have deciphered the **genetic** blueprint of a human DNA.

employ	고주파 신호들이 라디오 전파를 위해 이용된다.
endorse	절반을 겨우 넘는 영국 의원들이 논란이 되고 있는 수상의 참전 결정을 지지했다. 은행은 Kelly가 배서할 때까지 그녀의 수표를 받아들이는 것을 거절했다.
exponential	분석 전문가들은 제약 회사들이 급격한 속도로 성장을 계속할 것이라고 예상했다.
foremost	Colin Powell은 많은 사람들에 의해 미국 역사상 가장 뛰어난 아프리카계 미국 정부 관료로 여겨진다.
fragrance	Jane의 방은 달콤한 장미꽃 향기로 가득했다.
furthermore	게다가 일찍 결혼한 사람들 모두가 결국 이혼하게 된다는 것은 단정지어져서는 안 된다.
genetic	과학자들은 인간 DNA의 유전학적 청사진을 해독했다.

21 **imposing*** adj. **impressive, grand, magnificent** 강한 인상을 주는, 웅장한

[impóuziŋ]

The Empire State Building is an **imposing** structure situated in the heart of New York.

22 **luxurious*** adj. **sumptuous, rich, posh** 사치스러운

[lʌgʒú(:)riəs]
ascetic

Only the rich could have **luxurious** accommodations for long journeys.

23 **matter*** n. 1. **substance, material, stuff** 물질

[mǽtər]

Earthworms help to transport organic **matter** through the soil.

n. 2. **issue** 논점

With the increase in terrorism, national security is a **matter** of serious concern for the government.

24 **nurture*** v. **raise, rear, nurse** 양육하다

[nə́:rtʃər]
disregard

Parents always want to know the best way to **nurture** children.

25 **offset*** v. **balance, counterbalance, counteract** 상쇄하다

[ɔ́(:)fsèt]

Residents on the island claim that the high bridge toll is **offset** by lower housing rentals.

26 **partially** adv. **incompletely, fractionally** 부분적으로

[pɑ́:rʃəli]
completely

The motorcyclist was only **partially** to blame for the chain-reaction car crash.

27 **presumable*** adj. **probable, likely, possible** 있음직한

[prizjú:məbl]
unlikely

An undetected gas leak was the **presumable** cause of the explosion.

imposing	Empire State Building은 뉴욕 시내 한가운데 위치해 있는 웅장한 건축물이다.
luxurious	부자들만이 오랜 기간의 여행을 위해 사치스러운 숙박 시설을 취할 수 있을 것이다.
matter	지렁이들은 토양을 통해 유기 물질들을 나르는 것을 돕는다.
	테러 행위의 증가로 인해, 국가 안보는 정부의 심각한 관심 논점이다.
nurture	부모들은 항상 아이들을 양육하는 가장 좋은 방법을 알기를 원한다.
offset	섬 주민들은 높은 교량 통행료 때문에 낮은 주택 전세가가 상쇄된다고 주장했다.
partially	그 오토바이 운전자는 자동차 연쇄 추돌 사고에 부분적으로만 책임이 있을 뿐이었다.
presumable	감지되지 않은 가스 누출이 그 폭발의 가능한 원인이었다.

28 **principle*** n. **original method, precept, standard** 원칙, 규범

[prínsəpl]

Public schools were built on the **principle** that education should be free for all.

29 **purveyor**** n. **supplier** 공급업자

[pə(:)rvéiər]

The **purveyor** of wine didn't show up at the appointed time.

30 **replace**** v. **supersede, supplant, substitute** 대체하다

[ripléis]

Clean air in many cities had been **replaced** by smog.

31 **routine*** adj. **ordinary, normal, habitual** 보통의, 일상적인

[ru:tí:n]
unusual

Lucy took her daughter to the clinic every six months for a **routine** medical checkup.

32 **scold** v. **reprove, reproach, reprimand** rebuke 꾸짖다

[skóuld]
praise

Jennifer was severely **scolded** by her teachers for passing notes in class.

33 **sequence**** n. 1. **string, series, succession** 연속

[sí:kwəns]

Before stapling the papers, Jenna checked if the page numbers were in **sequence**.

n. 2. **order** 순서

Detectives talked to witnesses in order to establish the **sequence** of events leading up to the crime.

34 **startle**** v. **astonish, surprise, frighten, astound** 깜짝 놀라게 하다

[stá:rtl]

Roger was **startled** to see Peter there and fell off the chair.

principle	공립학교는 교육은 모두에게 무상으로 제공되어야 한다는 원칙하에 세워졌다.
purveyor	그 와인 공급업자는 약속 시간에 나타나지 않았다.
replace	많은 도시에서 깨끗한 공기가 스모그로 대체되었다.
routine	Lucy는 그녀의 딸을 정기적 의료 검진을 위해 6개월마다 병원에 데리고 간다.
scold	Jennifer는 수업 시간에 편지를 주고 받아서 선생님께 매우 혼났다.
sequence	Jenna는 종이를 호치키스로 고정시키기 전에 쪽수가 차례대로 놓여 있는지 확인했다.
	형사들은 범죄가 일어난 사건들의 순서를 정하기 위해 증인들과 이야기를 했다.
startle	Roger는 그곳에서 Peter를 보고 깜짝 놀라서 의자에서 떨어졌다.

35 typical**

[típikəl]
uncharacteristic

adj. **common, ordinary, usual, normal** 일반적인, 전형적인

The **typical** crimes of younger males are larceny and unlawful entry.

36 unshakable

[ʌnʃéikəbl]
changeable

adj. **firm, steadfast, fixed, unwavering** 흔들리지 않는, 확고한

The Amish are well known for an **unshakable** conviction in their religious beliefs.

37 yield**

[jí:ld]
appropriate

v. 1. **cede, surrender, submit, give in** 내주다, 굴복하다

The Taliban **yielded** their position to the enemy.

v. 2. **produce, generate, cause** 산출하다, 야기하다

No one expected that the fireplace would **yield** terrible accidents.

Quiz

Choose the synonym.

1. abrupt	ⓐ sharp, sudden hasty
2. bestow	ⓑ raise, rear, nurse
3. exponential	ⓒ firm, steadfast, fixed
4. nurture	ⓓ give, grant, confer
5. unshakable	ⓔ explosive, incremental

Answer 1. ⓐ 2. ⓓ 3. ⓔ 4. ⓑ 5. ⓒ

typical	남자 아이들의 전형적인 범죄는 절도와 불법 침입이다.
unshakable	암만파는 그들의 흔들리지 않는 종교적 신념으로 유명하다.
yield	탈레반은 그들의 위치를 적에게 넘겨주었다.
	어떤 이도 그 벽난로가 끔찍한 사고를 일으킬 것이라고 예상하지 않았다.

Hackers TOEFL Voca TEST DAY 37-39

Choose the synonym of the highlighted word in the sentence.

1. The governor received a solicitation for relief aid from state residents whose homes were damaged in a flood.

(A) request (B) frequency (C) proposal (D) grant

2. Many jazz musicians have tried to emulate the work of renowned artist Miles Davis.

(A) imitate (B) surround (C) parallel (D) gather

3. Some ominous evidence suggests that this disease may be contagious.

(A) covetous (B) obvious (C) headstrong (D) foreboding

4. Very few people in the modern world obtain their food supply by hunting.

(A) forbid (B) entitle (C) acquire (D) allot

5. A lawyer's duty is to advocate the cause of his client.

(A) hamper (B) support (C) permit (D) scare

6. Herbert and his wife, both outdoor enthusiasts, set up a business as purveyors of camping equipment and recreational clothing.

(A) depositors (B) suppliers (C) frequenters (D) locators

7. A typical classical curriculum will emphasize history, science, and mathematics.

(A) representative (B) elementary (C) voluntary (D) sociable

8. Hippocrates did not employ any aid to diagnosis beyond his own powers of observation and logical reasoning.

(A) advance (B) signify (C) use (D) cheat

9. The male pheasant-tailed jacana doesn't protect nor nurture its partner.

(A) soothe (B) ponder (C) imprison (D) raise

10. Kate abhorred her boss, who had a long history of mistreating employees.

(A) consulted (B) emulate (C) loathed (D) clasped

정답 p.419

TAKE A BREAK

Dreams Come True

DAY Hackers TOEFL Vocabulary

40 Hackers Voca

www.goHackers.com

1 **additive***

[ǽdətiv]

n. 1. **substance added in small amounts to another** 첨가제

Additives in food are used to improve nutrient value and enhance flavor.

adj. 2. **cumulative** 부가적인

Making sculpture is an **additive** process as it includes modeling, adding, and combining or building up materials.

2 **antiseptic*****

[æ̀ntiséptik]

adj. **clean, sterile, sanitary** 청결한, 위생적인

Surgical instruments must be absolutely **antiseptic** to reduce the risk of infection.

3 **assemble****

[əsémbl]
scatter

v. **gather, gather together, bring together, collect** 모으다

The family was **assembled** in the big white dining-room.

4 **asymmetric***

[èisəmétrik]
proportionate

adj. **unequal, lopsided, ill-proportioned** 균형을 잃은

While shopping with Jason, Sarah saw an exquisite gilded **asymmetric** mirror that she wanted for her bedroom.

5 **attire****

[ətáiər]

n. **clothing** 의상

Jeans are not appropriate **attire** for weddings.

additive	음식에 들어가는 첨가제들은 영양가를 높이고 맛을 더하기 위해 사용된다.
	조각 작품을 만드는 것은 자료를 모형에 맞추고, 첨가하고, 화합하거나 조립하는 것을 포함하는 부가적인 과정이다.
antiseptic	감염될 위험을 줄이기 위해서 수술 도구는 완전한 무균 상태여야 한다.
assemble	가족들이 크고 하얀 식당에 모였다.
asymmetric	Jason과 함께 쇼핑하면서 Sarah는 그녀의 침실에 두기 원했던 금박을 입힌 정교한 비대칭 거울을 보았다.
attire	청바지는 결혼식에 적절한 의상은 아니다.

6 **avid****

[ǽvid]

adj. 1. **greedy, avaricious, covetous** 탐욕스러운

Brian had an **avid** ambition to succeed.

adj. 2. **eager, enthusiastic** 열심인, 열렬한

The CEO of the company is an **avid** golfer and spends much of his free time on the links.

7 **basic***

[béisik]

n. **essential** 기본

Those texts examine various weather phenomena, including the **basics** of things such as winds, thunderstorms, tornadoes or hurricanes.

8 **bound***

[báund]

n. **limit, precinct, boundary** border 경계

The company's proposal exceeds the **bounds** of reason.

9 **cluster****

[klʌ́stər]
disperse

v. **group, gather, assemble** 모이다

The autograph seekers **clustered** around the celebrity.

10 **complex***

[kámpleks]

n. 1. **group of buildings** 복합 건물군

A new shopping **complex** is being built in town.

[kəmpléks]
simple

adj. 2. **elaborate, involved, complicated** compound 복잡한

Biologists seek to understand how **complex** species evolved from simpler ones.

11 **contrary***

[kántreri]
concordant

adj. **opposite, converse** 반대의, 반대되는

Contrary to popular belief, cavities are not caused by eating too many sweets.

---

avid	Brian은 성공하려는 탐욕스러운 야망을 가지고 있었다. 그 회사의 CEO는 아주 열렬한 골퍼이고 여가 시간의 대부분도 골프장에서 보낸다.
basics	그 문서들은 바람, 뇌우, 토네이도, 허리케인과 같은 것들에 관한 기초적 사실을 포함하여 다양한 기상 현상을 검토하고 있다.
bound	그 기업의 제안은 이성적으로 생각할 수 있는 범위를 넘어서는 것이다.
cluster	사인을 받으려는 사람들이 그 유명인 주위로 모였다.
complex	새로운 쇼핑 복합 건물이 도시에 지어지고 있다. 생물학자들은 어떻게 복잡한 종들이 단순한 종으로부터 진화했는지 이해하려고 애쓴다.
contrary	일반적인 믿음과는 반대로, 충치는 단것을 많이 먹어서 생기는 것이 아니다.

12 **customary****

[kʌ́stəməri]
occasional

adj. typical, habitual, traditional, **accustomed** 관례적인, 습관적인

It is **customary** to burn a flag when it becomes torn.

13 **dangle***

[dǽŋgl]

v. hang 매달리다

John sat on the desk with his legs **dangling** over the edge.

14 **devour**

[diváuər]

v. **eat, gulp, guzzle** 게걸스레 먹다

The men were so hungry after work that they each **devoured** three heaping platefuls of food.

15 **encapsulate***

[inkǽpsəlèit]

v. state briefly, condense, **summarize** 요약하다, 집약하다

The movie producer found it hard to **encapsulate** the life of the famous poet in a two-hour movie.

16 **faction***

[fǽkʃən]

n. side, **coalition, group** ring, party 파벌

The party is in danger of breaking into two or more **factions**.

17 **fragment****

[frǽgmənt]
whole

n. piece, particle, part, **portion** 조각, 부분

Detectives found a **fragment** of glass which would later help them solve the crime.

18 **ignite**

[ignáit]

v. set on fire, kindle, **inflame, fire** 불을 붙이다

Lightning strikes **ignited** the dry grasslands and caused a fire.

19 **impound**

[impáund]

v. contain, **confine, hold** 가두다

The car was **impounded** for being illegally parked.

customary	깃발이 찢어졌을 때 그것을 불태우는 것은 관례적이다.
dangle	John은 다리를 가장자리에 걸친 채 책상 위에 앉아 있었다.
devour	그 사람들은 일이 끝난 후 너무나 배가 고파서, 각각 수북이 쌓인 세 접시의 음식을 게걸스레 먹어 치웠다.
encapsulate	영화 연출자는 2시간의 영화 속에 유명한 시인의 삶을 집약시키기가 힘들다는 사실을 알았다.
faction	그 당은 두 개나 그 이상의 파벌로 나누어질 위험에 처해 있다.
fragment	형사들은 후에 범죄 해결에 도움이 된 유리 조각을 발견했다.
ignite	벼락들이 건조한 목초지에 불을 붙여서 화재가 났다.
impound	그 차는 불법 주차로 몰수당했다.

20 **innocuous***

[inákjuːəs]
pernicious

adj. **harmless** 해가 없는

The test proved the food additive to be **innocuous**.

21 **link****

[líŋk]

n. 1. **bond, connection, tie** 유대, 결합

The politician severed all **links** with his party.

v. 2. **connect, relate, associate** 관련짓다

Investigators had nothing to **link** the suspect to the crime.

22 **murmur****

[mə́ːrmər]

v. **grumble, mumble, mutter** 투덜거리다, 중얼거리다

Kevin **murmured** a few words of discontent as his mother scolded him.

23 **persistent***

[pərsístənt]
fleeting

adj. **continuous, constant, incessant, perpetual** 지속하는

The **persistent** sound of crickets chirping kept Steve from getting a good night's sleep.

24 **prospect***

[práspekt]

n. **possibility, chance, outlook** 가망성, 전망

There are good **prospects** for growth in the retail sector.

25 **random*****

[rǽndəm]
purposive

adj. **without planning, unpredictable, unsystematic** 마구잡이의

The choice of poems included in the collection seems somewhat **random**.

26 **realize***

[ríːəlàiz]

v. **be aware of, conceive, understand** grasp 알다, 이해하다

Whitney soon **realized** that the South would not readily accept change.

innocuous	그 실험은 그 조미료가 해가 없다는 것을 밝혀냈다.
link	그 정치가는 그의 정당과의 유대 관계를 모두 끊었다.
	수사관들은 그 용의자를 범죄와 관련지을 아무것도 가지고 있지 않았다.
murmur	Kevin은 엄마가 그를 꾸짖자 불만을 갖고 투덜거렸다.
persistent	귀뚜라미의 쉬지 않고 울어대는 소리 때문에 Steve는 잠을 제대로 잘 수 없었다.
prospect	소매업 부분의 성장에 대한 좋은 전망들이 있다.
random	그 시집에 포함되어 있는 시들의 선택은 다소 마구잡이인 것으로 보인다.
realize	Whitney는 남부가 쉽게 변화를 받아들이지 않을 것이라는 사실을 곧 깨달았다.

27 **reside in** | phr. **live in, dwell** 거주하다

Mary still lives in the house that she **resided in** as a child.

28 **robust**** | adj. **strong, vigorous, stalwart** sturdy 튼튼한, 강한

[roubʌ́st]
weak

Women generally prefer sweet delicate wines, while men like **robust** full-bodied wines.

29 **satisfy**** | v. **please, meet, gratify** satiate, suffice 만족시키다

[sǽtisfài]
pique

Sam tried to **satisfy** his master by doing all that he had been ordered to do.

30 **simple*** | adj. **unsophisticated, naive, unaffected, artless** 순진한

[símpl]
worldly

Kate was a **simple** country girl who had never been to a big city before.

31 **stamina*** | n. **endurance, perseverance, vitality** 지구력, 체력

[stǽmənə]

Long-distance runners must be endowed with tremendous **stamina**.

32 **staple*** | n. 1. **basic item, necessary commodity** 중요 상품

[stéipl]

The web site has the best shopping information based on the price comparison for **staples**.

adj. 2. **basic, principal** 기본적인, 주요한

Rice is the **staple** food of most Asian countries.

33 **terminate**** | v. **stop, finish, end** conclude 끝나다

[tə́:rmənèit]
initiate

It was an unfortunate marriage, which **terminated** in divorce.

reside in	Mary는 아직도 어렸을 때 살았던 집에서 산다.
robust	남자들이 감칠맛 나는 강한 포도주를 좋아하는 반면, 여자들은 보통 달고 미묘한 맛의 포도주를 선호한다.
satisfy	Sam은 그가 하도록 명령받은 모든 것을 함으로써 그의 주인을 만족시키려고 애썼다.
simple	Kate는 전에 대도시에 한번도 가본 적 없는 순진한 시골 소녀였다.
stamina	장거리 주자는 엄청난 끈기를 타고나야만 한다.
staple	그 웹사이트는 중요 상품들의 가격 비교에 기초한 최상의 쇼핑 정보를 가지고 있다.
	쌀은 아시아국들의 주된 식량이다.
terminate	그것은 불운한 결혼이었고, 이혼으로 끝이 났다.

34 treasure**　　v. **value, prize, cherish**　　소중히 하다

[trézər]

Richard **treasured** the time he spent with his grandfather.

35 unequal**　　adj. **unfair, asymmetric, uneven, unbalanced**　　불공평한, 균형을 잃은

[ʌníːkwəl]
symmetric

Class inequality was based on **unequal** access to material rewards and different life opportunities.

36 venture*　　v. **dare, chance, risk**　　과감히 ~하다

[véntʃər]

Lewis and Clark were the first team that **ventured** to explore the western frontier of North America.

Quiz

Choose the synonym.

1. dangle	ⓐ endurance, perseverance, vitality
2. customary	ⓑ habitual, accustomed, conventional
3. satisfy	ⓒ hang
4. persistent	ⓓ continuous, constant, incessant
5. stamina	ⓔ gratify, meet, satiate

Answer 1. ⓒ 2. ⓑ 3. ⓔ 4. ⓓ 5. ⓐ

treasure	Richard는 할아버지와 함께 했던 기억들을 소중히 여겼다.
unequal	계층 간의 불평등은 물질적 보상에 대한 불공평한 접근과 서로 다른 삶의 기회에 기초한 것이었다.
venture	Lewis와 Clark는 과감히 북아메리카의 서부 미개척지를 탐험했던 최초의 탐험대였다.

DAY 41 | Hackers TOEFL **Vocabulary**

Hackers Voca

www.goHackers.com

1 **ache***	v.	**hurt, pain**	아프다
[éik]		Muscles will usually **ache** the day after exercising.	
2 **advantageous****	adj.	**profitable, gainful, beneficial** helpful	이로운, 유익한
[ædvəntéidʒəs] detrimental		Pyeongtaek Harbor's location is **advantageous** as a trading base with China.	
3 **altitude***	n.	**elevation, height**	고도
[ǽltitjù:d] depth		The climate of the Middle Atlantic region varies with the **altitude**.	
4 **antiquity***	n.	**ancient times**	고대
[æntíkwəti]		Gold has been highly valued throughout **antiquity** and into modern times.	
5 **assist****	v.	**help, aid**	돕다
[əsíst] hamper		The man **assisted** the police with their inquiries.	
6 **brilliance***	n.	**radiance, luminosity, brightness**	광채
[bríljəns]		The degree of **brillance** of the star Algol changes every two and a half days.	

ache	근육은 보통 운동한 다음날 아플 것이다.
advantageous	평택 항구의 위치는 중국과의 무역 기지로서 유용하다.
altitude	중부 대서양 지역의 기후는 고도에 따라 다양하다.
antiquity	금은 예부터 현재에 이르기까지 줄곧 높은 가치를 지닌다.
assist	그 남자는 경찰의 질문에 협조했다.
brilliance	알골성의 광채의 정도는 매 이틀하고 반나절마다 변한다

7 **celestial**

[səléstʃəl]
terrestrial

adj. **heavenly** 하늘의

There are no sizable **celestial** bodies between Earth and Mars.

8 **cleave***

[klíːv]

v. 1. **split, dissect; rip** (쪼개어) 나누다 ; 찢다

To defeat Medusa, Perseus was given a sword by the Greek Gods that could **cleave** stone.

v. 2. **adhere, stick, cohere** cling 고수하다, 결합하다

The teacher has **cleaved** to her principles for 20 years.

9 **density***

[dénsəti]

n. **concentration** 농도, 밀도

The lower **density** of aluminum means that it is much lighter than an extremely dense element such as lead.

10 **desperate**

[déspərit]
composed

adj. **as a last resort; hopeless, critical** 필사적인 ; 절망적인

Desperate for a bank loan, David put up his house as collateral.

11 **encourage****

[enkə́ːridʒ]
discourage

v. **cheer up, hearten, motivate, prompt** 격려하다

The Secretary of State **encouraged** President John Adams to end the quarrel.

12 **encumber**

[inkʌ́mbər]

v. 1. **burden, weight, tax, oppress** (의무 · 짐 등을) 지우다

Heavy land taxes severely **encumbered** the poor farmers.

v. 2. **hinder, obstruct, impede, hamper** 저해하다

Government regulation can **encumber** economic growth rates.

celestial	지구와 화성 사이에는 큰 천체들이 없다.
cleave	Medusa를 이기기 위해, Perseus는 그리스 신들로부터 돌을 쪼갤 수 있는 검을 받았다.
	그 교사는 20년간 그녀의 원칙들을 고수해 왔다.
density	알루미늄의 낮은 밀도는 그것이 극도로 밀도가 높은 납과 같은 것에 비해 훨씬 가볍다는 것을 의미한다.
desperate	은행 대출에 필사적인 David는 자기 집을 담보로 내놓았다.
encourage	국무 장관은 John Adams 대통령에게 논쟁을 끝낼 것을 권했다.
encumber	과중한 토지세는 가난한 농부들에게 무거운 짐이 되었다.
	정부의 규제는 경제 성장률을 방해할 수 있다.

13 **enrich**

[inrítʃ]

v. enhance, **improve, better, upgrade** (질 · 가치 등을) 높이다

Public funding for the arts **enriches** cultural life.

14 **fade****

[féid]

wax; flourish

v. wane, **wither, vanish, wilt** 약해지다, 사라지다

Hopes for a peace settlement are beginning to **fade**.

15 **flee***

[flíː]

v. escape, **evade, avoid** 피하다, 도망하다

Although many criminals attempted to **flee** from Alcatraz Prison, the island penitentiary was nearly escape-proof.

16 **follow suit**

phr. **do the same things** 따라하다

After its competitors lowered fares, the airline had no choice but to **follow suit**.

17 **gigantic***

[dʒaigǽntik]

miniature

adj. huge, **immense, colossal** grand 거대한

Lincoln's program represented a **gigantic** expansion of presidential powers.

18 **hygiene*****

[háidʒi(ː)n]

n. cleanliness, sanitation 위생

Proper **hygiene** plays a vital role in the prevention of disease.

19 **impressive***

[imprésiv]

unremarkable

adj. striking, **moving, stirring** 인상적인, 감동적인

This Fourth of July, the city of Boston gave an **impressive** fireworks show that lasted almost four hours.

20 **instantaneous***

[ìnstəntéiniəs]

lengthy

adj. immediate, **prompt, swift, split-second** 즉각적인

Todd's **instantaneous** reaction to being fired was to scream at his boss, an action which he later regretted.

enrich	예술을 위한 공적 기금은 문화적 삶의 질을 높인다.
fade	평화 정착에 대한 희망들이 사라지기 시작하고 있다.
flee	많은 죄수들이 Alcatraz 교도소로부터 탈출을 시도했지만, 섬에 위치한 그 교도소는 탈옥이 거의 불가능했다.
follow suit	경쟁사들이 요금을 내리자, 그 항공사는 그대로 따라하는 수밖에 방법이 없었다.
gigantic	Lincoln의 계획은 대통령 권한의 대폭 확대를 나타내었다.
hygiene	적절한 위생 관리는 병을 예방하는 데 있어서 반드시 필요한 역할을 한다.
impressive	올해 7월 4일에 Boston 시는 네 시간 동안이나 지속된 감명 깊은 불꽃 놀이를 선보였다.
instantaneous	해고당한 데 대한 Todd의 즉각적인 반응은 그의 상사에게 소리를 지르는 것이었는데, 그는 나중에 이 행동을 후회했다.

21 **lusty***	adj. **vigorous, strong, robust** hearty	건장한, 원기왕성한
[lʌ́sti] effete	Arnold's **lusty** arm shows that he is in good shape.	
22 **mankind***	n. **human**	인류
[mǽnkáind]	The campaign was held to promote peace for **mankind**.	
23 **maturity**	n. **adulthood, manhood, majority**	성숙(기)
[mətjú(:)ərəti]	Humans reach reproductive **maturity** between the ages of twelve and nineteen.	
24 **mere**	adj. **insignificant**	단지, 대수롭지 않은
[míər]	The stock market gained a **mere** one percent for the entire year, causing investors to look elsewhere for profits.	
25 **modest**	adj. 1. **humble, unpretending; decent, proper**	겸손한 ; 예의바른
[mádist] impudent	Darwin was **modest** of his monumental achievements to the very end.	
	adj. 2. **small**	많지(크지) 않은
	The apartment Janet lives in is a **modest** one, but it satisfies her needs.	
26 **persist****	v. **endure, continue, remain, last**	지속되다
[pərsíst] cease	Fears **persisted** even after weather forecasters declared that the hurricane would not come ashore.	
27 **pile***	v. 1. **put together, collect; heap**	모으다 ; 쌓다
[páil]	The reporter **piled** together a series of documents to be used in his forthcoming article.	

lusty	Arnold의 강한 팔은 그가 건강하다는 사실을 보여 준다.
mankind	그 캠페인은 인류에게 평화를 촉진하기 위해 개최되었다.
maturity	인간은 12세에서 19세 사이에 성적으로 성숙한다.
mere	증권 시장은 한 해 동안 단지 1퍼센트의 수익만을 올려서 투자자들로 하여금 다른 곳으로 눈을 돌리게 만들었다.
modest	Darwin은 자신의 기념비적 업적에 대해 겸손했다. Janet이 사는 아파트는 별로 크지는 않지만, 그녀가 필요한 것들을 충족시켜 준다.
persist	기상 통보관들이 허리케인이 육상으로 근접하지 않을 것이라고 공표한 뒤에도 두려움은 계속되었다.
pile	그 기자는 이번에 실을 기사에 쓰기 위해 일련의 자료들을 모았다.

n. 2. **heap, stack, accumulation** 더미

The student was worried that he would never finish reading the **pile** of books assigned for that semester.

28 **pristine**

[prísti:n]

adj. **unspoiled, innocent, natural** 오염되지 않은

Chemical wastes from the factory polluted the once **pristine** river.

29 **proficient****

[prəfíʃənt]

adj. **expert, skilled, adept, adroit** 숙련된, 능숙한

Few North Americans are **proficient** in more than one language.

30 **sacred****

[séikrid]
profane

adj. **divine, holy** 신성한

Native Americans have pushed for laws that would preserve their **sacred** sites.

31 **scruple****

[skrú:pl]

n. **hesitation, uneasiness, qualms** 망설임, 양심의 가책

The man's **scruples** kept him from taking advantage of the opportunity.

32 **scrupulous***

[skrú:pjələs]
remiss

adj. 1. **careful, painstaking, meticulous** 세심한, 꼼꼼한

The police officer was praised for his **scrupulous** performance of duties.

adj. 2. **honest** 양심적인, 정직한

The **scrupulous** producer was fair to all those who auditioned.

33 **strike****

[stráik]

v. 1. **hit, bombard, assault** attack 치다, 공격하다

A man was **struck** and killed on the tracks by a passenger train yesterday evening.

pile	그 학생은 한 학기 동안 배정받은 책 한 더미를 다 못 읽을까봐 걱정했다.
pristine	공장에서 나오는 화학 폐기물들이 한때 깨끗했던 강을 오염시켰다.
proficient	북미 사람들은 한가지 이상의 언어에 능숙한 사람이 거의 없다.
sacred	아메리카 원주민들은 자신들의 신성한 유적을 보호하는 법을 요구해 왔다.
scruple	그 남자는 양심의 가책으로 그 기회를 이용하지 못했다.
scrupulous	그 경찰관은 꼼꼼한 근무 수행으로 칭찬을 받았다.
	그 정직한 제작자는 오디션을 받은 모든 사람들에게 공정했다.
strike	어젯밤 한 남자가 선로에서 여객 열차에 치어 사망했다.

n. 2. walkout, work stoppage 파업

The corporation reached a tentative agreement with some 1,600 technicians to end the **strike**.

34 unravel* [ʌnrǽvəl]

v. **explain, solve, figure out** 해명하다, 풀다

Hoffman has long studied ancient rocks to **unravel** the earth's early history.

35 vulgar [vʌ́lgər]

delicate

adj. **coarse, mean, rude** base 저속한

John never talks to a person who is **vulgar** in manner.

Quiz

Choose the synonym.

1. scrupulous	ⓐ hopeless, critical, as a last resort
2. desperate	ⓑ explain, solve, figure out
3. gigantic	ⓒ huge, enormous, immense
4. persist	ⓓ last, continue
5. unravel	ⓔ careful, painstaking, meticulous.

Answer 1. ⓔ 2. ⓐ 3. ⓒ 4. ⓓ 5. ⓑ

strike
unravel
vulgar

그 회사는 파업을 끝내도록 대략 1,600명의 기술자들과 잠정적인 합의에 도달했다.
Hoffman은 지구의 초기 역사를 풀기 위해 고대의 암석들을 오랫동안 연구했다.
John은 저속하게 구는 사람들과는 절대 이야기하지 않는다.

DAY 42 | Hackers TOEFL **Vocabulary**

Hackers Voca

www.goHackers.com

1 **account for****

phr. 1. **explain, justify, give a reason (for)** ~의 이유를 밝히다, 설명하다

The suspect couldn't **account for** his whereabouts last night.

phr. 2. **make up, comprise** 차지하다

Coffee exports **account for** nearly sixty percent of Ethiopia's gross national income.

2 **adjourn***

[ədʒə́ːrn]
advance

v. **suspend, postpone, delay** defer 연기하다

Court was **adjourned** when the witness suddenly fainted.

3 **adopt***

[ədɑ́pt]

v. **take up, choose, follow** ~을 채택하다, 차용하다

The U.N. Security Council **adopted** a resolution calling on Israel to withdraw its troops from Palestinian cities.

4 **adore***

[ədɔ́ːr]
execrate

v. **worship, esteem, revere** 숭배하다, 존경하다

Helen **adored** the singer and would do anything to please him.

5 **artificial****

[ɑ̀ːrtəfíʃəl]
natural

adj. **synthetic** 인위적인, 인조의

Christine's room was decorated with **artificial** flowers.

account for	용의자는 전날 밤 자신의 거처를 설명할 수 없었다. 커피 수출액이 에디오피아의 국민총소득의 60% 가까이 차지한다.
adjourn	그 목격자가 갑자기 기절했을 때 재판은 연기되었다.
adopt	유엔 안전 보장 이사회는 Israel에게 팔레스타인 도시들에서 군대를 철수할 것을 요구하는 결의안을 채택했다.
adore	Helen은 그 가수를 흠모했으며 그를 기쁘게 하는 것이라면 무엇이든 했을 것이다.
artificial	Christine의 방은 조화로 장식되어 있었다.

6 **attend** v. **wait on, serve** 돌보다, 시중들다

[əténd]

The wounded soldiers were **attended** to by army doctors.

7 **band*** n. **group, party, troop, squad** 집단, 무리

[bǽnd]

Bands of nomads continue to live in Saudi Arabia.

8 **besides*** adv. **in addition, as well, moreover** 게다가

[bisáidz]

Tom has the most experience for the job. **Besides**, he is very charismatic.

9 **circumstance**** n. **condition, situation** 상황

[sə́:rkəmstæ̀ns]

Under no **circumstances** are rare books allowed out of the library.

10 **crawl***** v. **creep, wriggle, inch** 기어가다

[krɔ:l]

Due to the accident, traffic on the road **crawled** along with difficulty.

11 **demolish*** v. **destroy, wreck** 파괴하다

[dimáliʃ]

Bombing **demolished** much of Tokyo in the Second World War.

12 **endure*** v. **survive, suffer, tolerate, persevere** 견디다

[endjúər]
give up

Bryan has **endured** a great many hardships in his life.

13 **enormous**** adj. **immense, vast, huge, tremendous** gigantic 거대한

[inɔ́:rməs]
tiny

China's **enormous** population poses a major challenge for the country's food production system.

attend	군의관들이 부상병들을 시중들었다.
band	유목민 집단들은 사우디아라비아에서 계속해서 살아가고 있다.
besides	Tom은 그 일에 가장 경험이 많은데다가 카리스마까지 풍부하다.
circumstance	어떤 경우에도, 희귀 서적을 도서관 밖으로 가져나갈 수 없다.
crawl	그 사고 때문에 그 길의 교통이 지체되었다.
demolish	도쿄의 많은 부분이 2차 세계 대전 때 폭격으로 파괴되었다.
endure	Bryan은 그의 일생에서 수많은 고난을 견뎌냈다.
enormous	중국의 거대한 인구는 국가의 식량 생산 체계에 대한 중대한 도전을 내포한다.

14 **fashionable**	adj.	**popular, up-to-date, trendy**	유행하는
[fǽʃənəbl]		Men growing their hair long became **fashionable** in the 1960s.	
15 **formulate**	v.	**state, express**	(명확히 · 체계적으로) 말하다
[fɔ́ːrmjəlèit]		The speaker **formulated** his ideas in clear and concise language that the audience understood easily.	
16 **hang***	v.	**dangle, suspend**	매달리다
[hǽŋ]		A painting **hangs** over the fireplace in the living room of the house.	
17 **immobility***	n.	**absence of motion**	부동 상태
[ìmoubíləti]		Prolonged **immobility** will cause bedsores and other severe medical conditions.	
18 **inflate***	v.	**bloat, expand, swell**	팽창하다
[infléit] deflate		The hot-air balloon slowly **inflated** and took off.	
19 **interrupt****	v.	**hinder, stunt, punctuate** intermit	가로막다, 중단시키다
[ìntərʌ́pt]		The TV show was **interrupted** by a very important news report.	
20 **manipulation**	n.	**deliberate alteration**	조작, 속임수
[mənìpjəléiʃən]		The broker's illegal **manipulation** of the stock market led to his arrest.	
21 **marvelous***	adj.	**wonderful, astonishing, amazing, miraculous**	경이로운, 놀랄만한
[mɑ́ːrvələs] ordinary, normal		It's **marvelous** what doctors can do with plastic surgery these days.	

fashionable	1960년대에 남자들이 머리를 길게 기르는 것이 유행했었다.
formulate	연설자는 그의 생각을 청중이 쉽게 이해하는 명확하고 간결한 언어로 말했다.
hang	그 집 거실에는 한 폭의 그림이 벽난로 위에 걸려 있다.
immobility	오랫동안 움직이지 않으면 욕창이나 그 외 심각한 질병의 원인이 될 것이다.
inflate	열기구가 천천히 팽창하더니 이륙했다.
interrupt	그 TV 쇼는 매우 중요한 뉴스 보고로 중단되었다.
manipulation	그 브로커는 불법적인 주식 조작으로 인해 체포되었다.
marvelous	요즈음 의사들이 성형 수술을 통해 할 수 있는 것들은 경이롭다.

22 **nevertheless*** | adv. **still, yet, nonetheless** 그럼에도 불구하고

[nèvərðəlés]

The rains have caused a lot of flooding in the southern part of the country, but **nevertheless** the residents refused to be evacuated.

23 **operate*** | v. **run, function, work** 작동하다

[ɑ́pərèit]

The new employee was trained to **operate** the machinery.

24 **outlive*** | v. **survive, outlast** 살아남다, ~보다 더(오래) 살다

[àutlív]

Jinny **outlived** her husband by thirty years.

25 **practicable*** | adj. **feasible, possible, workable** 실행 가능한

[prǽktikəbl]
impracticable

Ray chose the most **practicable** route to the town.

26 **resist*** | v. **withstand, confront** 저항하다

[rizíst]
submit

The colonists bravely **resisted** British imperialism.

27 **risky*** | adj. **dangerous, hazardous, perilous** 위험한

[ríski]
safe

Mountain climbing, bungee jumping, and sky diving are **risky** sports that are enjoyed by thrill seekers.

28 **saved*** | adj. **redeemed, rescued** 구원된, 구제된

[séivd]
condemned

According to Christianity, only people who are **saved** through the redemption of baptism will go to Heaven.

29 **severe**** | adj. 1. **harsh, extreme, rigorous, strict, unsparing** 극심한, 가차 없는

[səvíər]
tolerant

The schoolmaster firmly believed in **severe** disciplinary measures.

nevertheless	그 우기는 그 나라의 남부에 많은 홍수를 유발했음에도 불구하고 거주민들은 그곳을 떠나기를 거부했다.
operate	신입 사원은 기계를 작동하도록 훈련을 받았다.
outlive	Jinny는 그녀의 남편이 죽은 후 30년을 더 살았다.
practicable	Ray는 그 마을로 가는 가장 통행 가능한 길을 선택했다.
resist	식민지 주민들은 용감하게 영국의 제국주의에 저항했다.
risky	등산, 번지 점프와 스카이다이빙은 스릴을 찾는 사람들이 즐기는 위험한 스포츠이다.
saved	기독교 교리에 의하면 세례의 속죄를 통해 구원받은 사람들만이 천국에 갈 수 있다.
severe	그 교장은 엄한 훈육 방법에 대한 확고한 믿음을 가졌다.

adj. 2. **difficult, effortful, tough** 어려운, 까다로운

In his first year in office, Gerald Ford faced **severe** economic problems.

30 spontaneous [spɑntéiniəs]

adj. **voluntary, uncompelled, willing** 자발적인

Sarah's successful jump brought a **spontaneous** cheer from the crowd.

31 stagger** [stǽgər]

v. 1. **totter, falter, waver** 비틀거리다, 동요하다

Half drunk, the man **staggered** towards the door.

v. 2. **astonish, confuse, overwhelm** 당황시키다

John was completely **staggered** by the horrible sight.

32 thriller** [θrílər]

n. **suspenseful book/story/movie/play** 스릴을 주는 것

The couple decided to see a **thriller**.

33 toil* [tɔ́il]

v. **work hard, labor, strive** 힘들게 일하다

The student had been **toiling** away at this assignment all weekend.

34 touch off

phr. **start, arouse, provoke** 야기하다

The war in the Middle East **touched off** a panic in the oil markets.

35 utterly* [ʌ́tərli]

adv. **completely** 완전히

John was **utterly** surprised by the movie's ending.

severe	Gerald Ford 대통령은 임기 첫해에 심각한 경제 위기에 직면했다.
spontaneous	Sarah가 성공적으로 점프하자 군중으로부터 자발적인 환호가 나왔다.
stagger	반쯤 술이 취해서, 그 남자는 문을 향해 비틀거리며 나아갔다.
	John은 그 무시무시한 광경을 보고 굉장히 놀랐다.
thriller	그 커플은 스릴러물을 보기로 결정했다.
toil	그 학생은 주말 내내 이 숙제로 고생했다.
touch off	중동 지역의 전쟁은 석유 시장에 혼란을 야기했다.
utterly	John은 그 영화의 결말에 완전히 놀랐다.

36 **vacuum***
[vǽkjuəm]

n. **vacancy, emptiness, void** 진공, 공허

The shuttle moved past the earth's atmosphere and into the massive **vacuum** of outer space.

37 **valid***
[vǽlid]
groundless

adj. **just, sound, cogent** / logical 타당한

The farmers had a **valid** complaint against the railroad shippers.

38 **withhold**
[wiðhóuld]

v. **reserve; hold back, restrain** 보류하다 ; 억제하다

The landlord **withheld** the payment until the farmers completed the work.

39 **wonder***
[wʌ́ndər]
unconcern

n. **awe, astonishment, marvel** 경이로움, 놀라운 일

It was with a sense of **wonder** that people viewed the first landing on the moon.

Quiz

Choose the synonym.

1. adjourn — ⓐ sound, cogent, logical
2. circumstance — ⓑ condition, situation
3. interrupt — ⓒ dangerous, hazardous, perilous
4. risky — ⓓ hinder, stunt, punctuate
5. valid — ⓔ suspend, postpone, delay

Answer 1. ⓔ 2. ⓑ 3. ⓓ 4. ⓒ 5. ⓐ

vacuum	그 왕복선은 지구의 대기권을 지나서 외계의 대규모의 진공 상태 속에 들어갔다.
valid	그 농부들은 그 철도 수하물 운반자들에 대해 타당한 불평을 했다.
withhold	지주는 소작인들이 일을 끝마칠 때까지 급여 지불을 보류했다.
wonder	사람들은 인류가 달에 처음 착륙하는 것을 보았을 때 경이로움을 느꼈다.

Hackers TOEFL Voca TEST DAY 40-42

Choose the synonym of the highlighted word in the sentence.

1. Jerry used an ax to cleave the firewood into smaller pieces.
(A) place (B) raise (C) split (D) evade

2. The politician's utterly ridiculous statements were cause for scorn among his political opponents.
(A) plausibly (B) assuredly (C) completely (D) haltingly

3. Now known to be a toxic chemical, dioxin was once thought to be innocuous.
(A) deranged (B) noisome (C) preponderant (D) harmless

4. The encroachment of logging and development into the Amazon rain forest has meant that there are few pristine jungles in the area left.
(A) reticent (B) unspoiled (C) clamorous (D) ingrainedn

5. Despite being fifty years old, John showed his robust physical condition by completing a marathon.
(A) vigorous (B) urgent (C) orderly (D) harmonious

6. There are a seemingly infinite number of celestial bodies left for astronomers to chart.
(A) stationary (B) heavenly (C) evangelical (D) terrestrial

7. In many factories, robots assemble mechanical components.
(A) keep (B) hoist (C) shroud (D) put togather

8. The invitation specified that formal attire was expected at the banquet.
(A) odor (B) stack (C) felony (D) clothing

9. David encapsulated a 500 page report into an accessible twenty-five page summary.
(A) condensed (B) featured (C) redacted (D) locatedey

10. Asymmetric density may be a sign of breast cancer.
(A) costomary (B) dynamic (C) unequal (D) staple

정답 p.419

TAKE A BREAK

O You Whom I Often and Silently Come

Walt Whitman

O You Whom I often And Silently Come where you
are that I may be with you,
As I walk by your side near, or remain in
the same room with you,
Little you know the subtle electric fire that for
your sake is playing within me.

내가 가끔 조용히 찾아가게 되는 그대여...

그대와 함께 있고자,
내가 가끔 조용히 그대 있는 곳으로 가게 되는 그대여,
내가 그태 옆을 지나가거나,
가까이 앉았거나,
함께 같은 방안에 있을 때,
그대는 모르리라.
그대 때문에.
내 마음 속에서 흔들리는 미묘한 감동적인 불꽃을.

DAY Hackers TOEFL **Vocabulary**

43 Hackers Voca

www.goHackers.com

1 **advance****	v.	**improve, evolve, develop** progress	진보하다
[ədvǽns] delay		Nuclear technology has **advanced** considerably.	
2 **applicability**	n.	**relevance**	적절함, 적절성
[æ̀pləkəbíləti]		Attorneys questioned the **applicability** of evidence about the defendant's personality.	
3 **brittle***	adj.	**breakable**	부서지기 쉬운
[brítl] solid		The old woman's bones were so **brittle** that her leg broke when she slipped on ice.	
4 **careful****	adj.	**cautious, discreet, precautious**	주의 깊은
[kέərfəl] careless		The children were reminded to be **careful** when crossing the street.	
5 **convert***	v.	**transform, change**	바꾸다
[kənvə́ːrt]		Brown destroyed the Indian's cultures by trying to **convert** them to Christianity.	
6 **core****	n.	**center, heart**	핵심
[kɔ́ːr]		The **core** of Clinton's plan is to set up regional health alliances.	

advance	핵 기술은 상당히 진보해왔다.
applicability	변호사들은 피고인의 성격에 대한 증거가 적절한지에 대해 의심을 가졌다.
brittle	그 노부인의 뼈는 너무 부러지기 쉬워서, 빙판길에서 미끄러졌을 때 다리가 부러졌다.
careful	아이들은 길을 건널 때 조심하도록 주의를 받았다.
convert	Brown은 인디언들을 기독교로 개종하려 함으로써 그들의 문화를 파괴했다.
core	클린턴 대통령의 계획의 핵심은 지역 간 보건 당국의 제휴이다.

7 **countervail** | v. **oppose, counterbalance, offset** 상쇄시키다

[kàuntərvéil]

The decline in domestic consumer demand was **countervailed** by an increase in exports.

8 **curative*** | adj. **healing** 치유하는

[kjúərətiv]
irremediable

The scientists were surprised at the **curative** power of the new drug.

9 **disintegrate***** | v. **fall apart, crumble, break down** 붕괴되다, 분해되다

[disíntəgrèit]

The palace has **disintegrated** over the centuries and is now in ruins.

10 **divest*** | v. **deprive, strip** 박탈하다

[divést]

In some countries, people found guilty of treason are **divested** of their rights and citizenship.

11 **drive**** | v. 1. **propel, force, impel, compel** 억지로 ~하게 하다

[dráiv]
hinder

The prime minister was **driven** by the scandal to resign.

n. 2. **campaign, push, action** 운동

In the 1990s Lego enjoyed its greatest success with a spectacular **drive** to spread geographically.

12 **entangle** | v. **complicate, involve** 뒤얽히게 하다

[intǽŋgl]
disentangle

The separated couple became **entangled** in a lawsuit over the custody of their child.

13 **evolve** | v. **develop, progress, improve** 서서히 발전하다

[ivάlv]

The article **evolved** into a tightly argued piece of writing.

countervail	국내 소비자 수요의 감소는 수출의 증가로 상쇄되었다.
curative	그 과학자들은 새로운 약의 치료 효과에 놀랐다.
disintegrate	그 궁전은 수세기에 걸쳐서 무너져 내려서 지금은 폐허가 되어 있다.
divest	어떤 나라에서는 반역죄를 범한 사람들은 그들의 권리와 국적을 박탈당한다.
drive	수상은 그 스캔들로 인해 사임하도록 압력을 받았다.
	레고는 90년대에 세계 진출에 박차를 가하면서 최고의 전성기를 누렸다.
entangle	이혼한 커플이 자식의 양육권 소송에 휘말리게 되었다.
evolve	그 기사는 군더더기 없이 잘 짜여진 한편의 글로 서서히 발전했다.

14 **extant**

adj. **existing, living, remaining, surviving** 현존하는

[ékstənt]
extinct

Archaeologists work with **extant** pieces of civilization.

15 **hamper***

v. **prevent, impede, hinder, restrict** 방해하다

[hǽmpər]
aid

The development of a scientific approach to chemistry was **hampered** by several factors.

16 **hide***

n. 1. **fur, skin** (짐승의) 가죽

[háid]

Robby is asking for a blanket made from cow **hide** for his birthday this year.

reveal

v. 2. **camouflage, disguise, cloak, mask** 숨기다, 감추다

To avoid seeing her ex-husband, Maggie **hid** her face with dark sunglasses and a hat.

17 **immoral*****

adj. **improper, corrupt, sinful** 부도덕한

[imɔ́(:)rəl]

Most cultures would agree that stealing is **immoral**.

18 **incipient**

adj. **initial, beginning, commencing** 초기의

[insípiənt]
concluding

An accurate psychological evaluation is necessary to diagnose **incipient** psychotic symptoms in borderline mental patients.

19 **isolate***

v. **separate, segregate** 격리시키다

[áisəlèit]

Scientists have **isolated** the virus that causes SARS.

20 **joint***

v. **combine, connect** 접합하다, 연결하다

[dʒɔ́int]

The machine parts were **jointed** together and then welded.

extant	고고학자들은 현재까지 남아 있는 문명의 부분들을 갖고 작업을 한다.
hamper	화학에 대한 과학적인 접근의 발달은 여러 가지 요인들에 의해 방해를 받았다.
hide	Robby는 올해 그의 생일에 소가죽으로 만든 담요를 요구했다.
	Maggie는 그녀의 전남편과 마주치는 것을 피하기 위해, 그녀의 얼굴을 어두운 선글라스와 모자로 가렸다.
immoral	대부분의 문화는 절도가 부도덕하다는 점에 있어서 의견을 같이한다.
incipient	정상인들과 정신병자의 중간 상태에 있는 환자들에게서 정신 이상의 초기 증세를 진단하기 위해는 정확한 심리 평가가 요구된다.
isolate	과학자들은 SARS를 일으킨 바이러스를 격리시켰다.
joint	그 기계 부품들은 접합된 뒤 용접되었다.

21 **kindle**** | v. **ignite, fire, inflame** 불을 붙이다

[kíndl]
smother

Henry **kindled** the wood with a match.

22 **landscape*** | n. **scenery, outlook, scene** 풍경, 전망

[lǽndskèip]

Even though it was dark, a giant moon lit the road so brightly that we could see the **landscape** clearly.

23 **migrate**** | v. **travel, move around, immigrate, emigrate** 이동하다, 이주하다

[máigreit]

The five tribes agreed to **migrate** beyond the Mississippi.

24 **milestone**** | n. **important event, significant event** 획기적인 사건

[máilstòun]

The movie Toy Story was an entertainment **milestone** for the computer graphics industry.

25 **novel**** | adj. 1. **new, innovative, fresh, modern** 새로운

[návəl]
common, usual

Graphic calculators were highly **novel** in the 1960s.

adj. 2. **unusual, rare, strange** 신기한, 진기한

Joe's sister made a **novel** career choice when she decided to become a magician.

26 **out of the question**** | phr. **impossible** 불가능한

possible

Victory was **out of the question**.

27 **phenomenal*** | adj. **extraordinary, exceptional, remarkable, unusual** 놀랄 만한

[finάmənəl]

The discovery of the electron was a **phenomenal** advance in physics.

kindle	Henry는 성냥을 가지고 그 나무에 불을 붙였다.
landscape	비록 어두웠지만, 거대한 달이 매우 밝게 길을 비춰 주고 있어서 우리는 뚜렷하게 풍경을 볼 수 있었다.
migrate	그 다섯 부족들은 미시시피 강을 넘어 이주하는 것에 동의했다.
milestone	영화 토이스토리는 컴퓨터 그래픽 산업의 연예계 분야에서 획기적인 사건이었다.
novel	1960년대에 그래픽 계산기들은 굉장히 새로운 것이었다. Joe의 여동생은 마술사가 되기로 결정함으로써 흔치 않은 직업을 선택했다.
out of the question	승리는 불가능했다.
phenomenal	전자의 발견은 물리학을 놀랄 만큼 발전시켰다.

28 **plunge***

[plʌ́ndʒ]

v. **drop, dip, thrust** 떨어뜨리다, 던져 넣다

Mario cooked the peas by **plunging** them into boiling water.

29 **presently***

[prézəntli]

adv. **immediately, directly, soon** shortly 곧

Jane called to say she would be arriving **presently**.

30 **reckless***

[réklis]

adj. **careless, rash, heedless, inadvertent** 무모한, 부주의한

Tom's **reckless** driving caused the accident.

31 **sensitive***

[sénsitiv]
impervious

adj. **responsive, impressionable** 민감하게 반응하는

Because she was so **sensitive**, Jeniffer was easily brought to tears.

32 **serious***

[síəriəs]
light

adj. **solemn, important, momentous** 심각한, 중대한

Global climate change is the most **serious** environmental challenge that we face.

33 **simultaneous***

[sàiməltéiniəs]

adj. **concurrent, concomitant, synchronous** 동시에 일어나는

There was a flash of lightening and a **simultaneous** roll of thunder.

34 **soar***

[sɔ́ːr]
plummet

v. 1. **tower, rise, ascend** mount 높이 솟다

Khufu's pyramid **soars** 481 feet into the sky.

v. 2. **increase dramatically, shoot up** 급상승하다

Stock markets around the world **soared** on hopes for a global economic recovery.

plunge	Mario는 완두콩을 끓는 물에 넣어서 요리했다.
presently	Jane은 그녀가 곧 도착할 것이라는 사실을 말하기 위해 전화를 걸었다.
reckless	Tom의 부주의한 운전이 사고를 가져왔다.
sensitive	Jeniffer는 너무나 민감했기 때문에, 쉽게 눈물을 흘렸다.
serious	세계 기후 변화는 우리가 직면한 가장 심각한 환경적 도전이다.
simultaneous	번개의 섬광과 동시에 우뢰 소리가 있었다.
soar	Khufu의 피라미드는 481피트의 높이로 솟아 있다.
	전 세계적인 경제 회복이 기대됨에 따라 세계 주식 시장이 급상승세를 보였다.

35 **subservient*** adj. **secondary, subordinate** 부차적인, 종속적인

[səbsə́:rviənt]

In the 1960s it was widely accepted that women were inferior and should be **subservient** to men.

36 **subterranean*** adj. **underground, underneath** 지하의

[sʌ̀btəréiniən]

Mammoth Cave, in central Kentucky, contains several **subterranean** lakes and rivers.

37 **unlawful**** adj. **illegal, illicit, illegitimate** 불법적인

[ʌ̀nlɔ́:fəl]
justifiable

It was not **unlawful** for workers to engage peacefully in union activity.

Quiz

Choose the synonym.

1. careful	ⓐ travel, immigrate, emigrate
2. hamper	ⓑ subordinate, secondary
3. migrate	ⓒ illegal, illicit, illegitimate
4. subservient	ⓓ cautious, deliberate, prudent
5. unlawful	ⓔ hinder, impede, prevent

Answer 1. ⓓ 2. ⓔ 3. ⓐ 4. ⓑ 5. ⓒ

subservient 1960년대에 여성이 남성보다 열등하고 남성에게 종속되어야만 한다는 생각이 널리 받아들여졌다.
subterranean 켄터키 주의 중심부에 위치한 Mammoth Cave에는 여러 개의 지하 호수와 강들이 있다.
unlawful 노동자들이 평화적으로 노동조합 활동에 참여하는 것은 불법이 아니었다.

DAY Hackers TOEFL **Vocabulary**

44 Hackers Voca

www.goHackers.com

1 **absorb****

v. take in, **imbibe, soak up** 흡수하다

[əbzɔ́:rb]
exude

The sponge rapidly **absorbed** the water.

2 **accuse**

v. **indict, impeach, blame** charge 고발하다, 비난하다

[əkjú:z]
exculpate

Kate **accused** me of conspiring with Chris to make her marry him.

3 **a host of***

phr. a number of, **a multitude of** 많은 수의

There are **a host of** job opportunities for Computer Science majors after graduation.

4 **apathetic***

adj. indifferent, **unconcerned, uninterested** 무관심한

[æpəθétik]
alert

The masses are politically **apathetic**.

5 **array***

v. arrange, **display, exhibit** 배열하다, 진열하다

[əréi]
mess up

The street vendor **arrayed** his wares on the busy street corner.

6 **continual**

adj. **incessant, ceaseless** 끊임없는

[kəntínjuəl]
transient

The many factions and political parties caused almost **continual** turmoil.

absorb	그 스폰지는 물을 빨리 흡수했다.
accuse	Kate는 자신을 그에게 시집 보내려고 내가 크리스와 공모했다고 비난했다.
a host of	컴퓨터 공학 전공자들에게는 졸업 후 많은 취업의 기회가 있다.
apathetic	일반 대중들은 정치적으로 무관심하다.
array	길거리 행상인은 분주한 구석 자리에 자신의 상품을 배열했다.
continual	많은 파벌과 정당들은 거의 끊임없는 혼란을 일으켰다.

7 **design***

v. **intend, plan, project** 뜻을 품다, 계획하다

[dizáin]
accomplish

The officials' plan was **designed** to give aid to any European country suffering from nuclear reactor damage.

8 **discard***

v. **throw away, abandon, dispose of, cast aside** 버리다

[diskɑ́ːrd]
keep

Everyone should **discard** their paper, glass and plastic into a recycling box in order to keep the Earth green.

9 **elapse***

v. **pass, go by** 경과하다

[ilǽps]

It is normal for a few seconds to **elapse** between the flash and the thunder of lightning.

10 **furnish***

v. **provide, supply, replenish** 공급하다

[fə́ːrniʃ]
strip

The counselor **furnished** Tim the papers for his application.

11 **futile****

adj. **useless, ineffective, vain** 쓸모없는

[fjúːtl]
effective

It was **futile** to try to teach Jack French.

12 **guard***

v. **protect, defend, shield** 지키다

[gɑ́ːrd]
make vulnerable

Mayor Bob Walkup spent the night of Sept. 10 **guarded** by Tucson police in a location neither he nor police would reveal.

13 **locomotion****

n. **movement, motion** 운동, 이동

[lòukəmóuʃən]

Humans are one of the few animals capable of two-footed **locomotion**.

14 **metamorphose***

v. **change, transform, convert** (~으로) 변형, 변화하다(시키다)

[mètəmɔ́ːrfouz]

Caterpillars **metamorphose** into butterflies later in life.

design	공무원들의 계획은 핵원자로 피해로 고통받는 모든 유럽 국가들에게 원조를 제공하도록 계획되어 있었다.
discard	모든 사람들은 지구를 푸르게 보존하기 위해 종이, 유리, 플라스틱 등을 재활용 박스에 버려야 한다.
elapse	번개의 번쩍임과 천둥 사이에는 수 초가 경과하는 것이 일반적이다.
furnish	그 상담자는 Tim에게 신청을 위한 서류들을 주었다.
futile	Jack에게 프랑스어를 가르치려고 애쓰는 것은 쓸모없는 일이었다.
guard	Bop Walkup 시장은 Tucson 경찰에 의해 보호받으며, 그 자신도 경찰도 밝히지 않을 장소에서 9월 10일 밤을 보냈다.
locomotion	사람은 두 발로 이동할 수 있는 몇 안 되는 동물 중 하나이다.
metamorphose	모충은 일생의 말기에 나비로 변한다.

15 misconception [mìskənsépʃən]

n. **false belief, misunderstanding, fallacy** 잘못된 생각, 오해

It is a common **misconception** that driving is safer than flying.

16 multiplicity [mʌ̀ltəplísəti]

n. **variety, diversity; plurality, plenty** 다양성 ; 다수

There is a huge **multiplicity** of insect species.

17 native* [néitiv]

acquired

adj. **indigenous; innate, inborn, inherent** 토착의 ; 선천적인

Although Jane speaks excellent French, her **native** language is actually English.

18 needless to say***

phr. **obviously, of course, undoubtedly** 말할 필요도 없이

Needless to say, smoking is very bad for people's health.

19 passive* [pǽsiv]

active

adj. **inactive, inert** 수동적인, 활기 없는

For 2,000 years, women were confined to **passive** roles in society.

20 predicate* [prédəkeit]

v. 1. **affirm, assert, declare** 단언하다

The class lecture **predicated** the moral weakness of humans.

v. 2. **base, establish, found** 기초를 두다

The lawyer **predicated** his argument on all the known facts.

21 presence* [prézəns]

n. **existence, being** 존재

The coroner detected the **presence** of poison in the dead woman's blood.

misconception	자동차 운전이 비행보다 안전할 것이라는 생각은 흔하게 하는 오해이다.
multiplicity	곤충의 종류는 매우 다양하다.
native	Jane은 프랑스어를 완벽하게 구사하지만 실제 모국어는 영어이다.
needless to say	말할 필요도 없이 흡연은 건강에 매우 안 좋다.
passive	2,000년 동안, 여성들은 사회에서 수동적인 역할에 한정되어 있었다.
predicate	그 수업 강의는 인간이 도덕적으로 약하다고 단언했다.
	그 변호사는 그의 주장을 모든 알려진 사실들에 근거하였다.
presence	검시관은 죽은 여성의 혈액에 있는 독의 존재를 감지했다.

22 **progressively***	adv. **increasingly**	점차적으로
[prəgrésivli]	The government must clean up the air by setting **progressively** tighter pollution limits on power plants.	
23 **pungent****	adj. **sharp, piquant, tart**	신랄한, (맛 등이) 자극적인
[pʌ́ndʒənt] mellow	If frightened, a skunk will lift its tail and spray a **pungent** odor.	
24 **recover****	v. **retrieve, bring back, regain** reclaim	되찾다, 회복시키다
[rikʌ́vər] forfeit	Police have failed to **recover** the stolen jewelry.	
25 **regardless of**	phr. **in spite of**	~에 개의치 않고
	Regardless of the circumstances, a child should never be physically abused.	
26 **remainder***	n. **residue, remnant, rest**	나머지
[riméindər]	Lewis moved to Cambridge for the **remainder** of his life.	
27 **reputation***	n. **fame, renown**	명성
[rèpjutéiʃən] obscurity	Bill and Ted have a **reputation** for being irredeemable class clowns.	
28 **shelter***	v. **protect, shield, harbor** guard, safeguard	보호하다, 숨겨 주다
[ʃéltər]	The Quakers **sheltered** many runaway slaves.	
29 **spur****	n. 1. **stimulus, incitement, incentive**	자극
[spə́:r]	The tax cut was a much needed **spur** for the lagging economy.	

progressively	정부는 발전소에 점차적으로 더 엄격한 오염 한계 정도를 둠으로써 공기를 깨끗이 해야만 한다.
pungent	겁에 질리면 스컹크는 꼬리를 들고 자극적인 냄새를 뿌릴 것이다.
recover	경찰은 그 도난당한 보석류를 되찾는 데에 실패했다.
regardless of	어떤 상황이든지 간에, 아이들은 신체적으로 학대를 받아서는 안 된다.
remainder	Lewis는 그의 여생을 보낼 Cambridge로 이사를 했다.
reputation	Bill과 Ted는 구제할 길 없는 학급의 어릿광대들이라는 평판을 가지고 있다.
shelter	퀘이커 교도들은 많은 도망친 노예들을 보호했다.
spur	세금 감면은 경기침체를 극복하기 위해 필요한 자극이다.

v. 2. stimulate 자극하다

The Federal Reserve lowered interest rates in hopes of **spurring** the economy.

30 suggest**

[sədʒést]
express

v. implicate, point to, **indicate** hint, intimate 암시하다

The evidence **suggests** that Richard is guilty.

31 surge*

[sə́:rdʒ]

v. increase, rise 증가(상승)하다

After the World Cup, interest in local soccer teams **surged**.

32 terminal

[tə́:rmənəl]

adj. final, **last** 최종의

All passengers must depart the train at the **terminal** station.

33 transverse*

[trænsvə́:rs]

adj. cross, crosswise 가로지르는

The roof is held up by beams **transverse** to the main set of supports.

34 underscore

[ʌ̀ndərskɔ́:r]
downplay

v. reinforce, **emphasize, accentuate, underline** 강조하다

In a lecture on the importance of exercise, Dr. Jones **underscored** his belief that only one cure for obesity exists.

35 upbraid*

[ʌpbréid]
praise

v. **scold, berate, rebuke** 꾸짖다

The teacher **upbraided** the students for their carelessness.

36 vagabond**

[vǽgəbɑ̀nd]

adj. wandering, nomadic, **vagrant** 방랑하는

Having grown tired of a **vagabond** lifestyle, Rob settled down and found a steady job.

spur	연방 준비은행은 경제를 자극하기 위해 이자율을 낮추었다.
suggest	그 증거는 Richard가 유죄라는 사실을 암시한다.
surge	월드컵 이후에, 지역 축구팀에 대한 관심이 빠르게 증가했다.
terminal	종착역에서는 모든 승객들이 기차에서 내려야 한다.
transverse	그 지붕은 주 지지대를 가로지르는 들보에 의해서 지탱된다.
underscore	Jones교수는 운동의 중요성에 대한 강의에서 비만에 대한 치료법은 오직 하나 밖에 존재하지 않는다는 그의 믿음을 강조했다.
upbraid	그 교사는 학생들이 부주의하다고 꾸짖었다.
vagabond	방랑하는 삶의 방식에 지쳐왔기 때문에 Rob은 정착해서 안정된 직업을 찾았다.

37 vague** | adj. **uncertain, imprecise, obscure** indistinct 모호한

[véig]
express

In the darkness, we could see the **vague** shape of something approaching.

38 veracious* | adj. **honest, truthful, accurate** 진실한

[vəréiʃəs]
dishonest

Veracious lawyers and politicians are hard to come by.

39 vital** | adj. **essential, important, indispensable** 필수적인

[váitl]
needless

Taylor played a **vital** role in the memorable debates of 1850.

40 withstand** | v. **resist, endure** 버티다

[wiðstǽnd]
capitulate

His mother doesn't think Bill is capable of **withstanding** hardship for long.

Quiz

Choose the synonym.

1. apathetic ⓐ accentuate, reinforce, emphasize
2. metamorphose ⓑ regain, reclaim, retrieve
3. recover ⓒ transform, convert, change
4. underscore ⓓ resist, endure
5. withstand ⓔ unconcerned, indifferent, uninteresed

Answer 1. ⓔ 2. ⓒ 3. ⓑ 4. ⓐ 5. ⓓ

vague	어둠 속에서, 그 여자아이들은 다가오는 물체의 희미한 형체를 볼 수 있었다.
veracious	진실된 변호사와 정치인들은 만나 보기가 힘들다.
vital	Taylor는 1850년의 주목할만한 논쟁들에서 중요한 역할을 했다.
withstand	Bill의 어머니는 그가 오랫동안 고난을 견딜 수 있으리라고 생각하지 않는다.

DAY 45

Hackers TOEFL **Vocabulary**

Hackers Voca

www.goHackers.com

1 **abound****	v.	**overflow, fill with, teem** swarm with	풍부하다, 가득 차다
[əbáund] lack		Wild dolphins **abound** in Canada's Bay of Fundy.	
2 **abstract***	adj.	**theoretical, notional**	추상적인, 이론적인
[æbstrǽkt] concrete		The professor's lectures were so **abstract** that we failed to understand them clearly.	
3 **affliction***	n.	**woe, distress, sorrow** anguish	고뇌, 고통
[əflíkʃən] bliss		Her mother's death caused **affliction** to Kate's soul.	
4 **attachment***	n.	**emotional connection**	애착
[ətǽtʃmənt]		Many farmers have such a strong **attachment** to their land that they would rather starve than leave it.	
5 **beckon**	v.	**invite, call, summon**	호출하다
[békən]		The restaurant's owner **beckoned** the waiter over with a wave of his hand.	
6 **complicate*****	v.	**make difficult, entangle, involve**	복잡하게 하다
[kámpləkèit]		The project was **complicated** by the orders of many different managers.	

abound	야생 돌고래들은 캐나다의 Fundy 만에 풍부하다.
abstract	그 교수의 강의가 너무나 추상적이어서 우리는 정확히 그것들을 이해하지 못했다.
affliction	Kate의 어머니의 죽음은 그녀의 영혼에 고통을 가져왔다.
attachment	많은 농부들은 자신들의 땅에 대한 강한 애착을 가지고 있어서 땅을 떠나느니 굶는 편을 선택할 것이다.
beckon	그 음식점 주인은 손짓으로 웨이터를 불렀다.
complicate	그 프로젝트는 여러 명의 다른 경영자들이 내린 지시 때문에 복잡해졌다.

7 **consecutive*** — adj. successive, sequential — 연속적인

[kənsékjətiv]

The economy has been shrinking for three **consecutive** years due to high oil prices.

8 **consist of** — phr. be made up of — ~로 구성되다

The new fad diet in Hollywood **consists of** high protein meals and low-carbohydrate snacks.

9 **coordination*** — n. the harmonious functioning of parts — 공동작용

[kouɔ̀:rdənéiʃən]

Ballet dancers must develop great physical **coordination**.

10 **crowd** — n. throng, multitude, group, mass, host — 군중, 무리

[kráud]

The vast **crowd** assembled in the stadium.

11 **doctrine**** — n. principle, tenet, dogma — 원칙, 교리, 주의

[dάktrin]

The Buddha's **doctrine** allowed people to go about their daily lives with confidence.

12 **drastically**** — adv. strikingly, severely, extremely — 극심하게

[drǽstikəli]

In Arizona, a small reduction in rainfall can **drastically** influence the growth of trees.

13 **elegant*** — adj. sophisticated, delicate, polished graceful — 우아한, 세련된

[éləgənt]
crude

Chester A. Arthur will be remembered for being the most **elegant** president.

14 **entity**** — n. object, thing, individual — 개체, 실체

[éntəti]

The company is no longer an independent **entity**.

consecutive	고유가 때문에 경제가 3년 연속 위축되고 있다.
consist of	Hollywood에서 새로이 유행하는 식이요법은 고단백질의 식사와 저탄수화물 간식으로 이루어져 있다.
coordination	발레 무용수들은 상당한 신체적 조화 기능을 길러야 한다.
crowd	많은 군중들이 경기장에 모였다.
doctrine	부처님의 교리는 사람들이 자신감을 가지고 그들의 일상 생활을 영위하도록 해주었다.
drastically	애리조나에서는 강우량이 조금만 감소해도 나무들의 성장에 상당한 영향을 끼칠 수 있다.
elegant	Chester A. Arthur는 가장 우아한 대통령으로 기억될 것이다.
entity	그 회사는 더 이상 독립적인 개체가 아니다.

15 **era***

n. **epoch, period, age** time 시대

[érə]

The microchip opened the **era** of the personal computer.

16 **established**

adj. **certain, definite** 확정된

[istǽbliʃt]

The fact that America has an **established** church-going population says something important about its national values.

17 **facet***

n. **aspect** 양상

[fǽsit]

All individuals show different **facets** of their personalities, depending on their audience.

18 **flourish****

v. **thrive, prosper, blossom** 번성하다

[flə́:riʃ]
wither

Watercolor painting began to **flourish** in Britain around 1750.

19 **hue****

n. **tint, color, shade** 빛깔, 색

[hjú:]

The jewel shone with every **hue** under the lamp light.

20 **impair***

v. **damage, injure, deteriorate** 손상시키다, 약하게 하다

[impέər]
improve

Lack of sleep **impaired** Jane's concentration.

21 **inevitably**

adv. **without exception, unavoidably, necessarily** 불가피하게

[inévitəbli]

Large-scale printing of currency leads **inevitably** to inflation.

22 **infinite**

adj. **unlimited, limitless, immeasurable, boundless** 무한한, 끝없는

[ínfənit]

Scientists disagree as to whether the universe is **infinite**.

era	마이크로칩은 개인 컴퓨터의 시대를 열었다.
established	미국에 고정적으로 교회에 다니는 인구가 존재한다는 것은 미국의 국가적인 가치관에 대해 중요한 무언가를 말해 준다.
facet	모든 이들은 듣는 이에 따라 다른 성격적 양상을 보인다.
flourish	수채화는 1750년경에 영국에서 번성하기 시작했다.
hue	그 보석은 램프 불빛 아래에서 다양한 색깔로 빛이 났다.
impair	수면 부족은 Jane의 집중력을 손상시켰다.
inevitably	대량 통화 생산은 불가피하게 인플레이션을 낳는다.
infinite	과학자들은 우주가 무한한 것인지에 대해서 동의하지 않는다.

23 inflame [infléim]
soothe

v. **anger, arouse** 노하게 하다, 자극하다

Inflamed by the salary cut, many of the workers walked out of the factory in protest.

24 influential [ìnfluénʃəl]

adj. **important, powerful, potent** 영향력 있는, 유력한

Sigmund Freud was a highly **influential** psychiatrist.

25 jeopardize* [dʒépərdàiz]
protect

v. **threaten, endanger** 위태롭게 하다

Mary doesn't want to **jeopardize** her relationship with David.

26 marvel* [mɑ́ːrvəl]

n. **wonder** 경이로움

It's a **marvel** that Jane came back alive.

27 monotonous [mənɑ́tənəs]
varying

adj. **tedious, boring, dull, unvaried** 단조로운

Eric quit his job on the assembly line because his tasks were so **monotonous**.

28 notable* [nóutəbl]
unremarkable

adj. **remarkable, important, outstanding, noteworthy** 주목할만한

Professor Dixon's **notable** achievements in academia earned him the respect and admiration of his colleagues.

29 novelty* [nɑ́vəlti]
old story

n. **originality, freshness, newness, uniqueness** 참신함, 진기함

Fruits such as oranges and apples are **novelties** in some African countries.

30 oath* [óuθ]

n. **promise, vow, pledge** 맹세

Before the attorney could begin her questioning, the witness had to take an **oath** to tell the whole truth and nothing but the truth.

inflame	임금 감면에 격분한 많은 노동자들이 항의의 표시로 공장에서 걸어 나왔다.
influential	Sigmund Freud는 매우 영향력 있는 정신과 의사였다.
jeopardize	Mary는 David와의 관계를 위태롭게 하고 싶어하지 않는다.
marvel	Jane이 살아서 돌아오다니 놀라운 일이다.
monotonous	Eric은 자신의 임무가 너무 단조로워서, 조립 라인에서의 일을 그만두었다.
notable	Dixon 교수의 학계에서의 주목할 만한 업적은 그에게 동료들의 존경과 동경을 가져다 주었다.
novelty	오렌지나 사과와 같은 과일은 몇몇 아프리카 국가에서는 진기한 것이다.
oath	변호사가 질문을 시작하기 전에 증인은 모든 사실을 말할 것과 오직 사실만을 말할 것을 맹세해야 한다.

31 **on the contrary** phr. **conversely** 반대로

The audience was not hostile to the speaker; **on the contrary**, he was well-received.

32 **photosynthesis**** n. the production of special sugar-like substances that keeps plants alive 광합성

[fòutousínθəsis]

The students experimented with **photosynthesis** in their biology class.

33 **prodigious** adj. **wonderful, marvelous, amazing** astonishing 경이로운

[prədídʒəs]
commonplace

Many were amazed by Tom's **prodigious** musical talent.

34 **remedy**** n. **cure, treatment** 치료(법)

[rémidi]

The most effective **remedy** for boredom is work.

35 **speculate about*** phr. **hypothesize** 추측하다, 가정하다

The rookie failed to score in his first two games in regular-season, leaving some to **speculate about** his ability.

36 **strictly**** adv. 1. **tightly, severely; precisely** 엄격하게 ; 엄밀히

[stríktli]

Traffic rules are **strictly** enforced by the police department in the city.

adv. 2. **only** 순전히

The computers in the school library should be used **strictly** for educational purposes.

37 **trend**** n. **tendency, direction, inclination** 경향

[trénd]

The current **trend** is towards more part-time employment.

on the contrary	그 청중들은 연설자에게 적대적이지 않았다. 오히려 반대로 그는 청중의 호응을 받았다.
photosynthesis	그 학생들은 생물학 수업 시간에 광합성을 가지고 실험을 했다.
prodigious	많은 사람들이 Tom의 비범한 음악적 재능에 놀랐다.
remedy	지겨운 일상에 대한 가장 효과적인 치료법은 일하는 것이다.
speculate about	신인 선수는 정규 시즌에서 첫 두 경기 동안 점수를 내는 데 실패했기 때문에, 몇몇 사람들은 그의 능력에 대해 궁금해 했다.
strictly	그 도시에서는 교통 규칙이 경찰국에 의해 매우 엄격하게 시행되고 있다.
	학교 도서관에 있는 컴퓨터들은 순전히 교육용으로만 사용되어야 한다.
trend	좀 더 많은 파트타임 고용이 현재의 흐름이다.

38 **unencumbered by** phr. **free of** ~에 의해 방해받지 않는

Children are **unencumbered by** the concerns of the world.

39 **unwonted*** adj. **unusual, unordinary, extraordinary** 보통이 아닌, 드문

[ʌnwɔ́:ntid]
usual

The jeweler said that it is **unwonted** to find diamonds this large.

40 **vexing*** adj. **difficult, annoying, irritating** 성가신, 짜증나는

[véksiŋ]

Nothing is more **vexing** than slow service in a restaurant when one is hungry.

41 **votary*** n. **devotee, admirer, faithful follower** (특정 종교의) 신봉자

[vóutəri]
skeptic

Votaries of Judaism suffered persecution by Hitler.

Quiz

Choose the synonym.

1. affliction — ⓐ damage, injure, deteriorate
2. impair — ⓑ woe, distress, anguish
3. novelty — ⓒ unusual, unordinary, extraordinary
4. prodigious — ⓓ originality, freshness, newness
5. unwonted — ⓔ marvelous, amazing, astonishing

Answer 1. ⓑ 2. ⓐ 3. ⓓ 4. ⓔ 5. ⓒ

unencumbered by	아이들은 세상의 근심들에서 자유롭다.
unwonted	그 보석 상인은 이 정도 크기의 다이아몬드를 발견하는 일이 흔치 않다고 말했다.
vexing	배가 고플 때에 식당에서의 느린 서비스만큼 짜증나는 일은 없다.
votary	유대교의 신봉자들은 Hitler에 의한 종교적 박해로 고통을 받았다.

Hackers TOEFL Voca TEST DAY 43-45

Choose the synonym of the highlighted word in the sentence.

1. Bones become lighter and more brittle with age.
(A) judicial (B) heedful (C) breakable (D) gullible

2. Geochemical models suggest that the core of the Earth consists of a sphere of iron or iron sulfide.
(A) port (B) heart (C) error (D) edge

3. Angkor Wat at dawn was a prodigious sight for the tourists who had never been abroad.
(A) potent (B) ordinary (C) fretful (D) amazing

4. Despite incipient signs of recovery, the economy fell into a deeper recession.
(A) initial (B) final (C) ultimate (D) insufficient

5. The insulator absorbs heat during the day and slowly releases it at night.
(A) offends (B) blocks (C) notices (D) takes in

6. They made a futile attempt to escape their prison cell.
(A) dogged (B) innate (C) useless (D) lunatic

7. Ions play vital roles in the body's metabolic processes.
(A) famous (B) important (C) careful (D) ignorant

8. The boulder plunged down the cliff after it was dislodged by the rain storm.
(A) placed (B) vaulted (C) grated (D) dropped

9. The Viet Cong guerilla army used subterranean tunnels from which to attack American forces.
(A) underground (B) outdoor (C) hearty (D) designated

10. The unwonted behavior of the animals indicated to the farmer that a storm was approaching.
(A) urgent (B) imperious (C) unusual (D) ancillary

정답 p.419

TAKE A BREAK

Homestead Act

남북전쟁이 한참이던 1862년, 미국의회는 Homestead Act를 통과시켰다. 이 법률에는 5년간 일정한 토지에 거주하여 개척을 한 자(이민포함)에게는 160에이커의 토지를 무상으로 지급한다는 것과, 거주 시작 6개월이 지나면, 그 토지를 1에이커에 1달러 25센트의 염가로 구입할 수 있다는 것이 규정되어 있었다. 이것은 주로 미시시피강 이서(以西)의 미개척 지역을 신속히 개척하고 동부산업자본의 국내시장 확대를 촉진시키는 동시에 자영농민의 수를 늘리려는 것이었다. 이 법률에 의하여 1883년까지 약 2300만 에이커의 토지가 주어지고 정주자가 증가하여 프런티어(미개척지)의 소멸을 앞당기게 되었으나, 한편으로는 토지투기에 악용되기도 하였다. 특정한 개인이나 사적 집단이 아니고, 국가 또는 공공단체에 의하여 소유되는 토지인 공유지는 미국 역사적 개념상, 미국 토지정책에서 중요한 대상이 된다. 미국연방정부는 미시시피강 서쪽의 광활한 영역을 장악하여, 남북전쟁 때에 홈스테드(Homestead Act)로 자작농 조성을 촉진하였다. 그 후, 철도건설과 고등교육시설을 위해서 많은 공유지가 투입되었으며, 10세기 말부터는 공유지에 포함된 권리의 전면양도가 아니라, 국가에 의한 광산권의 유보와 같은 제약이 생겼다. 제 2차 세계대전 후부터는 석유자원의 채굴권·삼림보유 등의 목적으로, 공유지의 비 양도정책이 시행되었다.

DAY 46

Hackers TOEFL **Vocabulary**

Hackers Voca

www.goHackers.com

1 **alight***	v.	**land, come down, settle**	내리다
[əláit] rise		A mosquito **alighted** on the table.	
2 **alternate**	v.	**rotate, interchange**	번갈아 일어나다
[ɔ́:ltərneit] keep		Good luck and misfortune **alternate** with each other throughout our lives.	
3 **contain****	v.	**involve, comprise, hold**	포함(수용)하다
[kəntéin]		The declaration **contained** a basic principle.	
4 **deter***	v.	**preclude, prevent, inhibit** avert	막다, 방해하다
[ditə́:r] abet		Slavery **deterred** the development of the forces of production.	
5 **examine***	v.	**inspect, probe, scrutinize** investigate	정밀 조사하다
[igzǽmin]		The coroner dissected the bodies, and **examined** the internal organs.	
6 **fast**	adj.	**quick, swift, rapid** fleet	빠른
[fǽst] slow		The Olympic gold medal sprinter was known as the **fastest** man alive.	

alight	모기 한 마리가 탁자 위에 내려앉았다.
alternate	행운과 불운은 우리 인생에서 서로 번갈아 일어난다.
contain	그 선언서는 하나의 기본 원칙을 포함했다.
deter	노예 제도는 생산력의 발전을 방해했다.
examine	그 검시관은 시체를 해부하여 장기들을 정밀 조사했다.
fast	올림픽 단거리 경주 금메달리스트는 살아 있는 가장 빠른 사람으로 알려졌다.

7 **gist***

[dʒíst]

n. **core, kernel, essence** 핵심

Sarah understood the **gist** of the statement.

8 **gleaming***

[glíːmiŋ]

adj. **shining, luminous, brilliant** 반짝이는, 빛나는

John strode across the stage and took his seat at the **gleaming** black grand piano.

9 **guarantee**

[gæ̀rəntíː]

v. **insure, warrant** 보증하다

The link of medical institutions will **guarantee** better health care systems.

10 **hobby***

[hábi]

n. **pastime, diversion, avocation** 취미

One of my grandmother's **hobbies** is collecting teacups from around the world.

11 **inadequate****

[inǽdikwit]
adequate

adj. **insufficient, deficient** 불충분한

Because of **inadequate** preparation, the program ended in failure.

12 **inborn***

[ìnbɔ́ːrn]
acquired

adj. **innate, native, natural** 선천적인

Many believe that humans have an **inborn** sense of morality.

13 **inaccessible***

[ìnəksésəbl]
accessible

adj. **unreachable; unobtainable** 접근하기 어려운 ; 얻기 어려운

Certain Alpine villages are completely **inaccessible** during the winter.

14 **inclination****

[ìnklənéiʃən]

n. **preference, tendency, trend** 성향, 경향

The Mongols had little **inclination** to ally with other nomadic peoples of northern Asia.

---

gist	Sarah는 그 진술의 핵심을 이해했다.
gleaming	John은 무대를 가로질러 성큼성큼 걸어가서 반짝이는 검정색 그랜드 피아노 앞에 앉았다.
guarantee	의료 기관들의 연결은 더 나은 건강관리 제도를 보장할 것이다.
hobby	할머니의 취미 중 하나는 전 세계의 찻잔을 수집하는 것이다.
inadequate	불충분한 준비 때문에, 그 프로그램은 실패로 끝났다.
inborn	많은 이들이 인간은 타고난 도덕심을 가지고 있다고 믿는다.
inaccessible	어떤 알프스 산맥의 마을들은 겨울 동안 아예 접근이 불가능하다.
inclination	몽고인들은 북아시아의 다른 유목 민족들과 동맹을 맺으려는 의향이 거의 없었다.

15 **in proximity to**

phr. close to, **adjacent to, near, in the vicinity of** ~에 가까운

Those who work with or are **in proximity to** birds should be careful of avian flu.

16 **insight***

[ínsàit]

n. understanding, **perception** 통찰력, 직관

Nextel has **insight** into the mobile business market that Motorola would like to have.

17 **intent***

[intént]
accident

n. purpose, **intention, design** 의도

The officer declared his **intent** to enforce the law.

18 **intertwine***

[ìntərtwáin]

v. interweave, **intermingle, twine** 뒤엉키다

Joy and sorrow often **intertwine** within a person.

19 **join***

[dʒɔ́in]
disconnect

v. 1. connect, **link, unite, combine** 연결하다, 결합하다

The two nations are **joined** by economic dependency and political affiliation.

v. 2. meet 합류하다

The Mississippi River begins its course at the Canadian border and flows south until it **joins** the Gulf of Mexico.

20 **meddlesome****

[médlsəm]

adj. meddling, interfering, **intrusive** officious 간섭하는

Cinderella's daily life was intolerable because of her **meddlesome** stepsisters.

21 **multiply**

[mʌ́ltəplài]

v. increase, **expand, augment** 증가하다

The company's sales **multiplied** as a result of the ad campaign.

---

in proximity to	조류와 관련된 일을 하거나 조류와 가까운 곳에 있는 이들은 조류독감에 주의해야 한다.
insight	Nextel은 Motorola가 갖고 싶어하는 이동 전화 시장에 대한 통찰력을 가지고 있다.
intent	그 경찰관은 법을 집행하려는 그의 의도를 표명했다.
intertwine	기쁨과 슬픔은 종종 한 사람 안에 뒤엉켜 있다.
join	그 두 국가는 경제적 의존성과 정치적 제휴에 의해 연결되어 있다.
	미시시피 강은 캐나다의 국경에서 시작해서 멕시코만에 합쳐질 때까지 남쪽으로 흐른다.
meddlesome	Cinderella의 일상 생활은 간섭하기 좋아하는 그녀의 의붓 자매 때문에 견디기 힘들었다.
multiply	광고 캠페인의 결과 그 기업의 판매 실적이 배가되었다.

22 **myriad****
[míriəd]

adj. **innumerable, numerous, countless** many 무수한

A **myriad** of products are available for purchase at the store.

23 **naive**
[nɑːíːv]
sophisticated

adj. **ingenuous, simple, unaffected** 꾸밈없는, 순진한

Tom was hopelessly **naive** about the realities of combat and army life.

24 **outrage***
[áutrèidʒ]
placate

v. **anger, aggravate, offend, infuriate** 화나게 하다

Youthful Americans were **outraged** by social injustice.

25 **particularly****
[pərtíkjələrli]

adv. **especially, uniquely, specially** 특히

McDonald's and Lotteria are **particularly** popular with children and young adults.

26 **principal*****
[prínsəpəl]

adj. **central, major, main, primal, prime, chief** 주요한

Hemley was one of the **principal** authors of the WWF's 1997 tiger report.

27 **propel***
[prəpél]

v. **push, force out, drive, impel** 추진하다, 밀어내다

The force of the rapids managed to **propel** Francisca out of her kayak and right into the water.

28 **rigorous****
[rígərəs]
facile

adj. 1. **severe, demanding, harsh** 혹독한, 엄격한

Athletes should follow a **rigorous** training schedule to be competitive.

adj. 2. **precise** 정밀한

The specifications for the machine that the factory requires are **rigorous**.

myriad	그 상점에는 무수한 상품들이 판매되고 있다.
naive	Tom은 전투나 군생활의 현실에 대해 절망스러울 정도로 순진했다.
outrage	젊은 미국인들은 사회적 불의에 화가 났다.
particularly	맥도날드와 롯데리아는 특히 어린이와 젊은 사람들에게 인기가 좋다.
principal	Hemley는 WWF의 1997년 호랑이에 관한 보고서의 주요 저자들 중의 한 사람이었다.
propel	급류의 힘은 용케도 Francisca를 카약 밖으로 밀어내어 곧바로 물속으로 빠뜨렸다.
rigorous	운동선수들은 경쟁력을 갖추기 위해 엄격한 훈련 일정을 따라야 한다.
	공장이 요구한 기계의 설계 명세서는 매우 정밀하다.

29 **savor**** | n. **flavor, taste** 맛

[séivər]

Water from the valley of Mountain Taeduk in Yongin City is famous for its unique **savor**.

30 **scramble** | v. **mix up, jumble, muddle, tangle** 뒤섞다

[skrǽmbl]

The chef **scrambled** many different ingredients together to create his signature dish.

31 **seldom** | adv. **infrequently, rarely, hardly, scarcely** 거의 ~ 않다

[séldəm]

The temperature in the tropics **seldom** drops below twenty degrees.

32 **simulated** | adj. **artificial, imitated** 모조의, 가짜의

[símjəlèitid]

Simulated conditions of weightlessness were used at the space training facility.

33 **slight*** | adj. **small, minor, trivial** trifling 사소한

[sláit]

If Picasso had died before 1906, his mark on 20th century art would have been **slight**.

34 **sporadic**** | adj. **infrequent, occasional, irregular, intermittent** 산발적인

[spərǽdik]
regular

During World War II, many cities were subject to **sporadic** bombing raids.

35 **standstill*** | n. **complete stop, halt** 정지

[stǽndstìl]

During the Thanksgiving and the lunar New Year holidays in Korea, traffic comes to a **standstill** on the expressways as many people leave town to visit their parents.

36 **systematic** | adj. **methodical, organized** 조직적인

[sìstəmǽtik]

A **systematic** approach is needed to succeed in business.

savor	용인시 대덕산의 물은 그 독특한 풍미로 유명하다.
scramble	요리사는 여러 가지 재료를 같이 섞어 자신의 대표적인 요리를 만들었다.
seldom	열대 지방의 기온은 좀처럼 20도 아래로 내려가지 않는다.
simulated	인공적으로 만든 무중력 상태의 환경이 우주 탐사 훈련 시설에서 사용되었다.
slight	Picasso가 1906년 이전에 사망했다면, 20세기 예술에서의 그의 영향은 아주 적었을 것이다.
sporadic	2차 세계 대전 중, 많은 도시들이 산발적인 폭격의 대상이 되었다.
standstill	한국에서는 추석과 설 연휴가 되면, 많은 사람들이 부모님을 방문하기 위해 시내를 떠나기 때문에 고속도로가 정체된다.
systematic	사업에서 성공하려면 조직적 접근법이 필요하다.

37 through

[θrúː]

prep. **by, by means of** ~에 의하여

Ben achieved his goals **through** hard work and perseverance.

38 versatile

[vɔ́ːrsətil]

adj. **flexible, adaptable, all-around, many-sided** 다방면의

The **versatile** soccer player lined up as a forward and a defender for his club.

39 voluble*

[váljəbl]
reticent

adj. **talkative, loquacious, fluent** 입심 좋은, 유창한

The roommate that Jack had last semester was too **voluble**.

Quiz

Choose the synonym.

1. alight	ⓐ intermigle, interweave, twine
2. gist	ⓑ increase, expand, augment
3. intertwine	ⓒ settle, land, come down
4. multiply	ⓓ kernel, essence, core
5. voluble	ⓔ talkative, loquacious, fluent

Answer 1. ⓒ 2. ⓓ 3. ⓐ 4. ⓑ 5. ⓔ

through	Ben은 많은 노력과 인내로 그의 목표들을 달성하였다.
versatile	그 다재다능한 축구선수는 그의 클럽에서 공격수이자 수비수의 역할을 한다.
voluble	Jack이 지난 학기에 함께 했던 그 룸메이트는 너무 말이 많았다.

DAY 47

Hackers TOEFL **Vocabulary**

Hackers Voca

www.goHackers.com

1 **amiable** [éimiəbl] surly	adj.	**friendly, amicable, genial, cordial** The **amiable** Cassidy made many friends among her neighbors.	상냥한
2 **arduous**** [á:rdʒuəs] effortless	adj.	**difficult, laborious; strenuous** Tom's family had an **arduous** journey in the mountains this summer.	힘드는 ; 분투적인
3 **ascend*** [əsénd] descend	v.	**climb, mount, go up** Jack **ascended** the back stairs to carry his wife to their room.	올라가다
4 **atmosphere*** [ǽtməsfìər]	n.	**air, ambiance, aura** An **atmosphere** of optimism dominated the wedding reception.	공기, 분위기
5 **awe*** [ɔ́:] scorn	n.	**amazement, surprise, wonder** The complexity of the universe inspires great **awe**.	경외심
6 **completely*** [kəmplí:tli]	adv.	**totally, perfectly, entirely, utterly** A husband and wife should be **completely** honest with each other.	완전히

amiable	Cassidy는 상냥하여 주변에 친구가 많았다.
arduous	Tom의 가족은 이번 여름에 산에서 힘든 여행을 하고 왔다.
ascend	Jack은 부인을 그들의 방으로 옮기기 위해 뒷 계단을 올라갔다.
atmosphere	결혼 피로연에서는 낙관적 분위기가 지배적이었다.
awe	우주의 복잡함은 상당한 경외심을 불러일으킨다.
completely	남편과 아내는 서로 완전하게 정직해야 한다.

7 **cram****

[krǽm]

v. **jam, stuff** (쑤셔) 넣다

The kids **crammed** the fireplace full of pine-boughs.

8 **dilemma***

[dilémə]

n. **difficult situation, predicament, strait** 곤경

The disposal of wastes was a **dilemma** that had to be dealt with.

9 **discharge**

[distʃɑ́ːrdʒ]

v. 1. **release, set free, liberate** (군인 · 환자 등을) 해방시키다

The soldier was **discharged** from the army after being wounded.

v. 2. **release** 방출하다

The sun **discharges** a significant amount of ultraviolet radiation.

10 **enlist****

[enlíst]

v. **join in, enroll** 입대하다

Dasch **enlisted** in the German army at the age of 14.

11 **enterprise***

[éntərprὰiz]

n. **undertaking** (모험적인) 사업

Andrea soon discovered that her new **enterprise** was far more work than she had expected.

12 **escalate***

[éskəlèit]
diminish

v. **increase, intensify, mount, rise** 차츰 확대되다, 오르다

The civilians don't want the fighting to **escalate** into a full-scale war.

13 **estimate***

[éstəmèit]

v. **assess, evaluate, judge** value, appraise 평가하다

John tried to **estimate** the cost of the repairs.

cram	그 아이들은 벽난로에 소나무 가지를 가득 차게 쑤셔 넣었다.
dilemma	쓰레기를 처분하는 것은 해결되어야 하는 난제였다.
discharge	그 군인은 부상당한 후 군대에서 제대하였다.
	태양은 상당한 양의 자외선을 방출한다.
enlist	Dasch는 14살에 독일군에 입대했다.
enterprise	Andrea는 곧 그녀의 새로운 사업이 그녀가 예상했던 것보다 훨씬 더 어려운 일이라는 걸 알게 되었다.
escalate	일반 시민들은 전투가 전면적인 전쟁으로 발전되기를 바라지 않는다.
estimate	John은 수리 비용을 계산하려고 애썼다.

14 **green hand***

phr. **untrained worker** 미숙한 사람

Mr. Kim is a **green hand** at foreign trade.

15 **inclined**

[inkláind]

adj. 1. **apt, liable, prone, disposed** ~의 경향이 있는

Caucasians are more **inclined** to get skin cancer than other races.

adj. 2. **slanted, tilted** 경사진, 기울어진

The building was at an **inclined** angle after being damaged in the earthquake.

16 **incoherent***

[ìnkouhí(:)ərənt]

adj. **disordered, unintelligible** 두서 없는

Incoherent speech is a possible indicator of a head injury.

17 **innovate**

[ínəvèit]

v. **begin, create, pioneer** 시작하다

When people are free from bureaucratic constraints, they can often **innovate** more creatively.

18 **lading***

[léidiŋ]

n. **cargo, load, freight** 화물

The port of Singapore handles many tons of **lading** each year.

19 **original****

[ərídʒənəl]

banal

adj. 1. **imaginative, creative, inventive** 독창적인

Galileo had already started the deep process of **original** thinking.

last

adj. 2. **initial, primary, early** opening 처음의

The potato's **original** home is in the mountainous regions of South America.

green hand — Kim씨는 해외 무역에 미숙한 사람이다.

inclined — 코카서스인들은 다른 인종들에 비해 피부암에 더 많이 걸리는 경향이 있다.
그 빌딩은 지진에 손상을 입은 후 기울어진 상태였다.

incoherent — 두서 없는 말하기는 두부 손상의 척도가 될 수 있다.

innovate — 사람들은 관료주의적 제약으로부터 자유로울 때 좀 더 창조적인 혁신을 할 수 있다.

lading — 싱가포르 항구에서는 매년 상당량의 화물을 취급한다.

original — Galileo는 독창적인 사고의 심오한 과정을 이미 시작했었다.
감자의 원산지는 남아메리카의 산악 지방에 있다.

20 outrageous adj. **shocking, offensive, intolerable** 지나친, 엄청난

[autréidʒəs]

The company spokesman was fired for making **outrageous** statements.

21 picture** v. **represent, portray** depict 묘사하다

[píktʃər]

Johnson **pictured** Goldwater as a dangerous radical.

22 preliminary adj. **initial, introductory, preparatory** 서두의, 예비의

[prilímənèri]

Preliminary research indicates that solar radiation may have decreased by as much as 10 percent.

23 preoccupation* n. **fascination, absorption, obsession** 몰두, 강박 관념

[priːɑ̀kjupéiʃən]

Ford hoped his action would end the nation's **preoccupation** with Watergate.

24 preserve** v. **protect, save, maintain** conserve, keep 보호하다, 보존하다

[prizə́ːrv]

The senator took important steps to **preserve** the wildlife of his state.

25 radiant** adj. **bright, vivid, brilliant** beaming, glowing 빛나는

[réidiənt]

The window stood wide open, and the **radiant** moonlight streamed in.

26 research* v. **investigate, study, examine** scrutinize 조사하다

[ríːsəːrtʃ]

The reporter carefully **researched** the background of the soldiers who were implicated in the crime.

27 reverence n. **worship, veneration, homage** respect, awe 존경

[révərəns]
contempt

Ancestor **reverence** is an integral part of some Asian cultures.

outrageous	그 회사의 대변인은 지나친 발언을 해서 해고당했다.
picture	Johnson은 Goldwater를 위험한 과격론자로 묘사했다.
preliminary	예비조사는 태양 방사 에너지가 10%까지 감소했을 수도 있음을 나타냈다.
preoccupation	Ford는 자신의 조치로 나라가 워터게이트 사건에 더 이상 집착하지 않기를 바랐다.
preserve	그 상원 의원은 그의 주의 야생 생태계를 보존하기 위한 중요한 조치들을 취했다.
radiant	그 창문은 활짝 열린 채였고, 밝은 달빛이 비쳐 들어왔다.
research	그 기자는 범죄에 연루되었던 군인들의 배경을 신중하게 조사했다.
reverence	조상 경외와 숭배는 어떤 아시아의 문화에서 없어서는 안될 요소이다.

28 **reverse** v. **invert** 뒤집다

[rivə́:rs]

Europe has not only stopped its population growth but has actually **reversed** it.

29 **right** adj. **correct, proper, appropriate** 옳은, 적절한

[ráit]
wrong

All the evidence shows that the birth rate is falling and that we're moving in the **right** direction.

30 **satire*** n. **irony, sarcasm** 풍자

[sǽtaiər]

The columnist wrote a **satire** on the lives of the rich and the famous.

31 **segregate*** v. **seclude, separate, dissociate, disunite** 떼어놓다, 분리하다

[ségrigèit]
mix

The prisoners were **segregated** by gender at the prison camp.

32 **stable*** adj. **unchangeable, invariable, constant** steady, steadfast 안정된

[stéibl]
unstable

For 300 years, New Spain had been the most loyal and **stable** of all of Spain's colonies.

33 **strong**** adj. **robust, mighty** 강한

[strɔ́(:)ŋ]
weak

Angelou's biography became a **strong** source of inspiration for the boy.

34 **tease** v. **irritate, bother** annoy 괴롭히다

[tí:z]
soothe

The boy relentlessly **teased** the girl until she started to cry.

35 **tempting**** adj. **inviting, attractive, appealing, appetizing** 매력적인, 유혹하는

[témptiŋ]
repulsive

Jeniffer found the job offer to be too **tempting** to resist.

reverse	유럽은 인구 성장이 멈추었을 뿐만 아니라 사실상 성장을 뒤집어 감소하고 있다.
right	모든 증거는 출생률이 떨어지고 있고 우리가 바른 방향으로 가고 있다는 것을 보여 준다.
satire	특별 기고가는 부자와 유명인들의 삶에 대해 풍자한 글을 썼다.
segregate	죄수들은 감옥에서 성별에 의해 격리된다.
stable	300년 동안, New Spain은 모든 스페인 식민지들 중에서 가장 충성스럽고 안정된 식민지였다.
strong	Angelou의 전기는 그 소년에게 있어 강력한 영감의 원천이 되었다.
tease	그 소년은 소녀가 울 때까지 무자비하게 괴롭혔다.
tempting	Jeniffer는 그 취업 제의가 거절하기에는 너무 매력적이라는 것을 알았다.

36 type** — n. **kind, sort** — 유형

[táip]

Kate is the **type** of person anyone looks up to.

37 underlying* — adj. **fundamental, basic, elementary** — 근원적인, 기저의

[ʌ́ndərlàiiŋ]

The **underlying** theme of John Donne's poem 'The Flea' is marriage.

38 vein* — n. **blood vessel** — 정맥

[véin]

Everyone alive has blood pulsing through their **veins**.

Quiz

Choose the synonym.

1. amiable	ⓐ inviting, appealing, attractive
2. preliminary	ⓑ introductory, initial, preparatory
3. right	ⓒ kind, friendly, amicable
4. tempting	ⓓ correct, equitable, appropriate
5. underlying	ⓔ fundamental, basic, elementary

Answer 1. ⓒ 2. ⓑ 3. ⓓ 4. ⓐ 5. ⓔ

type	Kate는 누구나가 존경하는 유형의 사람이다.
underlying	John Donne의 시, 'The Flea'의 기저에 놓인 주제는 결혼이다.
vein	살아 있는 모든 이는 정맥을 통과하며 고동치는 혈액을 가지고 있다.

DAY 48

Hackers TOEFL **Vocabulary**

Hackers Voca

www.goHackers.com

1 **absolutely**** [ǽbsəlùːtli]
adv. **totally, utterly, completely** 전적으로
Political unity was considered **absolutely** essential for the stability of the nation.

2 **caption*** [kǽpʃən]
n. **title, heading** 표제
The **caption** of the photograph read, 'How to Reach Happiness.'

3 **categorize**** [kǽtəgəràiz]
v. **arrange in classes, classify, group** class 분류하다
Johnson doesn't like to be **categorized** as a socialist.

4 **complicated*** [kɑ́mpləkèitid]
simple
adj. **complex, intricate** 복잡한
The issue of abortion is **complicated** and debates about it are often left unresolved.

5 **conflicting**** [kənflíktiŋ]
similar
adj. **opposing, contrary, clashing** 상반(상충)되는
Studies on antioxidants like vitamins C and E have produced **conflicting** results.

6 **gratify*** [grǽtəfài]
exasperate
v. **please, satisfy, appease** 만족시키다
The journey was one of the most **gratifying** experiences of Peter's life.

absolutely	정치적 통일은 한 나라의 안정을 위해 전적으로 필수적인 것으로 여겨졌다.
caption	그 사진의 표제는 '행복에 도달하는 방법' 이다.
categorize	Johnson은 사회주의자로 분류되는 것을 좋아하지 않는다.
complicated	낙태라는 화제는 복잡하여 거기에 대한 토론은 종종 미결로 남겨진다.
conflicting	비타민C나 비타민E와 같은 산화 방지제에 대한 연구는 상반되는 결과들을 가져왔다.
gratify	그 여행은 Peter의 인생에서 가장 만족스러운 경험 중의 하나였다.

7 **in operation***

phr. **being used** 실시 중의, 효력을 가지는

Train service in the city is **in operation** until midnight.

8 **instrument***

[ínstrəmənt]

n. 1. **means, mechanism** 수단, 방법

Bob's greed was the **instrument** of his destruction.

n. 2. **apparatus, appliance, tool** device 기구, 도구

Galileo invented the telescope, an **instrument** which illustrates his great craftsmanship.

9 **intrude**

[intrú:d]

v. **trespass, encroach, violate** 침범(침해)하다

Corporations did not want the government to **intrude** on the business sector.

10 **key*****

[kí:]

n. 1. **tone** 어조, (음악) 조

Keith played that piece in a lower **key** than usual.

adj. 2. **essential, important, central** 필수적인, 중요한

The two ambassadors played a **key** role in negotiating a peace treaty between the hostile countries.

11 **legacy**

[légəsi]

n. **tradition, inheritance** heritage (전통적인) 유산

The idea of equality of opportunity is a **legacy** of the French Revolution.

12 **manufacture***

[mæ̀njufǽktʃər]

v. **make, build, construct, mass-produce** (대규모로) 제조하다

Germany **manufactures** some of the world's finest optical equipment.

in operation	도심에서 기차는 자정까지 운행한다.
instrument	Bob의 욕심은 그를 파괴하는 도구였다. Galileo는 망원경을 발명했는데, 이 도구는 그의 위대한 장인 정신을 보여 준다.
intrude	기업들은 정부가 그 사업 분야에 침범하는 것을 원하지 않았다.
key	Keith는 보통보다 낮은 조로 그 부분을 연주했다. 그 두 명의 대사들은 적대적인 두 나라 사이의 평화협정을 협상하는 데 있어 매우 중요한 역할을 하였다.
legacy	기회의 평등이라는 개념은 프랑스 혁명의 한가지 유산이다.
manufacture	독일은 세계에서 가장 미세한 광학 제품을 만든다.

13 **memorable** | adj. **notable, remarkable, noteworthy** 기억할 만한, 인상적인

[mémərəbl]

John F. Kennedy gave a **memorable** speech in Berlin.

14 **narrow** | v. **taper; limit** 좁아지다 ; 한정하다

[nǽrou]
broaden

As the race wound about the harbor, Ndugu's lead **narrowed** and the second place runner finally inched past him near the bridge.

15 **occasion*** | n. **event, affair** 행사, 사건

[əkéiʒən]

The opening of the new town library turned out to be quite an **occasion**.

16 **occasional*** | adj. **infrequent, irregular, sporadic** 가끔의

[əkéiʒənəl]
recurrent

Usually the family stays home on the weekends, with perhaps the **occasional** movie or dinner out on the town.

17 **oversee*** | v. **supervise, manage, control** 감독하다

[òuvərsíː]

It is the job of the foremen to **oversee** factory workers.

18 **oversight** | n. **mistake, blunder, slip** error 실수

[óuvərsàit]

Jane apologized for the **oversight**.

19 **peaceful*** | adj. **serene, tranquil, placid** quiet, calm 평온한

[píːsfəl]
bellicose, choleric

The Hopi people were very **peaceful**, and avoided war whenever possible.

20 **peak**** | n. **summit, maximum, pinnacle, height** apex 정점, 절정

[píːk]
nadir

The union reached its **peak** membership of 100,000 in 1912.

memorable	John F. Kennedy는 베를린에서 인상적인 연설을 했다.
narrow	항구쪽에서 경주 코스가 굽어지면서 Ndugu의 선두 위치는 점점 좁혀졌으며, 마침내 다리 근처에서 두 번째로 달려오던 주자가 그를 지나쳐 조금씩 나아갔다.
occasion	새로운 시내 도서관의 개관은 꽤나 특별한 사건이 되었다.
occasional	그 가족은 대개 주말에 집에 머물러 있으나, 아마 때로는 영화나 저녁 식사를 위해 시내로 나가기도 한다.
oversee	공장 직원들을 감독하는 것은 현장 주임의 일이다.
oversight	Jane은 그 실수에 대해 사과했다.
peaceful	Hopi족 사람들은 매우 평온했고, 언제든지 가능하면 전쟁을 피했다.
peak	그 노동조합은 1912년에 100,000명에 달하는 구성원들로 그 정점에 도달했다.

21 perforate
[pə́:rfərèit]
v. pierce, **punch, puncture, hole** 구멍을 내다
A hole puncher is used to **perforate** notebook paper.

22 postulate**
[pástʃəlèit]
v. propose, claim, **necessitate, call for** 요구하다
World peace **postulates** open communication between the nations of the world.

23 quit**
[kwít]
start
v. give up, **stop; resign, retire** 그만두다 ; 사직하다
The coach always reminds his players to never **quit**.

24 reinforcement*
[rì:infɔ́:rsmənt]
n. support 보강, 지원군
Arrival of **reinforcements** was decisive at the battle of Stalingrad.

25 remnant**
[rémnənt]
n. trace, remain, **relics** 잔재, 자취
It is possible that comets are primordial **remnants** from the formation of the solar system.

26 remove**
[rimú:v]
v. withdraw, extract, eliminate 끌어내다, 제거하다
Isaac's father **removed** him from Shrewsbury and enrolled him in the University of Edinburgh to study medicine.

27 role
[róul]
n. function, **duty, capacity** 역할, 기능
Central banks play a major **role** in regulating economies.

28 shudder*
[ʃʌ́dər]
n. tremor, **shiver, quiver** shake 떨림, 전율
A **shudder** ran through the hunter's body when he saw the bear.

perforate	펀처는 노트에 구멍을 내기 위해서 사용된다.
postulate	세계 평화는 나라 간의 열린 대화를 요한다.
quit	그 코치는 항상 선수들에게 결코 그만두지 말 것을 상기시킨다.
reinforcement	지원병들의 도착은 Stalingrad 전투에서 결정적인 것이었다.
remnant	혜성은 태양계가 생성되면서 생긴 옛 흔적일 가능성이 있다.
remove	Isaac의 아버지는 그를 Shrewsbury에서 빼낸 후 Edinburgh 대학에 등록시켜 의학을 공부하게 했다.
role	중앙 은행들은 경제를 규제하는 데 중요한 역할을 한다.
shudder	사냥꾼이 곰을 보았을 때 그의 온 몸은 전율로 흔들렸다.

29 **spread out** phr. **extend, broaden, stretch** 넓히다, 전개하다

condense

The market women had **spread out** their goods upon the pavement.

30 **strip*** v. **remove, divest, deprive** 제거하다

[stríp]

Before we can begin painting, we first need to **strip** the wallpaper off the walls.

31 **tactile***** adj. **tangible, touchable** 촉각으로 알 수 있는

[tǽktil]

Visually impaired people use **tactile** symbols in order to read.

32 **temporary*** adj. **makeshift, for a limited time, transient, transitory** 일시적인

[témpərəri]
permanent

The pill caused a few **temporary** side effects.

33 **tendency**** n. **trend, inclination, proneness** bent 경향, 성향

[téndənsi]

There has been a recent **tendency** among teachers to give more lenient punishments.

34 **underpinning*** n. **foundation, basis** 기초, 기반

[ʌ́ndərpìniŋ]

After a while, we found ourselves questioning the spiritual and moral **underpinnings** of the American way of life.

35 **unencumbered*** adj. **free** 방해 없는

[ʌ̀ninkʌ́mbərd]

Nick felt **unencumbered** after he took off all his scuba gear.

36 **version*** n. 1. **translation** 번역(물)

[və́:rʒən]

Erasmus published the Greek **version** of the New Testament in Latin.

spread out	시장의 여인들은 자신의 물건들을 포장도로 위에 펼쳐놓았다.
strip	페인트 칠을 하기 전에, 우리는 먼저 벽지를 벽에서 벗겨내야만 한다.
tactile	시각 장애자들은 만져서 알 수 있는 기호를 이용해서 글을 읽는다.
temporary	그 알약은 몇 가지 일시적인 부작용을 일으켰다.
tendency	최근에 교사들 사이에서 좀 더 관대한 처벌을 주는 경향이 있었다.
underpinning	얼마 후, 우리는 미국식 삶의 정신적, 도덕적 기준에 의문을 품었다.
unencumbered	Nick은 그의 스쿠버 장비를 모두 벗은 후에 자유로움을 느꼈다.
version	Erasmus는 라틴어로 된 신약 성경의 그리스어 번역판을 출판했다.

n. **2. variant, form** 이형, 판

An online **version** of "The Encyclopedia of New York State" will be available next year.

37 well-suited

[wélsjú:tid]

adj. **adequate, appropriate** 적절한

Daycare centers are **well-suited** to the needs of working mothers.

38 whole*

[hóul]
fractional, partial

adj. **entire, total, full** 전체의, 완전한

Pete ate the **whole** pizza in one sitting.

39 wit

[wit]

n. **humor** 재치

Mark Twain was known for his **wit**.

Quiz

Choose the synonym.

1. gratify	ⓐ summit, maximum, pinnacle
2. intrude	ⓑ please, satisfy, appease
3. peak	ⓒ trace, remain, relics
4. remnant	ⓓ trespass, encroach, violate
5. temporary	ⓓ makeshift, transient, transitory

Answer 1.ⓑ 2.ⓓ 3.ⓐ 4.ⓒ 5.ⓔ

version	뉴욕 주 백과사전의 온라인 형태는 내년에 이용 가능할 것이다.
well-suited	탁아소들은 일하는 엄마들의 요구에 적합한 곳이다.
whole	Pete는 앉은 자리에서 피자 한 판을 전부 먹어 치웠다.
wit	Mark Twain은 재치로 유명했다.

Hackers TOEFL Voca TEST DAY 46-48

Choose the synonym of the highlighted word in the sentence.

1. Custody of the child was to alternate between the mother and the father.
(A) depict (B) parry (C) solicit (D) interchange

2. Scientists believe we have an inborn urge to propagate our own genes.
(A) maladroit (B) innate (C) intricate (D) acid

3. The founders came together aggregated to discuss one of the principal elements of the Constitution.
(A) discourteous (B) major (C) gracious (D) august

4. Condensation begins when air is cooled at constant pressure.
(A) uniform (B) vast (C) bulky (D) culpable

5. The secretary was fired because she had a tendency to forget important messages for her boss.
(A) spite (B) shudder (C) trend (D) legacy

6. The soldier was discharged from duty after receiving a wound in combat.
(A) ordered (B) released (C) promoted (D) confiscated

7. With its radiant color and plantlike shape, the sea anemone looks more like a flower than an animal.
(A) fascinating (B) visible (C) brilliant (D) well-known

8. The roots of my neighbor's tree began to intrude upon my property.
(A) preserve (B) contain (C) trespass (D) negotiate

9. Greg had been a voluble child until the death of his mother, after which he became far more introverted.
(A) grandiose (B) trenchant (C) hortatory (D) talkative

10. The effects of the drug were temporary.
(A) transient (B) facile (C) offensive (D) headstrong

정답 p.419

시험 5분 전 *Do Your Best*

DAY Hackers TOEFL **Vocabulary**

49 Hackers Voca

www.goHackers.com

1 **absolve** [æbzάlv]

v. **pardon, forgive, exculpate, let off** 사면하다, 용서하다

The Hutton Inquiry **absolved** the Blair government of wrongdoing.

2 **ambling**** [ǽmbliŋ] hard

adj. **leisurely, slow, easy** 느긋한

The cowboys watched the horse's **ambling** walk to the fence.

3 **barter**** [bά:rtər]

v. **trade, exchange, swap** 교환하다, 교역하다

On the Gold Coast, the Europeans **bartered** gold for slaves.

4 **bombard** [bɑmbά:rd]

v. **strike, assault, assail** 공격하다

Warplanes **bombarded** the city until it was demolished.

5 **breeding** [brí:diŋ]

n. **reproduction, upbringing** 번식

The **breeding** of pandas in captivity is rare.

6 **bulky**** [bʌ́lki]

adj. **large, hulking, immense, gross, massive** 거대한

The laundry basket was heavy with several **bulky** wool sweaters.

absolve	Hutton 수사팀은 블레어 정부의 범죄 행위들을 사면했다.
ambling	카우보이들은 그 말이 울타리로 느릿느릿 걸어가는 것을 보았다.
barter	황금 해안에서 유럽인들은 금을 노예로 교환했다.
bombard	전투기들은 도시가 파괴될 때까지 공격을 했다.
breeding	갇힌 상태에서 판다의 번식은 매우 드물다.
bulky	그 세탁 바구니는 여러 개의 큰 모직 스웨터로 인해 무거웠다.

7 depict**

[dipíkt]

v. **represent, portray, picture** render, interpret 묘사하다

Political opponents **depicted** McKinley as Mark Hanna's puppet.

8 diminish*

[dimíniʃ]
intensify

v. **lessen, decrease, reduce, abate** shrink 줄다

Diminishing sea ice is contributing to the disappearance of seabirds called black guillemots.

9 duration*

[djuəréiʃən]

n. **length, term, span** 지속 기간

Hull enlisted on May 1, 1777, and served for the **duration** of the war.

10 emphasize*

[émfəsàiz]
downplay

v. **stress, make much of, highlight** 강조하다

The president **emphasized** the need for the entire country to be on high alert against terrorism.

11 exalted*

[igzɔ́:ltid]

adj. **superior, high, praised** 고귀한

Monet is an **exalted** artist because he created a new revolutionary technique.

12 favor*

[féivər]
animosity

n. 1. **kindness, good-will** 호의

The knight won the **favor** of the king.

n. 2. **approval, blessing, approbation** 찬성

The recent presidential polls show that the electoral votes are still in **favor** of the Democrats.

13 fervor**

[fə́:rvər]
apathy

n. **zeal, passion, ardor** enthusiasm 열정

John spoke with **fervor** as he confessed his love.

---

depict 정치적 반대파들은 McKinley를 Mark Hanna의 꼭두각시로 묘사했다.
diminish 바다 얼음이 줄어들어 검정 바다비둘기로 불리는 바닷새의 소멸을 가속화하고 있다.
duration Hull은 1777년 5월 1일에 입대하여 전쟁이 지속되는 동안 복무했다.
emphasize 대통령은 나라 전체가 테러리즘에 대해 매우 경계하고 있어야 할 필요성을 강조하였다.
exalted Monet는 새롭고 혁명적인 기술을 창조했기 때문에 매우 우수한 예술가이다.
favor 그 기사는 왕의 호의를 받았다.
최근의 대통령 선거 여론 조사는 선거인들이 여전히 민주당을 선호한다는 사실을 보여 준다.
fervor John은 그의 사랑을 고백할 때 열정적으로 말했다.

14 **foliage***	n. **leaves**		잎
[fóuliidʒ]	Dense **foliage** makes a great wind blocker and sun filter.		
15 **foster**	v. **rear, breed, nourish**	raise	기르다
[fɔ́(:)stər]	The family **fostered** a little Romanian boy for a few years.		
16 **free***	v. **liberate, deliver, emancipate**	release	해방시키다
[fríː] bond	In his will, Taylor ordered that his slaves be **freed** after the death of his wife.		
17 **further***	adj. **additional, extra, more**		그 이상의, 여분의
[fə́ːrðər] less	It was determined that the little girl would need **further** therapy to fully recover from the car accident.		
18 **guide***	v. **direct, lead, show**	conduct, escort	안내하다
[gáid] distract	**Guided** by the Indians, the pioneers safely passed through the channels.		
19 **inaction***	n. **lack of action or activity**		활동하지 않음
[inǽkʃən] activeness	As a result of Harry's **inaction**, the company lost a lot of money.		
20 **incursion**	n. **invasion, raid, foray**		침입
[inkə́ːrʒən]	The government warned that any **incursion** would be met with a violent response.		
21 **indispensable***	adj. **essential, necessary, requisite**		필수적인
[ìndispénsəbl] dispensable	Adam considered compromise an **indispensable** tool in a federal system.		

foliage	빽빽한 잎사귀들은 훌륭한 바람막이와 햇볕 여과기가 된다.
foster	그 가족은 몇 년간 어린 루마니아 남자아이를 양육했다.
free	그의 유언장에서, Taylor는 그의 노예들이 그의 부인의 사후에는 해방되어야 함을 명시했다.
further	그 어린 소녀가 자동차 사고에서 완전히 회복되려면 추가적인 치료가 필요하다는 진단이 나왔다.
guide	인디언들에게 안내를 받아, 개척자들은 안전하게 그 길들을 통과했다.
inaction	Harry의 근무 태만의 결과로, 그 기업은 많은 돈을 잃었다.
incursion	정부는 어떤 침략 행위도 격렬한 반발을 마주치게 될 것이라고 경고했다.
indispensable	Adam은 연방 제도에서 타협을 필수적인 도구로 간주했다.

22 **inimical****	adj. **unfriendly, hostile, antagonistic, opposed**	적대하는
[inímikəl] simpatico	Legend has it that certain objects are **inimical** to vampires, such as holy water, garlic and wooden stakes to the heart.	
23 **intervention***	n. **influence, interference**	간섭, 개입
[ìntərvénʃən]	Dick and Jane prefer to solve their quarrels at home without the **intervention** of a third party.	
24 **merge***	v. **combine, unite** blend	결합(융합)하다
[mə́ːrdʒ] separate	JAL and JAS said they would **merge** their operations fully in the near future.	
25 **pattern***	n. **design, figure**	도안, 무늬
[pǽtərn]	A common **pattern** in the quilts of European Americans in the Colonial period was the Amish cross.	
26 **permanent***	adj. **lasting, constant, everlasting** perpetual	불변의, 영구적인
[pə́ːrmənənt] temporary	The colonists decided to create a **permanent** settlement in the New World.	
27 **point***	n. **issue**	요점
[pɔ́int]	The **point** of the debate was lost on the audience, who did not understand the subject matter.	
28 **praise***	v. **acclaim, hail, laud** admire	칭송하다
[préiz] blame	Columbus doesn't deserve to be **praised** for the discovery of America.	
29 **precarious**	adj. **uncertain, unstable; delicate, touchy**	불확실한 ; 다루기 어려운
[prikέ(ː)əriəs]	The stock's recent fall put investors in a **precarious** position.	

inimical	전설에 의하면 특정한 것들이 흡혈귀에게 적대적이라고 하는데 성수, 마늘 그리고 심장에 나무 말뚝을 박는 것과 같은 것들이다.
intervention	Dick과 Jane은 제 3자의 간섭 없이 집에서 그들의 다툼을 해결하는 것을 선호한다.
merge	JAL과 JAS는 가까운 미래에 그들의 회사를 완전히 합칠 것이라고 말했다.
pattern	Amish Cross는 식민지 시대 유럽계 미국인들의 이불에 나타나는 흔한 무늬였다.
permanent	식민지 개척자들은 신세계에 영구적인 정착지를 만들기로 결정했다.
point	주제도 이해하지 못하는 청중은 그 논쟁의 요점을 파악하지 못했다.
praise	Columbus는 미국 대륙을 발견했다는 것으로 찬사를 받을 자격이 없다.
precarious	주식의 최근 하락은 투자자들의 입장을 불안정하게 만들었다.

30 **prototype**	n. **model**	원형, 모델
[próutətàip]	Companies often ask consumers to give their opinions on a **prototype** before they market the product to the public.	
31 **rapidly***	adv. **quickly, fast**	급속히
[rǽpidli]	Theodore's health declined **rapidly**, and in 1933, he died of cancer.	
32 **refine***	v. **improve, polish**	다듬어 좋게 하다
[rifáin]	The writing tutor suggested ways for the student to **refine** his essay and garner a better grade.	
33 **rent***	v. **lease, let**	임대하다
[rént]	John **rented** a house to stay in during the winter break.	
34 **source***	n. **origin, derivation**	근원, 출처
[sɔ́ːrs]	The electricians found the **source** of the trouble — a faulty connection.	
35 **sparsely****	adv. **lightly, thinly**	희박하게
[spɑ́ːrsli] compactly	Turkey's **sparsely** populated eastern regions are home to six million Kurds.	
36 **standpoint***	n. **perspective, point of view**	관점
[stǽndpɔ̀int]	From the coach's **standpoint** it looked like a touchdown, but the referee saw it in a different light.	
37 **stint****	v. **limit**	절약하다
[stínt]	The restaurant was famous for not **stinting** on the portions of any of its dishes.	

prototype	기업들은 일반 대중에게 제품을 출시하기 전에 소비자들에게 시제품에 대한 의견을 줄 것을 부탁하는 경우가 많다.
rapidly	Theodore의 건강은 급속히 나빠졌고, 1933년에 암으로 사망했다.
refine	그 작문 과목의 개인 교사는 학생에게 에세이를 다듬어 좋은 성적을 얻는 방법을 제시했다.
rent	John은 겨울 휴식 기간 동안 머무를 집을 임대했다.
source	전기 기사는 문제의 근원인 연결 장애를 발견했다.
sparsely	Turkey의 인구가 희박한 동부 지역은 6백만 쿠르드인들의 고향이다.
standpoint	코치의 관점에서는 그것이 터치다운처럼 보였지만 심판은 이를 다르게 보았다.
stint	그 식당은 푸짐한 양의 음식을 주는 것으로 유명하다.

38 **subsequently*** | adv. **later, successively, afterward** | 이후에

[sʌ́bsikwəntli]
prior

Taylor said he was a wealthy aristocrat, but this **subsequently** proved to be false.

39 **terrestrial*** | adj. **earthly, worldly** | 지상의, 속세의

[təréstriəl]
celestial

A lion is a **terrestrial** animal.

40 **unbridled*** | adj. **unrestrained, unrestricted, uncontrolled** | 억제되지 않은

[ʌ̀nbráidld]
restrained

Playing with someone who has such **unbridled** passion for music will be a huge inspiration.

Quiz

Choose the synonym.

1. inimical	ⓐ lightly, thinly
2. free	ⓑ necessary, requisite, essential
3. indispensable	ⓒ uncontrolled, unrestricted, unrestrained
4. unbridled	ⓓ unfriendly, hostile, antagonistic
5. sparsely	ⓔ liberate, release, emancipate

Answer 1. ⓓ 2. ⓔ 3. ⓑ 4. ⓒ 5. ⓐ

subsequently	Tylor는 그가 부유한 귀족이라고 말했지만, 이후에 그것은 거짓으로 판명되었다.
terrestrial	사자는 지상의 동물이다.
unbridled	음악에 그렇게 억제되지 않은 열정을 가지고 있는 사람과 함께 연주하는 것은 엄청난 자극제가 될 것이다.

DAY 50

Hackers TOEFL **Vocabulary**

Hackers Voca

www.goHackers.com

1 **acclaim****	n. 1. **praise, acclamation, applause, commendation**	갈채, 절찬
[əkléim] denouncement	The novel met with modest **acclaim**.	
	v. 2. **hail, praise, commend** applaud	격찬하다, 환호하다
	Christine was **acclaimed** as the magazine's person of the year.	
2 **active**	adj. **lively, brisk, energetic**	활기찬
[ǽktiv] inactive	Until Johnson died in 1895, he remained **active** in American politics.	
3 **administer****	v. 1. **manage, conduct, execute, supervise**	관리하다, 집행하다
[ədmínistər]	The king must have full power to **administer** justice.	
	v. 2. **give, deal**	가하다
	The lifeguard on-duty saved a young boy's life by **administering** CPR.	
4 **avail***	v. **be of use, serve**	도움이 되다
[əvéil] harm	Nothing could **avail** the dying patient.	

acclaim	그 소설은 평범한 칭찬을 받았다. Christine은 그 잡지의 올해의 인물로 선정되어 격찬을 받았다.
active	Johnson은 1895년 사망하기 전까지 미국 정치에서 활발하게 활동했다.
administer	왕이 재판권을 행사하기 위해서는 전권을 가져야 한다. 근무 중이던 인명구조원은 심폐소생술로 소년의 생명을 구했다.
avail	어떤 것도 죽어가는 환자에게 도움이 될 수 없었다.

5 **blossom** v. **flourish, bloom, thrive** 번영하다

[blɑ́səm]

European art and culture began to **blossom** during the Renaissance.

6 **cast*** v. **project, throw, hurl, pitch** 던지다

[kǽst]

The waves **cast** the driftwood far up on the shore.

7 **charge*** v. **impose responsibility** 책임을 지우다

[tʃɑ́:rdʒ]

Miss Wilson was **charged** with the duties of taking care of the youngest class.

8 **chiefly*** adv. **mainly** 주로

[tʃí:fli]

The arduous task was accomplished **chiefly** through slave labor.

9 **coherent**** adj. **logical, consistent** 논리적인, 일관성 있는

[kouhíərənt]
illogical

Wilson provided a **coherent** explanation of the demise of the Civil Rights Movement.

10 **count*** v. **matter, weigh, signify** 중요하다

[káunt]

The design of a product often **counts** more than its durability.

11 **discernible*** adj. **noticeable, detectable, observable, perceptible** 인식할 수 있는

[disə́:rnəbəl]
imperceptible

Steve had a **discernible** change of attitude toward the disabled after serving as a volunteer in a center for the physically challenged.

12 **distinguished**** adj. **marked, prominent, eminent** renowned 두드러진

[distíŋgwiʃt]
unremarkable

The most **distinguished** hero of the Battle of Bunker Hill was Peter Salem.

blossom	유럽의 예술과 문화는 르네상스 시기에 번영하기 시작했다.
cast	파도가 부목을 해안가 깊숙이 던져 놓았다.
charge	Wilson 여사는 가장 어린 학급을 돌보는 임무를 맡았다.
chiefly	몹시 힘든 일은 주로 노예들의 노동으로 이루어졌다.
coherent	Wilson은 공민권 운동의 쇠퇴에 대해 논리적인 설명을 제공했다.
count	제품의 디자인은 종종 그것의 내구성보다 더 중요하다.
discernible	Steve는 신체 장애자들을 위한 시설에서 자원 봉사를 한 후에, 장애인들을 향한 태도가 눈에 띄게 변하였다.
distinguished	Bunker Hill 전투에서의 가장 두드러진 영웅은 Peter Salem이었다.

13 **federate*****
[fédərèit]

v. **unite, amalgamate, consolidate** 연합하다

The republics **federated** to become the Soviet Union.

14 **frame**
[fréim]

v. **make, shape, mold** produce 만들다

Samson tried to **frame** a revolutionary scientific theory, and he succeeded.

15 **huge***
[hjú:dʒ]
diminutive

adj. **massive, mammoth, gigantic** colossal 거대한

The French owned a **huge** amount of land in the western part of the United States during the 18th century.

16 **inevitable****
[inévitəbl]
avoidable

adj. **certain, unavoidable, inescapable, fixed** 불가피한

Death is an **inevitable** facet of human life that is sometimes hard to cope with rationally.

17 **inspire***
[inspáiər]

v. **motivate, fire the imagination of** 고무하다

The professor tries to **inspire** his students everyday.

18 **intention***
[inténʃən]

n. **willingness, aim, design, intent, purpose** 의향, 의도

Margaret had no **intention** of helping Dennis with his homework after he teased her.

19 **livelihood***
[láivlihùd]

n. **occupation, job, living** 직업, 생계

Thousands of Enron employees lost their **livelihood** and their life savings.

20 **make****
[méik]

v. **create, constitute, form** compose 만들다, 구성하다

Christine plans to **make** a dress out of silk.

federate	공화국들이 연합하여 소련이 되었다.
frame	Samson은 혁신적인 과학이론을 만들기 위해 노력했고 그는 성공했다.
huge	18세기 동안 프랑스는 미국의 서쪽 부분에 거대한 땅을 소유했었다.
inevitable	죽음은 때로는 이성적으로 대처하기 힘든 인생의 한 단면이다.
inspire	그 교수는 매일 그의 학생들을 고무하려고 애쓴다.
intention	Margaret은 Dennis가 그녀를 놀리고 나자, 그의 숙제를 도와줄 의향이 없어졌다.
livelihood	수천 명의 Enron 사원들은 그들의 직업과 지금까지 저축한 돈을 잃었다.
make	Christine은 실크로 옷을 만들 계획을 한다.

21 **mark****

[má:rk]

n. 1. **note, notice, eminence** 유명, 명성

Vicky's parents have always encouraged her to marry a man of **mark**.

v. 2. **label** 표시하다

The young couple **marked** the tree by carving their initials in the bark.

22 **mechanism****

[mékənìzəm]

n. 1. **device, instrument, tool** apparatus 도구

Loud noises instinctively signal danger to any organism with a hearing **mechanism**.

n. 2. **means, method, technique** 방법

There has to be another **mechanism** for moving these boxes out.

23 **move****

[mú:v]

v. 1. **touch, affect, excite** impress 감동시키다

The audience in Peace Hall was deeply **moved** by the show.

v. 2. **pass, transfer, shift** 나아가다, 이동하다

Steve **moved** around in all directions to find his little son.

24 **oppress**

[əprés]

v. **maltreat, persecute** 억압(학대)하다

The administration promised to free **oppressed** peoples.

25 **pronounced****

[prənáunst]
insignificant

adj. **marked, significant, noticeable, distinct** 명백한, 뚜렷한

North Korean news anchors have a very **pronounced** manner of speaking.

mark	Vicky의 부모님들은 그녀에게 유명한 사람과 결혼하라고 항상 권해왔다. 그 젊은 커플은 나무의 껍질을 파서 자신들의 이니셜을 표시했다.
mechanism	큰 소음은 본능적으로 듣는 장치가 있는 모든 생물에게 위험하다는 신호를 보낸다. 이 상자들을 밖으로 옮기기 위한 다른 방법이 있어야 한다.
move	Peace Hall 안의 관중들은 그 쇼에 상당한 감명을 받았다. Steve는 사방으로 그의 아들을 찾기 위해 돌아다녔다.
oppress	행정부는 억압되어 있는 사람들을 해방시킬 것을 약속했다.
pronounced	북한의 뉴스 앵커들은 매우 뚜렷한 화법을 사용한다.

26 reward n. **recompense, prize, compensation, redress** 보답, 보상

[riwɔ́:rd]

The professor thinks reading Toni Morrison's literature is its own **reward**.

27 ripe* adj. **mature, mellow, developed** 무르익은, 성숙한

[ráip]
callow

The fruit that had fallen to the ground were not quite **ripe**.

28 roam* v. **wander, ramble, rove, stroll** stray 배회하다

[róum]

The unemployed **roamed** the country, hoping to find work.

29 sheen** n. **luster, brightness** 광채

[ʃí:n]

The girl's hair has a beautiful **sheen**.

30 situation n. **condition, position, status** 상태, 처지

[sìtʃuéiʃən]

The influx of weapons in schools creates a dangerous **situation** for teachers.

31 slender adj. **thin, slim; weak, fragile, delicate** 날씬한 ; 연약한

[sléndər]
obese

Catherine was **slender**, with delicate wrists and ankles.

32 speed* v. **go rapidly, hasten, race** 급속하게 진행하다, 서두르다

[spi:d]

The participants of the race **sped** past us on their way to the finish line.

33 sustenance* n. **fare, food, nourishment** 음식, 양식

[sʌ́stənəns]

Vacuum packed food is regarded as an important source of **sustenance** for astronauts.

---

reward	그 교수는 Tony Morrison의 문학 작품을 읽는 것은 그 자체로 보상이 된다고 생각한다.
ripe	땅에 떨어진 과일들은 잘 익지 않았다.
roam	그 실직자는 일자리를 찾기를 희망하면서 그 나라를 배회했다.
sheen	그 소녀의 머리카락은 아름다운 광채를 지니고 있다.
situation	학교 안으로의 무기 유입은 교사들에게 위험한 상황을 만들어낸다.
slender	Catherine은 날씬했고 가냘픈 허리와 발목을 가졌다.
speed	레이스 참가자들은 결승선을 향해서 속도를 내어 우리를 지나쳐갔다.
sustenance	진공 포장된 음식은 우주 비행사들에게 영양분의 중요한 원천으로 여겨진다.

34 **understand**** | v. comprehend, grasp, make head or tail of 이해하다

[ʌ̀ndərstǽnd]

It's easy to **understand** why the President wants a different farm bill.

35 **unparalleled*** | adj. unique, matchless, unequaled peerless, unrivaled 비길 데 없는

[ʌ̀npǽrəlèld]

The Williams sisters have had **unparalled** success in the realm of tennis.

36 **unquestionable*** | adj. definite, absolute, incontrovertible, indisputable 확실한

[ʌnkwéstʃənəbl]
doubtful

It is difficult to find a man of **unquestionable** honesty nowadays.

37 **veneration** | n. admiration, adoration, reverence 존경

[vènəréiʃən]

The general's treatment of his troops led to their **veneration** of him.

Quiz

Choose the synonym.

1. reward	ⓐ thin, weak, fragile
2. discernible	ⓑ unique, matchless, unequaled
3. frame	ⓒ make, shape, mold
4. slender	ⓓ recompense, prize
5. unparalleled	ⓔ noticeable, detectable, observable

Answer 1. ⓓ 2. ⓔ 3. ⓒ 4. ⓐ 5. ⓑ

understand	대통령이 다른 농장 법안을 원하는 이유를 이해하기란 쉽다.
unparalleled	Williams 자매는 테니스 분야에서 비길 데 없는 성공을 거두었다.
unquestionable	오늘날에는 의심할 여지없이 정직한 사람을 찾기 힘들다.
veneration	그 장군의 병사들에 대한 대우는 병사들의 존경으로 이어졌다.

DAY Hackers TOEFL Vocabulary

51 Hackers Voca

www.goHackers.com

1 **attempt**** v. **try, seek** 시도하다

[ətémpt]
accomplish

Thomas More **attempted** to create a Utopia in the New World.

2 **beneath*** prep. **below** ~할 가치가 없는

[biní:θ]
above

Vera considered it **beneath** her even to reply to Jeremy's spiteful remark.

3 **cohere**** v. **integrate, mingle, mix** 단합하다

[kouhíər]

The professor said some social groupings **cohere** through religious affiliation.

4 **collect*** v. **build up, accumulate, gather, pile up** 모으다, 쌓다

[kəlékt]
lose

Pauline **collected** her third gold medal at the Sydney Olympics.

5 **count for nothing*** phr. **be unimportant** 중요하지 않다

Mere beauty **counts for nothing**.

6 **creative*** adj. **inventive, imaginative** 창조적인

[kriéitiv]
unimaginative

One of the more **creative** uses for pasta is the spaghetti bridge building contest held by university engineering departments worldwide.

attempt	토마스 모어는 신대륙에 유토피아를 만들려고 시도했다.
beneath	Vera는 Jeremy의 짓궂은 말에 대답하는 것조차도 자신의 위신을 떨어뜨리는 것이라고 여겼다.
cohere	교수는 일부의 사회 집단들이 소속 종교를 통해 단합한다고 말했다.
collect	Pauline은 Sydney 올림픽에서 그녀의 세 번째 금메달을 모았다.
count for nothing	단순한 아름다움은 중요하지 않다.
creative	좀 더 창조적인 파스타의 사용법 중 하나는 전 세계 대학의 공학 학과에 의해 개최되는 스파게티 다리 쌓기 대회이다.

7 **disinterested*** adj. **impartial, unbiased, fair** just 공정한

[disíntərèstid]
prejudiced

It is imperative for a judge to be **disinterested**.

8 **distinguishable*** adj. **differentiated** 구별되는

[distíŋgwiʃəbl]
unrecognizable

Only the shine of the soldier's metal helmets was **distinguishable** in the gloom.

9 **erudite** adj. **logical, learned, educated, knowledgeable** 학식 있는

[érju(:)dàit]

Mr. Bertrand, the dean of journalism, is known in academic circles as an **erudite** and witty man.

10 **exceptionally** adv. **unusually, extraordinarily, abnormally** 유난히

[iksépʃənəli]

Exceptionally bright children sometimes do not get along with peers.

11 **final*** adj. **terminal, ultimate, conclusive** 마지막의, 궁극적인

[fáinəl]
initial

The president achieved a **final** agreement on limiting the proliferation of nuclear weapons.

12 **for the sake of*** phr. **for the purpose of** ~를 위하여

For the sake of peace, John avoids arguing over trivial matters.

13 **impartial*** adj. **disinterested, unbiased, unprejudiced, objective** 공정한, 공평한

[impá:rʃəl]
partial

The Proclamation of Neutrality urged American citizens to be **impartial**.

14 **impervious**** adj. **resistant, impenetrable** 불침투성의

[impə́:rviəs]

The new police vest is claimed to be **impervious** to bullets.

disinterested	판사는 반드시 공정해야만 한다.
distinguishable	그 병사의 금속 헬멧에서 나는 광택만이 어둠 속에서 분간되었다.
erudite	언론대 학장인 Bertrand씨는 학계에서 학식 있고 재치 있는 사람으로 알려져 있다.
exceptionally	유난히 영리한 아이들은 가끔 또래아이들과 어울리지 않는다.
final	대통령은 핵 무기의 확산을 제한하는 데 궁극적인 동의를 얻었다.
for the sake of	평화를 위하여, John은 사소한 문제들로 다투는 일을 피했다.
impartial	중립 정책 선언은 미국인들이 공정해질 것을 촉구했다.
impervious	새로운 경찰 조끼는 총알에 관통되지 않는다고 한다.

15 impolite

adj. **uncivil, rude, discourteous** coarse 무례한

[ìmpəláit]
polite, civil

Jack had never said an **impolite** word to Sarah in his entire life.

16 indifference

n. **unconcern, apathy, inattention** 무관심

[indífərəns]
interest

Alex received his son's criticism with complete **indifference**.

17 induce*

v. **persuade, instigate, urge** prompt 설득하여 ~하게 하다

[indjú:s]
check

His mother tried to **induce** Bill to see a doctor.

18 inhabitant*

n. **citizen, resident, dweller, tenant** 주민

[inhǽbitənt]

The **inhabitants** of the city have been asking for cleaner air and more police protection for their communities.

19 jolt*

n. **shock, impact** 충격

[dʒóult]

The famous Concord Coach could handle even the hard **jolts** of rough roads with ease.

20 luminous

adj. **bright, glowing, shining** 빛을 내는, 반짝이는

[lú:mənəs]

Luminous paints glow in the dark because of ingredients that release energy.

21 negligible*

adj. **insignificant, trivial, trifle** unimportant 하찮은

[néglidʒəbəl]
significant

Methyl bromide has a **negligible** effect on ozone depletion.

22 obscure**

adj. **uncertain, dim, faint, unclear, indistinct** 애매한

[əbskjúər]
lucid

The transition between slavery and feudalism remains **obscure**.

---

impolite	Jack은 평생 Sarah에게 무례한 말을 한마디도 하지 않았다.
indifference	Alex는 그의 아들의 비판을 완전히 무관심하게 받아들였다.
induce	Bill의 어머니는 그를 설득해서 진찰을 받게 하려고 노력했다.
inhabitant	그 도시의 주민들은 자신들의 공동체를 위해 좀 더 깨끗한 공기와 좀 더 많은 경찰의 보호를 요청해왔다.
jolt	그 유명한 Concord Coach는 울퉁불퉁한 길에서의 상당한 충격조차도 손쉽게 견뎌낼 수 있었다.
luminous	형광 페인트는 어둠 속에서 빛을 발하는데 이는 에너지를 방출하는 성분 때문이다.
negligible	브롬화메틸은 오존층의 감소에 거의 영향을 끼치지 않는다.
obscure	노예 제도와 봉건주의 사이의 변화는 애매한 상태로 남아있다.

23 **omnipresent***
[àmniprézənt]
limited

adj. **ubiquitous** 어디에나 존재하는

The Bible says that God is omnipotent and **omnipresent**.

24 **overpower***
[òuvərpáuər]

v. **overwhelm, subdue** vanquish, subjugate 압도하다

Dana felt **overpowered** by the strength of John's personality.

25 **peculiar****
[pikjú:ljər]
normal

adj. **strange, distinct, unusual, unique** eccentric 색다른, 독특한

The zoologists were puzzled by the animal's **peculiar** behavior.

26 **prohibitively***
[prouhíbitivli]
mildly

adv. **extremely, exorbitantly** 엄청나게

The cost of land in the city is **prohibitively** expensive.

27 **prophetic***
[prəfétik]

adj. **predictive** 예언적인

Hecuba was warned by a **prophetic** dream.

28 **proprietor***
[prəpráiətər]

n. **owner, landlord** 소유주

Harry is the **proprietor** of that store.

29 **protrude***
[proutrú:d]
withdraw

v. **stick out, extend, stretch out** 튀어나오다

A hockey stick, three shoes and a dirty sock all **protruded** from under the bed.

30 **proximity***
[praksíməti]
distance

n. **nearness, closeness** 근접

Proximity to a good school is a vital consideration for parents that plan on relocating to a new city.

omnipresent	성경은 신은 전능하고 어디에나 존재한다고 말한다.
overpower	Dana는 John의 강한 성격에 압도됨을 느꼈다.
peculiar	동물학자들은 그 동물의 희한한 행동에 당황했다.
prohibitively	그 도시의 땅값은 터무니 없이 비쌌다.
prophetic	Hecuba는 예언적인 꿈으로 경고를 받았다.
proprietor	Harry는 그 상점의 소유주이다.
protrude	하키 대와 세 켤레의 신발, 더러운 양말 모두가 침대 밑으로부터 튀어나와 있었다.
proximity	새로운 도시로 이사를 계획 중인 부모들에게는 좋은 학교의 인접성은 필수적인 고려 사항이다.

31 reliable adj. **trustworthy, dependable, credible** 믿을 수 있는

[riláiəbəl]
dubious

Jane wanted to know that there was someone **reliable** in her life.

32 resort to* phr. **turn to** 의지하다

The beggar finally **resorted to** staying at the charity house.

33 seek v. 1. **look for, search for, pursue** 찾다, 추구하다

[síːk]

The investigator **sought** the truth regardless of the consequences.

v. 2. **try out, strive, attempt, essay** 노력하다, 시도하다

Americans **sought** to free themselves from England during the Revolutionary War.

34 statue* n. **figure** 조각상

[stǽtʃuː]

The **Statue** of Liberty symbolizes hope and freedom for immigrants coming to America.

35 straight away phr. **immediately, right away** 즉시

The theft of the priceless painting was reported **straight away** by the security guards.

36 string* n. **series, chain** 일련, 연속

[stríŋ]

Michael Jackson had a **string** of hit albums in the 80's.

37 tangled* adj. **twisted together** 뒤엉킨

[tǽŋgld]
untangled

The girl's **tangled** hair was impossible to brush.

reliable	Jane은 그녀의 인생에 의지할만한 사람이 있다는 것을 알고 싶어했다.
resort to	그 거지는 마침내 자선 단체에 의지하게 되었다.
seek	그 수사관은 결과에 상관없이 진실을 찾아내려 했다.
	미국인들은 독립 전쟁 동안 영국으로부터 해방되고자 노력했다.
statue	자유의 여신상은 미국으로 이주해오는 사람들에게 희망과 자유의 상징이었다.
straight away	귀중한 그림의 도난은 경비원들에 의해 즉시 신고되었다.
string	Michael Jackson은 80년대에 일련의 히트 앨범을 냈다.
tangled	그 소녀의 머리카락은 뒤엉켜서 빗질을 할 수가 없었다.

38 **telling***	adj. **helpful, effective, valid** useful	효과적인
[téliŋ] ineffective	The inspector recently came across some very **telling** evidence.	
39 **track****	v. **follow, chase, trace; observe**	~을 쫓아가다 ; 진로를 관찰하다
[trǽk]	A bearded guy **tracked** Jane to her dormitory.	
40 **traditional***	adj. **usual, customary, conventional**	통상적인, 전통의
[trədíʃənəl]	These days shire horses are regarded more and more in their **traditional** role as work horses.	
41 **underneath****	prep. **below, beneath**	~의 아래에
[ʌ̀ndərníːθ] on	The little boy took shelter **underneath** the table.	

Quiz

Choose the synonym.

1. disinterested	ⓐ extremely, exorbitantly
2. erudite	ⓑ stick out, extend, stretch out
3. induce	ⓒ impartial, unbiased, fair
4. prohibitively	ⓓ logical, learned, educated
5. protrude	ⓔ persuade, instigate, urge

Answer 1. ⓒ 2. ⓓ 3. ⓔ 4. ⓐ 5. ⓑ

telling	그 수사관은 최근에 몇 가지 매우 효과적인 증거를 발견하게 되었다.
track	한 수염을 기른 사내가 Jane을 기숙사까지 쫓아갔다.
traditional	오늘날 shire 말들은 그들의 전통적인 역할인 마차말로서 높이 평가받고 있다.
underneath	어린 소년은 탁자 밑에 숨었다.

Hackers TOEFL Voca TEST DAY 49-51

Choose the synonym of the highlighted word in the sentence.

1. Being impervious to rain, the tent made a fine shelter during the storm.
(A) antagonistic (B) precarious (C) resistant (D) telling

2. Psychologists have found that lie detectors are simply not reliable.
(A) initial (B) trustworthy (C) notorious (D) decided

3. The notion of gender roles is not peculiar to sociology.
(A) aware (B) certain (C) unique (D) unchanging

4. Professor Stanton impressed his colleagues with his erudite exposition of the law.
(A) knowledgeable (B) jocular (C) trite (D) fatuous

5. Immediately following the Second World War, the United States enjoyed a period of unparalleled economic prosperity.
(A) imperious (B) peripatetic (C) matchless (D) jaundiced

6. Mrs. Strickland's face was pleasing, chiefly because of her kind brown eyes.
(A) infinitely (B) mainly (C) deliberately (D) potentially

7. Terrestrial radio communication entails the transmission of electromagnetic waves.
(A) bare (B) earthly (C) aquatic (D) fiery

8. Bananas spoil fairly rapidly after ripening.
(A) quickly (B) finally (C) alternately (D) remarkably

9. Some parents dislike the influence of the omnipresent media on their children.
(A) miserable (B) ubiquitous (C) obscure (D) tangled

10. Our president tried to diminish the risk of war.
(A) respect (B) evade (C) lessen (D) vaporize

정답 p.419

Courage 용기(勇氣)

Courage stands halfway between cowardice and rashness, one of which is a lack, the other an excess of courage.

용기는 비겁함과 무모함의 중간에 있다. 그 중 비겁함은 용기가 부족한 것이고, 무모함은 용기가 지나친 것이다.

– Plutarch 플루타르크

He who loses wealth loses much; he who loses a friend loses more; but he who loses courage loses all.

부(富)를 잃은 자의 손실은 크다. 친구를 잃은 자의 손실은 더 크다. 그러나 용기를 잃은 자는 더 이상 잃을 게 없다.

– Cervantes 세르반데스

Often the test of courage is not to die but to live.

용기가 시험 당하는 때는 대개 죽으려 하는 때가 아니라 살려고 하는 때이다.

– V.Alpierre V. 알피에르(이탈리아 극작가)

Courage without conscience is a wild beast.

양심 없는 용기는 야수(野獸)와 같다.

– R.G. Ingersoll R.G 잉거슬(미국정치가)

Courage is the ladder on which all the other virtues mount.

용기는 그 위로 다른 모든 미덕이 오를 수 있는 사다리이다.

– C.B. Luce C.B. 루스(미국 외교관, 작가)

TAKE A BREAK

DAY 52

Hackers TOEFL **Vocabulary**

Hackers Voca

www.goHackers.com

1 **abide***	v.	**inhabit, reside** remain	살다, 머물다
[əbáid] leave		The celestial Holy of Holies is the place where God **abides**.	
2 **accomplished***	adj.	**skilled, proficient**	숙련된
[əkámpliʃt]		Robin is an **accomplished** sculptor.	
3 **apprehend***	v.	**understand, grasp, comprehend**	이해하다
[æ̀prihénd] misunderstand		Modern physicists are struggling to **apprehend** the fundamental nature of all matter on a quantum level.	
4 **average****	n.	**mean, median**	중수, 평균(치)
[ǽvəridʒ]		New cars and trucks should get an **average** of 45 miles per gallon by 2010.	
5 **blend***	v.	**compound, fuse, combine, mingle**	섞다
[blénd] separate		The Indians **blended** Catholicism with their traditional beliefs.	
6 **block***	n.	1. **obstacle, barrier, blockade**	장애물
[blák]		Jennifer seems to have a mental **block** when it comes to writing.	

abide	거룩한 지성소는 하나님이 머무는 곳이다.
accomplished	Robin은 숙련된 조각가이다.
apprehend	현대의 물리학자들은 양자 수준에서 모든 물질의 근본적 속성에 대해 이해하려고 애쓰고 있다.
average	2010년경 새 차와 트럭들은 갤런당 평균 45마일을 달리게 된다.
blend	인디언들은 카톨릭 교리와 그들 전통 신앙을 혼합했다.
block	Jennifer는 쓰는 것에 관하여 정신적 장애를 가진 것으로 보인다.

v. 2. **prevent, hinder** 막다, 방해하다

Mr. Daniels couldn't get to work on time because his driveway was **blocked** by the garbage truck picking up trash in the neighborhood.

7 **compel****

[kəmpél]

v. **oblige, force, coerce** constrain 강요하다

Slave women were **compelled** to work tedious jobs all day long.

8 **constraint*****

[kənstréint]

n. **limitation, hindrance, confinement, restriction** 제한, 제약

Import taxes can act as a **constraint** on international trade.

9 **couple***

[kʌ́pəl]

n. **pair, brace, duo** 한 쌍

The new tax plan provides tax relief for married **couples** and expands retirement saving tax incentives.

10 **disorder****

[disɔ́ːrdər]

n. **chaos, disorganization, mess** confusion 무질서

The law was passed in an attempt to control civil **disorder**.

11 **encounter**

[enkáuntər]

miss

v. **meet, face** 마주치다

Bill **encountered** so many obstacles that delayed his promotion.

12 **erroneous***

[iróuniəs]

accurate

adj. **incorrect, mistaken, false** 잘못된

All of the team agreed that it was an **erroneous** conclusion.

13 **expertise****

[èkspəːrtíːz]

n. **art, craft, skill, mastery** 전문 기술

Joe has made a fortune with his **expertise** in computer programming for online games.

block	Daniel씨는 인근에서 쓰레기를 싣고 있는 쓰레기 트럭에 의해 그의 운전길이 가로막혀 있었기 때문에, 직장에 정시에 도착할 수가 없었다.
compel	노예 여성들은 하루 종일 지루한 일을 하도록 강요받았다.
constraint	수입 관세는 국제 무역에 제한 요소로 작용할 수 있다.
couple	그 새 세금법은 부부에게 세금 감면을 해주고 연금 저축에 대한 세금 혜택을 확대한다.
disorder	도시의 무질서를 통제하기 위한 시도로 그 법이 통과되었다.
encounter	Bill은 그의 승진을 늦추는 많은 장애를 만났다.
erroneous	그 팀의 모두는 그것이 잘못된 결정이라는 데 동의했다.
expertise	Joe는 온라인 게임을 프로그래밍하는 기술로 큰 재산을 벌었다.

14 **fame***

[féim]
disgrace

n. **renown, reputation, eminence** celebrity, honor 명성

Yanni is a musician of international **fame**.

15 **found***

[fáund]
dismantle

v. **create, set up, establish** 창설하다

Cal **founded** the after-school program to keep kids off the streets and away from drugs.

16 **imitate****

[ímitèit]
originate

v. **simulate, mimic, copy** reproduce, mock 흉내 내다, 모방하다

Children tend to **imitate** everything they see their parents doing.

17 **incredulous**

[inkrédʒuləs]
trustful

adj. **skeptical, doubtful, dubious** 의심 많은

Modern people are apt to be **incredulous** about ghosts.

18 **in opposition to***

in accordance with

phr. **counter to, con** ~에 반대하여

Most of the people who attended the rally are **in opposition to** war in the Middle East.

19 **means****

[mí:nz]

n. **method, way, process** 방법

Martin Luther King, Jr. had to find alternative **means** of protests.

20 **medium***

[mí:diəm]

n. **means, instrument** 매개

Silver circulated as a **medium** of exchange in the old colonial times.

21 **misleading***

[mislí:diŋ]

adj. **deceptive, deluding, confusing** 현혹시키는

Yetts gave customers false and **misleading** account statements.

fame	Yanni는 세계적 명성을 가진 음악가이다.
found	Cal은 아이들을 길거리와 마약으로부터 멀어지게 하기 위해 방과 후 프로그램을 세웠다.
imitate	아이들은 부모님이 하는 모든 것들을 모방하는 경향이 있다.
incredulous	현대인들은 유령에 대해 의심하는 경향이 있다.
in opposition to	집회에 참석한 대부분의 사람들은 중동에서 일어나는 전쟁에 반대한다.
means	Martin Luther King, Jr.는 다른 방법의 시위를 찾아야 했다.
medium	옛 식민지 시대에는 은이 교환의 매개로 통용되었다.
misleading	Yetts는 고객에게 잘못되고 현혹시키는 회계 서류를 주었다.

22 **onset***	n. **beginning, opening, outbreak**	시작
[ánsèt] end	At the **onset** of the 19th century, New York City was already a bustling commercial center.	
23 **overwhelm***	v. **overpower, crush**	압도(제압)하다
[òuvər*h*wélm]	The army quickly **overwhelmed** the rebels hiding out in abandoned buildings.	
24 **phenomenon***	n. **occurrence, appearance**	사건, 현상
[finámənàn]	The president began to deal with the global warming **phenomenon**.	
25 **pinnacle***	n. **the highest point, top, peak**	정상
[pínəkəl] bottom	Bryce Canyon is 56 square miles of badlands and towering **pinnacles**.	
26 **pinpoint**	adj. **precise**	정확한
[pínpɔ̀int]	Satellites can identify objects with **pinpoint** accuracy.	
27 **pliable**	adj. **smoothly shaped, easy to shape, easily shaped**	휘기 쉬운, 유연한
[pláiəbl]	Copper is an example of a **pliable** metal.	
28 **rear***	v. **raise, nurture, nurse**	기르다
[ríər]	Mrs. Brown painstakingly **reared** her three sons to be gentlemen.	
29 **repair**	v. **mend, amend, fix** remodel	고치다
[ripɛ́ər]	Doctors say they can **repair** the heart after coronary failure.	

onset	19세기 초반에, 뉴욕 시는 이미 분주한 무역의 중심지였다.
overwhelm	군대는 버려진 건물들 안에 숨어 있는 반군들을 재빨리 제압했다.
phenomenon	대통령은 지구 온난화 현상에 대처하기 시작했다.
pinnacle	Bryce Canyon은 56평방 마일의 황무지와 높이 치솟은 꼭대기들이다.
pinpoint	위성들은 매우 정확하게 물체를 확인할 수 있다.
pliable	구리는 휘기 쉬운 금속의 한 예이다.
rear	Brown 여사는 세 아들을 공들여 키워서 신사가 되게 했다.
repair	의사들은 심부전증을 일으킨 후에도 심장을 고칠 수 있다고 말한다.

30 **residue***

[rézidjù:]

n. **remain, remnant, remainder, dreg** 잔여

Chalky **residue** on the sole of Vincent's shoe proved that he had recently visited the murder scene.

31 **scanty**

[skǽnti]
plentiful

adj. **short, scarce, sparse, meager** 부족한

Because of his **scanty** breakfast, Billy felt hungry again.

32 **sense***

[séns]

n. **meaning, signification, denotation** significance 의미

The general was not a communist in the traditional **sense** of the term.

33 **shard**

[ʃɑ:rd]

n. **fragment, piece** 파편

Archaeologists were able to reconstruct the pot from the clay **shards** found on the site.

34 **substrate***

[sʌ́bstreit]
upper layer

n. **substratum, underlying layer** 하층, 기저

Geologists believe that under the rigid crust of the Earth's surface lies a semi-liquid **substrate**.

35 **subtle***

[sʌ́tl]

adj. **hardly perceived, imperceptible, elusive** 알아채기 어려운, 미묘한

The symptoms of pancreatic cancer are so **subtle** that it often goes undetected.

36 **suitable*****

[sú:təbl]

adj. **appropriate, proper, fit** 적절한

Jeans and a sweatshirt are not **suitable** attire for a formal event.

37 **tedious***

[tí:diəs]
absorbing

adj. **tiresome, irksome, wearisome** monotonous 지루한

McKinley's force – roughly 600 men – began the **tedious** but necessary task of digging a ditch.

residue	Vincent의 신발 밑창에 묻어 있는 초크의 잔여물은 그가 최근 살인 현장을 다녀왔다는 점을 증명했다.
scanty	부족한 아침식사 때문에 Billy는 시장기를 느꼈다.
sense	그 장군은 전통적 의미에서의 공산주의자가 아니다.
shard	고고학자들은 유적에서 찾은 토기 조각들로부터 토기를 재현해낼 수 있었다.
substrate	지질학자들은 지구 표면의 단단한 껍질 아래에 반유동액의 기저층이 놓여 있다고 믿는다.
subtle	췌장암의 증상들은 매우 알아채기 힘들어서 종종 발견되지 않는다.
suitable	청바지와 스웨터는 공식적인 행사에 입기에는 적합하지 않다.
tedious	약 600명 정도의 McKinley의 부대는 지루하지만 필요한 수로를 파는 일을 시작했다.

38 toxic*

[tάksik]

adj. **poisonous, noxious, toxicant, venomous** 유독한

Pollution from **toxic** chemicals threatens life on this planet.

39 ultimately**

[ʌ́ltimitli]

adv. **eventually, in the end, finally, after all, at last** 궁극적으로, 마침내

Citizens are **ultimately** accountable for the actions of their governments.

40 universally

[jùːnəvə́ːrsəli]

adv. **everywhere, generally, invariably** 도처에, 널리

There is no **universally** accepted religion or political philosophy.

41 usual***

[júːʒuəl]
unusual

adj. **typical, common, accustomed, familiar** 흔한, 보통의

As **usual**, John and Mary left their children at home with a babysitter when they went bowling.

Quiz

Choose the synonym.

1. abide	ⓐ mistaken, incorrect, false
2. erroneous	ⓑ remain, sojourn, reside
3. rear	ⓒ poisonous, noxious, toxicant
4. tedious	ⓓ tiresome, irksome, wearisome
5. toxic	ⓔ raise, nurture, nurse

Answer 1. ⓑ 2. ⓐ 3. ⓔ 4. ⓓ 5. ⓒ

toxic	유독 화학 물질에서 나오는 오염이 지구상의 생명체들을 위협한다.
ultimately	시민들에게는 궁극적으로 그들의 정부의 행동에 대한 책임이 있다.
universally	어디서나 받아들여지는 종교나 정치적 사상은 없다.
usual	평상시와 마찬가지로 John과 Mary는 볼링을 치러 가면서, 그들의 아이들을 보모와 함께 집에 남겨 두고 갔다.

DAY 53

Hackers TOEFL **Vocabulary**

Hackers Voca

www.goHackers.com

1 **adjacent****	adj.	**nearby, adjoining, neighboring**	인접한
[ədʒéisənt] remote		The land **adjacent** to the southern part of the Nile was called Upper Egypt.	
2 **alter****	v.	**modify, change, metamorphose** vary	변환하다
[ɔ́:ltər] fix		Vital coastal habitats are being **altered** or destroyed by construction and development.	
3 **bare***	adj.	**uncovered, exposed, naked, nude**	노출된, 벌거벗은
[bɛ́ər] covered		The workers dug ditches with their **bare** hands.	
4 **burden***	n.	**1. load**	짐, 부담
[bə́:rdən]		The people in the colony were groaning from the **burden** of taxation.	
exempt	v.	**2. tax, charge, load**	(짐 · 부담 등을) 지우다
		Argentina's interim government started to **burden** the people with heavy taxes.	
5 **clout****	n.	**influence, pull, power**	권력, 영향력
[kláut]		The largest cable company has enough **clout** to get discounts from programmers.	

adjacent	나일강 남부에 인접한 땅은 Upper Egypt라고 불렸다.
alter	중요한 해안 서식지가 건축과 계발로 변화되거나 파괴되었다.
bare	일꾼들은 맨손으로 도랑을 팠다.
burden	식민지의 사람들은 세금 부담으로 신음하고 있었다.
	아르헨티나의 임시 정부는 무거운 세금을 사람들에게 부과하기 시작했다.
clout	최대 규모의 유선 방송 회사는 프로그램 제작자들에게 할인을 받을 만큼의 영향력을 가지고 있다.

6 **commodity**** | n. **goods, product, merchandise** ware | 상품

[kəmάdəti]

Asian films and Asian stars are hot **commodities** in the American entertainment world.

7 **constellation*** | n. 1. **arrangement** | 배열

[kὰnstəléiʃən]

The astronomers spent the evening hours trying to identify **constellations** of stars in the night sky.

n. 2. **collection** | (유사 성질의) 모임, 집합체

The recent film festival held in France was attended by a **constellation** of movie stars, directors, and producers.

8 **daunt** | v. **intimidate, discourage, dishearten** | 위압하다

[dɔ́:nt]

Jeffrey was **daunted** by the 20,000 word thesis he had to write.

9 **delight** | v. **please, gratify, amuse, charm** | 기쁘게 하다

[diláit]

Mary was **delighted** to hear of her promotion.

10 **deluxe** | adj. **luxurious, lavish, opulent, rich** | 호화로운

[dəlʌ́ks]

The **deluxe** suite in the hotel offered spacious room and a fabulous view of the city.

11 **depressed**** | adj. 1. **concave, low, sunken** | 움푹 들어간, 내려 앉은

[diprést]

The center of the crater was **depressed** and couldn't be seen from afar.

animated | adj. 2. **downcast, melancholy, gloomy** | 우울한

The rainy day put Celeste into a **depressed** mood.

---

commodity 아시아 영화와 배우들이 미국 연예 세계에서 인기 있는 상품이다.
constellation 천문학자들은 밤하늘의 별자리를 확인하며 저녁 시간을 보냈다.
영화배우, 감독, 제작자들의 모임이 프랑스에서 열린 최근의 영화 축제에 참석했다.
daunt Jeffrey는 그가 작성해야 하는 2만 단어의 논문으로 인해 압도되었다.
delight Mary는 승진 소식을 들어 기뻤다.
deluxe 그 호텔의 호화로운 스위트룸에서는 넓은 방에 멋진 도시 전경까지 볼 수 있었다.
depressed 분화구의 중심은 움푹 패여서 멀리서는 보이지 않는다.
비 오는 날이 Celeste를 우울한 기분으로 만들었다.

12 **endless***　adj. **limitless, incessant, perpetual**　ceaseless　끝없는

[éndlis]

The maid walked up the **endless** stairs of the house in which Mr. Brown lived.

13 **especially****　adv. **notably, specifically, particularly**　특히

[ispéʃəli]

Environmentalists called for strict regulations on the use of pesticide, **especially** in agricultural areas.

14 **forbid***　v. **ban, inhibit, prohibit**　restrain　금하다

[fərbíd]
permit

The Islamic belief system **forbids** suicide and encourages patient perseverance.

15 **great****　adj. **outstanding, distinguished, magnificent**　뛰어난

[gréit]
insignificant

Yo-Yo Ma is a **great** musician who is widely renowned in many European and Asian countries.

16 **hold***　v. **include, contain, accommodate**　수용하다

[hóuld]

The classroom **holds** 30 students.

17 **impression****　n. 1. **image, idea, feeling**　sense　인상

[impréʃən]

Nicholson got the **impression** that Hoffman was emotionally disturbed.

n. 2. **influence, impact, effect**　영향, 효과

The way a parent acts makes a big **impression** on their children.

18 **inherent***　adj. **innate, built-in, congenital**　natural, intrinsic　선천적인

[inhíərənt]
adventitious

The need to be loved and recognized is an **inherent** part of the human psyche.

endless	그 가정부 Brown씨가 살고 있는 집의 끝없는 계단을 걸어 올라갔다.
especially	환경보호론자들은 살충제의 사용, 특히 농경지에서의 사용을 금지하는 엄격한 규제를 주장했다.
forbid	이슬람 신앙 교리는 자살을 금하고 인내를 권장한다.
great	Yo-Yo Ma는 많은 유럽과 아시아 국가에 널리 알려진 위대한 음악가이다.
hold	그 교실은 30명의 학생을 수용한다.
impression	Nicholson은 Hoffman이 감정적인 혼란 상태에 있다는 인상을 받았다.
	부모들이 행동하는 방식은 자녀들에게 강한 영향을 준다.
inherent	사랑받고 인정받기 원하는 욕구는 인간 심리의 선천적인 부분이다.

19 **instant***	n. **moment**	순간
[ínstənt]	The **instant** Sara saw a strange man lurking around her house, she knew he was the fellow the police were looking for.	
20 **in time****	phr. 1. **early**	일찍
tardily	Luckily Patrick arrived **in time** for work, even though he slept in an hour later than usual.	
	phr. 2. **eventually**	결국
	Some scientists believe that, **in time**, all diseases will be curable through gene therapy.	
21 **nocturnal***	adj. **active at night**	야행성의
[naktə́:rnəl] daytime	**Nocturnal** creatures have developed adaptations that allow them to hunt after dark.	
22 **overall***	adj. **general, total, comprehensive**	포괄적인, 전체의
[óuvərɔ̀:l]	A drop in the **overall** price of goods and services may signal a period of deflation.	
23 **process**	n. **method, procedure, system**	공정
[práses]	The **process** for making bricks was discovered in ancient times.	
24 **reach**	n. **area, expanse, stretch**	구역, 범위
[ri:tʃ]	The rafters paddled down a **reach** of the river that was known for its rapids.	
25 **reciprocal***	adj. **mutual**	상호적인
[risíprəkəl]	Though the two authors had different ideas about the same subject, they had a **reciprocal** respect.	

instant	Sara는 그녀의 집 근처에 숨어 있는 낯선 남자를 본 순간, 그가 경찰이 찾고 있던 사람이라는 걸 알아챘다.
in time	Patrick은 비록 평소보다 한 시간 늦게 일어났지만 다행히도 직장에 일찍 도착했다.
	몇몇 과학자들은 결국 모든 질병들은 유전자 요법을 통해 치료할 수 있을 것이라는 것을 믿었다.
nocturnal	야행성 동물들은 어두워진 후에도 사냥을 할 수 있게 적응해 왔다.
overall	상품과 서비스의 전반적인 가격의 하락은 디플레이션 기간이라는 신호를 보낸다.
process	벽돌 만드는 공정은 고대 시대에 발견되었다.
reach	뗏목 타는 사람들은 그 강에서 급류로 알려진 구역까지 노를 저어갔다.
reciprocal	그 두 작가들이 같은 주제에 대해 다른 생각들을 가지고 있음에도 불구하고, 그들은 서로 존경하고 있었다.

26 remarkable** [rimɑ́ːrkəbl]

adj. **incredible, significant, noteworthy** 놀라운, 상당한

Dickens had **remarkable** mental and physical energy.

27 routinely*** [ruːtíːnli]

adv. **commonly, generally, habitually** 일상적으로

John **routinely** forgot to turn off the lights when he went out.

28 sizable* [sáizəbəl]

adj. **large** 꽤 큰

The U.S. suffered a **sizable** trade deficit with Japan.

29 still** [stíl]

noisy

adj. 1. **calm, motionless, stationary** 정지한, 조용한

David had been dancing about like a child, but suddenly he stood **still**.

adv. 2. **nevertheless** 그럼에도 불구하고

The ride down the rapids is dangerous, but Mike **still** wants to try it tomorrow.

30 subdued* [səbdjúːd]

stimulated

adj. **reduced** 가라앉은, 약해진

The housing market is fairly **subdued** during the winter months.

31 touching* [tʌ́tʃiŋ]

unimpressive

adj. **moving** 감동적인

The scene of two lovers' parting at the station is the most **touching** in the movie.

32 trivial** [tríviəl]

crucial

adj. **frivolous, unimportant, insignificant, trifling** 사소한

The mayor's worries are **trivial** compared to those of countries which are at war or are suffering from famine.

remarkable	Dickens는 주목할만한 정신적, 심리적 에너지를 갖고 있었다.
routinely	John은 나갈 때 늘 불 끄는 것을 잊었다.
sizable	미국은 일본에 대해 꽤 큰 무역 적자를 냈다.
still	David는 어린 아이처럼 춤추면서 돌아다니다가 갑자기 멈춰 섰다.
	급류를 타고 내려가는 것은 위험한데도 Mike는 아직도 내일 시도해 보고 싶어한다.
subdued	주택 시장은 겨울 동안 다소 가라앉았다.
touching	두 연인이 역에서 이별하는 장면이 그 영화에서 가장 감동적이다.
trivial	시장의 염려는 전쟁 중이거나 기근으로 고통받고 있는 국가들에 비교하면 사소한 것이다.

33 transfer* v. **move, remove, relocate** 이동하다

[trænsfə́ːr]

Personal checks may ordinarily be **transferred** to other people by endorsement.

34 unintentionally* adv. **accidentally, casually, unconsciously** 무심코

[ʌninténʃənəli]
deliberately

Hope expressed her regret to Tommy even though she had damaged his car **unintentionally**.

35 variation** n. **variance, fluctuation, change, alteration** 변화

[vɛ̀əriéiʃən]

In Canada, the **variation** in temperature between the summer and winter is dramatic.

36 vociferous* adj. **noisy** 시끄러운

[vosífərəs]
quiet

The Customer Service Hotline received many **vociferous** complaints.

Quiz

Choose the synonym.

1. daunt — ⓐ variance, fluctuation, change
2. inherent — ⓑ innate, built-in, congenital
3. routinely — ⓒ discourage, intimidate, dishearten, dismay
4. variation — ⓓ commonly, generally, habitually
5. trivial — ⓔ frivolous, unimportant, trifling

Answer 1. ⓒ 2. ⓑ 3. ⓓ 4. ⓐ 5. ⓔ

transfer — 개인 수표는 보통 배서함으로써 다른 사람들에게로 건네진다.
unintentionally — Hope는 의도치 않게 Tommy의 차를 망가뜨리긴 했지만, 어쨌든 그에게 사죄의 뜻을 표했다.
variation — 캐나다에서는 여름과 겨울의 온도 변화 폭이 극심하다.
vociferous — 고객 서비스 연결망은 많은 시끄러운 불평을 들었다.

DAY **54** Hackers TOEFL Vocabulary

Hackers Voca

www.goHackers.com

1 **acquisition**	n.	**purchase, acquirement, attainment, procurement**	획득
[ǽkwizíʃən]		Tim's **acquisition** of a new car made his friends envious.	
2 **ancestor**	n.	**predecessor, antecedent, forefather, forebear**	조상, 선조
[ǽnsestər]		The **ancestors** of Native Americans came from Northern Asia.	
3 **capricious****	adj.	**unpredictable, fickle**	변덕스러운
[kəpríʃəs] constant		A leader should follow the way of righteousness with a steady, not **capricious** attitude.	
4 **collaboration**	n.	**cooperation, teamwork, alliance, association**	협동
[kəlæ̀bəréiʃən]		**Collaboration** between writers and artists led to a successful project.	
5 **colonize**	v.	**conquer**	식민지화하다
[kɑ́lənàiz]		The Spanish were the first Europeans to **colonize** America.	
6 **combine****	v.	**incorporate, mix, unite** join	통합하다, 결합시키다
[kəmbáin] part, alienate		The artist **combined** the richness of Venetian color and the vastness of Italian compositions.	

acquisition	Tim의 새 차 구입은 친구들의 부러움을 샀다.
ancestor	아메리칸 인디언들의 조상은 북방아시아 출신들이다.
capricious	지도자는 변덕스럽지 않은 확고한 태도로 정직한 방식을 따라야 한다.
collaboration	작가와 화가의 협동은 성공적인 작업을 만든다.
colonize	스페인 사람들은 미국을 식민지화한 첫 번째 유럽인이다.
combine	그 화가는 베네치아식 색감의 풍부함과 이탈리아식 구도의 방대함을 결합시켰다.

7 **complete** adj. **entire, total, whole, perfect** 전체의, 완전한

[kəmplíːt]

The **complete** encyclopedia set was thirty volumes.

8 **consequently*** adv. **as a result, hence, thus, therefore** 그러므로, 따라서

[kánsikwəntli]

China has made efforts to increase global trade which has **consequently** led to a more established economy.

9 **continuity** n. **uninterrupted connection, flow, succession** 연속성

[kàntənjúːəti]

The company pledged to provide **continuity** of service to its customers.

10 **disadvantage** n. **drawback, handicap, flaw, defect** 결점

[dìsədvǽntidʒ]

Pollution is a major **disadvantage** of living in a big city.

11 **dissemination** n. **spread, distribution, circulation, diffusion** 보급, 전파

[disèmənéiʃən]

The **dissemination** of literacy changed human society.

12 **documented*** adj. **recorded** 기록된

[dákjuməntid]

Because Rosie's case was well **documented** by her previous doctor, it was easy for her new physician to continue appropriate treatment.

13 **excite**** v. **stimulate, encourage, instigate** arouse 자극하다, 고무하다

[iksáit]
quiet

Students are **excited** by the numerous opportunities available to them in college.

14 **extent**** n. **scope, stretch, range, space** 범위

[ikstént]

To some **extent**, success depends on the strength of the economy.

complete	그 백과사전의 완전한 세트는 총 30권이다.
consequently	중국은 국제 무역의 증대를 위해 노력했으며 이는 경제의 안정을 가져왔다.
continuity	그 회사는 고객들에게 지속적인 서비스를 공급할 것을 약속했다.
disadvantage	환경 오염은 대도시에 살면서 겪게 되는 큰 단점이다.
dissemination	지식의 보급은 인간 사회를 바꾸어 놓았다.
documented	Rosie의 병세는 그녀의 이전 의사에 의해 잘 기록되어 있었기 때문에, 그녀의 새로운 의사는 적절한 치료를 하기가 쉬웠다.
excite	학생들은 대학에서 그들에게 주어진 수많은 기회들에 고무되었다.
extent	성공은 어느 정도 경제력에 달려 있다.

15 **from time to time*** phr. **now and then** 때때로, 이따금

Steve calls his elementary school teacher and his friends **from time to time**.

16 **fusion*** n. **union** 통합

[fjú:ʒən]

Sauber's work is a **fusion** of several different types of music.

17 **hunt*** v. **scour, seek** 뒤지다, 찾다

[hʌ́nt]

Ponce de Leon discovered Florida while **hunting** for the Fountain of Youth.

18 **illicit**** adj. **unlawful, illegitimate, illegal** 불법적인

[ilísit]
licit

The pirates are notorious for their **illicit** trade in drugs.

19 **improper*** adj. **unfit, inappropriate** 부적당한

[imprɑ́pər]
apposite, germane

John made **improper** advances to his friend's wife.

20 **incessant*** adj. **continuous, unceasing, everlasting** uninterrupted 끊임없는

[insésənt]
transient

The **incessant** sound of crickets kept John awake.

21 **infrequent** adj. **occasional; rare** 가끔의 ; 진기한

[infrí:kwənt]
frequent

Lately, Sylvia's trips home to see her parents have been **infrequent** due to financial difficulties.

22 **inhospitable*** adj. **unfavorable, unfriendly, desolate** 비우호적인, 황폐한

[inhɑ́spitəbəl]

The Sinai is one of the world's most **inhospitable** places.

from time to time Steve는 때때로 자신의 초등학교 시절 선생님과 친구들에게 전화하곤 한다.
fusion Sauber의 작품은 몇 종류의 음악 형태를 통합한 것이다.
hunt Ponce de Leon은 젊음의 샘을 찾아 헤매던 중에 플로리다를 발견했다.
illicit 해적들은 마약 불법 거래로 악명이 높다.
improper John은 친구 아내에게 부적절한 접근을 했다.
incessant 귀뚜라미의 끊임없는 소리 때문에 John은 잠을 이룰 수 없었다.
infrequent 최근에 Silvia는 경제적 어려움 때문에 부모님을 뵈러 집으로 여행하는 경우가 드물었다.
inhospitable 시나이 반도는 세계에서 가장 황폐한 장소 중 하나이다.

23 intact* adj. **undamaged, unaffected, complete, uninjured** 손상되지 않은

[intǽkt]
defective

The machine remained **intact** despite the explosion.

24 override* v. **cancel, annul, nullify** 무효로 하다

[òuvəráid]

The Senate **overrode** the president's veto by a single vote.

25 pore* v. **stare, gaze** 응시하다

[pɔ́:r]

Waiting to see the eclipse, the astronomer **pored** intently at the sky.

26 profusion* n. **abundance, wealth** 풍부

[prəfjú:ʒən]
dearth

Corn stalks grow in **profusion** on farmlands in the American Midwest.

27 proponent** n. **advocate, supporter, partisan, adherent, disciple** 지지자

[prəpóunənt]
opponent

Huxley's grandfather was a famous biologist and **proponent** of Darwin's theories.

28 prospective** adj. **future, soon-to-be, likely** 장래의

[prəspéktiv]

Most employers interview all **prospective** employees before making any hiring decisions.

29 pure* adj. **clear, clean, spotless** immaculate 흠없는, 결백한

[pjúər]

Jenny's ring is made of **pure** gold.

30 rough** adj. **uneven, rugged, bumpy** irregular 울퉁불퉁한

[rʌ́f]
flat

The merchants completed the trip over the **rough** mountain road to Price.

intact	그 기계는 폭발에도 불구하고 손상되지 않은 채 있었다.
override	상원은 한 표 차이로 대통령의 거부권을 무효로 만들었다.
pore	식을 보기 위해 기다리면서 천문학자는 하늘을 골똘히 응시하였다.
profusion	옥수수 줄기는 미국 중서부 지역의 농장에서 풍부하게 자란다.
proponent	Huxley의 할아버지는 유명한 생물학자요 다윈의 이론을 지지하는 사람이었다.
prospective	대다수의 고용주들은 채용 결정을 내리기 전에 항상 모든 입사 지원자들을 면접한다.
pure	Jenny의 반지는 순금으로 만들어진 것이다.
rough	그 상인들은 Price로 가는 거친 산길의 여정을 마쳤다.

31 **stand for*** | phr. **symbolize, represent** ~를 나타내다

Students who have never studied chemistry do not know what the symbols in the periodic table **stand for**.

32 **stationary**** | adj. **unmoving, motionless, immobile** 정지한

[stéiʃənəri]
moving

A **stationary** target is easy to aim at.

33 **submarine*** | adj. **underwater** 해저의

[sʌ́bmərìːn]

The professor's research project is related to **submarine** plant life.

34 **submerge** | v. **plunge, inundate, immerse, submerse** 물에 담그다, 물속에 넣다

[səbmə́ːrdʒ]

If the polar ice caps melt due to global warming, there is a danger that some coastal cities will be **submerged** underwater.

35 **surmise**** | v. **speculate, guess, suppose, conjecture** hypothesize 추측하다

[səːrmáiz]

Without any hard evidence to rely upon, researchers can only **surmise** how the death of King Tutankhamen occurred.

36 **suspect** | v. **believe, consider, suppose, guess** 생각하다, 추측하다

[səspékt]

The chairman **suspected** that the board members would replace him.

37 **sustainable*** | adj. **endurable, bearable** 견딜 수 있는, 고갈되지 않는

[səstéinəbl]
unsupportable

Biotechnology may enable us to manufacture plastics from **sustainable** carbon sources.

38 **unequaled**** | adj. **matchless, unparalleled, peerless** 무적의

[ʌ̀níːkwəld]

Michael's talent for playing guitar was **unequaled** in the class.

stand for	화학을 한번도 공부해보지 않은 학생들은 원소주기표의 기호들이 무엇을 나타내는지 모른다.
stationary	정지해 있는 목표물은 겨냥하기 쉽다.
submarine	그 교수의 연구 과제는 해저 식물 생태와 관련이 있다.
submerge	만약 극지방의 만년설이 지구 온난화로 인해 녹는다면 몇몇 연안 도시들이 물속에 잠길 위험이 있다.
surmise	어떤 신뢰할만한 근거도 없기 때문에, 연구자들은 Tutankhamen 왕이 어떻게 죽었는지에 대해서는 추측만 할 뿐이다.
suspect	그 의장은 위원회의 회원들이 의장 자리를 다른 사람으로 바꿀 것이라고 생각했다.
sustainable	생명 공학은 우리로 하여금 고갈되지 않는 탄소 자원을 가지고 플라스틱을 제조할 수 있도록 해줄 것이다.
unequaled	Michael의 기타 연주에 대한 재능은 학급에서 견줄 사람이 없었다.

39 **unsurpassed*** adj. **superior, superlative** 비길 데 없는

[ʌ̀nsərpǽst]

J. R. R. Tolkien's ability to create an entire world of medieval fantasy is truly **unsurpassed**.

40 **unwittingly*** adv. **unintentionally** 무의식 중에

[ʌ̀nwítiŋli]

John **unwittingly** erased the file.

41 **urge** n. **compulsion, impulse, drive** 충동

[ə́ːrdʒ]

The **urge** to succeed drove Wally Amos to build a financial empire out of his grandmother's chocolate chip cookie recipe.

42 **with little regard to** phr. **with little attention to** ~를 거의 고려하지 않고, ~에 상관없이

Sam filled out the form **with little regard to** the instructions.

Quiz

Choose the synonym.

1. acquisition	ⓐ unmoving, motionless, immobile
2. capricious	ⓑ purchase, attainment, procurement
3. incessant	ⓒ plunge, inundate, immerse
4. stationary	ⓓ unpredictable, fickle
5. submerge	ⓔ continuous, unceasing, everlasting

Answer 1. ⓑ 2. ⓓ 3. ⓔ 4. ⓐ 5. ⓒ

unsurpassed	중세 시대 공상물의 모든 세계를 창조해내는 J. R. R. Tolkien의 능력은 실로 비길 데가 없다.
unwittingly	John은 무의식 중에 그 파일을 지웠다.
urge	성공하고자 하는 충동은 Wally Amos로 하여금 할머니의 초콜릿 칩 쿠키의 요리법에서 출발한 금융 제국을 건설하도록 이끌었다.
with little regard to	Sam은 지시 사항은 거의 고려하지 않고 서식에 기입했다.

Hackers TOEFL Voca TEST DAY 52-54

Choose the synonym of the highlighted word in the sentence.

1. The arithmetic average of a set of values is obtained by adding the values together and dividing by the number of items in the set.

(A) mean (B) allusion (C) chaos (D) dishonor

2. Megan routinely takes her dog out for a walk around the neighborhood before breakfast and occasionally after dinner.

(A) ultimately (B) regularly (C) particularly (D) unintentionally

3. In Korea, bronzeware was probably first used about the 8th century BC, though some scholars surmise that it predates the 10th century.

(A) determine (B) prove (C) speculate (D) refuse

4. The defendant's weak alibi received incredulous looks from the jury.

(A) fortuitous (B) intransigent (C) radiant (D) skeptical

5. There appeared to be an endless wave of soldiers advancing upon them.

(A) incessant (B) prodigious (C) adept (D) fast

6. There was a vociferous response from the crowd in response to the referee's poor judgment.

(A) mind (B) noisy (C) urgent (D) radiant

7. Two teams of researchers were excited by their success in obtaining a new form of matter.

(A) dismayed (B) stimulated (C) soothed (D) bothered

8. Only in the twentieth century did this pharaoh reach fame, for his tomb was found nearly intact.

(A) queer (B) lasting (C) wily (D) unimpaired

9. The collapse of the Mycenaean civilization was the result of its own weaknesses combined with natural catastrophes.

(A) incorporate (B) attained (C) submitted (D) donated

10. Bats are nocturnal creatures that prefer to move about and hunt at night.

(A) accomplished (B) pliable (C) active at night (D) unpredictable

정답 p.419

TAKE A BREAK

멕시코 전쟁

1845년 대통령 J.K. 포크는 목화재배 확대를 바라는 대농장주(大農場主) 들의 요구에 따라 멕시코와 텍사스 매수교섭을 벌였으나 실패하였다. 양국 군대간의 충돌은 계속되었고, 미국의회는 1846년 5월 11일 멕시코에 대하여 정식으로 전쟁을 선포하였다. 이 전쟁은 노예문제를 둘러싼 대립격화를 두려워한 대서양 연안의 각 주(州)의 반대에도 불구하고 미국군의 승리로 끝났다. 1848년 2월 양국은 과달루페-이달고 조약을 체결, 미국은 희망하는 서부의 영토확장을 달성하였지만, 정치적으로 남부의 발언권이 증대되고, 노예제를 둘러싼 논쟁이 더욱 격화되는 결과를 가져왔다.

원래 인디언들의 땅이었던 텍사스에 백인이 나타난 것은 1591년 에스파냐의 피네다가 최초였다. 17세기 후반부터 에스파냐 인이 텍사스에 정착하기 시작하여 1691년에는 에스파냐 령이 되었다. 점점 늘어나던 미국인 이주자들이 1835년 반란을 일으켰지만 알라모 요새의 싸움에서 패배하였다. 하지만 센해싱트 싸움에서는 멕시코 군을 격파하고 이듬해에는 독립을 이룩하여 텍사스 공화국을 세웠다. 1845년 미국에 병합되어 그 해 12월 29일 텍사스 주(州)가 되었다. 이러한 발전과정 때문에 텍사스 주에는 멕시칸 이라고 부르는 메스티소의 비율이 높다.

D A Y **55** | Hackers TOEFL Vocabulary

Hackers Voca

www.goHackers.com

1 **abandonment***	n. **desertion, forsakenness**	유기
[əbǽndənmənt] reclamation	The lost child felt a sense of **abandonment** as he stood on the street corner unable to find his parents.	
2 **abuse**	v. 1. **misuse, ill-use**	오용하다
[əbjú:z]	Many adults **abuse** alcohol, especially when they have problems.	
esteem, honor	v. 2. **maltreat, mistreat**	학대하다
	The slave was **abused** by his master so much that he ran away.	
3 **accommodate****	v. 1. **adjust to, adapt, suit, fit**	맞추다, 적응시키다
[əkámədèit]	The building was renovated to **accommodate** the needs of handicapped people.	
	v. 2. **lodge, make room for, hold** contain	수용하다
	The resorts were carefully planned to **accommodate** large numbers of tourists.	
	v. 3. **provide for**	공급하다
	The five-star hotel **accommodated** guests with impeccable service and luxurious amenities.	

abandonment	길을 잃은 아이는 부모님을 찾지 못한 채 길 모퉁이에 서 있으면서 버려진 느낌을 받았다.
abuse	특히 문제가 생긴 경우에, 많은 성인들은 알코올을 남용한다.
	그 노예는 주인에게 심하게 학대 받아서 도망을 갔다.
accommodate	그 건물은 장애인들의 필요를 충족시키기 위해서 새로이 개조되었다.
	그 휴양지는 많은 관광객들을 수용하기 위해 세심하게 설계되었다.
	그 최고급 호텔은 흠 잡을 데 없는 서비스와 고급스런 시설을 손님들에게 제공했다.

4 affront

[əfrʌ́nt]
laud

v. **offend, insult, abuse** 모욕하다

Many older people were deeply **affronted** by Bill's impudent manners.

5 aggressive*

[əgrésiv]
unassertive

adj. **forceful, pushing; offensive, militant** 적극적인 ; 공격적인

The conglomerate is planning an **aggressive** marketing strategy to expand its presence internationally.

6 as well as*

phr. **in addition to, also** 또한, ~뿐만 아니라

There were politicians and artisans at the banquet, **as well as** some foreign visitors.

7 cardinal

[ká:rdinəl]

adj. **fundamental, primary, principal, essential** 기본적인

Obedience to elders is a **cardinal** principle of Confucianism.

8 cautious

[kɔ́:ʃəs]

adj. **careful, prudent, discreet, wary** 신중한, 조심스러운

The hikers chose a **cautious** approach in unfamiliar territory.

9 celebrate*

[séləbrèit]

v. **commemorate, observe** 축하하다

The couple chose to **celebrate** their love by renewing their wedding vows.

10 continuous*

[kəntínjuəs]
interrupted

adj. **uninterrupted, unceasing, consecutive** 연속적인

Timmy is excited that the NBC TV network is going to televise five **continuous** hours of 'Saturday Night Live.'

11 derive**

[diráiv]

v. **originate, trace; obtain, draw** 유래를 찾다 ; 끌어내다, 얻다

The name of the city was **derived** from the Spanish word for 'village.'

affront	많은 연장자들은 Bill의 무례한 태도로 심하게 모욕을 받았다.
aggressive	대기업은 국제적으로 자신의 존재를 확장시키기 위해 적극적인 마케팅 전략을 계획하고 있다.
as well as	파티에는 외국 손님들뿐만 아니라 정치인들과 장인들도 있었다.
cardinal	어른들께 순종하는 것은 유교의 기본적인 원칙이다.
cautious	익숙하지 않은 지역에서 하이커들은 조심스러운 길을 택했다.
celebrate	부부는 그들의 결혼 서약을 새로이 함으로써 그들의 사랑을 축하하기로 했다.
continuous	Timmy는 NBC TV 채널에서 연속으로 5시간 동안 '토요일의 나이트 쇼'를 방영해줄 것이라는데 매우 흥분했다.
derive	그 도시의 이름은 '마을'을 뜻하는 스페인어에서 나온 것이다.

12 **despite*** | prep. **notwithstanding** ~에도 불구하고

[dispáit]

Despite a lack of money for college, Jerry Mcglow managed to obtain a good education.

13 **dim**** | adj. **obscure, faint, weak** 희미한

[dím]
bright

Rosie flipped on a **dim** lamp that filled the room with light and shadows.

14 **disgusting*** | adj. **offensive, sickening, nauseating, displeasing** 정말 싫은, 지긋지긋한

[disgʌ́stiŋ]

The pictures of prisoners being maltreated by prison wardens were **disgusting**.

15 **exposition*** | n. **exhibition, display, presentation** 전시, 진열

[èkspəzíʃən]

Since it was a rainy day, Brad and Alison decided to attend the Porsche **exposition** being held at the local trade center.

16 **extraneous*** | adj. **unneeded, unnecessary, irrelevant, unrelated** 부차적인, 관계없는

[ikstréiniəs]
integral

The dream sequence struck the audience as **extraneous** and somewhat out of keeping with the rest of the play.

17 **feed**** | v. **nourish; graze** 기르다, 부양하다 ; 먹이를 먹다

[fíːd]

John must continue to work to **feed** his family.

18 **happen** | v. **occur, befall** (사건이) 발생하다

[hǽpən]

Many people hope a tragedy like World War II will never **happen** again.

19 **impartially*** | adv. **fairly, without bias** 공명정대하게

[impáːrʃəli]
prejudicially

The votes were **impartially** counted and sent to the judge who will announce the winner.

despite	Jerry Mcglow는 대학 학비가 부족함에도 불구하고 좋은 교육을 받을 수 있었다.
dim	Rosie는 방을 빛과 그림자로 채우는 희미한 조명등을 탁 켰다.
disgusting	교도관들 의해 고문당한 죄수들의 사진은 정말 보기 싫은 것들이었다.
exposition	그날은 비가 왔기 때문에, Brad와 Alison은 지역 무역 센터에서 열리는 Porsche 전시회에 참석하기로 했다.
extraneous	꿈 장면은 관객들에게 연극의 다른 부분과 관계없고 다소 어울리지 않는 듯한 느낌을 주었다.
feed	John은 그의 가족을 부양하기 위해 일을 계속해야 한다.
happen	많은 사람들이 제2차 세계 대전 같은 비극이 다시는 일어나지 않기를 바란다.
impartially	표는 공정하게 세어져서, 우승자를 발표 할 심판원에게 보내졌다.

20 **indeed*** adv. **in truth, in fact, surely, really** 정말로

[indíːd]

Indeed, the demand for manual labor is growing smaller every day with the advent of increased computer technology.

21 **innovation**** n. **novelty, new idea** 새로이 채택(도입)한 것

[ìnouvéiʃən]

Built-in cameras and web browsing capabilities are some recent **innovations** in cellular phone technology.

22 **jeer** v. **scoff, mock, scorn** ridicule, sneer 조롱하다

[dʒíər]
toady

A band of children began to **jeer** at Sam and threw stones.

23 **noticed**** adj. **observed** 주목받는

[nóutist]

The young actress tried to get **noticed**.

24 **nourish*** v. **feed, nurture, breed** 기르다, 키우다

[nə́ːriʃ]

Many educational programs aim to **nourish** students' souls as well as their minds.

25 **outcome** n. **result, consequence, end, conclusion** 결과

[áutkʌ̀m]

Most observers were surprised by the **outcome** of the election.

26 **paramount** adj. **supreme, sovereign, chief, principal** 최고의, 주요한

[pǽrəmàunt]

The company's **paramount** concern was its declining sales.

27 **ponder**** v. **think of, weigh** muse 심사숙고하다

[pándər]

Mr. Kinley **pondered** over the letter so long that his wife noticed his preoccupation.

indeed	실제로 육체 노동에 대한 요구는 나날이 증가하는 컴퓨터 기술의 출현과 함께 점점 줄어들고 있다.
innovation	내장형 카메라와 인터넷 검색 기능은 최근에 휴대폰에 새로 도입된 기술이다.
jeer	한 무리의 아이들이 Sam을 놀리기 시작하더니 돌을 던졌다.
noticed	젊은 여배우는 주목을 받기 위해 노력했다.
nourish	많은 교육적 프로그램들은 학생들의 정신뿐만 아니라 기상을 기르는 것을 목표로 한다.
outcome	대부분의 입회자들은 선거의 결과에 놀랐다.
paramount	그 회사의 가장 주요한 관심사는 감소하는 판매 실적이었다.
ponder	Kinley씨가 편지에 대해 너무 오랫동안 심사숙고해서 그의 아내는 그가 몰두하고 있다는 것을 알아챘다.

28 **prepare*** v. ready, **prime, arrange** 준비하다

[pripέər]

Robert's friends are **preparing** a surprise birthday party for him.

29 **procurement**** n. obtaining 획득, 확보

[proukjúərmənt]

Nowadays, the **procurement** of a visa to the US is really difficult.

30 **produce*** v. yield, **generate, procreate** 생기게 하다

[prədjúːs]

Gas can be **produced** from coal.

31 **propose*** v. suggest, **offer, proffer** 제안하다

[prəpóuz]
withdraw

The supervisors **proposed** that office procedures be revamped to improve efficiency.

32 **prosperous*** adj. thriving, **successful, flourishing** 번영하는

[prάspərəs]
decrepit

For most Americans, the 1920s were **prosperous** years.

33 **purpose**** n. goal, aim, end, function, **object** 목적

[pə́ːrpəs]

The **purpose** of John's thesis is to analyze the end of the Civil War.

34 **scent**** n. fragrance, perfume, **odor** 향기, 냄새

[sént]

The hounds followed the wolf's **scent**.

35 **spring up*** phr. suddenly arise, **emerge** 갑자기 나타나다

fade

Fast-food restaurants are **springing up** all over town.

prepare	Robert의 친구들은 그를 위해 깜짝 생일 파티를 준비하고 있다.
procurement	근래에 미국 비자 받기가 정말 어렵다.
produce	가스는 석탄으로부터 생겨날 수 있다.
propose	그 감독관들은 효율성을 높이기 위해 사무 진행 절차의 혁신을 제안했다.
prosperous	미국인 대부분에게 1920년대는 번영하는 해였다.
purpose	John의 학위 논문의 목적은 남북 전쟁의 결말을 분석하는 것이다.
scent	사냥개들은 늑대의 냄새를 따라갔다.
spring up	패스트푸드점이 온 시내에 갑자기 생겨나고 있다.

36 **stubborn** | adj. **obstinate, dogged, rigid** persistent, headstrong 완고한, 완강한

[stʌ́bərn]
docile

Japan's **stubborn** adherence to the absurd policy would jeopardize its relations with other countries.

37 **subsistence*** | n. **survival, existence, living** 생존

[səbsístəns]

Farming is a hard means of **subsistence**.

38 **territorial*** | adj. **of or relating to territory** 영토의

[tèrətɔ́:riəl]

The two countries have a **territorial** dispute over the island.

39 **threatening***** | adj. **intimidating, menacing, aggressive** 위협적인

[θrétəniŋ]

Many large predators appear **threatening** in their natural environments.

Quiz

Choose the synonym.

1. accommodate	ⓐ scoff, mock, ridicule
2. jeer	ⓑ survival, existence, living
3. stubborn	ⓒ adapt, suit, fit
4. subsistence	ⓓ fragrance, perfume, odor
5. scent	ⓔ obstinate, dogged, rigid

Answer 1. ⓒ 2. ⓐ 3. ⓔ 4. ⓑ 5. ⓓ

stubborn	일본이 불합리한 정책을 완고하게 고수한다면 다른 나라들과의 관계를 위태롭게 할 것이다.
subsistence	농사는 고된 생존 수단이다.
territorial	두 나라는 그 섬을 두고 영토 분쟁을 했다.
threatening	많은 거대 육식 동물들은 그들이 속한 자연환경에서 위협적으로 보인다.

Hackers Voca

1 **ancient****	adj. **prehistoric, antique, old** aged	고대의, 옛날의
[éinʃənt] modern	Most **ancient** Greek philosophies denied the existence of God.	
2 **annihilate****	v. **remove, abolish, exterminate** eradicate	전멸시키다
[ənáiəlèit] restore	Old economic folkways were **annihilated** by the Industrial Revolution.	
3 **antagonist**	n. **opponent, adversary, enemy** foe	반대자, 적
[æntǽgənist] supporter	Hamilton faced his **antagonist** before the duel began.	
4 **arrange***	v. **order, array**	배열하다
[əréindʒ] jumble	Ann **arranged** a number of candles in a rough circle around the room.	
5 **clutch**	v. **grasp, grab, grip, seize, snatch**	꽉 붙잡다
[klʌ́tʃ]	The mountain climber **clutched** for the top of the cliff.	
6 **contour***	n. **outline**	윤곽
[kántuər]	The **contours** of the Atlantic coast are very irregular.	

ancient	대부분의 그리스 철학들은 신의 존재를 부인했다.
annihilate	오래된 경제 관습은 산업 혁명에 의해 전멸되었다.
antagonist	Hamilton은 결투가 시작되기 전 상대방을 직시했다.
arrange	Ann은 많은 초들을 방 주변에 엉성한 원 모양으로 배열했다.
clutch	등산가들은 절벽의 꼭대기를 꽉 붙잡았다.
contour	대서양 해안의 윤곽은 매우 불규칙적이다.

7 **contradictory** adj. **opposite, paradoxical, contrary** inconsistent 모순된

[kὰntrədíktəri]

The voters were puzzled by General Howe's **contradictory** behavior.

8 **converse*** adj. **opposite, reverse** 반대의

[kənvə́:rs]

John's opinion is the **converse** of his brother's.

9 **dependent*** adj. **reliant, relying on** 의존하는

[dipéndənt]
autonomous

All of Tom's friends noticed that his girlfriend was very **dependent** on him, but he refused to see it.

10 **depose*** v. **oust** 쫓아내다

[dipóuz]
inaugurate

The trustees of Princeton **deposed** the president in 1902.

11 **distress** n. **pain, agony, anguish** anxiety, torment 고통

[distrés]
comfort

The treasury couldn't find a solution to the increasing economic **distress**.

12 **diverge*** v. **separate, deviate** 갈라지다

[daivə́:rdʒ]
converge

About four miles outside town the road **diverges**, with the I-5 heading north and Route 66 leading west.

13 **diversity*** n. **variety** 다양함

[daivə́:rsəti]
homogeneity

The cultural **diversity** of the United States is particularly obvious in larger cities.

14 **divert** v. **redirect, reroute, avert, deflect, switch** 전환하다

[daivə́:rt]

Management decided to **divert** pension funds into the general budget.

contradictory	유권자들은 Howe 장군의 모순된 행동에 당황했다.
converse	John의 의견은 그의 형제와 반대이다.
dependent	Tom의 모든 친구들은 그의 여자 친구가 그에게 너무 의존적임을 알아챘지만 그는 그것을 인정하려 하지 않았다.
depose	프린스톤의 이사들은 1902년에 총장을 몰아내었다.
distress	재무부는 증가되어 가는 생활고에 대한 해결 방안을 찾아낼 수 없었다.
diverge	마을에서 4마일 정도 벗어난 곳에서 길이 갈라져, 북쪽으로 향하는 I-5와 서쪽으로 향하는 66번 도로로 나뉜다.
diversity	미국의 문화적 다양성은 특히 대도시일수록 확연하다.
divert	경영자는 연금비를 일반 예산으로 전환하기로 결정했다.

15 enable*
[inéibl]
hinder

v. **permit, allow, facilitate** ~을 가능케 하다

Mikhail Gorbachev and his moderate politics of perestroika and glasnost **enabled** the Cold War to finally end.

16 equilibrium
[ì:kwəlíbriəm]

n. **balance, evenness, stability, symmetry** 평형

Markets are in **equilibrium** when suppliers sell all of their stock and customers have as much product as they need.

17 exclusively
[iksklú:sivli]

adv. **only, entirely, solely, totally** 오로지

The St. Patrick's Day party was an **exclusively** Irish affair.

18 ferry*
[féri]

v. **transfer, carry, convey, transport** 수송하다

Arrangements have been made to **ferry** troops across the river.

19 hole**
[hóul]

n. **pit, pore, opening** cavity, hollow 구멍

A **hole** in the ozone layer lets the dangerous rays come through.

20 in fact

phr. **actually, precisely, really** 사실상

Alex thought that he was getting paid $10/hr, but **in fact** his salary was slightly less than $8/hr.

21 legitimate
[lidʒítəmit]
illegitimate

adj. **lawful, legal, licit, valid** 합법적인

The Mafia uses **legitimate** businesses to hide illicit activity.

22 neat*
[ní:t]
messy

adj. **orderly, trim, tidy** 정돈된, 단정한

The room was **neat** and clean enough, with pink-flowered wallpaper.

enable	Mikhail Gorbachev 자신과 그의 온건 정책인 페레스트로이카와 글라스노스트는 마침내 냉전이 종식될 수 있도록 했다.
equilibrium	공급자가 재고량을 전부 팔고 고객들이 자신들이 필요로 하는 만큼 상품을 가질 수 있게 되면 시장이 평형 상태에 놓이게 된다.
exclusively	'성패트릭 기념일' 파티는 오로지 아일랜드인들의 축제였다.
ferry	군대를 강 건너로 수송할 준비가 갖추어져 있었다.
hole	오존층에 난 구멍은 유해 광선들이 통과할 수 있게 한다.
in fact	Alex는 그가 시간당 10달러를 지급받고 있다고 생각했었지만, 사실상 그의 급료는 시간당 8달러에 약간 못 미쳤다.
legitimate	마피아들은 불법적인 활동들을 은폐하기 위해 합법적인 사업을 이용한다.
neat	그 방은 분홍 꽃무늬의 벽지를 바른 단정하고 깨끗한 방이었다.

23 notion**
[nóuʃən]
n. opinion, **view**; concept, general idea 의견 ; 개념
The **notion** that one is born with a tabula rasa has long been abandoned by most psychologists.

24 perennial
[pəréniəl]
adj. persistent, **constant**, **continual**, **long-lasting** 장기간 계속되는
Flooding is a **perennial** occurrence along China's Yellow River.

25 persecute
[pə́:rsikjù:t]
v. **oppress**, **harass**, **molest** torment 박해하다, 괴롭히다
The Jews were heavily **persecuted** because of their religious beliefs.

26 portion*
[pɔ́:rʃən]
n. part, segment, **fragment** section 부분
The most useful **portions** of the collection have been photocopied.

27 prestige*
[prestí:dʒ]
n. status, **influence**, **distinction** 지위, 명성
Being enrolled at a top university gives a student **prestige**.

28 prized*
[práizd]
adj. outstanding, prominent, valued 높이 평가받는
Mother's **prized** orchids won first place in the flower show.

29 result**
[rizʌ́lt]
origin
n. sequence, product, **outcome** effect, consequence 결과
The gold came in as a **result** of trade with the south of Europe.

30 rich**
[rítʃ]
destitute, sparse
adj. fertile, abundant affluent, ample 비옥한, 풍부한
Unfortunately rural areas are losing a lot of **rich** agricultural soil by creating pavement.

notion	인간은 백지 상태로 태어난다는 의견은 대부분의 심리학자들에게 버림받아져 왔다.
perennial	홍수는 황허 강 연안에 장기간 지속하는 현상이다.
persecute	유대인들은 그들의 종교적인 신념 때문에 심하게 박해를 받았다.
portion	소장품 중 가장 유익한 일부 작품들이 복사되었다.
prestige	최고의 대학에 입학하는 것은 학생에게 명성을 안겨 준다.
prized	어머니가 가장 아끼는 난초들이 꽃 전시회에서 대상을 받았다.
result	남유럽과의 교역의 결과물로써 금이 들어 왔다.
rich	불행히도 시골 지역은 포장도로 건설에 의해서 많은 비옥한 농토를 잃고 있다.

31 **series** n. sequence, string, succession 일련, 연속

[sí(:)əri:z]

Europe's Thirty Years War was a long **series** of smaller conflicts.

32 **sole*** adj. only, single, solitary 유일한

[sóul]

Although the king was the **sole** ruler, the nobility of the nation kept a wary eye on his activities.

33 **stingy** adj. parsimonious, miserly, mean 인색한

[stíndʒi]
generous

Richard is much too **stingy** to buy anyone a drink.

34 **suggestion*** n. implication, hint, overtone 암시

[sədʒéstʃən]

There was never any **suggestion** of criminal involvement in the suicide case.

35 **supervise**** v. direct, oversee, control, manage 감독하다

[sú:pərvàiz]

The teachers take turns in **supervising** the children during recess.

36 **surmount*** v. overcome, conquer 극복하다

[sərmáunt]

Jason tried to **surmount** the obstacles but failed.

37 **trade*** v. barter, exchange, swap 교역하다

[tréid]

During the American Colonial Period, local tribes often **traded** goods with the settlers because they had no money.

38 **unchanged*** adj. even 불변의

[ʌntʃéindʒd]
changing

Despite fluctuating market conditions, the value of Donald's stock portfolio has remained remarkably **unchanged**.

series	유럽의 30년 전쟁은 일련의 소규모 분쟁의 연속이었다.
sole	왕이 유일한 통치자이긴 했지만, 그 나라의 귀족들은 왕의 행동들을 경계했다.
stingy	Richard는 누구에게 음료수 하나도 사지 않을 정도로 인색하다.
suggestion	그 자살 사건에는 범죄적 관련성에 대한 암시가 조금도 없었다.
supervise	교사들은 휴식 시간 동안 번갈아 가며 아이들을 감독한다.
surmount	Jason은 장애들을 극복하려고 노력했지만, 결국 실패했다.
trade	미국 식민지 시대 동안, 지역 부족들은 식민지 주민들과 물건을 교환했는데 그 이유는 그들이 돈이 없었기 때문이다.
unchanged	불안정한 시장 상태에도 불구하고 Donald의 유가 증권 가격은 놀랍게도 변함없이 유지되었다.

39 **underway*** [ʌ̀ndərwéi]

adj. **continuing, in progress, already commenced** 진행 중인

Negotiations are **underway** for the surrender of Mullah Mohammad Omar.

40 **uneven*** [ʌníːvən]

adj. **rough, rugged, bumpy** 울퉁불퉁한

The drive to grandmother's house took longer than expected because the road was so **uneven**.

41 **uninterested*** [ʌ̀níntəristid]

adj. **indifferent, unconcerned** 무관심한

Jenny seemed **uninterested** in Alex's exciting stories.

42 **way** [wéi]

n. **method, means** 방법

The proprietor kept looking for a **way** to cut costs without adversely affecting the business.

Quiz

Choose the synonym.

1. contradictory	ⓐ separate, deviate
2. persecute	ⓑ overcome, conquer
3. diverge	ⓒ barter, exchange, swap
4. trade	ⓓ oppress, harass, molest
5. surmount	ⓔ opposing, paradoxical, contrary

Answer 1. ⓔ 2. ⓓ 3. ⓐ 4. ⓒ 5. ⓑ

underway	Mullah Mohammad Omar를 항복시키기 위한 협상이 진행 중에 있다.
uneven	도로가 매우 울퉁불퉁했기 때문에 할머니 댁에 가는 데 생각보다 시간이 더 걸렸다.
uninterested	Jenny는 Alex의 흥미진진한 이야기에 무관심해 보였다.
way	그 경영자는 사업에 불리하게 영향을 끼치지 않으면서 원가를 낮추는 방법을 계속 찾고 있었다.

DAY Hackers TOEFL **Vocabulary**

57 Hackers Voca

www.goHackers.com

1 **apply**	v.	**use, employ, utilize**	사용(적용)하다
[əplái]		Marie is looking for a job where she can **apply** her knowledge of Spanish.	
2 **appreciate***	v.	**recognize, value, esteem**	(진가를) 인정하다
[əpríːʃièit] disapprove		Daniel's sacrifices will be **appreciated** by future generations.	
3 **available***	adj.	**accessible, obtainable, usable**	사용할 수 있는, 이용할 수 있는
[əvéiləbəl]		Books were **available** to the masses for the first time with the invention of Guttenberg's printing press.	
4 **capitalize on***	phr.	**take advantage of**	(좋은 기회 · 사실)을 이용하다
		Dental Technologies Inc. will **capitalize on** the growing demand for restorative dental products.	
5 **consumption***	n.	**use, waste**	소비, 소모
[kənsʌ́mpʃən] production		The eighteenth amendment banned the sale or **consumption** of alcohol anywhere in the U.S.	
6 **detract***	v.	**reduce, diminish, lessen**	(가치 · 명성 등을) 줄이다
[ditrǽkt] intensify		Any scratches on the frame of a guitar will **detract** from its monetary value.	

apply	Marie는 그녀의 스페인어 지식을 활용할 수 있는 직업을 찾고 있다.
appreciate	Daniel의 희생은 후세에 의해 인정받을 것이다.
available	Guttenberg의 인쇄술 발명으로 책이 대중에게 처음으로 이용 가능하게 되었다.
capitalize on	치과 기술 회사는 치아 회복 상품들에 대한 수요가 증가하고 있는 기회를 이용할 것이다.
consumption	헌법 18조의 수정조항(미국의 1920년의 금주법)은 미국 내의 어디서도 주류의 판매나 소비를 금했다.
detract	기타의 몸체에 난 조그마한 흠집도 그것의 금전적 가치를 떨어뜨릴 것이다.

7 **dimension***

n. **size** 크기

[diménʃən]

It was important that Leenie accurately measure the **dimensions** of her bedroom before deciding what size of bed to buy.

8 **erect***

adj. 1. **upright, vertical, perpendicular** 직립한, 수직의

[irékt]
recumbent

Hominids walked **erect** and learned to share food with one another.

demolish

v. 2. **build, construct, set up** 세우다

Nearly $4.8 billion was used to **erect** more than some 200 garbage facilities.

9 **exceptional***

adj. **abnormal, unusual, extraordinary** 예외적인

[ikséptʃənəl]
average

A prior restraint of publication would be allowed only in the most **exceptional** cases.

10 **express*****

v. **communicate, represent, disclose, reveal** 표현하다, 나타내다

[iksprés]
hint

The editor **expressed** his dissatisfaction with the articles submitted by the newly hired reporters.

11 **expressly**

adv. **definitely, clearly** 명백히, 확실히

[iksprésli]
vaguely

Sarah stated **expressly** that she needed the money by tomorrow.

12 **fit**

v. **adjust, customize, modify, shape** 적응시키다, 맞추다

[fít]

The tailor **fitted** the suit to his customer's size.

13 **habitual***

adj. **customary, regular, usual** accustomed 습관적인, 평소의

[həbítʃuəl]
sporadic

As Chris grew older, he became an increasingly **habitual** liar.

dimension	어떤 크기의 침대를 살지 결정하기 전에 Leenie가 침실의 크기를 정확하게 측정하는 것이 중요했다.
erect	인간은 직립 보행을 했고 음식을 다른 사람과 나누는 것을 배웠다.
	200개 이상의 쓰레기 처리장을 세우는 데 거의 48억이 쓰였다.
exceptional	출판물에 대한 사전 제재는 가장 예외적인 경우에만 허용될 것이다.
express	그 편집장은 새로 고용한 기자들이 제출한 기사에 대한 불평들을 나타냈다.
expressly	Sarah는 내일까지 돈이 필요하다는 것을 명백히 말했다.
fit	그 재단사는 옷을 고객의 사이즈에 맞추었다.
habitual	Chris는 성장하면서 점점 습관적인 거짓말쟁이가 되었다.

14 **harness****

[hɑ́ːrnis]

v. **utilize** 이용하다

The ancient Egyptians **harnessed** the power of water for agriculture.

15 **implausible****

[implɔ́ːzəbl]

adj. **unbelievable, improbable** 믿기지 않는, 그럴 듯하지 않은

The author was criticized for basing his book on an **implausible** theory.

16 **institute****

[ínstitjùːt]
abrogate

v. **establish, start** 수립하다, 설립하다

An attempt to **institute** a new order of society is being carried out in Russia.

17 **juncture****

[dʒʌ́ŋktʃər]

n. **connection, junction** 연결

A weakened **juncture** was responsible for the collapse of the building.

18 **long**

[lɔ́(ː)ŋ]

v. **desire, crave, yearn, pine** 바라다

The elderly often **long** for a return to their youth.

19 **mysterious***

[mistíəriəs]

adj. **puzzling, mystic, inscrutable** 불가사의한, 신비한

The **mysterious** symbols in the underground cave attracted archaeologists from all over the world.

20 **obsolete****

[ɑ̀bsəlíːt]
current

adj. **unused, out of use; out of date, outdated** 안쓰이는 ; 시대에 뒤진

The pager is now becoming **obsolete** because of advances in mobile communications.

21 **omit*****

[oumít]

v. **exclude** 제외하다

Some researchers **omit** data that doesn't agree with their hypothesis from their final reports.

harness	고대 이집트인들은 농경에 수력을 이용했다.
implausible	그 작가는 믿기 힘든 이론에 바탕하여 책을 만든 것에 대해 비판받았다.
institute	사회의 새 질서를 수립하려는 시도가 러시아에서 진행되고 있다.
juncture	약화된 접합 상태가 그 건물이 붕괴하게 된 원인이다.
long	노인들은 자주 젊은 시절로 돌아가기를 바란다.
mysterious	그 지하 동굴에 새겨진 불가사의한 기호들은 전 세계에서 온 고고학자들을 사로잡았다.
obsolete	이동통신의 발달로 호출기는 이제 쓸모가 없어지고 있다.
omit	어떤 연구원들은 최종 보고서에서 가설과 맞지 않는 데이터를 제외한다.

22 **owing to***

phr. **because of** ~ 때문에

Owing to an increase in the cost of raw materials, the company has decided to raise the prices of its entire product line by five percent.

23 **point out**

phr. **indicate, show** 가리키다, 지시하다

The tour guide **pointed out** historic buildings as the bus passed them.

24 **prevail****

[privéil]

v. **triumph, dominate, master, overcome** 이기다, 압도하다

The northern states **prevailed** in 1865, freed the slaves and introduced adult male suffrage.

25 **recede****

[risí:d]

proceed

v. **withdraw, retreat** 물러나다

The sound of the siren **receded** into the distance.

26 **reluctant****

[rilʌ́ktənt]

adj. **unwilling, disinclined, loath** averse 꺼리는

Many school educators are **reluctant** to add sex education to the lower grades.

27 **scour***

[skáuər]

v. 1. **search, hunt, seek** 탐색하다, 찾아다니다

Spanish explorers **scoured** South America for gold deposits.

v. 2. **rub, polish, scrub, scrape** 문질러 닦다

Carol used soap and a sponge to **scour** the dirty dishes.

28 **signal**

[sígnəl]

v. **indicate, beckon, sign, gesture** 신호하다, 신호로 알리다

The police officer **signaled** for traffic to move on.

owing to	원료비의 상승으로 인해, 그 회사는 모든 생산품들의 가격을 5%까지 올리기로 하였다.
point out	여행 가이드는 버스가 역사적인 건물들을 지나쳐 가자 그것들을 가리켰다.
prevail	1865년 북부 지역이 승리해서 노예들을 해방시키고 성인 남자에게 투표권을 주었다.
recede	사이렌 소리가 멀리 사라져 갔다.
reluctant	많은 학교 교육자들은 저학년 학생들에게 성교육을 추가하기를 꺼린다.
scour	스페인 탐험가들은 금 매장지를 찾아 남아메리카를 탐사했다.
	Carol은 더러운 접시들을 닦기 위해 비누와 스폰지를 사용했다.
signal	그 경찰관은 운전자들에게 움직이라는 신호를 보냈다.

29 **silhouette** | v. outline | 윤곽을 그리다

[sìluét]

Detectives **silhouetted** the shape of the dead body.

30 **slightly** | adv. somewhat, **a little** | 약간, 조금

[sláitli]

This year's bar exam was **slightly** harder than the one last year.

31 **stretch*** | v. 1. extend, **lengthen** | 늘리다

[strétʃ]
shorten

The interstate highways **stretched** American mobility to new distances.

n. 2. area, reach, **expanse, extent** | 범위, 널리 퍼진 지역

The land area of Russia encompasses a **stretch** of 17 million square kilometers.

32 **surrounding*** | n. environment, **condition, situation, atmosphere** | 주변 환경

[səráundiŋ]

Elephants that are relocated often take months to adapt to their new **surroundings**.

33 **susceptible*** | adj. prone, vulnerable, **liable, subject to** | (영향을) 받기 쉬운, 감염되기 쉬운

[səséptəbl]
invulnerable

Thanks to her healthy immune system, Mrs. Ferguson was not **susceptible** to catching the virus.

34 **tout** | v. praise, **hype, ballyhoo** | 크게 선전하다

[táut]

The spokesman **touted** his company's new product offering.

35 **trifling**** | adj. trivial, unimportant, **petty** | 하찮은

[tráifliŋ]

Maxwell broke away from the **trifling** conversation he was involved in.

silhouette	탐정들은 시체 모양의 윤곽을 그렸다.
slightly	올해의 변호사 시험은 지난해보다 약간 더 어려웠다.
stretch	주간 고속도로는 미국인의 이동 능력을 잘 알려지지 않은 먼 곳까지 확장시켰다.
	러시아의 땅은 1,700만km에 이르는 지역을 포함한다.
surrounding	다른 지역으로 옮겨진 코끼리들이 새로운 주변 환경에 적응하는 데는 종종 몇 달이 걸린다.
susceptible	Ferguson 부인은 건강한 면역 체계 덕분에 바이러스에 잘 감염되지 않았다.
tout	그 대변인은 회사의 새 제품에 대해 크게 선전했다.
trifling	Maxwell은 자신이 참여하고 있던 하찮은 대화에서 벗어났다.

36 **turbulence** [tə́:rbjuləns]

n. agitation, tumult, commotion, turmoil 동요, 혼란

The **turbulence** in the plane caused some passengers to panic.

37 **unsuitable*** [ʌnsú:təbl]

proper

adj. unfit, improper, unseemly, inappropriate 부적당한

Films that are rated R are **unsuitable** for children under the age of 17.

38 **void** [vɔ́id]

useful

adj. useless, ineffectual, vain 쓸모없는

The terms of exclusive contract will be null and **void** on July 22, 2010.

39 **wielding*** [wí:ldiŋ]

adj. using, exerting, exercising (권력 등을) 행사하는

The Molasses Act was a good example of the British **wielding** control over America.

Quiz

Choose the synonym.

1. detract ⓐ rub, polish, scrub
2. habitual ⓑ reduce, diminish, lessen
3. institute ⓒ prone, vulnerable, liable
4. scour ⓓ establish, start
5. susceptible ⓔ customary, regular, accustomed

Answer 1. ⓑ 2. ⓔ 3. ⓓ 4. ⓐ 5. ⓒ

turbulence	기내의 혼란으로 몇몇 승객들이 공포에 떨었다.
unsuitable	R로 등급이 매겨진 영화는 17세 미만의 어린이들에게는 부적합하다.
void	독점 계약의 조항들은 2010년 7월 22일에 무효화될 것이다.
wielding	당밀 조약은 미국에 대해 영국이 영향력을 행사하는 좋은 예이다.

Hackers TOEFL Voca TEST DAY 55-57

Choose the synonym of the highlighted word in the sentence.

1. The teacher's explanation that sneezing trees were responsible for wind seemed implausible even to the first grade students.

(A) improper (B) unbelievable (C) infrequent (D) unconcerned

2. The court impartially ruled that the murderer be sentenced to life imprisonment.

(A) frequently (B) indiscreetly (C) inconsistently (D) fairly

3. The inverse relationship between interest rates and inflation is one of the cardinal principles of macroeconomics.

(A) delirious (B) hermeneutic (C) fundamental (D) gregarious

4. Procurement of funds for the national pension program was made difficult due to budget shortfalls.

(A) obtaining (B) extraction (C) gradient (D) addition

5. Chemical pesticides can easily annihilate insect populations unless the insects develop immunity.

(A) broach (B) exterminate (C) modify (D) enhance

6. Polygraph tests should not be used as the sole evidence of guilt.

(A) adequate (B) excellent (C) only (D) reliable

7. Some Westerners detract the effectiveness of acupuncture analgesia, suggesting it as nothing more than placebo.

(A) reduce (B) intensify (C) enhance (D) vary

8. With each new scientific development, medical practices from just a few years ago became obsolete.

(A) awkward (B) clean (C) unused (D) refined

9. Poor nutrition and fatigue makes the human body more susceptible to disease.

(A) impervious (B) unsuitable (C) prone (D) jaded

10. Today, where once prosperous cities covered the Mesopotamian plain, there is only desert.

(A) thriving (B) grand (C) blameless (D) meek

정답 p.419

The Road Not Taken　가지 않은 길

Robert Frost

Two roads diverged in a yellow wood,
And sorry I could not travel both
And be one traveler, long I stood
And looked down one as far as I could
To where it bent in the undergrowth;

Then took the other, as just as fair,
And having perhaps the better claim,
Because it was grassy and wanted wear;
Though as for that the passing there
Had worn them really about the same.

And both that morning equally lay
In leaves no step had trodden black.
Oh, I kept the first for another day!
Yet knowing how way leads on to way,
I doubted if I should ever come back.

I shall be telling this with a sigh
Somewhere ages and ages hence:
Two roads diverged in a wood, and I—
I took the one less traveled by,
And that has made all the difference.

노란 숲속에 난 두 갈래 길
아쉽게도 한 사람 나그네
두 길 갈 수 없어 길 하나
멀리 덤불로 굽어드는 데까지
오래도록 바라보았다.

그리곤 딴 길을 택했다. 똑같이 곱고
풀 우거지고 덜 닳아 보여
그 길이 더 마음을 끌었던 것일까.
하기야 두 길 다 지나간 이들 많아
엇비슷하게 닳은 길이었건만.

그런데 그 아침 두 길은 똑같이
아직 발길에 밟히지 않은 낙엽에 묻혀 있어
아, 나는 첫째 길을 후일로 기약해 두었네!
하지만 길은 길로 이어지는 법이라
되돌아올 수 없음을 알고 있었다.

먼 훗날 어디선가 나는
한숨 지으며 이렇게 말하려나
어느 숲에서 두 갈래 길 만나, 나는—
덜 다닌 길을 갔었노라고
그래서 내 인생 온통 달라졌노라고.

TAKE A BREAK

DAY 58 Hackers Voca

www.goHackers.com

1 **apparent****

[əpǽrənt]
obscure

adj. 1. **clear, obvious, evident** conspicuous, plain 명백한

It is becoming more **apparent** that the same problems are going to continue.

adj. 2. **seeming, likely, probable** 외견상, 그럴듯한

Despite a few **apparent** differences most branches of Christianity are fundamentally similar.

2 **appreciable*****

[əpríːʃiəbl]

adj. **noticeable, detectable** 눈에 띄는

Global warming has caused an **appreciable** rise in sea levels.

3 **ardent****

[áːrdənt]
composed

adj. **enthusiastic, passionate, fervent** intense 열정적인

Tyler began his political career as an **ardent** nationalist.

4 **authentic**

[ɔːθéntik]

adj. **genuine, true, real, bona fide** 진짜의

The British Parliament houses **authentic** copies of the Magna Carta.

5 **authorize**

[ɔ́ːθəràiz]

v. **empower, accredit, commission, enable** 권위를 부여하다

The accountant was **authorized** to look into the company's financial records.

---

apparent	똑같은 문제들이 계속 될 것이라는 게 점점 더 명백해지고 있다.
	몇 가지의 외견상 차이에도 불구하고, 대부분의 기독교 종파는 기본적으로 유사하다.
appreciable	지구 온난화는 눈에 띄는 해수면의 상승을 초래했다.
ardent	Tyler는 열정적인 국가주의자로서 그의 정치 경력을 시작했다.
authentic	영국 의회는 대헌장의 원본을 보관하고 있다.
authorize	그 회계사는 그 회사의 재정 기록을 조사할 수 있는 권리를 부여받았다.

6 broad appeal*** phr. **wide popularity** 폭넓은 인기

A politician must have **broad appeal** to win an election.

7 capture** v. **seize, catch, snare** 붙잡다, 포획하다

[kǽptʃər]

The African people were **captured** in local wars and sold into slavery.

8 channel v. **direct, guide, convey** (의도하는 방향으로) 돌리다

[tʃǽnəl]

The new governor decided to **channel** more funds into education.

9 cherish v. **value, prize, treasure, esteem** 소중히 여기다

[tʃériʃ]

The long-separated siblings **cherished** the chance for a reunion.

10 comprehensive** adj. **complete, extensive, far-reaching** 포괄적인

[kàmprihénsiv]

Before entering a foreign market, firms do a **comprehensive** evaluation of the country in question.

11 convince* v. **persuade, assure, induce** 확신시키다, 설득하다

[kənvíns]
discourage

The explorers were **convinced** that they would find treasure.

12 crust* n. **exterior, surface, outer layer** 표면, 외피

[krʌ́st]
endothelium

Bright areas represent ancient **crust** left-over from the Moon's formation.

13 execute* v. **perform, achieve, transact** 수행하다

[éksikjù:t]

Peter **executed** his work with satisfaction.

broad appeal	정치가는 선거를 이기려면 광범위한 사람들에게 호소력을 가져야 한다.
capture	아프리카인들은 내전에서 포로로 잡혀 노예로 팔렸다.
channel	그 새로 부임한 주지사는 더 많은 자금을 교육 쪽으로 돌리기로 결정했다.
cherish	오랫동안 헤어진 형제들은 재회의 기회를 소중히 여겼다.
comprehensive	해외 시장에 진입하기 전에 회사들은 대상이 되는 국가에 대해서 포괄적인 평가를 한다.
convince	탐험가들은 보물을 발견할 수 있을 것이라고 확신했다.
crust	밝은 부분은 달의 형성시 생긴 오래된 표면 잔여물을 드러낸다.
execute	Peter는 만족하며 그의 일을 수행했다.

14 **expect**** | v. **predict, anticipate, await, reckon on** 기대(예상)하다

[ikspékt]

Although Alice didn't **expect** anything for her birthday, her husband bought her a day at the spa.

15 **figure*** | n. **amount, number** 수치, 합계

[fígjər]

Fourth-quarter profits will grow 10.4% over last year's **figures**.

16 **fragrant*** | adj. **aromatic, perfumed, savory** 향기로운

[fréigrənt]
fetid

People sat in the chocolate house and enjoyed the **fragrant** hot cocoa.

17 **gainful**** | adj. **profitable, paying, lucrative** 벌이가 되는

[géinfəl]

Teresa was happy about her **gainful** employment.

18 **gap*** | n. **opening, hole, break** 틈, 구멍

[gǽp]

There was a large **gap** between Paul's two front teeth.

19 **given**** | adj. **particular, specified** 정해진

[gívən]

Harry and Ron hurried to the train station to reach the meeting place at the **given** time.

20 **incisive** | adj. **penetrating, biting, acute** sharp 예리한, 신랄한

[insáisiv]
maundering

Madison had a more subtle and **incisive** political sense than anyone else.

21 **irreversible*** | adj. **permanent, irrevocable** 되돌릴 수 없는

[ìrivə́:rsəbəl]
reversible

Chuck's addiction to alcohol has resulted in **irreversible** damage to his liver lining.

expect	비록 Alice는 그녀의 생일날 아무 것도 기대하지 않았지만, 그녀의 남편은 그녀에게 온천에서 하루를 보낼 수 있는 티켓을 사주었다.
figure	4사분기의 이익은 지난 해의 수치보다 10.4% 증가할 것이다.
fragrant	사람들은 초콜릿 집에 앉아서 향기로운 핫코코아를 즐겼다.
gainful	Teresa는 벌이가 되는 취직에 기뻐했다.
gap	Paul의 앞니 두 개 사이에는 큰 틈이 있다.
given	Harry와 Ron은 정해진 시간에 모임 장소에 도착하기 위해 서둘러 기차역으로 갔다.
incisive	Madison은 다른 누구보다 더 치밀하고 예리한 정치적 감각을 가졌다.
irreversible	Chuck의 알코올 중독이 그의 간 내부에 돌이킬 수 없는 손상을 가져왔다.

22 **locale**** [loukǽl]

n. **place** 장소

The artists must choose a suitable **locale** for taking good pictures.

23 **ooze**** [ú:z]

v. **seep, pass through slowly** (물 · 공기 등이) 새다

The youth didn't realize that he had been injured until blood began **oozing** out of a puncture wound on his leg.

24 **penetrate*** [pénətrèit]

v. **go through, pierce, enter, permeate** 관통하다, 스며들다

Carbon dioxide created a 'greenhouse effect,' allowing solar energy to **penetrate** the atmosphere.

25 **pervade*** [pəːrvéid]

v. **spread, permeate, penetrate** 널리 퍼지다, ~에 스며들다

Social idealism **pervaded** the theological atmosphere of the time.

26 **phase*** [féiz]

n. **period, stage, step** 시기, 단계

The first **phase** of construction on the fort was completed before the War of 1812.

27 **pinion**** [pínjən]

n. **feather, plumage** 깃털

A peacock displayed his beautifully colored **pinions**.

28 **pitiful** [pítifəl]

adj. **pitiable, pathetic, piteous** 불쌍한

There was something so **pitiful** in the movements of Diana's hands.

29 **predicament**** [pridíkəmənt]

n. **difficult situation, dilemma, plight** 곤경

Ford's poor policy decisions contributed to the automaker's financial **predicament**.

locale	화가는 좋은 그림을 그리려면 적절한 장소를 선택해야 한다.
ooze	그 청년은 자신의 다리에 난 상처에서 피가 흘러 나오기 시작할 때까지 자신이 다쳤다는 사실을 몰랐다.
penetrate	이산화탄소는 온실 효과를 일으켜 태양 에너지가 대기를 관통할 수 있게 했다.
pervade	사회적 이상주의가 그 당시의 신학적 분위기에 스며들었다.
phase	요새 건설의 첫 번째 단계가 1812년의 전쟁 전에 완성되었다.
pinion	공작은 아름답고 화려한 색채의 깃털을 뽐냈다.
pitiful	Diana의 손놀림에는 뭔가 불쌍한 것이 있었다.
predicament	Ford의 서투른 정책 결정은 자동차 제조업자의 재정난에 일조했다.

30 **sanction***
[sǽŋkʃən]
interdiction

n. **approval, permission, ratification** 허가, 승인

The special envoy acted only with the **sanction** of the president.

31 **snatch***
[snǽtʃ]

v. **seize, grab, clutch** (와락) 붙잡다

The cat **snatched** a mouse in the corner.

32 **subjective***
[səbdʒéktiv]
objective

adj. **personal, individual** 개인적인

The way the Greeks recorded their history was highly **subjective**.

33 **sweat***
[swét]

n. **perspiration** 땀

After jogging, Joe wiped off the **sweat** from his face.

34 **therefore***
[ðέərfɔ̀ːr]

adv. **consequently, accordingly, hence, thus, thence** 그 결과

Giles was constantly falling asleep in history class, and **therefore** scored very poorly on the final exam.

35 **trap***
[trǽp]

n. **pitfall, snare, lure, bait** 함정, 덫

Jack has fallen into a **trap** devised by two tricky veterans, Bill and Danny.

36 **tricky***
[tríki]

adj. 1. **difficult, complicated, problematic** 어려운, 까다로운

The recipe was **tricky** and called for some expertise in cake baking.

dull, candid

adj. 2. **cunning, sly, astute, wily** 교활한

Jason is **tricky** enough to cheat on exams without getting caught.

sanction	특사는 대통령의 허가에 의해서만 행동했다.
snatch	고양이는 구석에 있는 쥐를 붙잡았다.
subjective	그리스인들이 자신들의 역사를 기록한 방법은 매우 주관적이었다.
sweat	조깅을 마치고 Joe는 얼굴에서 땀을 닦았다.
therefore	Giles는 역사 시간에 끊임없이 잠에 빠져들었으며, 그 결과 기말 시험에서 매우 나쁜 성적을 얻었다.
trap	Jack은 교활한 두 베테랑, Bill과 Danny가 꾸민 함정에 빠졌다.
tricky	케이크를 구워낼 때의 조리법은 어렵고 약간의 전문적 기술도 필요로 했다.
	Jason은 솜씨가 교묘해서 시험에서 걸리지 않게 부정 행위를 할 수 있다.

37 unique**
[ju:ní:k]

adj. **particular, distinct, original** 특유의, 독특한

All people have a **unique** set of fingerprints which may be used to identify them.

38 unrestricted*
[ʌ̀nristríktid]
restricted

adj. **unlimited, unbridled** 제한이 없는

Military personnel and their families have **unrestricted** access to all base facilities.

39 vice*
[váis]
virtue

n. **wickedness, evil** 악

Some people see smoking and drinking as serious **vices**.

40 win
[wín]
lose

v. **obtain, gain, procure** earn, acquire 얻다

South Carolinians **won** a reputation for hard fighting.

Quiz

Choose the synonym.

1. authentic — ⓐ penetrating, biting, acute
2. incisive — ⓑ pitiable, pathetic, piteous
3. pitiful — ⓒ seize, hold, clutch
4. snatch — ⓓ veritable, genuine, true, real
5. trap — ⓔ pitfall, snare, lure

Answer 1. ⓓ 2. ⓐ 3. ⓑ 4. ⓒ 5. ⓔ

unique — 모든 사람들은 신분 확인에 이용될 수 있는 독특한 지문을 갖고 있다.
unrestricted — 군대의 병사들과 그 가족들은 모든 기지 시설에 접근하는 것이 제한되어 있지 않았다.
vice — 어떤 사람들은 흡연과 음주를 심각한 악으로 본다.
win — South Carolina 사람들은 분투하는 것으로 명성을 얻었다.

DAY

59

Hackers TOEFL **Vocabulary**

Hackers Voca

www.goHackers.com

1 **abundant****

[əbʌ́ndənt]
scarce

adj. **plentiful, ample, bountiful** 풍부한

Plants are extremely **abundant** on the east coast of North America.

2 **acute***

[əkjú:t]
blunt

adj. 1. **keen, sharp, poignant** penetrating 예리한

Richard made **acute** observations regarding the book.

adj. 2. **severe, critical, dire** 심한, 심각한

The EPA has documented many cases of **acute** injury and death from fires.

3 **admit***

[ədmít]
shut out

v. **let in, accept, receive** ~을 들이다

The annual ball at the Beverly Hills Country Club only **admits** Hollywood's biggest stars.

4 **affiliation***

[əfiliéiʃən]
opposition

n. **association, relationship, connection, alliance** 결연, 제휴

The Democratic and Republican parties refuse to build any kind of **affiliation** because of fundamental differences.

5 **arrangement****

[əréindʒmənt]

n. **configuration, structure** 배열

The random **arrangement** of crystals in snowflakes makes each one unique.

abundant	북아메리카의 동부 해안에는 식물들이 지극히 풍부하다.
acute	Richard는 책에 관한 예리한 관찰을 했다.
	EPA(미국 환경 보호국)는 화재로 인한 심각한 부상과 사망 사례들을 상세히 기록해 왔다.
admit	Beverly Hills Country Club에서 해마다 열리는 무도회는 오직 할리우드의 대형 스타들만을 받아들인다.
affiliation	민주당과 공화당은 근본적인 차이 때문에 어떠한 형식의 결연도 쌓기를 거부했다.
arrangement	눈송이 결정의 일정하지 않은 배열은 각각의 눈송이가 독특한 모습을 가지게 해준다.

6 **assault***

[əsɔ́:lt]
defend, protect

v. **attack, aggress, assail** 공격하다

Lee was arrested for allegedly **assaulting** Anderson at their Malibu home in 1998.

7 **bias***

[báiəs]
justness

n. **prejudice** 편견

The senator's words betray a deeply conservative political **bias**.

8 **civil**

[sívəl]
uncouth

adj. **polite, courteous, civilized** 예의 바른

The CEOs of the competing companies found it difficult to be **civil** to each other even in public.

9 **coalesce**

[kòuəlés]

v. **combine, unite, amalgamate, fuse, merge** 합체하다, 연합하다

The former enemies **coalesced** in the face of a greater threat.

10 **coat**

[kóut]

v. **cover, apply, smear, spread** 입히다, 칠하다

The baker **coated** his cake with a layer of sugary icing.

11 **congenial**

[kəndʒí:njəl]

adj. **favorable, pleasant, affable, agreeable, friendly** 친절한, 호의적인

The host kept a **congenial** attitude in spite of tensions.

12 **contaminate**

[kəntǽmənèit]
purify

v. **pollute, stain, corrupt** 오염시키다

The river was rapidly **contaminated** with toxic wastes.

13 **course*****

[kɔ:rs]

n. **progression, process** 진행, 진전

The **course** of human history has shown that civilizations rise and fall.

assault	Lee는 1998년 Malibu의 집에서 Anderson을 폭행한 혐의로 체포되었다.
bias	그 상원 의원의 말은 극히 보수적인 정치적 편견을 드러내었다.
civil	경쟁하는 회사의 CEO들은 대중 앞에서조차 서로 예를 차리기가 어려웠다.
coalesce	예전의 적들이 더 큰 위협에 맞서서 연합하였다.
coat	그 제빵사는 그의 케이크에 설탕층을 입혔다.
congenial	그 집주인은 긴장감에도 불구하고 친절한 태도를 유지했다.
contaminate	강은 독성 있는 쓰레기들로 급속하게 오염되었다.
course	인류 역사의 진행 과정은 문명이 흥하고 망한다는 것을 보여 주어 왔다.

14 **debatable***
[dibéitəbəl]
incontrovertible

adj. **questionable, arguable, disputable** 논쟁의 여지가 있는

A rapid recovery in the first or second quarter is still **debatable**.

15 **determine***
[ditə́ːrmin]

v. 1. **calculate, figure** (관찰 · 조사 등으로) 확인하다, 단정하다

The income earned by a student's mother and father is used to **determine** how much financial aid each university will offer.

v. 2. **decide, resolve, settle, judge** 결정을 내리다

The playoff series between the teams will **determine** the league champion.

16 **devoid****
[divɔ́id]
full

adj. **free from, empty, destitute** void ~가 없는

The sequel appears to be **devoid** of the wit and humor that characterized the first movie.

17 **domestic*****
[dəméstik]

adj. **home, family, household** 가정의

If both the husband and wife work, they should share the **domestic** chores.

18 **dominated**
[dɑ́mənèitid]

adj. **governed, controlled, directed** 지배되는

The leadership of North Korea is **dominated** by the autocratic rule of Kim Jong-Il.

19 **exercise****
[éksərsàiz]

v. **practice, use** 실행하다, 행사하다

Students must **exercise** care in citing sources in all their written assignments.

20 **exhibit****
[igzíbit]

v. **display, set forth, show, present, demonstrate** 보여 주다, 나타내다

The dancer **exhibited** grace and dignity despite the difficult situation.

debatable	1, 2분기의 빠른 회복은 여전히 논쟁의 여지가 있다.
determine	학생의 어머니와 아버지가 벌어들이는 수입은 각 대학이 얼마만큼의 재정적 원조를 지원할 것인가를 정하는 데 이용된다.
	그 팀들 간의 우승 결정전 시리즈는 리그의 우승팀을 결정하게 될 것이다.
devoid	그 영화의 속편은 전작의 특징이었던 재치와 유머가 없어 보인다.
domestic	남편과 아내가 둘 다 일한다면, 가사를 분담해야 한다.
dominated	북한의 지도권은 김정일의 독재적 통치에 의해 지배된다.
exercise	학생들은 보고서 작성시 자료 인용을 조심스럽게 해야 한다.
exhibit	그 무용가는 힘겨운 상황에도 불구하고 기품과 위엄을 보여주었다.

21 **extol***

[ikstóul]
decry

v. **applaud, laud, exalt** commend 칭찬하다

The professor is quick to **extol** the works of E. B. White.

22 **feasible****

[fíːzəbəl]
impossible

adj. **possible, viable, workable** practicable 실행할 수 있는

Workfare is a **feasible** solution to teaching people how to become independent.

23 **flexible****

[fléksəbəl]
rigid

adj. **pliable, adjustable, adaptable, plastic** 융통성 있는, 유연한

The **flexible** tongue can be used to shape a wide variety of sounds.

24 **global***

[glóubəl]

adj. **worldwide, universal, ecumenical** 세계적인

A prophet foretold that a **global** war would break out in the near future.

25 **heed*****

[híːd]
disregard

v. 1. **listen to, consider, pay attention to** 주의하다

Palestinian militants **heeded** Arafat's call to halt suicide bombings and armed attacks.

n. 2. **attention, notice, caution** 주의

Students must pay **heed** to the school's warnings about not taking drugs if they want to avoid severe punishment.

26 **inquiry***

[ínkwəri]

n. **scrutiny, examination, investigation** research 조사

Warner's committee investigated the accident after the Navy completed its **inquiry**.

27 **issue***

[íʃuː]

n. **matter, point, question** 논점

Nowhere in their documents did they address the **issue** of racial slavery.

extol	그 교수는 E. B. White의 작품을 재빨리 칭찬했다.
feasible	노동 재교육은 사람들이 자립하는 방법을 가르치는 것에 대한 실행 가능한 해결책이다.
flexible	유연한 혀는 매우 다양한 소리를 내는 데 사용된다.
global	한 예언자는 세계 전쟁이 가까운 미래에 발생할 것이라고 예언했다.
heed	팔레스타인 투사들은 자살 폭탄과 무장 공격을 중지하라는 아라파트의 요구에 주의를 기울였다.
	만약 학생들이 엄중한 처벌을 피하고 싶다면, 마약을 복용하지 말라는 학교측의 경고에 주의를 기울여야 할 것이다.
inquiry	Warner의 위원회는 해군 조사가 완료된 후 사고를 조사할 것이다.
issue	그들은 논문 어디에서도 인종적 노예 제도에 관한 논점은 말하지 않았다.

28 **potential****

[poutén∫əl]
actual

adj. **prospective, possible, latent, dormant** 가능성 있는, 잠재적인

The rise of antislavery sentiment was a **potential** threat to national unity.

29 **potentially***

[pətén∫əli]

adv. **possibly** 아마도

Anna accidentally swallowed a **potentially** fatal substance.

30 **prone****

[proun]

adj. **tending, susceptible, inclined** disposed ~하는 경향이 있는

Ben is very **prone** to writing things on the backs of letters.

31 **share***

[∫ɛər]

n. **portion, part, allotment** 몫

Bob's roommate was constantly late with his **share** of the rent.

32 **status****

[stéitəs]

n. **standing, prestige, position, rank** 지위

The document showed how the social **status** of men could be destroyed by alcohol.

33 **strength****

[stréŋkθ]
weakness

n. **force, power, might** 힘

Cuban-Americans have attained political **strength** commensurate with their numbers.

34 **tempt**

[témpt]
discourage

v. **attract, decoy, lure** induce, allure 유혹하다, (마음을) 끌다

Einstein was **tempted** to return to Germany to become a research director.

35 **urgent***

[ə́ːrdʒənt]

adj. **pressing, imperative, exigent** 긴급한

The next morning, Jeannie got an **urgent** call from Tony.

potential	반노예 제도 감정이 일어나는 것은 국가 단합에 잠재적인 위협이었다.
potentially	Anna는 우연히 치명적일 수도 있는 물질을 삼켰다.
prone	Ben은 편지 뒷면에 뭔가를 쓰는 경향이 있다.
share	Bob의 룸메이트는 항상 임대료 중 자신의 몫을 늦게 지불했다.
status	그 문서는 사람의 사회적 지위가 음주에 의해 어떻게 무너질 수 있는지를 보여 주었다.
strength	쿠바계 미국인들은 그들의 숫자에 비례하는 정치적 힘을 획득했다.
tempt	Einstein은 독일로 돌아가서 연구팀장이 되는 데 마음이 끌렸다.
urgent	다음날 아침, Jeannie는 Tony로부터 급한 연락을 받았다.

36 utilize* [jú:təlàiz]
v. employ, **make use of** 이용하다
In the future, every house may be equipped with a heating system that **utilizes** solar energy.

37 vaguely*** [véigli]
adv. unclearly, **ambiguously, indefinitely** 불분명하게
Due to the age of the photograph, Jenna could only **vaguely** see the people's faces.

38 vigorous** [vígərəs]
lethargic
adj. strong, energetic, **tough** sturdy 힘찬, 강력한
Adams' European experience made him a **vigorous** supporter of Washington's policy.

39 vow* [váu]
n. pledge, **promise** 서약
After the couple recited their **vows**, they were declared married.

Quiz

Choose the synonym.

1. acute — ⓐ attract, decoy, lure
2. prone — ⓑ strong, tough, sturdy
3. tempt — ⓒ inclined, susceptible, tending
4. vigorous — ⓓ pledge, promise
5. vow — ⓔ keen, sharp, poignant

Answer 1. ⓔ 2. ⓒ 3. ⓐ 4. ⓑ 5. ⓓ

utilize — 미래에는 모든 가구가 태양 에너지를 이용하는 난방 시스템을 갖추게 될지도 모른다.
vaguely — 사진이 오래 되어서 Jenna는 사람들의 얼굴을 흐릿하게 볼 수밖에 없었다.
vigorous — Adams의 유럽에 대한 경험은 그를 Washington의 정책에 대한 강력한 지지자로 만들었다.
vow — 그 커플이 서약을 낭독한 후 그들의 결혼이 선포되었다.

DAY Hackers TOEFL **Vocabulary**

60 Hackers Voca

www.goHackers.com

1 **a great deal*** | phr. a lot, **in abundance** | 많음, 많이

Christopher travels **a great deal** due to his job as a pilot.

not many

2 **added*** | adj. extra, **additional, supplemental** | 여분의, 추가의

[ǽdid]

Colette had a deadbolt fitted on her door as an **added** safeguard against crime in her neighborhood.

3 **albeit** | conj. although, **even though, notwithstanding** | 비록 ~이지만

[ɔ:lbí:it]

Many third-world economies are growing steadily, **albeit** slowly.

4 **allow*** | v. enable, **permit, let** | 허용하다

[əláu]

reject

When the Civil War began, blacks weren't **allowed** to fight in the Union army.

5 **antecedent*** | n. predecessor, **ancestor** | 선조

[æ̀ntisí:dənt]

descendant

Fossils of the prehistoric animal eohippus have proven its lineage as an **antecedent** of our modern horse.

6 **apart from** | phr. except for | ~을 제외하고

Jack's essay is very good, **apart from** a few grammatical errors.

a great deal	Christopher는 조종사라는 그의 직업 때문에 여행을 매우 많이 한다.
added	Colette은 이웃에서 저질러졌던 범죄에 대한 추가적인 보안으로 그녀의 문에 꼭 들어맞는 빗장을 철저하게 채웠다.
albeit	많은 제3 세계 국가들의 경제는 느리긴 하지만 꾸준하게 성장하고 있다.
allow	남북 전쟁이 시작되었을 때 흑인들이 북부 연합군에서 싸우는 것은 허락되지 않았다.
antecedent	선사 시대 동물인 에오히푸스의 화석은 그것이 현 시대 말의 조상의 혈통임을 증명한다.
apart from	Jack의 에세이는 약간의 문법상 오류를 제외하면 매우 훌륭하다.

7 **application***
[æpləkéiʃən]

n. use, **employment, appliance** 이용

A micro computer has a wide range of **applications** for mobile businesses.

8 **augment**
[ɔːgmént]

v. add, increase 증가시키다

Many professors **augment** their salaries by providing consultation services for private companies.

9 **avenue*****
[ǽvənjùː]

n. means, **channel** 수단

The Internet opened new **avenues** to accessing information.

10 **cease***
[síːs]
continue

v. stop, halt, **terminate** 중지하다

The rain had **ceased**, but a strong wind still blew from the southwest.

11 **clean****
[klíːn]
dirty

adj. 1. **unstained, clear, pure** 깨끗한

The picnickers made many efforts to keep the environment **clean**.

adj. 2. hygienic, antiseptic 살균의, 위생적인

It is important to have a **clean** dressing to avoid infection and reduce scarring.

12 **cumulate**
[kjúːmjəlèit]

v. build up, **accumulate, amass, collect** 쌓아 올리다, 모으다

There are many ways to **cumulate** points in pinball.

13 **demise**
[dimáiz]

n. end, **fall, death, decease** 멸망, 서거

The Battle of Midway ensured the **demise** of the Japanese Empire.

application	소형 컴퓨터는 이동 전화 사업에 광범위하게 사용될 수 있다.
augment	많은 수의 교수들이 사기업들에게 컨설팅 서비스를 제공하는 방법으로 수입을 증가시킨다.
avenue	인터넷은 정보를 얻는 새로운 길을 열어 주었다.
cease	비는 멈췄지만 남서쪽에서 오는 강한 바람이 계속 불었다.
clean	피크닉을 즐기던 사람들은 자연 환경을 깨끗하게 유지하기 위해서 많은 노력을 했다.
	감염을 막고 흉터를 줄이기 위해서는 위생적인 붕대를 감는 것이 중요하다.
cumulate	핀볼에서 점수를 모으는 방법은 많다.
demise	미드웨이 해전은 일본 제국의 멸망을 확고하게 했다.

14 **detest** [ditést]

v. strongly dislike, hate, abominate, abhor 혐오하다

Romantic artists and authors **detested** the rationalism of their era.

15 **dilute** [dailú:t]

v. reduce, thin, weaken 묽게 하다, 약화시키다

Chemists used water to **dilute** the strong alcohol.

16 **disrupt**** [dìsrʌ́pt]

v. interrupt, interfere with, upset 중단시키다, 혼란시키다

Professor Gumpert's lecture was **disrupted** by two students talking in the back of the classroom.

17 **diverse*** [daivə́:rs]
identical

adj. dissimilar, varied, various, manifold 다양한

Russell's genius lies in getting people of **diverse** backgrounds to work together.

18 **drill*** [dríl]

n. practice, exercise 연습, 훈련

The soldiers were ordered to attend daily calisthenic **drills** of sprinting, push-ups, and jumping jacks.

19 **ease*** [í:z]
aggravate

v. alleviate, relieve, mitigate 완화시키다

Patrick **eased** Amanda's worries about her surgery by explaining the whole process to her step by step.

20 **empty**** [émpti]
full

adj. vacant, hollow, void unoccupied, blank 텅 빈

There was an **empty** bottle which had contained milk.

21 **engaged**** [engéidʒd]

adj. busy, occupied 바쁜

Jennifer was so **engaged** in the conversation that she hadn't noticed that her husband had left.

detest	낭만주의 예술가들과 작가들은 당대의 합리주의를 혐오했다.
dilute	화학자들은 독한 알코올을 묽게 하기 위해 물을 사용했다.
disrupt	Gumpert 교수의 강의는 강의실 뒤쪽에서 이야기하는 두 명의 학생에 의해 방해를 받았다.
diverse	Russell의 천재성은 다양한 배경의 사람들을 함께 일하도록 하는 데 있다.
drill	군인들은 매일 실시되는 구보, 팔굽혀펴기, 팔벌려뛰기 등의 유연 체조 훈련에 참석하도록 지시를 받았다.
ease	Patrick은 Amanda에게 수술의 전 과정을 차근차근 설명해 줌으로써 그녀의 우려를 완화시켰다.
empty	우유가 들어 있던 빈 병이 있었다.
engaged	Jennifer는 대화하느라 바빠서 그녀의 남편이 나가는 것도 알아채지 못했다.

22 **engrossed** [ingróust]

adj. **absorbed, occupied, preoccupied** 몰두한

Bright children become **engrossed** in books at an early age.

23 **even**** [í:vən]

uneven, rugged

adj. 1. **flat, level, horizontal, plane** 평평한

The vase should be placed on an **even** surface to keep from spilling.

adj. 2. **unchanging, constant** 한결같은

The runners in the marathon ran at an **even** pace.

24 **exceed**** [iksí:d]

v. **go beyond, surpass, have a greater number than** 능가하다

Christine's yearly income **exceeded** Jack's total earnings from the previous 14 years.

25 **exude**** [igzjú:d]

v. **release, emit, give off** 방출하다

Human skin **exudes** sweat as a cooling mechanism.

26 **extreme*** [ikstrí:m]

moderate

adj. **intense, excessive, ultimate** unreasonable 극심한, 극단적인

Brian was an **extreme** conservative when it came to his political views.

27 **imprecise** [ìmprisáis]

adj. **inexact, inaccurate, loose** 부정확한

Predicting earthquakes is a highly **imprecise** science.

28 **inauspicious*** [ìnɔ:spíʃəs]

favorable

adj. **unfavorable, ominous** 불길한

The Middle East peace talks were off to an **inauspicious** start.

engrossed	영리한 아이들은 어린 나이에 책에 몰두하게 된다.
even	꽃병은 쏟아지지 않도록 평평한 표면 위에 놓여져야 한다.
	마라톤의 선수들은 일정한 속도로 달렸다.
exceed	Christine의 연간 수입은 Jack의 지난 14년간의 총수입을 초과한다.
exude	인간의 피부는 냉각 절차로써 땀을 방출한다.
extreme	Brian은 그의 정치적 관점에 있어서는 극도로 보수주의자였다.
imprecise	지진을 예측하는 일은 매우 부정확한 과학 분야이다.
inauspicious	중동 평화 회담은 좋지 않은 출발로 시작되었다.

29 **mask****

[mǽsk]

v. disguise, camouflage, pretend, cover 가장하다, 감추다

The spy tried to **mask** his enmity under an appearance of friendliness.

30 **merit***

[mérit]
fault

n. value, **worth, excellence** 가치, 장점

The great **merit** of the poems is that they make us aware of previously unperceived possibilities.

31 **perspective****

[pəːrspéktiv]

n. **view, prospect, vista** 전망

The data provides a fascinating new **perspective** on the pattern of industrial development.

32 **predominantly**

[pridάmənəntli]

adv. primarily, mainly, **predominately** 주로

Indonesia is a **predominantly** Muslim country.

33 **prey***

[préi]

n. victim 희생자

After the lion killed its **prey**, the vultures hovered above, waiting to feed on the remains.

34 **recast***

[riːkǽst]

v. transform 고쳐 만들다

The cabinet was completely **recast** after the inauguration of the new president.

35 **skip**

[skíp]

v. **spring, jump, leap** 깡충 뛰다

The children were **skipping** about in the park.

36 **submit**

[səbmít]
resist

v. **yield, surrender, obey** 복종(굴복)하다

The criminals will **submit** to the judgment of the majority of town.

mask	그 스파이는 다정한 외모 속에 적의를 가리려고 했다.
merit	시의 큰 장점은 우리로 하여금 이전에 감지하지 못한 가능성을 깨닫게 한다는 것이다.
perspective	그 자료는 산업 발달 유형에 대한 매혹적인 새로운 전망을 제시한다.
predominantly	인도네시아는 주로 이슬람을 믿는 국가이다.
prey	사자가 사냥감을 죽이고 나자, 독수리들이 남은 것을 먹기 위해 기다리며, 그 위를 맴돌았다.
recast	새 대통령 취임식 후에 각료들이 완전히 바뀌었다.
skip	아이들은 공원에서 뛰어다니고 있었다.
submit	그 범죄자들은 마을의 다수의 판결에 복종할 것이다.

37 **sustain****

[səstéin]

v. 1. **support, bear, uphold** 지탱하다

The old shelf cannot **sustain** the weight of the books.

abandon

v. 2. **maintain, continue** 유지(지속)하다

Only one planet is able to **sustain** human life in our solar system.

38 **trace****

[tréis]

n. **imprint, vestige, mark** sign 자취, 흔적

The results of the blood test showed **traces** of an illegal drug in the patient's blood.

39 **urban**

[ə́ːrbən]

rural

adj. **civic, municipal** 도시의

Urban crime has increased in Los Angeles by 5% over the past three years.

Quiz

Choose the synonym.

1. antecedent — ⓐ hate, abominate, abhor
2. detest — ⓑ unfavorable, ominous
3. engrossed — ⓒ imprint, vestige, mark
4. inauspicious — ⓓ predecessor, ancestor
5. trace — ⓔ absorbed, occupied, preoccupied

Answer 1. ⓓ 2. ⓐ 3. ⓔ 4. ⓑ 5. ⓒ

sustain 오래된 선반은 그 책들의 무게를 지탱할 수 없다.
우리 태양계에서 오직 한 행성만이 인간의 삶을 유지할 수 있다.

trace 혈액 검사 결과, 환자의 혈액에서 불법적인 약물 복용의 흔적이 나타났다.

urban Los Angeles에서의 도시 범죄는 지난 3년간 5% 정도 증가하였다.

Hackers TOEFL Voca TEST DAY 58-60

Choose the synonym of the highlighted word in the sentence.

1. Seeing a strange fluid oozing out of a cut on his arm, Greg realized that the wound was infected.
(A) seeping (B) loosening (C) clamoring (D) streaming

2. An atmosphere of distrust pervaded the air.
(A) imputed (B) verified (C) liberated (D) permeated

3. Hearing thunder in the distance and seeing storm clouds was inauspicious for the charity group's picnic plans.
(A) urgent (B) unfavorable (C) propitious (D) impending

4. Water is present in abundant quantities on and under the Earth's surface.
(A) plentiful (B) jovial (C) ingenious (D) stark

5. Runoff from a factory contaminated streams and rivers for several dozen square miles.
(A) bemoaned (B) polluted (C) agitated (D) infected

6. Jamie failed to heed his mother's warning about talking to strangers.
(A) account for (B) brace (C) resort to (D) listen to

7. The university president's congenial relationship with the city business community resulted in donations to several departments and colleges.
(A) gracious (B) ambulatory (C) friendly (D) residual

8. Many tribes submitted peacefully to being moved to the West.
(A) yielded (B) adjusted (C) baited (D) eased

9. In China the worship of royal antecedents was central to the maintenance of the dynasty.
(A) predecessors (B) religionists (C) families (D) rulers

10. The people's ardent desire for freedom was the basis of the French Revolution.
(A) authentic (B) incisive (C) enthusiastic (D) unrestricted

정답 p.419

TAKE A BREAK

TOEFL을 마치고 모두 함께 원 샷!

드디어 해방이다 ~.

Hackers TOEFL Voca

TEST Answer Key

DAY 01–03	**1.** (C)	**2.** (A)	**3.** (B)	**4.** (C)	**5.** (A)	**6.** (C)	**7.** (B)	**8.** (A)	**9.** (B)	**10.** (C)
DAY 04–06	**1.** (D)	**2.** (A)	**3.** (B)	**4.** (C)	**5.** (A)	**6.** (C)	**7.** (B)	**8.** (A)	**9.** (C)	**10.** (A)
DAY 07–09	**1.** (B)	**2.** (C)	**3.** (B)	**4.** (B)	**5.** (B)	**6.** (B)	**7.** (A)	**8.** (D)	**9.** (A)	**10.** (B)
DAY 10–12	**1.** (B)	**2.** (D)	**3.** (A)	**4.** (B)	**5.** (D)	**6.** (C)	**7.** (A)	**8.** (A)	**9.** (C)	**10.** (B)
DAY 13–15	**1.** (B)	**2.** (B)	**3.** (A)	**4.** (B)	**5.** (C)	**6.** (B)	**7.** (A)	**8.** (C)	**9.** (C)	**10.** (B)
DAY 16–18	**1.** (A)	**2.** (C)	**3.** (C)	**4.** (D)	**5.** (A)	**6.** (A)	**7.** (C)	**8.** (B)	**9.** (A)	**10.** (A)
DAY 19–21	**1.** (C)	**2.** (B)	**3.** (C)	**4.** (C)	**5.** (B)	**6.** (B)	**7.** (C)	**8.** (D)	**9.** (A)	**10.** (C)
DAY 22–24	**1.** (A)	**2.** (C)	**3.** (A)	**4.** (B)	**5.** (B)	**6.** (D)	**7.** (C)	**8.** (A)	**9.** (D)	**10.** (B)
DAY 25–27	**1.** (C)	**2.** (A)	**3.** (D)	**4.** (D)	**5.** (A)	**6.** (C)	**7.** (B)	**8.** (B)	**9.** (C)	**10.** (A)
DAY 28–30	**1.** (C)	**2.** (A)	**3.** (B)	**4.** (B)	**5.** (C)	**6.** (D)	**7.** (A)	**8.** (D)	**9.** (D)	**10.** (B)
DAY 31–33	**1.** (A)	**2.** (B)	**3.** (C)	**4.** (B)	**5.** (A)	**6.** (D)	**7.** (A)	**8.** (A)	**9.** (C)	**10.** (B)
DAY 34–36	**1.** (C)	**2.** (A)	**3.** (B)	**4.** (B)	**5.** (B)	**6.** (D)	**7.** (D)	**8.** (B)	**9.** (A)	**10.** (D)
DAY 37–39	**1.** (A)	**2.** (A)	**3.** (D)	**4.** (C)	**5.** (B)	**6.** (B)	**7.** (A)	**8.** (C)	**9.** (D)	**10.** (C)
DAY 40–42	**1.** (C)	**2.** (C)	**3.** (D)	**4.** (B)	**5.** (A)	**6.** (B)	**7.** (D)	**8.** (D)	**9.** (A)	**10.** (C)
DAY 43–45	**1.** (C)	**2.** (B)	**3.** (D)	**4.** (A)	**5.** (D)	**6.** (C)	**7.** (B)	**8.** (D)	**9.** (A)	**10.** (C)
DAY 46–48	**1.** (D)	**2.** (B)	**3.** (B)	**4.** (A)	**5.** (C)	**6.** (B)	**7.** (C)	**8.** (C)	**9.** (D)	**10.** (A)
DAY 49–51	**1.** (C)	**2.** (B)	**3.** (C)	**4.** (A)	**5.** (C)	**6.** (B)	**7.** (B)	**8.** (A)	**9.** (B)	**10.** (C)
DAY 52–54	**1.** (A)	**2.** (B)	**3.** (C)	**4.** (D)	**5.** (A)	**6.** (B)	**7.** (B)	**8.** (D)	**9.** (A)	**10.** (C)
DAY 55–57	**1.** (B)	**2.** (D)	**3.** (C)	**4.** (A)	**5.** (B)	**6.** (C)	**7.** (A)	**8.** (C)	**9.** (C)	**10.** (A)
DAY 58–60	**1.** (A)	**2.** (D)	**3.** (B)	**4.** (A)	**5.** (B)	**6.** (D)	**7.** (C)	**8.** (A)	**9.** (A)	**10.** (C)

Hackers TOEFL Voca

Confu Voca

www.goHackers.com

A

1. **abide** [əbáid] 살다, 머물다 inhabit, reside
   abode [əbóud] 주소 address, residence

2. **absolve** [æbzálv] 사면하다, 용서하다 pardon, forgive, exculpate, let off
   absorb [əbsɔ́:rb] 흡수하다 take in, imbibe, soak up

3. **accede** [æksí:d] 동의하다 agree, assent
   accept [əksépt] 받다, 얻다 receive, acquire, get

4. **acceleration** [əksèləréiʃən] 촉진 precipitation, haste, impetuosity
   accretion [əkrí:ʃən] 축적(물) accumulation

5. **adapt** [ədǽpt] 적응시키다 adjust, modify
   adept [ədépt] 숙련된 skillful, expert
   adopt [ədápt] ~을 채택하다 take up, choose, follow

6. **adore** [ədɔ́:r] 숭배하다 worship, esteem, revere
   adorn [ədɔ́:rn] 장식하다 decorate, ornament, embellish

7. **advance** [ədvǽns] 발전 progress, improvement, development
   advent [ǽdvent] 출현 arrival, introduction, appearance

8. **afford** [əfɔ́:rd] 주다 provide, give, grant
   affront [əfrʌ́nt] 모욕하다 offend, insult, abuse

9. **aggravate** [ǽgrəvèit] 1. 성나게 하다 annoy, irritate
   2. 악화시키다 intensify, worsen
   aggregate [ǽgrəgit] 집합적인, 총계의 entire, total

10. **alight** [əláit] 내려 앉다 land, settle, come down
    alike [əláik] 동일한 identical, same, equal

11. **allay** [əléi] 달래다 soothe, relieve, mitigate
    alley [ǽli] 통로 lane, path, way
    alloy [ǽlɔi] 혼합하다 mix, blend, mingle
    ally [ǽli] 동맹을 맺다 confederate, affiliate, associate

12. **antipathy** [æntípəθi] 반감 dislike, disgust, hatred
    antiquity [æntíkwəti] 고대 ancient times, classical times

13. **appreciate** [əprí:ʃièit] 평가하다 value, estimate
    appropriate [əpróupriit] 적당한 suitable, proper

14. **assemble** [əsémbl] 모으다 gather, collect
resemble [rizémbl] 닮다 be similar to, be like, take after

15. **assent** [əsént] 동의하다 accord, agree
ascend [əsénd] 올라가다 climb, mount, go up

16. **assault** [əsɔ́:lt] 공격하다 attack, aggress, assail
assert [əsə́:rt] 주장하다 claim, declare, maintain
assort [əsɔ́:rt] 분류하다 categorize, classify, codify

17. **attempt** [ətémpt] 시도하다 try, seek
tempt [témpt] 유혹하다 attract, decoy, lure

B

18. **band** [bænd] 군대, 무리 troop, squad, party
bond [bɑnd] 결속, 속박 tie, link, attachment

19. **banish** [bǽniʃ] 추방하다 expel, exile, deport
vanish [vǽniʃ] 사라지다 disappear, fade
vanquish [vǽŋkwiʃ] 압도하다 overpower, overwhelm, subjugate

20. **bait** [beit] 함정 trap, lure
beat [bi:t] 치다 pound, thrash, batter

21. **bare** [bɛər] 벌거벗은 uncovered, naked, nude
bear [bɛər] 산출하다 yield, provide, produce

22. **belittle** [bilítl] 과소평가하다 downplay, detract
brittle [brítl] 부서지기 쉬운 breakable

23. **blank** [blæŋk] 텅 빈 vacant, empty, hollow
brink [briŋk] 경계 verge, rim, margin

24. **bloat** [blóut] 확장하다 expand, increase, swell
blot [blɑt] 얼룩 stain, spot, soil

25. **board** [bɔ:rd] 판재 lumber, log, timber
bode [boud] 징조가 되다 foretell, presage

26. **broad** [brɔ́:d] 넓은 extensive, wide, far-reaching
brood [bru:d] 심사숙고하다 contemplate, consider, ponder

C

27. **celebrity** [səlébrəti] 유명인, 명성 a famous person, hero, notable
celerity [səlérəti] 속력 velocity, speed

28. **chart** [tʃɑ:rt] 지도를 만들다 map, design
charter [tʃɑ́:rtər] 임대하다 lease, rent, hire

29. **clarify** [klǽrəfài] 명료하게 하다 elucidate, clear up
classify [klǽsəfài] 분류하다 categorize, arrange, assort

30. **coarse** [kɔ:rs] 무례한 rough, crude, ill-mannered
coerce [kɔ:rs] 강요하다 compel, oblige, force

31. **command** [kəmǽnd] 명령 direction, mandate, order
commend [kəménd] 맡기다, 칭찬하다 entrust, laud, praise, exalt, applaud

32. **complement** [kɑ́mpləmənt] 보충, 보완 supplement
compliment [kɑ́mpləmənt] 칭찬, 경의 commendation, honor, tribute

33. **compound** [kɑ́mpaund] 복잡한 complex, involved, complicated
confound [kɑnfáund] 혼란시키다 confuse, disturb, disconcert

34. **congenial** [kəndʒí:njəl] 친절한, 호의적인 favorable, pleasant, affable
congenital [kəndʒénitəl] 선천적인 inborn, inherent, innate

35. **constrain** [kənstréin] 억제하다 bind, inhibit, restrain
constraint [kənstréint] 제한, 제약 limitation, hindrance, confinement

36. **contour** [kɑ́ntuər] 윤곽 outline
detour [dí:tuər] 우회로 indirect course

37. **contest** [kɑ́ntest] 경쟁 competition, contention
context [kɑ́ntekst] 배경 setting

38. **converge** [kənvə́:rdʒ] 한데 모이다 meet, come together, merge
converse [kənvə́:rs] 반대의 opposite, reverse

39. **capacious** [kəpéiʃəs] 넓은 ample, spacious
capricious [kəpríʃəs] 변덕스러운 unpredictable, fickle

40. **counterbalance** [káuntərbæ̀ləns] 상쇄하다 offset, balance, counteract
outbalance [àutbǽləns] ~보다 뛰어나다 preponderate, overbalance, outweigh

41. **cover** [kʌ́vər] 숨기다 conceal, hide, obscure
covert [kóuvərt] 비밀의 underground, secret, clandestine

42. **crash** [kræʃ] 박살내다 smash, shatter, crush, break
clash [klæʃ] 충돌하다 collide, smash, bump

D

43. **decent** [dí:snt] 예의바른 nice, modest
descent [disént] 하강 falling, descending

44. **defer** [difə́:r] 연기하다 suspend, postpone, delay, procrastinate
deter [ditə́:r] 막다, 방해하다 preclude, prevent, inhibit

45. **deride** [diráid] 조소하다 sneer, jeer, ridicule, scorn
derive [diráiv] 유래하다 stem, originate

46. **desperate** [déspərit] 1. 필사적인 as a last resort
2. 절망적인 hopeless, critical
disparate [díspərit] 전혀 다른 different, contrary

47. **devise** [diváiz] 고안하다 invent, plan, figure out
device [diváis] 장치 instrument, tool, mechanism

48. **devour** [diváuər] 게걸스레 먹다 gulp, guzzle, eat
devout [diváut] 독실한 pious, devoted, saintly

49. **dip** [dip] 던져 넣다 plunge, drop, thrust
deep [di:p] 심오한 profound, abysmal

50. **discreet** [diskrí:t] 분별력 있는 judicious, prudent, considerate
discrete [diskrí:t] 별개의 distinct, separate, different

51. **dispose** [dispóuz] 배치하다 array, arrange, place in order
depose [dipóuz] 쫓아내다 oust

52. **distract** [distrǽkt] 산만하게 하다 divert, perturb
detract [ditrǽkt] 줄이다 reduce, diminish, lessen

53. **divest** [divést] 제거하다 strip, remove
divert [divə́:rt] 즐겁게 하다 entertain, amuse, please

54. **divulge** [divʌ́ldʒ] (사실 등을) 밝히다 reveal, disclose, unveil
deluge [délju:dʒ] 물에 잠기게 하다 flood, inundate, swamp, submerge

55. **drag** [dræg] 끌어 당기다 pull, haul, tug, heave
dreg [dreg] 잔여 residue, remain, remnant, leftover

E

56. **enroll** [inróul] 등록하다 register, sign up for
enthrall [inθrɔ́:l] 매혹하다 fascinate, captivate, enchant, mesmerize

57. **eternal** [i(:)tə́:rnəl] 끊임없는 ceaseless, constant, uninterrupted
ethereal [i(:)θí(:)əriəl] 비현실적인 unsubstantial, unreal, dreamlike

58. **evolve** [iválv] 서서히 발전하다 develop, progress, improve
involve [inválv] ~을 수반하다 include, entail
revolve [riválv] 회전하다 rotate, circulate, circle

59. **exacerbate** [igzǽsərbèit] 더욱 심하게 하다 intensify, aggravate
exaggerate [igzǽdʒərèit] 과장하다 overstate, play up
exasperate [igzǽspəreit] 화나게 하다 provoke, enrage

60. **exalt** [igzɔ́:lt] 칭찬하다 extol, applaud, laud, commend
exert [igzə́:rt] 발휘하다, 노력하다 apply, exercise, wield

61. **expel** [ikspél] 내쫓다 exclude, throw out
impel [impél] 재촉하다 force, compel

62. **exploit** [éksplɔit] 업적 feat, accomplishment
explicit [iksplísit] 명백한 clear, unambiguous, definite

63. **extant** [ékstənt] 현존하는 existing, living, remaining, surviving
extend [iksténd] 1. 걸쳐있다 stretch, reach
2. 확장하다 expand, enlarge
extent [ikstént] 범위 scope, stretch, range, space

64. **extract** [ikstrǽkt] 추출하다 draw, pull out
protract [proutrǽkt] (기간을) 연장하다 prolong

F

65. **fad** [fæd] 유행 fashion, style, vogue, mode
fade [feid] 사라지다 wane, vanish, wither

66. **faint** [feint] 희미한 indistinct, dim, feeble
feign [fein] ~인 체하다 pretend, assume, affect

67. **fair** [fɛər] 공정한 disinterested, impartial, unbiased, just
fare [fɛər] 음식 sustenance, food

68. **favor** [féivər] 호의 kindness, good-will
fervor [fə́:rvər] 열정 zeal, passion, ardor

69. **fickle** [fíkl] 하기 쉬운 volatile, whimsical
trickle [tríkl] 졸졸 흐르다 dribble, run, drop

70. **flair** [flɛər] 재주, 재능 talent, aptitude, knack
flare [flɛər] 번쩍이다 flash, flame, glare

71. **flee** [fli:] 피하다, 도망하다 escape, evade, avoid
fleet [fli:t] 빠른 swift, quick, speedy, rapid

72. **foliage** [fóuliidʒ] 잎 leaves
forage [fɔ́(:)ridʒ] 찾아다니다 search, rummage, hunt

73. **fragment** [frǽgmənt] 조각, 부분 piece, particle, part, portion
fragrant [fréigrənt] 향기로운 aromatic, perfumed, savory

74. **freight** [freit] 화물 cargo, shipment, load
fright [frait] 공포 dismay, terror, panic

75. **fuse** [fju:z] 녹다 melt, dissolve
fusion [fjú:ʒən] 통합 union

G

76. **gasp** [gæsp] 숨이 차다 pant
grasp [græsp] 잡다 clasp, grip, clutch

77. **genetic** [dʒənétik] 유전적인 hereditary, inborn, inheritable
genial [dʒí:njəl] 다정한 cordial, friendly, kindly
genuine [dʒénjuin] 진짜의 true, real, authentic

H

78. **hail** [heil] 격찬하다, 환호하다 acclaim, praise, commend, applaud
haul [hɔ:l] 끌어당기다 pull, tug, drag

79. **harass** [hǽrəs] 박해하다 persecute, oppress, molest
harness [há:rnis] 이용하다 utilize

80. **heart** [hɑ:rt] 핵심 core, center
hearty [há:rti] 건강한, 원기 왕성한 lusty, vigorous, strong

81. **hectic** [héktik] 매우 흥분한 feverish, fervid
tactic(s) [tǽktik] 전술, 책략 strategy, maneuver

I

82. **illicit** [ilísit] 불법적인 unlawful, illegal, illegitimate
elicit [ilísit] 이끌어 내다 evoke, draw, educe

83. **impart** [impá:rt] 주다 give, bestow, grant, confer
impartial [impá:rʃəl] 공평한 unbiased, just, fair, disinterested

84. **impetuous** [impétʃuəs] 격렬한 rash, impulsive
impetus [ímpitəs] 자극 stimulus

85. **imprudent** [imprú:dənt] 경솔한 short-sighted, indiscreet
impudent [ímpjədənt] 뻔뻔스러운 brazen, insolent, rude

86. **incentive** [inséntiv] 자극 encouragement, spur
inceptive [inséptiv] 처음의 initial, original, first

87. **incise** [insáiz] 새기다 carve, cut, engrave
incite [insáit] 자극하다 provoke, inflame, spur

88. **incredible** [inkrédəbl] 놀랄 만한 miraculous, marvelous, wonderful
incredulous [inkrédʒələs] 의심 많은 skeptical, doubtful, dubious

89. **inert** [inə́:rt] 움직일 수 없는 motionless, inactive, stationary
invert [invə́:rt] 거꾸로 하다 reverse

90. **influx** [ínflʌ̀ks] 유입 arrival, inrush, inflow
reflux [rí:flʌ̀ks] 간조, 썰물 ebb

91. **ingenious** [indʒí:njəs] 재능이 있는 skillful, adroit, resourceful, inventive
ingenuous [indʒénjuəs] 솔직한 frank, candid, open, naive

92. **inhabit** [inhǽbit] 거주하다 live, occupy, dwell, abide, reside
inhibit [inhíbit] 금지하다 hinder, limit, ban, prohibit, forbid

93. **intend** [inténd] 목표하다 aim, attempt
intent [intént] 의도 purpose, intention

94. **interpret** [intə́:rprit] 설명하다, 해석하다 construe, explain, explicate
interrupt [ìntərʌ́pt] 가로막다, 중단시키다 hinder, stunt, punctuate

95. **intimate** [íntəmit] 친숙한 close, familiar
intimidate [intíməděit] 위압하다 frighten, pressure, daunt

96. **intricate** [íntrəkit] 복잡한 complex, elaborate, complicated
intrigue [intrí:g] 1. ~의 호기심을 돋구다 attract, interest
2. 음모 plot, conspiracy

97. **invaluable** [invǽljuəbl] 매우 귀중한 precious, priceless
invariable [invɛ́(:)əriəbl] 불변의 constant, consistent, unchanging

98. **inveigh** [invéi] 통렬히 비판하다 rail, object, criticize strongly
inveigle [invéigl] 꾀다, 얻어내다 entice, coax

L

99. **label** [léibəl] 표시하다 mark
labor [léibər] 힘들게 일하다 toil, strive

100. **lack** [læk] 부족하다 need, want
lag [læg] 꾸물대다, 뒤처지다 linger

101. **lash** [læʃ] 묶다, 매다 tie, bind
rash [ræʃ] 무분별한 reckless, hasty, imprudent

102. **laud** [lɔ:d] 찬양하다 praise, exalt, applaud
load [lɔ:d] 부과하다 burden, charge

103. **loath** [louθ] 꺼리는 reluctant
loathe [louð] 혐오하다 abhor, abominate

104. **lethal** [lí:θəl] 치명적인 fatal, mortal, deadly
lethargic [ləθá:rdʒik] 무기력한, 활발치 못한 dull, languid

105. **luster** [lʌ́stər] 광채 sheen, brightness, radiance, brilliance
lusty [lʌ́sti] 건강한 vigorous, strong, robust, hearty

M

106. **maim** [meim] 손상시키다 cripple, disable, ruin
main [mein] 주요한 chief, prime, principal

107. **mass** [mæs] 집단 aggregation, collection, accumulation, pile
mess [mes] 혼란 confusion, muddle

108. **meditate** [méditèit] 숙고하다 ponder, contemplate
meditative [méditèitiv] 사색적인 speculative, reflective

109. **migrate** [máigreit] 이동하다 travel, move around, immigrate
mitigate [mítəgèit] 완화하다 alleviate

110. **minuscule** [mínəskjù:l] 작은 minute, small
muscular [mʌ́skjələr] 강한 strong, athletic, robust

111. **mold** [mould] 만들다 frame, make, shape
molt [moult] 탈피하다 shed, discard

112. **mutation** [mju:téiʃən] 변이, 변화 change, alteration, modification
mute [mju:t] 무언의 quiet, silent, dumb, still, speechless

113. **mystic** [místik] 신비한 mysterious, puzzling, inscrutable
mythical [míθikəl] 전설적인 legendary, mythological, fabulous

N

114. **novel** [návəl] 1. 새로운 new, innovative, fresh
2. 신기한, 진기한 unusual, rare, strange
novelty [návəlti] 참신함, 진기함 originality, newness

115. **noisome** [nɔ́isəm] 유해한, 불쾌한 noxious, stinking
noisy [nɔ́izi] 시끄러운 vociferous
nosy [nóuzi] 호기심이 강한 curious, inquisitive

O

116. **obscure** [əbskjúər] 모호한 unclear, uncertain, ambiguous, indistinct
obvious [ábviəs] 명백한 plain, manifest, evident, clear, apparent

117. **outflow** [áutflòu] 유출 effluence, efflux
overflow [òuvərflóu] 범람 runoff

P

118. **pair** [pεər] 한 쌍 couple, brace, duo
pare [pεər] 껍질을 벗기다, 삭감하다 peel, reduce, whittle, trim

119. **peel** [pi:l] 껍질을 벗기다 pare
peer [piər] 필적하다 match, equal

120. **pinpoint** [pínpɔ̀int] 정확한 precise
standpoint [stǽndpɔ̀int] 관점 perspective, point of view

121. **plain** [plein] 분명한 clear, distinct, obvious
plane [plein] 평평한 even, level, horizontal, flat

122. **plumage** [plú:midʒ] 깃털 feather
plunge [plʌndʒ] 던져 넣다 drop, dip, thrust

123. **poor** [puər] 초라한 shabby, ragged, beggarly
pore [pɔ:r] 응시하다 stare, gaze

124. **precede** [prisí:d] 앞서다, 우선하다 come before, antecede, forerun
recede [ri:sí:d] 물러나다 withdraw, retreat

125. **precipitate** [prisípitèit] 촉진시키다 quicken, trigger, accelerate
precipitous [prisípitəs] 성급한 sudden, hasty, rash

126. **preliminary** [prìlíimənèri] 예비의 introductory, preparatory
primarily [práimerəli] 주로 mainly, chiefly, principally

127. **prestige** [prestí:dʒ] 지위, 명성 status, influence, distinction
vestige [véstidʒ] 흔적 remnant, trace, shadow

128. **prevalent** [prévələnt] 널리 퍼진 widespread, universal
prevent [privént] ~을 막다 preclude, avoid, impede

129. **principal** [prínsəpəl] 주요한 central, major
principle [prínsəpl] 원칙, 규범 precept, standard

130. **probe** [proub] 조사하다 examine, explore, investigate
prone [proun] ~의 경향이 있는 inclined, disposed, liable, tending

131. **profuse** [prəfjú:s] 풍부한 abundant, plentiful, copious
propose [prəpóuz] 제안하다 suggest, offer, proffer

132. **propel** [prəpél] 추진하다 push, drive, force
proper [prápər] 적당한 suitable, appropriate, adapted, fitting

R

133. **radical** [rǽdikəl] 1. 근본적인 fundamental, basic
2. 급진적인 extreme, revolutionary
radiant [réidiənt] 빛나는 bright, brilliant, beaming, glowing

134. **rational** [rǽʃənəl] 이성적인 sensible, reasonable
rationale [ræ̀ʃənǽl] 근거 grounds, excuse

135. **reap** [ri:p] 획득하다, 수확하다 obtain, harvest, gather
rip [rip] 쪼개다, 찢다 cleave, split
ripe [raip] 무르익은 mature, mellow, developed

136. **real** [rí:əl] 실제의 actual, factual, genuine
rear [riər] 기르다 breed, raise, nurture

137. **refuge** [réfju:dʒ] 피난처 sanctuary, haven
refuse [rifjú:z] 거절하다 decline, rebuff

138. **refute** [rifjúːt] 반박하다 contradict, disprove
repute [ripjúːt] 명성 fame, distinction, reputation

139. **relevant** [réləvənt] 관련된, 적절한 applicable, pertinent, germane
reverent [révərənt] 독실한 devout, fervent

140. **renounce** [rináuns] 거절하다 reject, refuse, decline
renown [rináun] 명성 fame, repute, distinction

141. **replace** [ripléis] 대신하다 supersede, supplant, substitute
repress [riprés] 억제하다 check, suppress, subdue, quell

142. **request** [rikwést] 간청하다 sue, supplicate, solicit, beseech
require [rikwáiər] 요구하다 demand, enjoin

143. **resolute** [rézəljùːt] 단호한 resolved, decided, determined
resolve [rizálv] 결정하다 determine, decide

144. **respectable** [rispéktəbl] 존경할 만한 estimable, honorable
respectful [rispéktfəl] 공손한 courteous, polite, civil

145. **reveal** [rivíːl] 드러내다 disclose, divulge, unveil
revere [rivíər] 숭배하다 worship, venerate, respect

146. **reverse** [rivə́ːrs] 거꾸로 하다 invert
revert [rivə́ːrt] 되돌아가다 return, revisit

147. **ridicule** [rídəkjùːl] 조롱하다 mock, jeer
ridiculous [ridíkjələs] 어리석은 absurd, silly

S

148. **scan** [skæn] 조사하다 examine, scrutinize, investigate
scant [skǽnt] 줄이다 minimize, reduce, decrease

149. **scarce** [skɛərs] 희귀한 rare
scare [skɛər] 겁주다 terrify

150. **scatter** [skǽtər] 퍼뜨리다 disperse, dissipate, spread out
shatter [ʃǽtər] 박살내다 break, pulverize, smash

151. **scoop** [skúːp] 긁어 모으다 gather up
scope [skoup] 범위 extent, range, space

152. **scorn** [skɔːrn] 경멸하다 disdain, despise
scour [skáuər] 1. 탐색하다 search, hunt
2. 문질러 닦다 rub, polish, scrub

153. **scrap** [skræp] 파편 fracture, piece, portion
scrub [skrʌb] 문지르다 scour

154. **secret** [síːkrit] 비밀의 underground, clandestine, covert
secrete [sikríːt] 분비하다 release, produce, discharge

155. **seethe** [siːð] 끓다 boil, bubble, simmer
soothe [suːð] 달래다 relieve, allay, mitigate

156. **serve** [səːrv] 봉사하다 assist, succor
sever [sévər] 나누다 separate, rend
severe [sivíər] 가혹한 rough, harsh

157. **shade** [ʃeid] 음영 cross-hatching
shed [ʃed] 발산하다 emit, radiate, diffuse

158. **shoddy** [ʃádi] 조악한 inferior, poor, base
shudder [ʃʌ́dər] 떨림, 전율 tremor, shiver, quiver

159. **shred** [ʃred] 조각 piece, scrap
shrewd [ʃruːd] 예리한 astute, keen, acute

160. **shrivel** [ʃrívəl] 위축되다 shrink, contract, diminish
swivel [swívəl] 회전하다 whirl, spin, revolve
shiver [ʃívər] 떨다 tremble, quake

161. **simulate** [símjəlèit] 1. 흉내 내다 imitate, copy
2. 가장하다 pretend, feign
stimulate [stímjuléit] 자극하다 prompt, activate, spur

162. **slather** [slǽðər] (흠뻑) 칠하다 daub, coat, cover, plaster
slaughter [slɔ́ːtər] 학살하다 massacre, butcher, kill

163. **snare** [snɛər] 함정 trap, lure, bait
sneer [sniər] 조소하다 jeer, deride, ridicule

164. **solicitation** [səlìsitéiʃən] 권유 invitation, entreaty, request
solicitude [səlísitjùːd] 근심 concern, anxiety

165. **speculation** [spèkjəléiʃən] 추측 supposition, conjecture, surmise
speculative [spékjəlèitiv] 1. 이론적인 academic, abstract
2. 사색적인 thoughtful, reflective

166. **spin** [spin] 회전하다 rotate, wheel
spine [spain] 척추 backbone

167. **sprig** [sprig] 가지 twig, branch, stick
spring [spriŋ] 뛰다 skip, jump, leap

168. **stagnant** [stǽgnənt] 침체한 inert, inactive
stringent [stríndʒənt] 엄격한 severe

169. **strain** [strein] 1. 잡아당기다 stretch, tighten
2. 긴장 tension
strait [streit] 곤경 dilemma

170. **statue** [stǽtʃuː] 조각상 figure
status [stéitəs] 지위 standing, position, prestige

171. **sting** [stiŋ] 따끔따끔하게 하다 smart, tingle
stingy [stíndʒi] 인색한 parsimonious, miserly, mean

172. **stirring** [stə́ːriŋ] 감동적인 impressive, moving
string [striŋ] 일련, 연속 series, chain

173. **strife** [straif] 불화 conflict, discord
strike [stràik] 치다 pound, slap, hit
strive [straiv] 노력하다 endeavor, try

174. **stun** [stʌ́n] 놀라게 하다 amaze, astound, daze
stunt [stʌ́nt] 중단시키다 interrupt, hinder, stop

175. **style** [stail] 유행 vogue, mode, fashion
stylus [stáiləs] 첨필 pen

176. **subdue** [səbdjúː] 정복하다 conquer, subjugate, defeat
submerse [səbmə́ːrs] 가라앉다 dip, sink
subscribe [səbskráib] 동의하다 agree, assent

subsidize [sʌ́bsidàiz] 보조금을 주다 back, finance, fund
subtract [səbtrǽkt] 제하다 deduct, discount

177. **subsistence** [səbsístəns] 생존 survival, existence, living
substance [sʌ́bstəns] 물질 matter, material, stuff

178. **surface** [sə́ːrfis] 표면 covering, face, exterior
surpass [sərpǽs] 능가하다 exceed, outrun, excel

179. **suspect** [səspékt] 추측하다 surmise, imagine, conjecture
suspend [səspénd] 1. 연기하다 defer, postpone
2. 멈추다 stop, cease, arrest
suspicion [səspíʃən] 의혹 doubt, mistrust, distrust

180. **summarize** [sʌ́məràiz] 요약하다 encapsulate, condense
surmise [səːrmáiz] 추측하다 speculate, suppose, conjecture

181. **swamp** [swɑmp] 습지 bog, marsh
swap [swɑp] 교역하다 exchange, trade

182. **synchronize** [síŋkrənàiz] 동시에 일어나다 occur at the same time
synchronous [síŋkrənəs] 동시에 일어나는 concomitant, simultaneous

T

183. **tailored** [téilərd] 맞추어진 adapted, fitted
tapered [téipərd] 좁아진 narrow, tapering

184. **tatter** [tǽtər] 갈기갈기 찢다 shred
totter [tɑ́tər] 비틀거리다 dodder

185. **temperament** [témpərəmənt] 기질 disposition, make-up, temper, nature
temperate [témpərit] 알맞은 moderate, self-restrained
temporary [témpərèri] 일시적인 transient, fleeting

186. **tenant** [ténənt] 주민 resident
tenet [ténit] 원칙 principle, doctrine, dogma

187. **tendency** [téndənsi] 경향 trend, inclination
tender [téndər] 부드러운 soft, delicate, mild

188. **terrestrial** [təréstriəl] 지구의, 지상의 earthly, worldly
territorial [tèritɔ́:riəl] 영토의 of or relating to territory

189. **touch** [tʌtʃ] 감동을 주다 impress, move, strike, stir
tough [tʌf] 단단한 firm, strong, hard, sturdy

190. **track** [trǽk] 쫓아가다 follow, chase, trace
tract [trækt] 지역 region, area
trek [trek] 이동하다 migrate, rove, travel

191. **transfer** [trænsfə́:r] 이동하다 move, remove, relocate
transform [trænsfɔ́:rm] 변형시키다 convert, change, alter

192. **transparent** [trænspέ(:)ərənt] 명백한 clear, obvious, lucid, limpid
transport [trænspɔ́:rt] 옮기다 carry, convey

193. **transverse** [trænsvə́:rs] 가로지르는 cross, crosswise
traverse [trǽvə:rs] 가로지르다 cross, pass, go over
travesty [trǽvisti] 풍자적 변형 parody, lampoon, mockery

U

194. **underline** [ʌ̀ndərláin] 강조하다 underscore, emphasize, accentuate
underlying [ʌ́ndərlàiiŋ] 근원적인 fundamental, basic, elementary

195. **urge** [ə:rdʒ] 충동 compulsion, eagerness
urgent [ə́:rdʒənt] 긴급한 pressing, imperative, exigent

V

196. **vagarious** [vəgέ(:)əriəs] 변덕스러운 changeable, whimsical, capricious
vigorous [vígərəs] 힘찬, 강력한 strong, energetic, tough

197. **vagary** [vəgέ(:)əri] 예측 불허의 변화 uncertainty, caprice, impulse
vague [veig] 모호한 uncertain, imprecise, obscure

198. **vain** [vein] 헛된 futile, useless
vein [vein] 정맥 blood vessel

199. **variable** [vέ(:)əriəbl] 변하기 쉬운 changeable, inconstant, fickle, unsteady
various [vέəriəs] 다양한 diverse, varied

200. **velocity** [vəlásəti] 속도, 신속함 speed, rapidity, celerity
vivacity [vivǽsəti] 활기 activity, liveliness

201. **vigilant** [vídʒələnt] 방심하지 않는 wary, awake, watchful
vigorous [vígərəs] 원기 왕성한 strong, robust, sturdy, powerful

202. **voluble** [váljəbl] 입심 좋은 talkative, loquacious
valuable [vǽljuəbl] 귀중한 precious, dear, priceless

203. **vociferous** [vousífərəs] 시끄러운 noisy
voracious [vɔːréiʃəs] 탐욕적인 insatiable, greedy, gluttonous

204. **ware** [wɛər] 상품 good, merchandise
wary [wɛ́(ː)əri] 조심하는 alert, careful, cautious
weary [wí(ː)əri] 피곤한 tired, exhausted

205. **wander** [wándər] 배회하다 ramble, roam, rove
wonder [wʌ́ndər] 경이로움 awe, astonishment, marvel

206. **wield** [wíːld] 행사하다, 발휘하다 exert, exercise, apply
yield [jiːld] 굴복하다 cede, submit, surrender

207. **withdraw** [wiðdrɔ́ː] 물러가다 retire, retreat, secede
withhold [wiðhóuld] 보류하다 reserve, retain

Hackers TOEFL Voca

Index

www.goHackers.com

A

INDEX A

B

INDEX C

D

E

F

G

H

J

K

L

M

N

O

P

Q

R

S

T

U

V

W

Y

Z